DATE DUE

MY 29 97			
AG 8 97			
SE 8 97			
NO 17 08			
API 9 01			
OC 23 01			
MR 26 02			
MR 11 03			
AP 2 03			
AP 21 03			
MY 14 03			
JE 03			
OC 8 03			
MY 12 08			

DEMCO 38-296

guitarmaking

TRADITION AND TECHNOLOGY

12

guitarmaking
TRADITION AND TECHNOLOGY

A Complete Reference

for the Design & Construction

of the Steel-String Folk Guitar

& the Classical Guitar

William R. Cumpiano and Jonathan D. Natelson

photographs by Clyde Herlitz / line drawings by William R. Cumpiano

Riverside Community College
Library
DEC '96   4800 Magnolia Avenue
Riverside, California 92506

CHRONICLE BOOKS
SAN FRANCISCO

ML 1015 .G9 C85 1994

Cumpiano, William R.

Guitarmaking, tradition and
technology

Published in 1993 by Chronicle Books.
Copyright © 1987 by William R. Cumpiano and Jonathan D. Natelson
All rights reserved. No part of this book may be reproduced without written permission from the Publisher.

Printed in the United States of America
Designed by Jane McWhorter and Louis Vasquez
Cover Design by Todd Reamon, Green Studios

Originally published by Rosewood Press
31 Campus Plaza Road
Hadley, MA 01035

Library of Congress Cataloging-in-Publication Data

Cumpiano, William R.
    Guitarmaking, tradition and technology : a complete reference for
the design and construction of the steel-string folk guitar and the
classical guitar / William R. Cumpiano, Jonathan D. Natelson ;
photographs by Clyde Herlitz ; line drawings by William R. Cumpiano.
        p.   cm.
    Originally published: Amherst, Mass. : Rosewood Press, c1987.
    Includes bibliographical references (p.) and index.
    ISBN: 0-8118-0640-5 (pb). -- ISBN: 0-8118-0615-4 (hc).
    1. Guitar--Construction. 2. Natelson, Jonathan D.   I. Title.
II. Title: Guitarmaking, tradition and technology.
ML1015.G9C85   1994
787.87'1923--dc20

                                        93-6160
                                         CIP
                                         MN

Distributed in Canada by Raincoast Books,
112 East Third Avenue, Vancouver, B.C. V5T 1C8

10 9 8 7 6 5 4 3 2 1

Chronicle Books
275 Fifth Street
San Francisco, CA 94103

CONTENTS

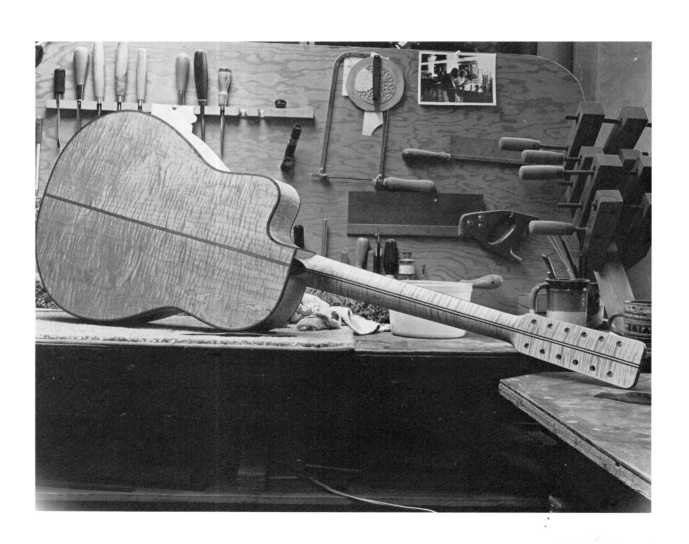

ACKNOWLEDGMENTS

We were introduced to the world of guitarmaking in the New York City workshops of master luthier Michael Gurian. Michael's extraordinary breadth of knowledge about fretted instrument construction was the wellspring from which many of the techniques in this book were derived. We thus wish to express our enduring gratitude for the opportunity to have first learned from an artisan of such remarkable ability and for his permission to make public in this way many of the techniques that we learned at his workshop. Our best wishes and our combined dedication of this effort go out to him.

Our special appreciation goes to Clyde Herlitz, whose technically superb photographic record of the entire guitarmaking sequence has made an unprecedented contribution to the woodworking literature; to Sam Bittman, who administered the complex final stages of production; and to Jim McWilliams, who provided us with the original design concept.

We are also most grateful to the following people: Steve Sauve of Sauve Guitars in North Adams, Massachusetts, who gave us room and kept us sane during preparation of the original manuscript; Steve Toplitz of the Amherst Music House and Guitar Workshop in Amherst, Massachusetts, for his advice and encouragement; R.B. "Sam" Blair, who helped with the documentation; Luthier Brian Dunn of Tucson, Arizona, whose superb workmanship graces some of the following pages; Edith Leu, who so patiently typed our enormous manuscript; Ellen Fitzpatrick, who provided superb editorial assistance; Tim White, who gave us technical assistance on guitar acoustics; Barbara Lampert, who provided access to the musical instrument collection of the Boston Museum of Fine Arts; Herbert Buck of the Dictaphone Corporation, who generously made dictating equipment available when we needed it; Art Halliday of the Franklin Glue Company, who provided us with technical information on glues; the Cook-Horton Company, for technical advice on fretwire manufacture; Dick

Boak of the C.F. Martin Organization and of the Church of Art in Nazareth, Pennsylvania, for information, illustrations and continuing support; and David Coulter of Coulter & Bass Design in Providence, Rhode Island, John Donegan, and Fran Ferry, who furnished additional photographs.

Each of us would also like to make the following personal acknowledgments:

WRC: My consuming love for this ancient craft evolved at the side and by the example of Michael Millard, the Williamsville, Vermont guitarbuilder whose instruments bring joy and beauty to this world. To Michael and to the world-class luthier Manuel Velazquez and the late C.F. Martin III, both of whom generously gave me their time and support, I give my thanks and my boundless admiration.

My appreciation also:

to my mother, Marion Weinfeld Cumpiano, who taught me to love learning; and my father, Willie Cumpiano, who showed me how work is love made visible;

to those who have so lovingly and generously supported me: Frederic Weinfeld, Charles Weinfeld, Laura Cumpiano Vda. de Levy and Esther Cumpiano Vda. de O'Reilly; and my old friend, Anne Walter, who made an early investment into the first Stringfellow studio, and who I hope will accept a copy of this book as interest; my love and appreciation goes out to all of them; and finally to those who provide the joyful fabric of existence, those beautiful people who populate my daily life and provide me with love and support on an ongoing basis: Jeanette Rodriguez, Jason Lugo, Ina Cumpiano, Arsalaan Fay of Douglas Harps, luthier Cat Fox, Al Ell, Rusty Annis, Flo and Rich Neuman, Bob Hasenstab, Ellen Davis, the magnificent Ed Vadas and the Fabulous Heavyweights, Domingo de Jesus, Clara Ruiz, Pamela McGeary, Nancy Hill, Lisa Tremblay, Rob Goldberg, Guillermo Cuellar, Jeffrey Elliott, Cyndy Burton, Manuel Rodriguez, German Velazquez, Chris Kleeman, Rajnar Vajra, Jackie Barceloux, John Dandurand, Joe Bel-

mont, Andy May, Kevin Jones, Michael Dresdner, and to my long-lost brothers Harry Becker and the late Howard Greene (may happiness follow them forever); to all and to many more, my truest thanks.

JDN: I am forever indebted to the dozens of friends, relatives, guitarbuilders, guitarists, and guitar enthusiasts who provided support and encouragement over the many years of effort required to make this book actually happen.

My love and gratitude go first to my mother, Ruth Natelson Pollack, for her often tested but always unflagging support and unconditional love.

Very special thanks go to my dear friends Steve Sauve and Sandy Kelly, who put me up (and put up with me) through the long winter when the manuscript for this book was written.

I am also grateful to Frederic Hand and Edward Flower, two brilliant players who gave generously of their time to provide me with advice so critical to improving my instruments; to the Honorable Bruce W. Kauffman, in respect and affection, for his immeasurable contribution to my writing skills; and to those whose support and encouragement have buoyed me along the way: Bob and Toni Ceisler; Andy and Sara Krulwich; Abigail Child and Henry Hills; Rebecca Ruggles Radcliffe; David and Susan Malony; Minna, Matty, Christine, and the rest of the Walsh clan; John Senior and Nancy Kimmons; Peter and Susan Safronoff; Peter and Nancy Blasini; Carol O'Brien Hardman; Richard Lamarita; Joel Leskowitz; Richard Ross-Podoloff; and Karma, who will live forever in my heart.

Finally, yet above all, I dedicate my work in this world to His Holiness Maharishi Mahesh Yogi, and to Maharishi's Master, Swami Bramhananda Saraswati, Jagadguru Bhagwan Shankaracharya of Jyotir Math.

VIVA FUI IN SILVIS
SUM DURA OCCISA
SECURI DUM VIXI TACUI
MORTUA DULCE CANO

I was alive in the forest
I was cut by the cruel axe
In life I was silent
In death I sweetly sing

—— Inscription on the face frets of an Elizabethan lute

PREFACE

At the time we first considered writing this book, several texts and a variety of technical publications on guitarmaking already existed. We observed, however, that when the quality of the information was good, it could only be found either in summary form or in obscure or widely diffused sources. To our dismay, we also found a remarkable amount of published misinformation, most of it coming from amateurs or experimenters with little knowledge of or regard for the traditions of this ancient craft. The literature was thus at best inadequate and, at worst, outright misleading—a minefield for the unwary student.

All of this suggested to us a need for a comprehensive text on guitarmaking based upon traditional methods. Our idea was to create something that could be used either as a workshop manual for the student guitar builder or simply as a general reference on good guitarmaking technique—for woodworkers who might simply be interested in seeing how it's done, or for guitar players and enthusiasts who would benefit from learning how good instruments are made.

We also wanted our readers to appreciate the importance of historic precedents to modern guitar design and construction techniques. The current state of the art descends directly from the work of brilliant artisans from an earlier age, master builders such as Joachim Tielke, Louis Panormo, Antonio de Torres, Christian Frederick Martin, Manuel and Jose Ramirez, Hermann Hauser, and others, all of whose work has been emulated and further refined by a small number of contemporary masters. We felt that by taking a close and critical look at the work of these great makers, the aspiring luthier could avoid a great deal of reinvention and wasted effort.

What follows then, is an illustrated account of two different guitars, from two divergent traditions, being made—a steel-string folk guitar and a classical guitar. In addition to a step-by-step construction sequence, we have provided technical and historical discussions about many aspects of guitar design and construction. Each of these discussions appears concurrently with the relevant procedure on the guitar, explaining why we do it this way and how the methods we use evolved over time.

The critical reader should be aware that many of the techniques in this book have advanced or exotic variations that simply could not be included because of space limitations and necessary conceptual boundaries. Also, we do not claim that this book demonstrates the only way to build a good guitar. Our purpose essentially was to document a complete sequence of guitar-making procedures—most of which evolved from a very old tradition and all of which have worked effectively for us as professional guitar builders—in sufficient detail to allow a thoughtful amateur with modest resources to do an excellent job.

For those students who intend to build a guitar from this book, a few caveats are in order. Each procedure should be read all the way through before the first step is actually begun. Try to anticipate potential problems, especially those that may be peculiar to your own work environment, and think them through. We suggest doing dry runs (going through the step as described but leaving out the glue) as often as necessary to make your movements more fluid and to work out any unanticipated problems. Also, note that the two guitars being made are progressing simultaneously, so you must notice where steps or procedures are marked "steel-string only" (SS), or "classical only" (CL). Where neither distinction is made, you can assume that the step is identical for both.

Finally, be aware that although the process of making a guitar is rather long and complex, it need not be intimidating. We will be following your progress with tips and suggestions, anticipating many of the pitfalls before they appear. You should not expect to create a work of art on the first try, but we have seen many beginners produce excellent results simply by applying a modicum of intelligence and determination. Above all, if a first guitar is treated as a learning experience and not as some kind of personal test, you are certain to come away delighted and inspired.

CHAPTER 1

MECHANICS

The guitar is a refined musical cabinet that must respond freely to the complex blend of signals produced by its six strings. It must also bear, with little distortion, the unremitting stresses imposed upon it by string tension. The luthier's task is to make these often conflicting requirements work well and work together.

Our discussion of the guitar and the interrelationship of its parts begins with the stretched string. Over the centuries, strings have been made from natural fibers such as silk and hair, from the sinews and intestines of animals, and from lengths of drawn metal wire. In more recent years, synthetic materials such as nylon have come into widespread use. Each of these different string materials has a profound effect upon the structural and acoustic characteristics of the instrument.

Strung with wire, the acoustic guitar is under far greater tension than if strung with animal gut or nylon. This fact determines virtually all the

The Guitar's Anatomy

structural differences between the American folk guitar (steel-string) and the classical guitar, the two members of the guitar family that comprise the focus of this book.

Similarly, the nature of the musical tones produced by these guitars is determined by the choice of string material. Each tone is composed of a fundamental (determining the audible pitch of the note) and an accompanying chorus of harmonics which—depending on the string material—we hear as the metallic shine of brass or the dry crispness of nylon.

The strings' complex signals are coupled to the guitar's neck and soundbox by the nut, saddle, and bridge. The nut and saddle are fashioned from slivers of dense, hard-wearing material. The nut supports the open strings at the neck end. The saddle, fit snugly into a slot in the bridge, supports the strings at the soundbox end.

The array of six strings is stretched along the neckshaft. Located under the strings is a hardwood fingerboard. Raised metal bars, called frets, are let into slots in the fingerboard, providing a series of durable stops for the strings. The fretboard (the fretted fingerboard) can be likened to a decoder, selecting from an infinite number of possible pitches only those that are notes in the scale familiar to our civilization: the chromatic twelve-tone scale.

The guitarmaker chooses a scale length that is appropriate for the guitar being built, and then determines the location of the frets for that scale length according to a mathematical formula. The actual distance between the nut and saddle (the string length) is the sum of the scale length plus a small increment called the *compensation,* which allows the string to produce accurate pitch even though it must be stretched by a small amount each time it is fretted.

The difference between the shortest and longest familiar scale lengths on modern, full-sized guitars is only about an inch. Yet different lengths will impart noticeably different sound characters and different playing qualities, factors of no small importance to the luthier. The reason for this effect is that at any given pitch, a longer string must be tighter than a shorter one. Greater tension means that the string's output will be incrementally greater, its "feel" and the harmonic structure of its tone different.

String tension is created and maintained at the neck's tilted headpiece by means of tuning machines, or pegs. The tilt of the headpiece imparts downward pressure that holds the string against the nut, ensuring a positive string stop. The headpiece must withstand considerable torsional force and is therefore stiffened with laminations of wooden sheets called headpiece veneers. Tension is maintained at the bridge by knotting the strings at its tie block or by pinning the string ends into holes.

The bridge multiplies the strings' effect by leverage; the strings' mechanical advantage (and thus the tension load) increases in proportion to the height of the bridge above the soundboard. The bridge's own mass, composition, and stiff-

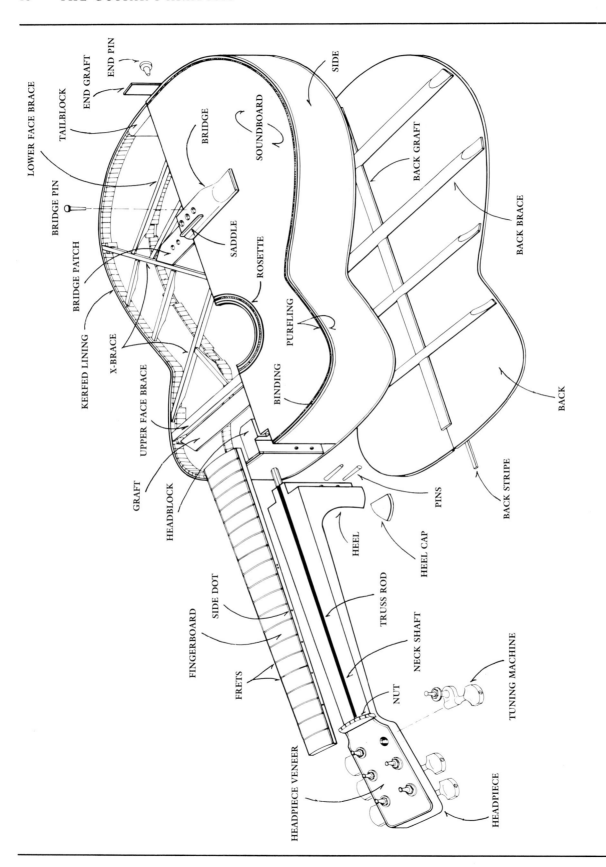

END PIN

END GRAFT

TAILBLOCK

LOWER FACE BRACE

BRIDGE PIN

BRIDGE

SIDE

SOUNDBOARD

BACK GRAFT

BRIDGE PATCH

SADDLE

BACK BRACE

KERFED LINING

ROSETTE

X-BRACE

PURFLING

UPPER FACE BRACE

BINDING

BACK

GRAFT

HEADBLOCK

BACK STRIPE

PINS

FINGERBOARD

HEEL

SIDE DOT

HEEL CAP

FRETS

TRUSS ROD

NECK SHAFT

TUNING MACHINE

NUT

HEADPIECE VENEER

HEADPIECE

1–1. Exploded view of the steel-string guitar.

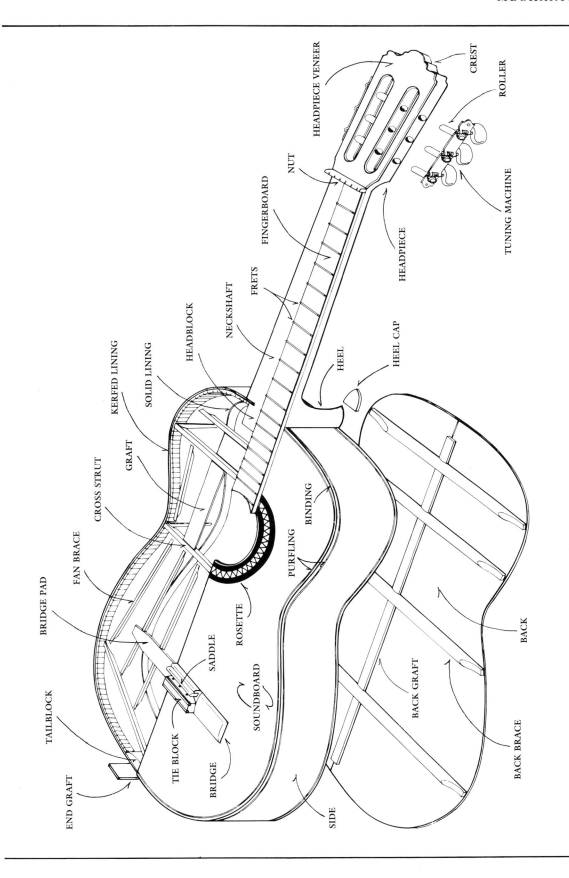

CREST

ROLLER

HEADPIECE VENEER

NUT

TUNING MACHINE

FINGERBOARD

HEADPIECE

FRETS

NECKSHAFT

HEADBLOCK

SOLID LINING

KERFED LINING

GRAFT

HEEL

HEEL CAP

CROSS STRUT

FAN BRACE

BRIDGE PAD

BINDING

PURFLING

TAILBLOCK

SADDLE

ROSETTE

BACK

END GRAFT

TIE BLOCK

BRIDGE

SOUNDBOARD

BACK GRAFT

BACK BRACE

SIDE

1–2. Exploded view of the classical guitar.

ness further modulate the string signal as it is transferred to the box.

The soundboard is reinforced with a pattern of wooden struts (braces). The pattern on the soundboard is designed to transmit the twisting forces away from the bridge and toward the more rigid rim of the sides.

The back, too, is braced to keep it from distorting under load, maintaining the integrity and dimensional accuracy of the soundbox. The back receives and dissipates a considerable part of the forces traveling down the neckshaft and across the neck/body joint to the headblock. These forces can be spread with an extension to the headblock called the *foot*. The foot, however, can be replaced with an extra back brace, a practice that we believe spreads these forces over a wider surface and thus better protects the integrity of the thin back plate.

Back and soundboard are directly coupled by the sides and indirectly coupled by the volume of air in the soundbox. The luthier thus must determine and control the resilience of these plates, since they must respond and interact with each other.

The resilience and strength of the plates are further enhanced by arching them. An arch is achieved by shaping the braces and by contouring the rim of the sides. This "doming" of the plates helps them to resist the distorting effect of

string tension and also allows them to expand and contract safely in response to changes in the moisture content of the surrounding air.

The principal effect of string tension is to force the nut and saddle closer to each other by folding the guitar away from the strings. Tension on the tuning-machine rollers forces the neck into a long, slow curve. Tension at the saddle and bridge causes the bridge to twist around its longitudinal axis. Since the bridge is glued securely to the resilient soundboard, its twisting causes the soundboard area below the bridge to bulge and the area ahead of the bridge to hollow slightly. Over time, these tensional forces can cause progressive distortion, changing the angle of the neck in relation to the body, and raising the strings away from the neck until the guitar's playability is seriously impaired.

A poor solution to the problem of distortion would be to structure the guitar so massively that the soundbox and neck could never be affected by string tension. This would inevitably result in radically choking the guitar's response and spoiling its sound. To achieve a favorable balance between structure and compliance, the forces of string tension must be anticipated and taken into account by thoughtful design and construction. Rather than making the guitar into a totally unyielding structure, the skilled luthier builds

a controlled resilience into a minimally adequate structure.

The Neck/Body Joint

The central focus of the string tension originating at both ends of the string largely falls in the region of the headblock. The luthier must therefore utilize a joining system for the neck and soundbox that is fail-safe and appropriate for the guitar being built.

The Spanish Method of neck/body connection is best used for handbuilding low-tension guitars. It is an ancient, single-piece system. The block at the end of the neck is divided into a heel and a headblock by two vertical saw cuts into which the guitar's sides are inserted. The heel thus stays outside the soundbox, and the headblock ends up inside (Fig. 1-3a).

Conversely, the most suitable connecting system for the quantity production of high-tension guitars is the two-piece tapered dovetail neck/body joint (Fig. 1-3b). Unlike the Spanish Method, it is reversible; it is made so as to be disassembled at some future date. This feature anticipates the need for restoring the neck to its original attitude relative to the soundbox after having been distorted by years of strain under the pull of wire strings.

Making the two matching and interlocking members of the dovetail, however, requires accuracy most easily achieved with the aid of jigs, fixtures, and high-speed shaping machinery. We thus have adopted (and describe in this book) an alternate reversible joint for high-tension guitars, suitable for the handbuilder: the pinned mortise-and-tenon neck-joint system (Fig. 1-3c). This is an ancient joint, found in traditional house framing. In 1972, it was first adopted for use in limited production guitarmaking at the workshop of Michael Gurian. Like the Spanish Method, it consists primarily of essentially straight saw cuts. Like the dovetail, however, it also consists of a separate heel and headblock that tighten and interlock together. Although this joint requires a special set of home-made utensils for its construction, assembly, and disassembly, it is a marvelously simple design. It relies on two wooden taper pins that are tightly pressed into tapered holes in the headblock; by connecting with corresponding holes in the heel, the tenon draws the neck in snugly. Like the very best cabinetmaking joints, it requires no glue to achieve its strength. Finally, it can be made to come apart for neck resetting by simply popping out the pins.

AESTHETICS

Traditionally, the areas reserved for decorative treatment are the soundhole, the edges and corners, the bridge, the

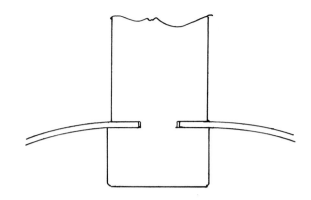

1–3a. Spanish-style slotted headblock neck/body connection.

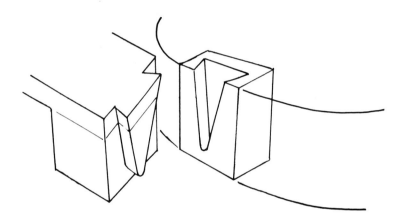

1–3b. Dovetail neck/body joint.

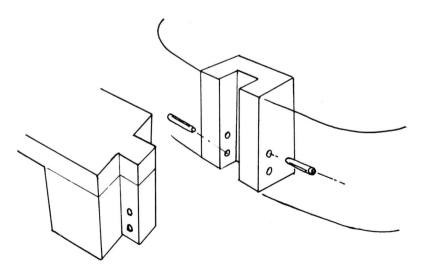

1–3c. Pinned mortise-and-tenon neck/body joint.

headpiece and—on folk guitars—the fingerboard.

The main decorative focus is usually on the soundhole rosette. Also, all the seams of the soundbox are closed and covered by strips called bindings. The meetings of the bindings and the plates are often decorated with ribbonlike strips of contrasting materials called purflings. The seam between the back plates is ornamented by a purfling called the back stripe. The seam between the terminus of the sides at the butt end of the guitar, called the end graft, is also sometimes embellished with purflings.

Additionally, the top of the headpiece is decoratively shaped into the luthier's distinctive crest.

The luthier who seeks to create an integrated decorative scheme for the guitar must plan and prepare all the decorative materials at the earliest stages of the guitar's construction. For example, if a ribbon of dyed purflings arranged in a selected sequence is to be repeated on the sides, back stripe, end graft, rosette, and soundboard, the motif should be inlaid around the soundhole and down the back plate before the soundbox is assembled, with sufficient material left over for the subsequent binding steps. This is what was done on the classical guitar made for this book. (On the steel-string, the elements of the instrument were integrated with repeating wood species:

ebony was selected for the headpiece veneer, fingerboard, bridge, binding, and end graft. An "accidental" sworl of pale figuring can be detected in each.)

The beginner with modest resources and facilities need not go to these lengths to come up with a visually pleasing result. The best way to achieve a rich, refined appearance is through simplicity and restraint. Modern decorative binding and purfling should not compete with but should show off the natural beauty of the tone woods. We recommend that the beginner start with a basic binding scheme, increasing the level of complexity in measured stages on subsequent instruments. A simple, tasteful design executed flawlessly is infinitely more impressive than a complicated scheme done poorly. Before commencing, the beginner should look ahead to Chapter 11, Purfling & Binding, and start thinking about the guitar's decoration.

ACOUSTICS

Unlike the violin, which has been the subject of acoustic research for more than fifty years, the guitar has been widely studied from the perspective of acoustic physics only since the last decade. Moreover, even with modern testing instruments, the guitar has been a far more complex subject for study than the vio-

lin. The guitar's production of sound in the low- and mid-frequency ranges has been explored and documented to some degree; its behavior in the higher frequency range seems, at present, to defy analysis.

As a result, the study of guitar acoustics currently seems to be of little direct technical use to the practicing luthier. It has, however, ably served to dispel many myths common in the popular media and in advertisements, and even some myths perpetrated by established luthiers themselves. Thus, guitar acoustics should be of more than passing interest to the student of guitar-making—not so much to learn what a guitar is, but to learn what it is not.

For example, we can learn from acoustics that a guitar is not an "amplifier" of the string signal; that the soundboard is not the sole sound generator; that the guitar cannot be acoustically subdivided into bass and treble halves; that the neck is not acoustically inactive; that sound does not radiate in "waves" from the bridge or travel down the braces like cars on a highway. Acoustical study will also shake the notion that sound is like a wind that must blow unencumbered through the soundbox, or that it must be channeled with baffles or reflected off the back, or that it is like a fluid soaking through the wood.

Reduced to its essence (and

freed from popular misconceptions), the guitar is a device built to release the kinetic energy found in its strings and to transform some of that energy into audible, controllable sound. When tightened and plucked, the musical string will produce a sustaining signal of pulses. These are composed of a blend of distinct pure tones whose frequencies are related mathematically (rather than randomly), as Pythagoras first discovered in ancient Greece. This highly organized information is then coupled to the guitar's soundboard and neck by the nut, saddle, and bridge. Rather than amplify (which would require a power supply), the guitar fritters most of the strings' energy away as heat, causing the guitar actually to warm up, albeit imperceptibly, as it is played. Only a small fraction of the strings' energy leaves the guitar as sound. The guitar's structure *transforms* that fraction by the energy storing and discharging process called resonance.

The tones we actually hear result from at least two acoustic mechanisms. One is a complex acoustic energy field radiating from the exterior surfaces of the guitar. The other, a series of rapid pressure fluctuations occurring at the soundhole (termed a "point-source" mechanism by acousticians), produces sound in the manner of a reflex enclosure (like many loudspeakers).

Several joint efforts by acoustic researchers and luthiers have produced guitars conforming to theoretical acoustical models, but these experiments as yet appear to be inconclusive. Until more definite and generally accepted results have been obtained, guitar design will continue to derive principally from the intuition, experience, and effort of those great builders who determined its traditional form.

CHAPTER 2

Although it is far beyond the scope of this book to engage in a detailed discussion of wood and woodworking technology, we feel that every student luthier should be familiar with the basics. This chapter is a distillation of what we think the luthier should know about wood, glue, abrasives, and tools. Readers who seek more in-depth discussions of these subjects should consult the Bibliography.

WOOD

Among nature's bounties, few contribute more to the quality of human life than wood. It has remarkable versatility as an engineering material and a natural beauty that graces any object for which it is used.

When wood is used to make stringed instruments, both its structural properties and aesthetic qualities are employed. Transcending these considerations, however, is a more esoteric purpose: the creation of music. In learning to cope with the natural characteristics of wood, the luthier thus

Materials & Tools

shares the concerns of the engineer and the cabinetmaker; in addition, however, the luthier must consider the material's acoustic purpose.

The Tree

The natural properties of wood that are of greatest significance to the luthier can be best understood by first considering the source—the tree.

All trees fall into two groups: those that yield softwood lumber (gymnosperms) and those that yield hardwood (angiosperms). When cut in cross section, both softwood and hardwood logs display growth layers around a central core (*pith* or *medulla*). When formed on the basis of yearly growth, these layers are known as *annual rings*. The outer rings, which conduct sap (nutrients in water solution) in the living tree, are called *sapwood*. Sapwood is always pale and undistinguished in appearance. The wood closer to the pith consists of cells that no longer conduct sap but instead serve only to support the tree. This is the *heartwood*, which

displays the characteristic color, figure, and fragrance of the species.

Most of the wood cells in a tree grow with their axes oriented vertically (*longitudinal cells*). Some cells, however, grow horizontally, radiating from the pith. These are called *medullary rays* or simply *rays*, and they demark the planes along which a log will split when cleft with a maul or froe. The end-grain of a log often will display checks running along ray planes (i.e., radially from the pith). The rays are very important to the luthier, as is seen below.

Quarter Sawing

When a log is cut into lumber, the sawn faces of each board will intersect the growth rings in various ways (Fig. 2-1). A lumber face that is perpendicular (or nearly so) to the annual rings is called the *radial* face, and when that is the wide face of the board, the lumber is said to be *quarter-sawn* or to have *quarter-grain* or *vertical grain*. The lumber face more or less parallel to

the annual rings (Fig. 2-1) is the *tangential* face, and when that is the wide face of the board, the lumber is said to be *flat-sawn, flat-grain,* or *slab-cut*. When the annual rings intersect the wide face of a board at an oblique angle, the lumber is said to be *skew-cut*.

These distinctions are critical to the luthier, for almost all instrument wood of choice is quarter-sawn. Quarter-sawing enhances acoustic qualities, bending properties, and dimensional stability.

To understand some of the advantages of quarter-sawn wood, it helps to visualize a piece of wood as a series of laminations, one next to another, each representing a growth layer. The layers are tied together by the ray cells, which pass through the piece perpendicular to the laminations. A piece in which the rays run straight across will have greater lateral rigidity than one in which the rays run through at an angle. This is especially noticeable in softwoods typically chosen for guitar soundboards: a quarter-sawn sheet of spruce will be dramatically stiffer and livelier than a skew-cut piece from the same log. These qualities translate into structural efficiency and acoustic responsiveness.

Similarly, the side-by-side "laminations" of quarter-sawn wood support one another during the bending process. With flat-sawn wood, the layers may separate as the fibers are stretched and bent.

Moisture Content

When lumber is freshly cut, it contains a large percentage of water by weight. In many species, the water weight exceeds the dry weight of the wood. The ratio of water weight to the dry weight of the wood is expressed as *percent moisture content*.

The water in wood exists in two forms: as *free* water, which is in the cell cavities, and as *bound* water, which is in the cell walls. When lumber is cut, the wood immediately begins to lose free water by evaporation; when the free water is gone, the wood begins to lose the bound water. Because the cell walls are swollen with bound water, the wood will shrink when the bound water begins to evaporate. The wood will continue to shrink as long as it loses bound water, and it will continue to lose bound water until it reaches a moisture balance with the surrounding atmosphere, the *equilibrium moisture content* (EMC). The EMC varies according to the temperature and relative humidity of the environment. These factors, of course, vary according to the season, the regional climate, and the location—indoors or outdoors—of the wood.

The story does not end here, however. Wood is *hygroscopic*—that is, it will take on as well as lose water, and shrink or swell in response to environmental temperature and humidity changes.

Shrinkage and swelling on the tangential face of a board is substantially greater than that on the radial face. Because of this unevenness in dimensional change over the surface of a board, it will warp, twist, bow, or otherwise distort if left to react to the environment without restraint. But if the radial faces are directly opposite one another, as in quarter-sawn lumber, the differential shrinkage and swelling

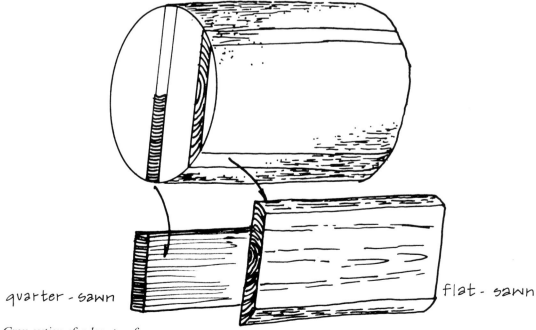

quarter - sawn   flat - sawn

2–1. *Cross section of a log: two faces.*

will occur at right angles and the board usually will not warp. This explains why we say that quarter-sawn wood has greater dimensional stability than flat-sawn or skew-cut wood.

Even when quarter-sawn wood is used, however, the luthier must remain extremely sensitive to shrinkage and swelling caused by environmental changes. When an instrument is assembled, the wood plates that previously had been free to shrink and swell are locked in a permanent relationship to one another. The wood, therefore must be dimensionally stable; i.e., at equilibrium with the shop atmosphere before it is used.

Moreover, the shop atmosphere must be at a medium relative humidity to reduce the degree of dimensional changes during the life of the instrument. If the instrument is assembled in a very humid atmosphere, it is likely to crack when brought into a dry environment; conversely, if assembled in a very dry atmosphere, it may buckle and distort due to swelling in a more humid environment. At normal indoor temperatures, a relative humidity of forty to fifty-five percent is ideal for guitar assembly. Our shop atmosphere is dehumidified with an air conditioner in the summertime and is humidified in the wintertime. We try to avoid assembling in the midst of seasonal changes.

Also important to the luthier is the fact that moisture leaves end-grain surfaces at least ten times as fast as it leaves side-grain surfaces. During drying, therefore, the end-grain surfaces will shrink rapidly and split (called *end-checking*) if left exposed. Every piece of instrument wood stored in a luthier's shop should be end-coated, at least until thoroughly seasoned, to retard moisture loss through the end-grain and thus avoid end-checking. We dip the ends in melted paraffin, but any moisture-proof material completely coating the ends will do.

When buying wood, then, the luthier must be aware of its moisture condition. The supplier will usually indicate whether or not the wood has been dried; if it has not, or if its moisture condition is suspect, the pieces must be end-coated and stacked with air spaces in between and all around until equilibrium with the shop atmosphere is reached. In the wintertime, if the wood has been stored in an open-air yard or an unheated warehouse, even if it is at EMC in that atmosphere, it must be brought into the shop environment and gradually acclimated to the shop's different temperature and relative humidity conditions.

GLUE

For centuries the glues most frequently chosen by luthiers have been organic protein compounds made from animal hides. Since World War II, however, several synthetic glues developed for industrial applications have gained acceptance for instrument making. Most commonly used are the polyvinyl acetate (PVA) glues, white liquids that dry to a hard, translucent film.

In more recent years, PVA glues have been modified to improve their heat and solvent resistance, creating a new family of adhesives. These are yellow liquids sometimes referred to as aliphatic resin (AR) glues.

Although many other glues are commonly used in woodworking, such as plastic resins, resorcinals, caseins, mastics, and epoxies, we generally recommend only animal (hide) and PVA (white and yellow) glues for instrument construction. We do, however, use epoxies and cyanoacrylate for repair work.

The choice between animal and PVA glue is a matter of personal preference. We find the PVA glues to be far more convenient and generally more durable than hide glue, and we do not subscribe to the belief held by some luthiers that the organic nature of animal glues make them more suitable for instrument construction. While certain aspects of bowed instrument construction make hide glue clearly the adhesive of choice, for guitar building we use white and yellow PVA's almost exclusively. For the guitars to be built from this book, therefore, we will instruct the student to follow our lead and use only white and yellow glues.

The choice between white and yellow glue for various parts of the instrument depends largely upon the amount of stress to which the joint will be subjected and the desirability of a reversible joint—that is, a joint that can later be taken apart without damage to the instrument.

Although white glues are extremely strong under normal conditions, they begin to release at quite moderate temperatures (about 130° to 140°F), especially in a humid environment. Yellow glues will withstand much higher temperatures, even in wet conditions. White glues are also subject to a phenomenon known as *cold flow* or *creep*—specifically, the plastic deformation of the hardened film—which can result in the failure of a continually stressed joint. This problem is negligible with yellow glues. Thus, the white glues are used where stress is relatively low and where the joint may well require disassembly in the future (such as the glue seam under the fingerboard). The yellow glues are for more permanent, durable joints, particularly in high-stress areas (such as the soundboard centerseam).

Regardless of the type of glue used, whether animal or synthetic, all wood-glue joints are functionally similar. A wood-glue joint is usually described as having five parts: the two pieces of wood; the two interpenetrating areas of wood and glue; and the glue line itself. The glue attaches itself to the mating surfaces of the wood by molecular *ad*hesion and holds itself together by *co*hesion. The principal strength of most glues is in *ad*hesion rather than *co*hesion; thus, ordinarily, the thinner the glue line, the stronger the joint. (Epoxy, which has enormous cohesive strength, is a notable exception to this rule.)

A thin glue line is obtained primarily by having smooth, flat mating surfaces on the parts being glued and sufficient clamping pressure properly distributed to average out remaining irregularities in the mating surfaces. It should be clearly understood, however, that massive clamping pressure is unnecessary on a well-prepared joint, especially when gluing softwoods. Pressure serves only to bring the mating surfaces together and hold them snugly until the glue has enough strength to do the job itself.

The amount of glue spread is an important factor in the success of the joint. If too much glue is spread, greater pressure may be required just to make it flow out from between the two pieces sufficiently to ensure a thin glue line. On the other hand, the glue must be spread sufficiently to ensure wetting of both mating surfaces. As soon as the glue is applied, it begins to be absorbed into the wood; if insufficient glue remains in the joint after it is closed and under pressure, a "starved," weak joint results.

Also critical is the amount of time the glue has to set before pressure is applied. If the glue precures before pressure is applied, the glue line will be thick and weak. Glues have limited assembly times: usually only a few minutes after spreading with the mating surfaces apart (*open* assembly time), and somewhat longer after the joint is closed and awaiting clamping pressure (*closed* assembly time).

Pressure is distributed on wide surfaces with *cauls*, appropriately shaped pieces of scrap wood inserted between the clamp and the workpiece. The clamping forces spread through the caul at about a 45-degree angle in all directions from the clamp jaws. The number of clamps and the thickness of the caul must be adjusted accordingly to ensure that pressure is being applied to the entire surface being glued.

Wood surfaces to be glued should be freshly machined, planed or sanded, and then wiped or blown off before gluing to avoid contamination in the joint. This is especially necessary when working with ebony and rosewood, for they exude oily extractives that can interfere with gluing. If the surfaces are machined, the tool knives must be sharp. Dull cutting tools will leave a burnished, glazed, or burned surface to which glue will not adhere well.

Ready-to-use glues have finite shelf lives. We buy glue in small quantities frequently rather than buying large containers less often. As synthetic glues age, they often become difficult to spread; sometimes they "skin" over so rapidly that they are virtually impossible to spread.

ABRASIVES

All abrasive materials serve the purpose of removing irregularities from a surface, whether it be wood, metal, glass, finish coatings, or whatever. Abrasives are typically minerals that may be in block form (sharpening stones), in composites (grindstones, cut-off wheels), coated on paper or cloth (sandpaper), or suspended in liquids or pastes (rubbing and polishing compounds). Our primary concern in this discussion is with coated abrasives to be used on both bare and finish-coated wood.

Coated abrasives are manufactured by adhering jagged mineral fragments to a backing material. The mineral coatings may be *closed coat,* in which case the particles are immediately adjacent to one another so that the backing is completely covered, or *open coat,* in which case the mineral parti-

cles are set with spaces in between, thus only covering about fifty to seventy percent of the backing surface.

Three natural and two synthetic minerals are used for virtually all commercially manufactured coated abrasives. The natural minerals are flint (actually quartz), emery, and garnet; of these we use only garnet on bare wood surfaces. The synthetics are aluminum oxide and silicon carbide, of which we use only silicon carbide on finish-coated surfaces.

The minerals are attached to paper, cloth, or fiber backings. For hand sanding, we use only light- or intermediate-weight paper backings (depending on the grit). Heavyweight paper, cloth, and fiber backings are used for machine-sanding applications; these are inappropriate for hand sanding because they tend to crease when folded around a sanding pad, leaving a jagged edge that can mar the surface being sanded.

When the particles are attached to a waterproof backing, liquid sanding lubricants (such as water) can be used with the coated abrasive. We refer to this as "Wetordry" paper. (Wetordry is a 3M Company trade name for waterproof sandpaper.) We use extra-fine-grit Wetordry paper with liquid lubricants for sanding finish-coated surfaces and also use it dry for extreme refinement of some unfinished surfaces, such as the ebony fingerboard, metal frets, and bone nut and saddle.

Grit size is determined by the number of openings per lineal inch on the screen through which the mineral particles are sifted in preparation for adhesion onto the various backings. We use #100-, #120-, and #220-grit open-coat garnet papers for sanding bare wood. When sanding finishing materials, we use a bluish-gray dry silicon carbide paper specifically formulated to minimize loading; #220- and #320-grits are used on undercoats, while #400 and #500 grits are used on topcoats. We use #360 and #500 Wetordry without lubricants for polishing bare woods, such as on the fingerboard, and #500 and #600 with lubricants on finish topcoats. Our practice has generally been to buy 8½-inch or 9 × 11-inch sheets and cut or tear them into smaller segments (six to a sheet) for hand sanding.

When smoothing a surface with coated abrasives, we choose an initial grit coarse enough to remove major irregularities without requiring an excessive amount of sanding, but not so coarse that the scratches left behind by the grit are more difficult to remove than the original irregularities. Basically, only the first grit used should actually work on initial surface irregularities; each succeeding grit should function primarily to reduce the scratches from the previous grit. It is essential to progress from one grit to the next systematically to ensure that scratches from the previous grit are thoroughly removed. For example, progressing directly from #400-grit to #600-grit on a finished surface will make thorough removal of the #400 grit scratches far more difficult than if #500-grit were used in between the two.

When sanding a flat surface, it is absolutely essential to wrap the paper around a block or pad of felt, rubber, cork, or similar material. The block serves to ensure that the sandpaper is not dug into the surface with bare fingers. We use felt blocks (available from finish-supply houses) when dry sanding and rubber pads when wet sanding. We also use thin rubber pads for working in very tight places. The use of a material with some give, rather than, say, a block of wood, dramatically prolongs the useful life of the sandpaper. (Note, however, that a flat, hard block, such as wood, is necessary when sanding two adjacent surfaces of extremely dissimilar hardnesses, such as pearl and spruce, to avoid creating irregularities.)

We also sand almost all curved surfaces with a block or pad, using sandpaper *without* a block or pad only for very specialized operations. Felt blocks can be either firm or soft; the firm blocks are best for flat surfaces and the softer blocks best for curved surfaces.

On finishing materials, fine-grit sandpaper is followed by rubbing and polishing compounds. These are discussed along with finishes in Chapter 14.

TOOLS

Most guitarmaking tools are simply woodworking tools of the sort available from hardware stores, industrial suppliers, or mail-order tool catalogs. The difference between instrument making and most other forms of woodworking, however, is in the extremely close tolerances to which the parts must be made and, therefore, the precision with which the wood must be worked. The tools, then, must be capable of producing precision work. Many of the woodworking tools we use are designed for patternmakers, who require a similar level of precision. Other ordinary tools may be of sufficient quality that they can be modified for precise work. Still others, however, are simply not well suited and should be avoided.

The following is a basic list of tools that we use for guitarmaking, with a brief discussion of requirements for each tool or category of tools. The student may wish to expand on this list. A few additional special tools will be required occasionally during the procedures; because these are typically required for a single step only and are not of general utility to the instrument maker, we have excluded them from the basic list.

Chisels

We use long-bladed chisels for most of our work; these are sold as *paring* or *patternmaker's* chisels. If the student has a set of short-bladed (*butt* or *cabinetmaker's*) chisels, these will do, but if buying new chisels for guitarmaking, choose paring chisels from a catalog tool supplier.

All chisels should be made of high-quality tool steel; although the best chisels are expensive, they are worth it. If you buy paring chisels, start with a ¼-inch and a 1-inch, and fill the set in from there. You should also have a ¼-inch butt chisel for close work where the ¼-inch paring chisel might be cumbersome. A ½-inch butt chisel will be useful as a "glue" chisel, for cleaning up glue squeeze-out. (This can be an inexpensive chisel sharpened as usual but with the edge burnished back with #600-grit sandpaper.) Finally, a ³⁄₃₂-inch chisel, long or short, will be essential for certain very fine operations. If difficult to find, a ³⁄₃₂-inch chisel can be fashioned by grinding down a ⅛-inch chisel on a belt sander. If you grind this or any other tool, do not let it get hot enough to discolor.

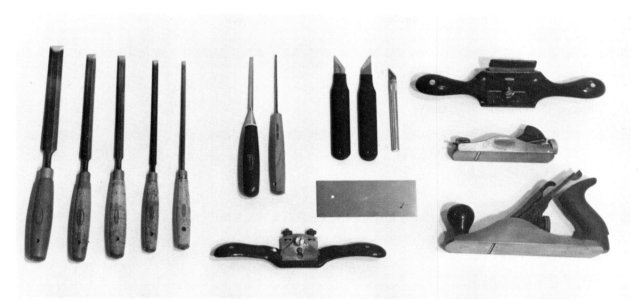

2–2a.   Edge tools. Shown, clockwise from left to right, are paring (long-blade) chisels; a ¼-inch butt (short-blade) chisel for close work; a ³⁄₃₂-inch chisel for special operations; violin-makers' knives (also called skew knives or skew chisels); a razor knife; a scraper plane; a block plane; a smoothing plane (03 or 04); a scraper; and a spokeshave.

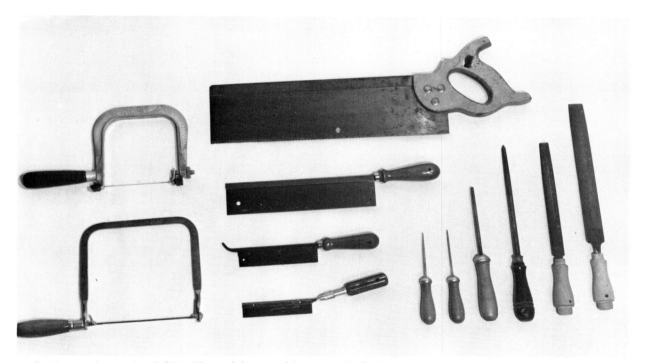

2–2b.   Saws and rasps (wood files). Shown, left top and bottom: a jeweler's saw (for cutting shell inlay); a coping saw; middle, top to bottom: a backsaw; a dovetail saw; a miniature backsaw; a razor saw; right: miniature files; a rat-tail file; a round rasp (or file); and half-round rasps (or files).

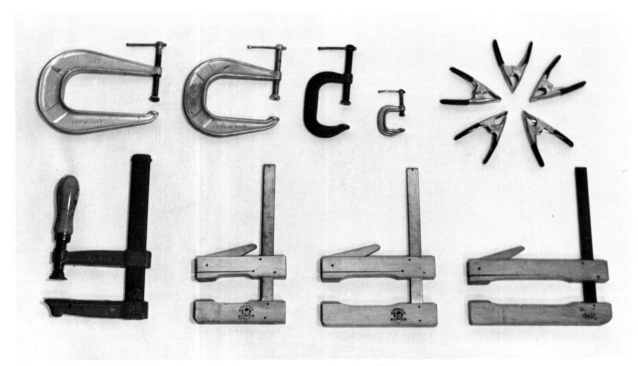

2–2c. Clamps. Shown, from left to right, are: at top, deep-reach (also called deep-throat) C-clamps; regular C-clamps; small spring clamps; at bottom, bar clamp; 4-inch, 6-inch, and 8-inch reach cam clamps.

Planes

The basic planes required are a block plane and either a #03 or #04 smoothing plane. Some hardware-store varieties are good quality, but avoid cheap discount-store planes. A good plane is truly a tool to be used for a lifetime and longer, so consider the expense of high-quality planes a wise investment.

With an old plane or even a new one, performance will be greatly enhanced by smoothing and truing the bottom (*sole*) on a flat abrasive surface, and sanding off all sharp corners. Progressively finer grits of emery paper taped to a piece of plate glass will provide a good surface for grinding the plane sole. Number 120-grit garnet sandpaper or a similar grit of emery cloth will eliminate sharp corners.

Knives

We use a *violinmaker's* knife for carving operations. This is sometimes referred to as a *skew* knife; it has a chisel-type blade ground at an angle and beveled on both sides for carving in either a right-hand or left-hand direction. These knives are also available beveled on only one side, in which case they are called *skew chisels*. For carving with skew chisels, two—one for each direction—are necessary. Skew knives and chisels are available from general tool catalogs, but the best ones are found in instrument-makers' supply catalogs.

For a multitude of small cutting and scribing operations, we use a *razor* knife. This has a pencil-shaped metal handle and inexpensive replaceable blades. The best-known razor knife is the X-acto knife, available at most hobby stores. Disposable blade scalpels, available from surgical-supply houses, also make excellent razor knives.

Saws

It is helpful to have a large backsaw or crosscut saw around for a few large cuts on guitar parts, but large hand-saws are not really essential in guitarmaking. If you do not own such a saw, try to borrow one before going out to buy it. What you must have, however, is a variety of *dovetail* saws. These are very fine cutting backsaws available from tool catalogs and sometimes in hardware stores. Get a 10- to 12-inch dovetail saw for all-purpose use; an 8- to 10-inch saw for frets (see Chapter 12 on fretting tools first); a miniature backsaw for small work such as the set-up (see Chapter 16); and a *razor* saw for superfine kerf cuts. The most common razor saw is made by X-acto and is available at hobby stores.

Drills

A good hand drill will always have two pinion gears; a drill with only one pinion gear will quickly bind up and eventually fall apart. The crank must operate smoothly during all drilling operations, lest you spoil a piece of work with a jerky movement. Drill bits should be made of high-speed steel. A full set of bits from 1/16 inch to 1/2 inch in 1/64 inch steps is nice to have, but most of the sizes are not really necessary. Brad-point bit sets are especially helpful for certain operations, but again,

only a few sizes are really important. If you do not think you will have other uses for a drill set, it is probably best to read along and buy drill bits as required.

Measuring Tools

These are extremely important to the guitarmaker. Rulers should have various scales: large (such as 1/16 inch) for easy reading and small (1/64 inch or 1/50 inch) for precise measurements. Better rulers are made of stainless steel with engraved markings; aluminum rulers are not as dimensionally stable and are usually of lower quality. The basic measuring tools required are a 6-inch and a 36-inch ruler.

A note on measuring scales is pertinent here. We use standard English fractional scales for all measurements except those pertaining to the fingerboard and scale length. For the fret spacings on the fingerboard, a decimal scale is easier to use. Thus, we describe the scale length, for example, as 25.4 inches rather than as a fraction, so that mathematical division for the frets can be carried out directly. Conversion charts for fractions to decimals and vice versa are available at many hardware stores; they can also be found on many small measuring tools such as 6-inch rulers and micrometers.

Also in our category of measuring tools are straightedges

and squares. (We sometimes use a ruler as a "straight edge" but when we refer to a *straightedge,* we mean the tool used specifically for checking the straightness of a surface.) An 18-inch straightedge is an invaluable tool for guitarmaking. This can be bought as an already-milled straightedge (very expensive) or as a piece of 18-inch bar stock you can have ground at a machine shop. Also, a good 18-inch machinist's combination square will have a heavy-duty graduated ruler, which makes a fine straightedge.

The basic square required is a 4- or 6-inch tool-steel machinist's square. Buy a good one. A 6-inch machinist's combination square will double as a 6-inch ruler (and can be used as a small straightedge); thus, you may decide that it is worth buying.

Clamps

You can never have too many clamps, but good ones are shockingly expensive, so try to get along with the basic set. Remember, though, to buy only cast-iron or cast-steel clamps. Cheap pressed or stamped-steel clamps are virtually worthless, and cast aluminum clamps will not permit cranking to anywhere near the level of pressure available with cast-iron or cast-steel clamps.

For metal clamps, you will need the following (minimum quantities in parentheses): 4-

inch-opening C-clamps (four); 2½- to 3-inch-opening deep-reach (at least 3-inch reach) C-clamps (two); and 4-inch or 5-inch-reach sliding bar (12-inch bar) clamps (two). You will also need a very-deep-reach C-clamp for gluing the bridge—about 5 inches of reach for the steel-string and about 6 inches of reach for the classical.

You will also need quick action (*cam*) clamps for a multitude of operations. We have a whole lot of these, but you can get by with eight: 4-inch reach (four); 6-inch reach (two); and 8-inch reach (two). These operate in much the same way as do metal bar clamps, but instead of having a screw and handle for compression, one of the padded wooden jaws has a cam that applies pressure when thrown.

Finally, you may wish to buy small spring clamps for gluing the interior linings of the guitar. Before doing so, refer to the discussion in Chapter 9 on applying kerfed linings.

Files

Some files are made for wood only and some for metal only; you should know the difference before you buy. Basic wood files for guitarmaking are 8-inch, 10-inch, and 12-inch half-round wood files, and for the classical builder, a small wood rattail and a ½-inch round rasp. For fretwork you will need an 8- to 10-inch flat mill file and a 12- to 14-inch flat mill file that checks out straight on at least one side. Take your straightedge to the hardware store and check out the 12-inch and 14-inch mill files to get one that is straight enough for fret work. Also nice to have is a 3-inch segment of a mill file (about 1 inch across) for various small filing jobs. We call this a *file stub*.

A set of needle files is useful for carving the crest of the classical headpiece, finishing the notches in the nut, and other small operations.

Other Tools

A wonderful tool for carving the neck, and one we consider essential, is the *spokeshave*. The spokeshave operates like a plane but has a very short sole and side-mounted handles for working in areas where a plane cannot reach. High-quality spokeshaves, available from tool catalogs, are usually reasonably priced.

Also essential are several simple and inexpensive tools that have dozens of applications. A 6-inch tool-steel scraper blade is better for our type of work than a small scraper with a handle; scraper blades are sold through catalogs and in hardware stores. Thicknesses are often noted in metric, so look for a 0.8-millimeter (about 1/32-inch) scraper as the basic tool; other thicknesses are generally necessary only for specialized operations. You also will need an ordinary scratch awl, a protractor (plastic is fine), and a plastic drafting triangle.

For checking consistency of thickness of the guitar plates, you will need an outside caliper. This need not be an elaborate tool, but it should be sturdy enough to provide readings without excessive flex. A vernier caliper is a necessary tool for obtaining actual thickness measurement. Very inexpensive vernier calipers are available from catalog suppliers and are generally adequate; for more precise measurement (for instance, in thousandths), you will pay quite a bit more. Good dial calipers are very expensive and no more accurate than vernier calipers; they are, however, a little quicker to read.

Specialized Tools

Several of these, such as the fretting hammer, flush-cutting end nipper (horizontal jaw pliers), and fret file, are described in the fingerboard and set-up chapters. The end nipper has a variety of uses, however, so buy one to start out but wait until the fingerboard chapter to modify it as required there. A set of feeler gauges (available through auto-parts suppliers) is very good to have, but wait until you reach the fingerboard chapter to decide just what you need. Also very useful are an inspection light and mirror for examining interior parts after the soundbox is assembled. The mirror is like a dentist's mirror but larger; it can be found in hardware stores and tool catalogs. The inspection light is nothing more than an ordinary socket with a low-wattage bulb; an in-line on/off switch makes it easier to use. For prying apart glue joints in the event of errors, pick up a 5-inch-wide joint knife and dull its leading edge so that it will enter a tight seam but not cut into the wood. You may not need this tool, but it is very nice to have around just in case.

Note: For the purfling and binding, an additional specialized guitarmaking tool is required in some instances. This is the purfling cutter, which is described in Chapter Eleven.

Power Tools

We consider a hand-held electric router to be indispensable for a wide variety of operations. Thus, although hand tools are emphasized for the most part in this book, we assume that the student will add a router to the basic tool list. An expensive router is unnecessary; look for a basic one-half- to one-horsepower router. Almost all operations can be done with a straight bit; ¼ inch is the size usually supplied with a new router. Other bits are discussed elsewhere in this book as they are required.

A straight-line edge guide has various uses, and a laminate-edge trimming guide is required for routing the binding-and-purfling ledges (see Chapter Eleven). These are available as accessories from power-tool suppliers.

Vises

The very best vise to use for luthierie is a universal woodworking vise with jaws that swivel to hold irregularly shaped objects. The student, however, can make do with an ordinary tabletop or woodworker's bench vise. The jaws must be padded with belt or sole leather to avoid marring wood surfaces; a thick padding also will permit an ordinary vise to hold some irregular shapes.

It is actually possible to build a guitar with no vise at all; the workpieces can be held with clamps to the workbench when necessary.

Sharpening Stones

Chisels, plane and spokeshave blades, knives, and other cutting tools must be razor sharp for best results. A good set of sharpening stones is expensive, but no woodworker should be without them. We use medium and fine "India" stones and a hard "Arkansas" stone for all cutting tools.

Sharpening stones must be lubricated during use. The choice of lubricants depends upon the type of stone; we use oilstone for all sharpening operations. Many commercial stone oils are available, but we have found nothing that works better than a one-to-one mixture of mineral oil and kerosene. The stone oil not only lubricates and cools during the sharpening process, but also has the important function of floating metal particles off the surface of the stones so that the metal is not impregnated into the stone. As the oil on a stone gets dirty with metal grit, it must be wiped away and fresh oil applied.

A Note on Sharpening

Sharpening is a skill that can take a long time to master; we recommend obtaining a text that describes the process in detail or seeking the advice of an experienced woodworker. Basically, however, sharpening is simply a process whereby the tool edge is ground until a burr develops on the side of the edge opposite the stone. The burr is worked back and forth by flipping the tool over and over on the stone until the burr gets finer and finer and finally peels off, leaving a razor edge. Finally, the tool is stropped on a smooth, hard piece of leather.

The original bevel must always be maintained on plane and spokeshave blades. On chisels and knives used for guitarmaking, however, the bevel must be softened into a "belly." This is somewhat different from sharpening for other woodworking purposes, but it is essential for fine shaving during brace and neck carving (Fig. 2-3). We almost never carve with gouges and we never use a mallet. Many woodworkers "hollow grind" their chisels, but this is inappropriate for the kind of work that the luthier's chisel is expected to do.

Sharpening a scraper blade is very simple, but there are many different types of edges required for different applications, and this complicates matters somewhat. The basic edge is produced with one or two shots with a file, as in Fig. 2-4. The file leaves a burr that is rather rough and irregular; this will leave deep

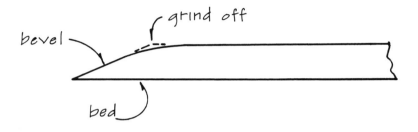

2–3.   *The luthier's "bellied" chisel.*

2–4.   *Sharpening the scraper by grinding a burr with a flat file.*

scratches in a surface if left unburnished. An unburnished
edge is excellent for scraping
off an old finish but is unsuitable for smoothing operations.
To burnish, the edge must be
straightened up with a burnisher (the smooth tang of a
round file will work well as a
burnisher) and then turned
over, as shown in Fig. 2-5.

For an ultrasmooth edge,
the scraper also can be sharpened with a fine-cutting stone.
This will leave an almost perfectly square edge with an ultrafine burr. As is, the edge
will work well for very fine
operations such as leveling a
finish; if turned further with a
burnisher, it will work well for
fine-smoothing bare wood.

2–5. For smooth cutting, the burr is turned with a hardened burnisher or, as shown here, with the smooth area at the tang end of a rattail file.

CHAPTER 3

A few preliminary steps are required before actual construction begins. Certain implements must be made and certain crucial dimensional requirements must be calculated. In this chapter the student makes the necessary implements, and we provide and describe a layout drawing illustrating how we coordinate the guitar's dimensional requirements.

IMPLEMENTS

Many guitarbuilding systems require elaborate molds for side bending and for assembly of the guitar. Molds provide a solution—albeit superficial—to some of the difficulties associated with aligning fragile surfaces in precise interrelationship during enclosure of the soundbox. For the same reason, production systems invariably use molds, permitting consistent mass production by factory workers who are not, strictly speaking, luthiers.

We feel, however, that making molds is an unnecessary drain on the student's time

Preparation & Planning

and energy. In our view, mold assembly systems represent an encumbrance, rather than a solution, for the aspiring hand-builder.

We use a traditional system of construction that we describe as *free-standing assembly* or, simply, *free assembly,* in which the guitar is built on a flat guitar-shaped workboard without the use of a mold. Although maintaining alignment and symmetry is more challenging in free assembly than it is with mold assembly, we feel that the advantages are well worth the extra care required. By dispensing with molds we are free to build almost any shape we desire, without having to make a new mold for each. This enables us to build truly custom instruments—the player can request any shape or size and we can deliver it. Moreover, in our experience, the student is liable to treat the mold as a means of holding the guitar's shape even if the sides are improperly bent. This can bind permanent deforming stresses into the instrument, which are likely to impair the instru-

ment's tone and may ultimately result in structural failure.

In making implements for free assembly, we begin with a template, which consists of a piece of sheet metal, Masonite, or even just heavy cardboard, cut out to represent one-half the soundbox outline (Fig. 3-1). After the template is constructed, we make an assembly workboard, which is a guitar-shaped lamination of plywood about 1½ to 2 inches thick. The only other implements we will make in this chapter are sanding boards—sheets of plywood or particle board faced with sandpaper.

In later chapters we will describe several more simple implements that can be made as the instrument progresses.

PROCEDURE: MAKING A TEMPLATE

Modern classical-guitar templates vary within a relatively limited size range. Lower bout widths range from 14 inches to 14⅝ inches. Anything in the 14½-inch area would be considered grand concert size, while anything under 14¼ inches would be considered a small box. Body lengths range from about 18¾ inches to 19½ inches.

Steel-string templates vary far more widely, starting at about the same size as the smaller classicals (14 inches wide across the lower bout), but ranging up to 17 inches and sometimes even 18 inches in width. The smaller boxes (14 to 15 inches) are often preferred by folk artists. Between 15 and 16 inches is a popular size among performers of solo instrumental music. This size range is often chosen for recording instruments because it tends to produce a more even, or "flat," response. The widely used "dreadnought" shapes are guitars about 16 inches wide with typically bass-rich response that can be played hard (especially with a flat pick) without distorting. Guitars sometimes referred to as jumbo size typically range from 16¼ inches to 17½ inches in width and, when properly constructed, have a deep, powerful tone. These are favored by many blues musicians. Body lengths on steel-string guitars range from about 18¾ inches to 20½ inches.

We recommend that the beginner start with a steel-string body size in the middle range, measuring between 15½ and 16 inches wide at the lower bout and 19½ to 20 inches in length. A balanced tone will be easiest to achieve in that range.

You can trace a template from an actual guitar of your desired size and shape by laying the guitar face down on a large sheet of paper and penciling around half its outline. For best results, use a pencil ground in half lengthwise, and press its flat face against the guitar's sides as you swing around the curves in a single stroke. Determine the centerline accurately (calculate its location across the fretboard) and connect it at the top and bottom with a ruler. To design your own template, follow the simple instructions below. (The figures in parentheses in the following procedure correspond to the templates used for the guitars depicted in this book.)

TOOLS
36-inch ruler
scissors or razor knife
optional: French curve
optional: coping saw or
　bandsaw
optional: scratch awl
optional: metal cutting
　shears
optional: metal file

MATERIALS
heavy paper or cardboard,
　24 × 9 inches
optional: ⅛-inch pressboard
　(Masonite) or ¹⁄₁₆-inch
　aluminum, same
　dimensions as cardboard

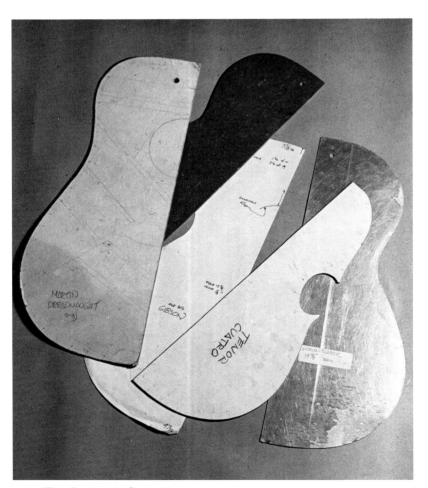

3–1. *Templates made from various materials.*

Step 1—Drafting the Parameters

On a sheet of graph paper, draw a straight line with a ruler to the desired length of the soundbox (SS, 20 inches; CL, 19¼ inches). Next, measure out to a parallel line the distance that denotes the desired width of the lower bout, as shown in Fig. 3-2 (SS: 8 inches; CL: 7³⁄₁₆ inches), then to a parallel line for the waist (SS: 4⅞ inches; CL: 4½ inches), and then to one for the upper bout (SS: 5⅞ inches; CL: 5⁵⁄₁₆ inches). Measure down from the top of the template to locate the position of the deepest point on the waist (SS: 6⅞ inches; CL: 7 inches).

Step 2—Drawing the Curves

The upper bout must begin at the top of the template as a straight line for a short distance before beginning to curve. On the steel-string, the straight portion is not less than 1½ inches and must be at a 90-degree angle to the centerline. On the classical, the straight portion is slightly less than 1 inch and is at slightly *less* than a 90-degree angle to the centerline.

The sharpness or roundness of the waist curve is a personal touch, but remember that the sides must eventually be shaped to match; tighter, sharper curves will compound the beginner's difficulties and

increase the chances of side breakage.

Finally, the lower bout must end at the bottom of the template, either along a straight

line square to the straight edge (SS) or along a very flattened curve (CL).

With these strictures in mind, sketch in the connecting

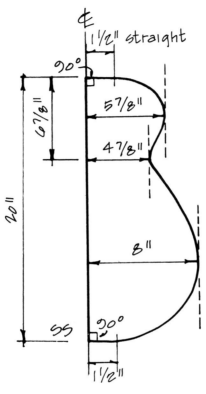

3–2. Dimensional layout—steel-string and classical templates.

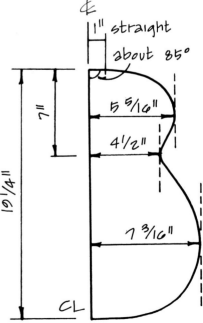

curves freehand. Keep refining the curves with the pencil, trying to make all the transitions smooth and graceful. Sketch lightly at first, and make your line bolder as the curves are refined by your eye. A compass and a French curve can help.

Step 3—Cutting Out the Template

You can now cut out the template with a scissor or razor knife, trying to retain the smooth continuity of the curves. This paper template will serve adequately for the purpose of making a guitar from this book. You can, however, make a more durable template by tracing your paper template onto heavy cardboard, scoring it repeatedly with a razor knife until you cut through; or on pressboard by sawing as close as possible to the traced pencil line with a coping saw or bandsaw and filing the edge smoothly down to the line.

A cardboard or pressboard template can be used to make an aluminum template. Lay the pressboard template on 16-gauge (1/16-inch) aluminum sheet and trace its outline with a scratch awl. Cut closely to the scratch line with metal shears, taking care not to pucker or wrinkle the sheet in any way. Finally, file the soft metal down to the line. File all the sharp edges smooth and round.

Step 4—Notching the Waist

Cut or file (as appropriate) a tiny V-notch precisely at the deepest point on the waist of the template.

PROCEDURE: MAKING THE ASSEMBLY WORKBOARD AND WORKBOARD SHIM

The assembly workboard is a flat plywood construction platform, cut out to approximate the guitar's shape, upon which the major assembly steps are performed. The bottom of the workboard has a rectangular protruding stub that provides a platform for a squaring tool during several assembly steps, as well as a "foot" for stowing the workboard when it must be put aside. A hole is drilled through the workboard precisely where the center of the guitar's soundhole will be; a bolt and wingnut will be sent through the workboard at this point, tightening onto a clamping "shoe," a small rectangular piece of wood that serves to clamp the guitar's soundboard face down to the workboard.

The workboard shim is a sheet of paper cut out to match the guitar outline and edged with 1/8-inch-thick sheet cork (such as can be purchased in rolls at variety and discount stores). It serves to lift the guitar's rim off the workboard, allowing clearance for the soundboard arch and permitting the guitar to lie on the workboard without rocking.

TOOLS
long ruler or straightedge
template
drill and 11/32-inch bit
electric saber saw or
   bandsaw
rattail file
wood file
razor knife
weights (e.g., cinder blocks)

SUPPLIES
glue and spreader (spatula,
   brush, or the like)
5/16-inch flat-head machine
   screw, 4½ inches long,
   and matching wingnut
   and washers

MATERIALS
two sheets ¾-inch AA or
   AC plywood, 36 × 18
scrap block 1¾ × 1 × 7
   inches
one sheet stiff paper at least
   21 × 16 inches
one sheet 1/8-inch cork at
   least 21 × 16 inches (1/8-
   inch cardboard will do if
   cork is unavailable)
CL only: one 3 × 12-inch
   piece of 1/8-inch
   pressboard, such as
   Masonite

Step 1—Making the Workboard

The two pieces of ¾-inch plywood must be glued together to form a single 1½-inch piece. Unless you have very large clamps, it will be difficult to apply clamping pressure in the middle of 18-

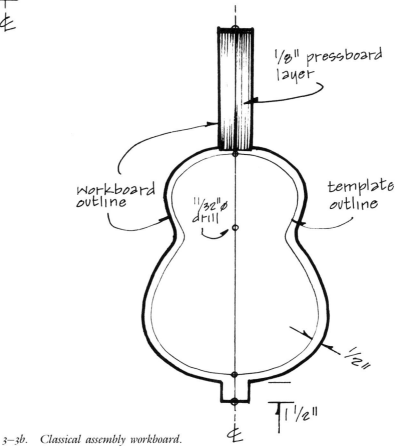

3–3a. Steel-string assembly workboard.

tra ½ inch or so around the outline, saw out the workboard to the guitar's shape, including the neck extension. Round the edge with a rasp. (See Figs. 3-3a and 3-3b.)

From the top of the guitar outline, measure down and mark approximately where the soundhole center will be located (for both guitars, 5⅞ inches). Drill through the workboard at that point with the ¹¹⁄₃₂-inch bit.

The clamping shoe is a simple rectangular block with an ¹¹⁄₃₂-inch hole drilled at mid

inch-wide sheets. The simplest way to glue up the two sheets is to weight them with several large cinder blocks.

Find a surface that you know is flat. Lay down enough newspaper to protect against glue squeeze-out. Lay the first plywood sheet down and spread glue over it evenly. Place the second sheet on top and weight with at least four large cinder blocks.

Let the glue dry for at least two hours. Remove the weights, and draw a centerline lengthwise on the smoothest (or flattest) face. Draft the guitar outline with the template. The neck segment should be 3 inches wide and should extend about 12 inches from the top of the outline. Leaving an ex-

3–3b. Classical assembly workboard.

length. The edges should be beveled with a file or rasp (Fig. 3-4).

The workboards in our shop have two additional holes drilled in the neck segment to accept two large ½-inch machine bolts (let in so they are flush with the workboard's surface); these actually bolt right through our worktable so that the main body of the workboard overhangs the edge of the table.

Step 2—Making the Workboard Shim

Draw the guitar outline on a sheet of stiff paper and cut it out with a razor knife or scissors. Now repeat this process on a sheet of ⅛-inch cork and cut out the center so it looks like Fig. 3-5a or 3-5b. (Note in the classical guitar that the center is only partially cut out, leaving a wider expanse of cork across the upper bout.) Apply glue to the undersurface of the cork and glue the cork and paper together, making sure the centerlines and edges line up. Note the small dotted-line rectangles that represent additional shims; these must be glued on later to span the distance between the sound-board and workboard directly under the clamping shoe.

The neck extension of the classical workboard is layered with a 3 × 12-inch piece of ⅛-inch pressboard (such as Masonite) to bring the surface of the neck extension up to the same level as the top of the workboard shim. Fig. 3-6 shows the finished classical workboard.

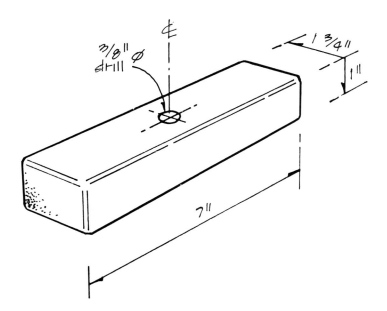

3-4. *Clamping shoe for assembly workboard.*

SANDING BOARDS

Sanding boards are used wherever a flat abrasive surface is needed. The large sanding board consists of a *flat* 18(to 20)×24(to 28)-inch piece of plywood or particle board, faced with fairly coarse sandpaper (about #80 grit). If you can come by a wide sanding belt, you can cut a single sheet of sandpaper large enough to cover the whole board; otherwise you will have to lay up smaller sheets. The sandpaper can be glued to the sanding board with spray adhesive or white glue. Sometimes a wide piece of plywood will warp if it is coated on one side and not the other; you may thus wish to put sandpaper on both sides if you can.

The small sanding board is about 5 × 10 inches, and is similarly faced with fairly coarse paper. We have several small sanding boards, with different grits for different applications. The other grits are handy, but not essential.

LAYOUT

The scale length and string spacing chosen for any particular guitar will determine the fingerboard taper and sound-hole position. When designing a new instrument, we plot these dimensions on a layout drawing to ensure that they do not conflict disastrously on the finished guitar. The layout drawings shown in Figs. 3-7a

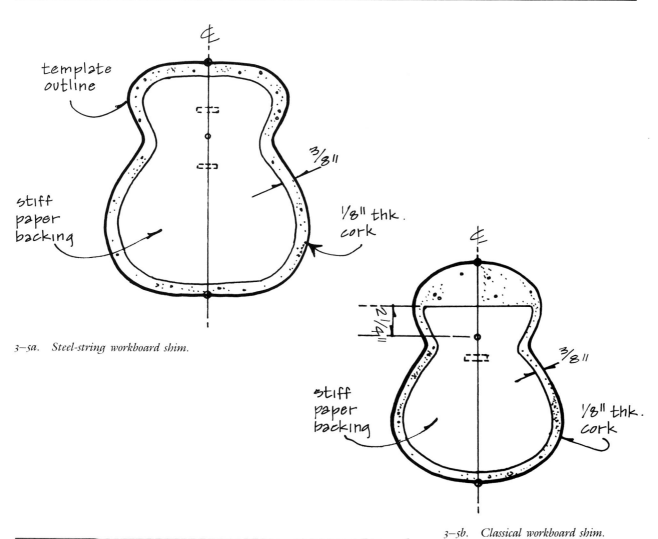

template outline

stiff paper backing

3/8"

1/8" thk. cork

3–5a.   *Steel-string workboard shim.*

2 1/4"

3/8"

stiff paper backing

1/8" thk. cork

3–5b.   *Classical workboard shim.*

3–6.   *Classical workboard and shim with pressboard addition to neck extension.*

and 3-7b are representative of the full-sized drawings we did for the guitars built in this book. The layout instructions below can be followed either as an exercise to produce a full-sized layout with the dimensions we will actually use or to create a layout for a different scale length or string spacing.

On a long sheet of paper, draw a straight line about 27 inches long. This represents the centerline of the guitar. Near one end, make a mark (A) and draw a line through it perpendicular to the centerline. This represents the front edge of the nut.

Measure down the centerline from A and place a mark (B) at the scale length (SS: 25.4 inches; CL: 25.6 inches).

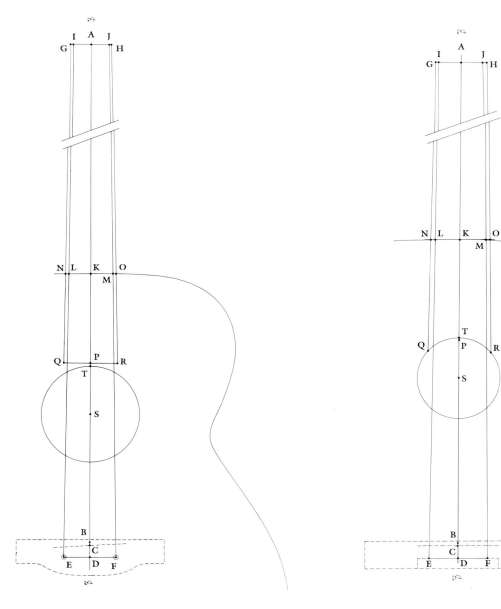

3–7a. *Steel-string layout.*

3–7b. *Classical layout.*

Make another mark (C), adding the compensation increment to locate the midpoint of the saddle (SS: add .15 inch; CL: add .10 inch). Finally, place a mark (D) a little further down the centerline (SS: add ½ inch; CL: add ⅜ inch) and draw a perpendicular line through it to denote the string apertures in the bridge. On that perpendicular line, you will add marks E and F, which represent the two outer strings and determine the overall spacing of the strings at the bridge. On the guitars in this book, that spacing is SS: 2⅛ inches; CL: 2^{11}⁄₃₂ inches (the typical ranges for string spacing at the bridge are SS: 2–2¼ inches; CL: 2⁵⁄₁₆–2⅜ inches).

Back at the perpendicular line through point A, add marks G and H, determining the desired width of the fingerboard at the nut. On the guitars in this book, that width is SS: 1^{11}⁄₁₆ inches; CL: 2^{1}⁄₁₆ inches (the typical ranges for nut width are SS: 1½–1⅞ inches; CL: 2–2⅛ inches). Measure in from G and H ⅛ inch on each side and add marks I and J to indicate the outer string positions at the nut.

The outer strings are delineated by connecting I to E and J to F. We then measure down the centerline from A and mark K to denote the neck/body joint location at either the twelfth or fourteenth fret, depending upon which is appropriate for the guitar being

built. For the guitars in this book, the distance A to K will be SS: 14³⁄₃₂ inches (fourteenth fret); CL: 12^{51}⁄₆₄ inches (twelfth fret). Draw a perpendicular line through K traversing the outer strings at marks L and M. Measure out from L and M ³⁄₁₆ inch on each side and mark at N and O to denote the edges of the fingerboard at the neck/body joint.

Again measuring from mark A down the centerline, make a mark P at the soundhole end of the fingerboard. On the steel-string, P will be at the (imaginary) twenty-first fret location, 17^{27}⁄₃₂ inches from A; on the classical, P will be at the nineteenth fret location, 17^{1}⁄₁₆ inches from A. Measure down from P on the steel-string 2⅛ inches and on the classical 1⅝ inches to mark S, the soundhole center. Draw in the soundhole with a compass set at a radius of SS: 2 inches; CL: 1^{11}⁄₁₆ inches. Mark T where the top of the soundhole intersects the centerline. The distances from K to S and from K to T will be very useful when laying out the soundboard for the rosette and bracing patterns.

On the steel-string, draw a perpendicular line through P and then run lines from G through N and from H through O intersecting the perpendicular line through P at points Q and R. On the classical, simply run lines from G through N and from H through O to the soundhole

edge at points Q and R. These lines will delineate the fingerboard taper.

With the full-sized layout thus drawn, the fingerboard dimensions can be derived to ensure that the fingerboard taper corresponds to the chosen string spacing. (On the guitars built in this book, however, we provide actual fingerboard outline dimensions in Chapter 12, where the fingerboard will be made.) The layout also ensures that the soundhole will be accurately located on the blank soundboard so that the fingerboard ends at an appropriate spot.

Note: The outer treble string position on the classical at point J is represented in Fig. 3-7b to be slightly further inboard of the fingerboard edge than point I on the bass side. This is because the actual location of the outer treble string notch on the classical is ³⁄₁₆ inch from the fingerboard edge, rather than ⅛ inch, to give greater clearance all along the treble edge. The strings thus form a slightly asymmetrical pattern on an otherwise symmetrical fingerboard. For purposes of laying out the symmetrical fingerboard taper, however, we use the symmetrical dimension of ⅛ inch on both the bass and treble sides. When the layout is completed, the outer treble string line can be erased and moved over if the student wishes to see the actual layout as it will appear on the finished guitar.

CHAPTER 4

NECKSTOCK TIMBERS

The principal criteria for choosing suitable neck wood for the acoustic guitar are stability (limited reaction to environmental changes), working ease, and strength-to-weight ratio. The relative importance of each of these criteria varies depending upon the specific type of instrument being built.

Of all the tone woods, far and away the most versatile timber for neckstock is Honduras mahogany (*Swietenia macrophylla*). It grows from southern Mexico through Central America, Colombia, and Venezuela into the Amazon Basin to northern Bolivia and eastern Peru. For woodworking generally, the species is so stable and easy to work that it is often used as a standard for rating other tropical species. These characteristics, combined with its excellent strength-to-weight ratio, also make it the standard material for neckstock timber.

Other varieties of mahogany, such as Cuban (*Swietenia mahogani*) and various African species (*Khaya,* spp.), are also

The Neck & the Headpiece

used for neckstock, but these are appreciably heavier than Honduras without a proportionate increase in strength.

On lower-tension (nylon-strung) instruments, builders often accept a slight decrease in strength in exchange for a significant decrease in weight. Thus, for most flamenco and many classical guitars, the timber of choice is Spanish cedar (*Cedrela,* spp.), an aromatic timber found widely in Latin America. Spanish cedar enjoys a strength-to-weight ratio and stability comparable to Honduras mahogany but is about fifteen to twenty percent lighter on the average. Although somewhat coarser than mahogany, it is similarly easy to work.

Conversely, where strength and stiffness are of paramount concern, North American rock maple (*Acer saccharum*) is typically the timber of choice. Over the years, maple has been widely used on production steel-string guitars because it has been common and inexpensive. Although in most parts of the country maple is now comparable to mahogany

in price and availability, it continues to be found on production acoustic and electric guitars. Rock maple is an extremely strong, tough material, but because this characteristic is coupled with relatively high weight, it is seldom used on lightly constructed instruments such as classical guitars. Maple with a curly figure is highly prized as neck material, especially when it is used in conjunction with curly-maple back and sides. The spectacular shimmering optical effect of curly maple (also called tiger maple or fiddleback maple) is especially startling when enhanced by the curved cross section of the neckshaft (Fig. 4-1). Other varieties of maple can also be used, but none of these are as stiff as rock maple.

We have also seen rosewood used for neckstock on some instruments, but we do not recommend its use, especially for beginners.

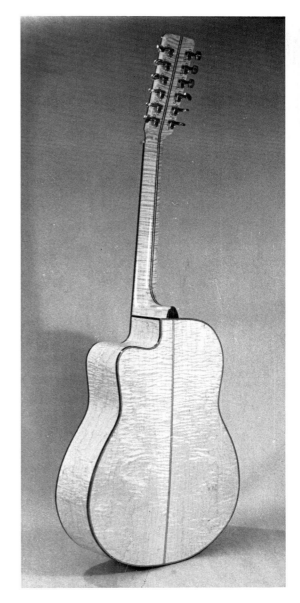

4–1. A highly figured curly-maple neck can be used for dramatic effect in combination with a curly-maple soundbox. The curly-maple twelve-string guitar shown was built at Stringfellow Guitars.

Many domestic hardwoods can be and have been used successfully on good acoustic guitars and, where more exotic species are unavailable, these should be considered. Cherry, walnut, and birch are examples of local woods that are usable as neck material. Although these and other "woods of opportunity" are less desirable than the woods of choice mentioned above, the luthier's budget and lack of access to the material may compel an acceptable compromise.

Regardless of the species chosen, the material used for the neck should be straight-grained and free of defects. Quarter-sawn material is best, but for relatively homogeneous species such as mahogany, it is not essential.

Acoustic Considerations

Contrary to some popular beliefs suggesting that the neck participates only minimally in sound production of the instrument, many neck resonances can be shown to occur at significant amplitudes. We can only speculate, however, about the specific effect of using one material as compared to another. All other things being equal, we can presume that a guitar with a mahogany neck, for example, will produce a different response than one with, say, a maple neck. Any claim by a builder of effective control over this factor, however, must be viewed with some skepticism. Thus, for ex-

ample, the claim is sometimes made that a rosewood neck will enhance sound quality. In truth, however, the contribution of the neckstock timber can be undone as well as enhanced by a bewildering variety of other factors. The most that we can say is that the student builder should seek to use traditional materials of good quality, and leave more esoteric decisions about the choice of timber to a time when most other factors have been brought under control.

PROCEDURE: CONSTRUCTING THE NECK BLANK

In a mass-production setting, the guitar neck blank is often cut in one piece from a single slab of mahogany. Sometimes the slab is laid up as a sandwich of lumber and veneers, producing contrasting stripes down the center of the neck.

The handbuilder can improve on the factory product (and conserve materials in the process) by constructing the neck blank from separate pieces for the headstock, shaft, and heel. Although more time consuming, the joined headstock is structurally sounder because of its grain orientation (Fig. 4-2). By avoiding a short-grain headstock, the builder reduces the likelihood of fracture due to shock. Also, neckstock lumber is more readily available and less expensive when purchased in smaller di-

mensions rather than in thick slabs. And even if thick slabs can be obtained, waste is reduced by the use of multipiece as compared to one-piece construction.

When building a neck with separate stock for heel and headpiece, it also becomes possible to laminate the shaft by itself either to strengthen the shaft or because material of sufficient width is unavailable. Thus, with imagination, a strong, elegant neck can be built up from pieces that might otherwise be considered waste.

In the following procedure the shaft and headstock are cut from a straight-grained, accurately dressed mahogany billet; the heelblock is glued under the shaft opposite the headstock and can consist of either a single block of mahogany or a stack of segments cut from a mahogany billet similar to that used for the shaft (Fig. 4-3). A single block simplifies the heelblock-gluing procedure, but it may be easier to obtain another billet rather than a block. Some highly regarded luthiers, in any case, believe that the stacked heelblock provides a marginal increase in shock resistance over the single block. The heelblock later will be shaped into a heel and neck-to-body joint.

The headstock is attached with a scarf glue joint. The mahogany billet is cut through its width at a 15-degree angle, producing a shaft section and headstock section. The sawn faces of the two sections are smoothed, and the headstock is then glued to the underside of the shaft, forming a continuous face for subsequent gluing of decorative veneers.

The 15-degree cut provides an adequate gluing surface to maintain the integrity of the scarf joint while also providing sufficient downward string tension on the nut. Torres used this angle for his headpieces. Instruments made by some great builders, notably Hermann Hauser and Manuel Velazquez, however, utilize a shallower angle, evidently to increase the available gluing surface for the scarf joint. Other builders use a steeper angle, increasing the downward tension on the nut. The choice is purely a matter of priorities, but extremes should be avoided. In particular, the student should observe that increasing the angle of the headstock both decreases the available gluing surface and increases the tension on the joint. We therefore discourage a radical increase in the angle of the scarf.

The neck blank is most easily assembled on a workboard that permits clamping from all

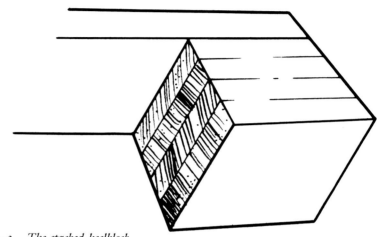

4–3. The stacked heelblock.

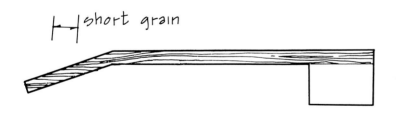

In a one-piece neck blank, the headstock grain runs parallel to the shaft producing a short-grained configuration.

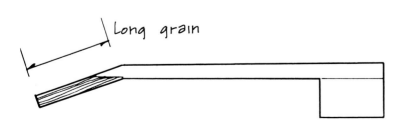

The long-grained configuration of the joined headstock produces a more shock-resistant neckblank.

4–2. Headstocks: one-piece and joined.

directions. This need be no more than a reasonably flat section of lumberyard variety 2 × 6 that is about 3 feet long; one end is clamped to the workbench; the other end is left overhanging.

TOOLS
6-inch machinist's square
protractor
36-inch ruler
block plane
backsaw or fine-tooth
    crosscut saw (see Step 2)
scraper
small and large sanding
    boards
optional: marking gauge
glue chisel
sharp pencil
two bar and several cam
    clamps (min. 6-inch
    opening)
four C-clamps (4-inch
    opening, min. 3-inch
    reach)

IMPLEMENTS
workboard
two small, rectangular scrap
    blocks
two cauls, ¾ × 3 × 2
    inches (SS) or × 2½
    inches (CL)
thin hardwood caul, 2 × 4
    inches

SUPPLIES
AR yellow glue

MATERIALS
two 24 × 3 × ¹¹⁄₁₆(to ¾)-
    inch dressed mahogany
    billets, or one billet as
    above plus one well-
    squared mahogany block,
    3 × 3 × 4 inches (SS)
    or 4⅝ inches (CL)

Step 1—Layout

Measure 7 inches (SS) or 8 inches (CL) from one end of the billet and, with a square, draw a line across its top surface. Using the protractor, draw a diagonal line on the side of the billet at a 15-degree angle from the top edge, starting at the initial 7- or 8-inch mark (Fig. 4-4). Flip the billet over and, with the square, draw a line across the underside, starting at the end of the diagonal line. These will be the guidelines for the 15-degree-angle saw cut.

Step 2—Making the Cut

This cut must be made with a sharp, well-set backsaw or a fine-tooth crosscut saw. If your saw is dull or in need of a set, it will be virtually impossible to make the cut accurately.

Clamp the billet to the workbench with a piece of waste stock underneath. (It is most convenient to make this cut at elbow height.) Begin the cut adjacent to, not on, the diagonal line. Start the cut very slowly, keeping its entry accurately parallel to the line.

Continue through the billet with long, deliberate strokes, pausing frequently to examine your progress. Wandering can be overcome somewhat by flexing the saw back to the guidelines.

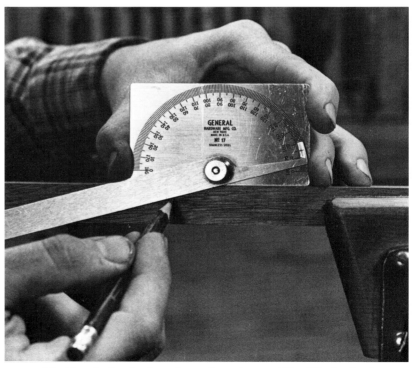

4-4. *Marking the headstock angle on the mahogany billet. The headstock segment in the photo has been measured off from the left.*

Step 3—Truing Angled Surfaces

The two segments must be stacked and clamped as shown in Fig. 4-5. The fresh-cut surfaces should form a continuous angled plane, with the knife edge at the bottom just at the end of the workboard.

If the knife edge of the headstock piece is not parallel to the beginning of the angled surface on the shaft, align the two segments so that the overcut of one and the undercut of the other average out, crossing at the center. The original guideline at the beginning of the angled surface of the headstock should still be visible. If it is not, draw it again with the square.

Begin planing with a coarse setting to remove large irregularities on the angled surface. If the knife edge recedes and the plane strikes the workboard, loosen the clamp and move the segments forward to the edge, realigning carefully before clamping. Similarly, if your guideline is obliterated, redraw it further back before proceeding. You should have at least ½ inch extra stock for trial and error.

After the surfaces are approximately level and continuous, read the surface in all directions with the edge of the square (Fig. 4-6). Adjust the plane for a fine cut, and remove material as necessary to improve the reading. Alternately plane and read the result until the surface is free from hollows and lumps.

4–5. Planing the sawn faces of the scarf joint. The headstock and scarf segments are stacked as shown to ensure a continuous face for the headstock after the scarf is glued.

4–6. The flatness and continuity of the angled surfaces of both the headstock and the shaft are verified during the truing operation by reading the surface longitudinally, laterally, and diagonally with a straightedge.

Finally, scrape off the fine plane marks with a sharp scraper. Flex the blade gently while refining the surfaces, and read the results with a straight-edge and backlight. Proceed until you are satisfied that the entire surface is flat and smooth.

Alternate: The foregoing plane-and-scraper technique for truing the surfaces of the scarf joint makes considerable demands upon the patience and manipulative skills of the woodworker. If you, as a beginner, become frustrated by repeated unsuccessful attempts to achieve a true surface, use the small sanding board instead of the plane and scraper. Although sanding does not yield as perfect a gluing surface as does an edge tool, it will produce an adequate glue joint.

Short, vigorous straight-line strokes with the sanding board on the angled surface should quickly yield accurate results. Watch that the knife edge and the seam between the two segments remain parallel to the guideline drawn on the headstock. If they begin to converge, it means that the surface is tipped; it must be replaned until they are parallel again to avoid a crooked result when the headstock is glued.

Step 4 (SS Only)—Reducing Headstock Thickness

The steel-string guitar headstock must be reduced in thickness to ½ inch before assembly to accommodate standard tuning machinery.

Set a marking gauge to ½ inch and scribe a line around the two sides and the end of the headstock segment. If you have no gauge, measure off two points on each of the two sides and the end of the piece and connect them with a pencil and ruler. Accurately connect the ends of the lines across the angled surface.

Secure the headstock segment in the vise, smaller face up. Adjust the plane to a coarse setting and hog the bulk of the waste material off the headstock face (Fig. 4-7). As you approach the line, reduce the plane setting to a fine cut. Favor the edges of the surface until you closely approach, but do not obliterate, the guidelines, leaving the center portion to bulge slightly. Then work the bulge down,

4–7. Reducing the thickness of the steel-string headstock segment to accommodate standard tuning machinery. (The classical headpiece is left at full thickness.)

avoiding the edges. Leave the center to swell very slightly. Scrape the center down slowly, checking constantly with a straightedge. Remove the segment from the vise and stroke on the sanding board in either short, deliberate, straight-line, and unidirectional strokes or, carefully, in a circular motion. Check your progress often. Stop when your guidelines are almost, but not quite, obliterated.

Step 5—Getting Ready

When the headstock segment is glued to the underside of the shaft, the oblique angle of the scarf joint causes clamping forces to be directed down the length of the headstock and the shaft. With the glue acting as a lubricant, the two segments can slide past one another or, if stopped at their ends, can torque upward unless secured by additional clamps.

The longitudinal forces must be countered by stop blocks at each end; the torquing forces must be countered by clamping both segments down to a scrupulously flat work surface. When the glue dries, the pieces must not have shifted, even by the smallest amount. Thus, three sets of clamps must be used: two stop-block clamps, three hold-down clamps (two for the shaft and one for the headstock), and four C-clamps on the scarf joint itself.

Place the headstock and

shaft segments on edge on the neck workboard. They should sit square or very nearly so; if they do not, the edge of the billets should be planed or jointed to minimize tipping.

Arrange the two pieces in the configuration in which they will be glued, with the headstock and angled surface of the shaft forming an uninterrupted flat show face. Then trace a pen mark on the board or work surface along the headstock and shaft, as well as at the two ends, so that the pieces can be removed and accurately realigned during the subsequent steps.

Clamp the two stop blocks at the end marks. Place the two segments back on the line, in between the stop blocks. The segments should positively butt up against the stop

blocks, follow the traced line on the board, and maintain the linear continuity of the headstock show face. If they do not, adjust the stop blocks until the segments sit accurately between them. Remove the headstock segment.

Carefully apply the two shaft hold-down clamps without tipping the shaft or moving it away from the pen line (Fig. 4-8).

Step 6—Gluing the Scarf Joint

Read the following text and then perform the operation as described without actually applying any glue—a dry run—in order to familiarize yourself with the manipulation of the various clamps and cauls.

Apply a generous film of

4–8. *The scarf joint ready for gluing. The square is used to ensure that the shaft is not tipping. Note the guideline along which the headstock will sit when clamped. Although this photo shows bar clamps used as hold-downs, cam clamps will serve equally well.*

AR glue to the angled surface of the headstock and replace the segment under the shaft, abutting the stop block and along the guideline on the workboard. Apply the headstock hold-down clamp about two inches from the seam, using light pressure only.

Place the scarf-joint cauls on opposite sides of the glue seam. Keep the edges of the cauls just within the headstock and shaft knife edges. Apply two C-clamps to the lower part of the cauled joint. Tighten them just sufficiently to hold them in place. Apply two more C-clamps so that the four clamps are in a rectangular arrangement. Alternate the clamps so that the handles approach from both sides of the joint to allow more room for their manipulation (Fig. 4-9).

Tighten down all the clamps firmly in the following sequence: stop-block clamps; shaft hold-downs; headstock hold-down; scarf-joint clamps in rotation. Clean up the bulk of the squeeze-out with the glue chisel. Let dry for at least forty-five minutes.

Step 7—Evaluating and Truing

Remove the clamps and chip or scrape off remaining dried squeeze-out. Scrape any drips off the assembly board before putting it aside.

Evaluate the glue joint. If the two segments have shifted badly, either laterally or longitudinally, it may be necessary to saw them apart, resurface, and reglue. The ultimate result must be a headstock that is not crooked and that presents a flat gluing surface for the decorative veneers. If you are satisfied with the joint, the gluing face may be surfaced with straight, unidirectional strokes on the large sanding board.

Step 8—Marking for the Heelblock

If the guideline at the beginning of the angled surface of the shaft has disappeared, use the square to draw a new line across the shaft precisely where the angled surface begins. Draw a second line parallel to the first, $\frac{3}{16}$ inch (SS) or $\frac{1}{8}$ inch (CL) toward the heelblock end of the shaft. Measure down the shaft from the second line the distance from the nut to the fourteenth fret—14.08 inches (SS)—or the twelfth fret—12.80 inches (CL). Draw a third line across the shaft, parallel to the first two, at that point.

Finally, draw a fourth line parallel to the first three, $\frac{15}{16}$ inch (SS) or $1\frac{5}{8}$ inch (CL) further toward the end of the shaft. Using a square positioned on the top surface of the shaft, continue the fourth line down the side of the shaft. This last line will denote the location of the end of the heelblock (see Step 10).

Note: Steel-string only—If you plan to make the subsequent cuts with a table saw, draw another line on the side of the shaft $\frac{1}{8}$ inch further toward the end, and align the heelblock to that mark *instead* of to the fourth line.

4-9. *The scarf joint glued. Note that C-clamps alternate handle direction to avoid crowding.*

Step 9—Preparing the Stacked Heel Pieces or the Heelblock

If you happen to have obtained a single, well-squared block for the heel, you need only one accurate gluing surface. If you have obtained a billet similar to that used for the neckshaft and headstock, it must be cut into segments, all but one of which must be surfaced on both faces. If the block or billet has been machined (dressed) by your supplier, its surfaces should be ready for gluing as is, without further preparation.

For the guitars built from this book, a billet cut for a stacked heel must yield a sufficient number of segments to total not less than 3 inches in height. As the steel-string heelblock is 3 × 3 × 4 inches and the classical heelblock is 3 × 3 × 4⅝ inches, the segments must be 4 inches long for the steel-string or 4⅝ inches long for the classical.

Step 10—Gluing the Heelblock

A one-piece block can be glued with the neckshaft clamped face down on the workboard. Apply a moderate amount of AR glue to the dressed face of the block. Place the glued face on the neckshaft with the end of the block aligned to the registry line on the side of the shaft. Move the block in a tight circular motion until the glue starts to grab; then realign the block to the mark and to the edges of the shaft.

Position one bar clamp (with the handle up) toward one end of the block and tighten it gently, making sure that the bottom jaw is *flat* against the bottom of the workboard. If the block starts to slide in one direction or another, jockey the clamp and tighten gently again. Continue until the block stops moving while remaining in proper alignment.

Position the second clamp toward the other end of the block. When the block is stable and correctly aligned, gradually snug down both clamps, watching for movement. If the block does not remain cor-rectly aligned, loosen the clamps and readjust.

To clamp a stacked heel, we use a different procedure. Lay a piece of waxed paper on the workboard, covering the area where the heelblock will be glued together. Clamp the neckshaft on its side on the workboard. The segments that make up the stack must be first laid up dry. Align the stack to the mark on the side of the neckshaft. Position stop blocks on either side of the stack and clamp them in place (Fig. 4-10).

Remove the segments from the workboard, apply a moderate amount of glue to one face of the first block, and press it back against the underside of

4–10. *Clamping the stacked heel. The stop block keeps the pieces in the stack from sliding around under clamping pressure. Note that the block on top of the stack is faced with waxed paper, as is the workboard underneath the stack.*

the shaft between the stop blocks. Apply glue to one face of each successive block, pressing it in place. Place a caul (a scarf-joint caul will do) on the stack, overlapping the neck-shaft and the bottommost segment. Clamp down with light pressure.

Use a thin caul to protect the top surface of the neck-shaft and apply the two clamps to the stack, as shown in the photo. Tighten gradually.

After three minutes, remove the stack hold-down caul and stop blocks. Let the assembly dry for about one hour before removing the clamps.

Step 11—Cleaning Up, Trimming the Neckshaft and Height of the Heelblock

Remove glue squeeze-out with the glue chisel and scraper. Smooth the side faces of the heelblock by stroking the neck blank on edge on the large sanding board.

Cut back any overhang of the neckshaft so that the ends of the shaft and the heelblock present a continuous face. Clean up the surface by stroking upright on the sanding board.

Note: Steel-string only—If you are using a table saw and, in accordance with the instructions in Step 8, aligned the heelblock ⅛ inch past the fourth line, trim the heelblock and shaft together to the fourth line, making the cut dead square to the surface of the shaft.

Finally, trim the heelblock so that the height of the heel-block and shaft taken together is 3⅛ inch (SS) or 3¹¹⁄₁₆ inch (CL). Mark guidelines all around the bottom of the heelblock and saw off the excess; on the table saw, trim with the shaft pressed against the rip fence.

Step 12—Laying Out the Shaft

Draw a centerline down the middle of the neckshaft by finding the midpoints on the second and third lines drawn across the shaft in Step 8 and connecting them with a straight line that travels to the end of the shaft. Using the square, carry the centerline down the end of the neck blank and then back along the bottom of the heelblock.

Refer to the layout drawing (Chapter 3) and, measuring outward from the centerline, draft the outline of the fingerboard onto the shaft.

PROCEDURE: CLASSICAL ONLY— SLOTTING THE HEELBLOCK AND TRIMMING THE HEADBLOCK

The neck-to-body joint on the classical guitar consists of two slots cut into the heelblock, which will receive the sides during soundbox assembly. The slots are cut at the location of the twelfth fret, divid-

ing the heelblock into the *heel,* which will remain part of the neck, and the *headblock,* which will live inside the guitar body. After the slots are cut, the sides of the headblock must be trimmed to final dimension.

We use a table saw to make these cuts on our own instruments, but we provide a hand tool procedure below.

TOOLS
12-inch dovetail saw or 8- to 10-inch backsaw
machinist's square
sharp pencil
clamps as needed
6-inch ruler

IMPLEMENTS
hardwood veneer or other hard, thin material, 2½ × 5 inches
small sanding board

Step 1—Marking the Heelblock

From each end of the third line drawn across the shaft in Step 8 of the neck-blank construction procedure (the neck/body junction line), mark a point ¹⁄₁₆ inch toward the end of the neck blank. Connect those points to the midpoint of the third line (Fig. 4-11a). Starting at the ends of the resulting slanted lines, continue them down the side faces of the heelblock as in Fig. 4-11b. Accurately connect the ends of those lines across the bottom of the heelblock. Measure ¹⁄₁₆ inch from the line across the bottom toward the headstock along the bottom centerline.

Connect that point with the ends of the cross line to form a shallow triangle, as in Fig. 4-11c.

The slanted lines on the top of the shaft and bottom of the heelblock, along with the lines on the sides of the heelblock, will be the guidelines for sawing the slots into which the sides will be fitted. Draw additional 7/32-inch lines on either side of and parallel to the top and bottom centerlines to denote the bottom limit of the slot cuts, leaving a 7/16-inch web between the heel and the headblock.

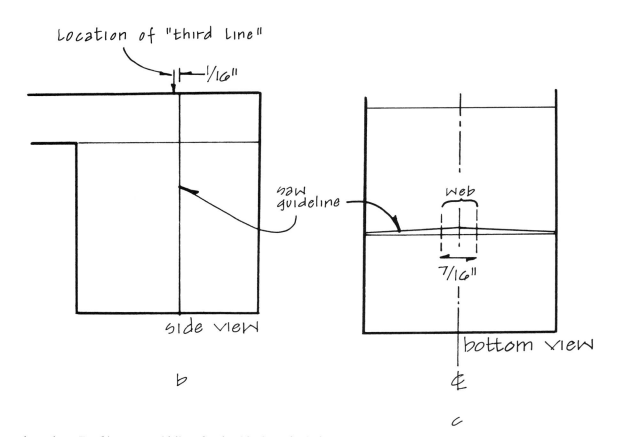

4–11a, b, and c. Drafting saw guidelines for the side slots (classical).

Step 2—Cutting the Slots

The entry cuts for the slots must be made adjacent to the lines drawn down the sides of the heelblock. These cuts must be made with a fairly rigid saw so that the entry line does not waver. The saw should leave a kerf of about .040 to .050 inch, which is fairly typical for a 12-inch dovetail saw or an 8- to 10-inch backsaw. A piece of hard, thin material must then be inserted into the initial saw kerf, enabling you to make a second cut directly adjacent to the first, widening the kerf to .080- to .100-inch in order to receive the sides. The insert must protrude an inch or so from the heelblock so that it can be used as a flush guide for the adjacent cut. In Fig. 4-13, the operation is shown using a piece of hardwood veneer for the insert. A piece of formica or sheet plastic will work equally well.

4–12. Making the initial saw cut for the slots in the Spanish heel. The thumb and forefinger are used as a fence to guide the saw.

Clamp the neck blank on its side to the workbench. The entry cut must be made on the side of the line away from the headpiece. Use the thumb and forefinger as a guide along the line (Fig. 4-12), and slant the saw so that it will enter and cut parallel to the slanted lines on the top of the shaft and the bottom of the heelblock. Proceed slowly, keeping the saw as level as possible. The saw must follow both slanted lines all the way down, stopping when it reaches the boundaries of the 7/16-inch web.

Withdraw the saw and insert the veneer or other thin material. Press the saw against it and, holding as shown in Fig. 4-13, cut slowly and carefully to the depth of the initial kerf. The resulting double kerf should be sufficiently wide to allow insertion of the sides.

4–13. Making the adjacent saw cut to widen the slot. A piece of hardwood veneer or other hard, thin material is inserted into the initial saw kerf to guide the adjacent cut.

Repeat the operation for the other side of the heelblock.

Step 3—Trimming the Headblock to Width

The final width of the headblock will be 2 inches. Mark 1 inch on either side of the centerline and, with the square, draw guidelines on the top, end, and bottom of the headblock.

Clamp the neck vertically, as shown in Fig. 4-14. (If you have a side-mounted woodworker's vise, use that to hold the shaft.) It is critical that you *do not* touch the end-grain face of the heel with the saw. For this reason, we recommend that you insert a piece of veneer or other hard, thin material into each slot to protect the end-grain face of the heel while making the cut.

Cut straight down with a backsaw or crosscut saw outside the guidelines. Work slowly and carefully, keeping the saw as level as possible.

Clean up the saw marks on the sides of the headblock with the small sanding board. Again, it is *critical* that you do not cut into the end-grain face of the heel with the edge of the sanding board; thus, you may wish to keep the veneer in place while sanding off the saw marks. (See Fig. 4-15 for plan view.)

Using #120-grit garnet sandpaper, knock off the sharp vertical edges of the end-grain face of the headblock.

4-14. *Sawing the cheeks of the headblock. Note that a scrap of veneer is inserted into the slot to protect the end-grain face of the heel.*

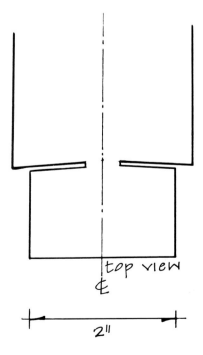

4-15. *Plan view.*

TRUSS RODS

As the steel-string guitar evolved from its original gut-string predecessors early in this century, players demanded narrower, longer necks and higher-tension strings for increased loudness, comfort, and expanded musical ranges. Because of higher tension and smaller neck cross section, neckshaft distortion was the inevitable result. This eventually required the insertion of an internal stiffener, called the *truss rod*, inside the shaft.

It was later discovered that a small amount of "give" in the neckshaft produced better playability than an unyieldingly straight neckshaft. This resulted in the development of adjustable truss rods that could be tightened to adjust and control the neck's response to string tension. This permitted the setting of an ideal neck-to-string relationship regardless of the neck's stiffness or the gauge of the strings being used.

Unfortunately, most popular truss-rod designs in use today possess several serious technical drawbacks. Most notable are their reliance on the compression of the neck to operate and the need to cut a large access hole in the headpiece right at the spot where it suffers maximum stress.

We have selected a truss-rod design with none of these drawbacks. Its original application appears to have been inside banjo necks early in this century, but its use inside guitars is quite recent. The "over-and-under" design does not rely on neck compression to operate and it distributes the bending forces evenly along a curve to which the plane of the fingerboard is tangential. It is extremely powerful; it can force the strings flush against the frets, so it needs very little adjustment to be effective.

Our truss rod has its adjusting nut located inside the headblock, driven with a small 5/16-inch open-end wrench or a 5/16-inch socket on a 1/4-inch drive ratchet with an extension piece.

PROCEDURE: STEEL-STRING ONLY— TRUSS-ROD FABRICATION

Our steel-string guitar uses an "over-and-under" adjustable truss rod (Fig. 4-16). It is fabricated from a single 36-inch length of 3/16-inch circular cross-section steel rod, which is available in many hardware stores, junkyards, and metal supply houses. The steel rod is heated with a torch and then folded upon itself by bending it around a pin and hammering the fold flat. One of the arms is threaded and the other is cut slightly shorter. A metal cap is fabricated, which stops the short arm but allows the threaded arm through. An adjusting nut is turned onto the longer threaded end.

Warning: a shiny, untarnished metal surface on the rod may indicate the presence of a heavy metal plating (i.e., chromium). When heated, the plating vaporizes, releasing toxic fumes in small amounts. Occasional exposure may not present a health problem, but frequent exposure is indeed hazardous. It is best to file the plating off for several inches in each direction from the focus of the flame. (Vacuum the filings up afterwards.)

TOOLS
hammer
center punch
vise (metal jaws)
drill (hand-, electric-, or
    drill-press)
hacksaw
smooth mill file, single cut
die for 10-32 N.F. thread
die handle or open-end
    wrench
oil can
small anvil or metal block
    (hammering surface)

MATERIALS
36 × 3/16-inch-diameter
    steel rod (circular cross
    section)
3-inch length of 3/4 × 3/16-
    inch-thick cold rolled-steel
    bar
gummed metal flashing tape

Step 1—Folding the Rod

Measure 17 inches away·
from one end of the rod. At
that point file a V-notch about
1/16-inch deep. Now, fix a
short length of rod or wedge-
shaped scrap metal into a vise.
It will serve as a bending
pivot.

Focusing the flame from a
propane torch on the filed
notch, twirl the rod slowly until a portion about 2 inches
long glows cherry red (Fig.
4-17). You must now work
very quickly; if you take too
long, the rod will lose its heat
and the rod arms will refuse to
fold flat.

Hook the V-notch onto the
pivot and pull the rod ends
quickly together (Fig. 4-18).

Hold the ends tightly with one
hand and, with the other,
whack the hot fold with a hammer on an anvil (Fig. 4-19).
(Many metal vises have a miniature built-in anvil. Any small
chunk of flat steel will also
serve.) Hammer until there is
no gap whatsoever between
the arms. The arms should lay
flat and parallel when you are
done. Do not hammer the fold
unnecessarily.

After the rod has cooled, cut
one arm of the rod to a length
of 16 1/8 inches with a hacksaw.
Cut the other arm to 15 3/8
inches.

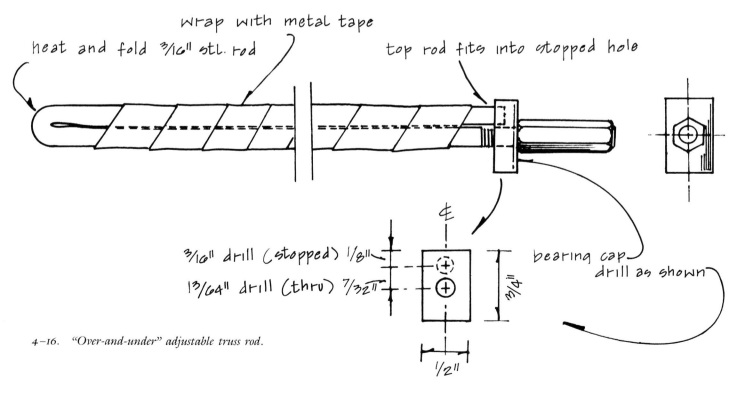

4–16. "Over-and-under" adjustable truss rod.

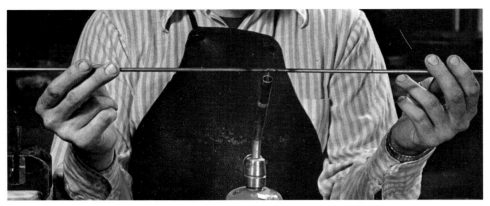

4–17. Heating the truss-rod stock prior to bending.

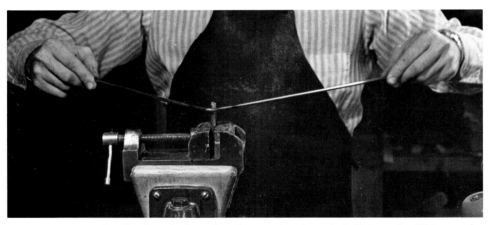

4–18. Bending the heated stock around a pivot pin held in a vise. This must be done quickly to avoid cooling of the heat-softened area.

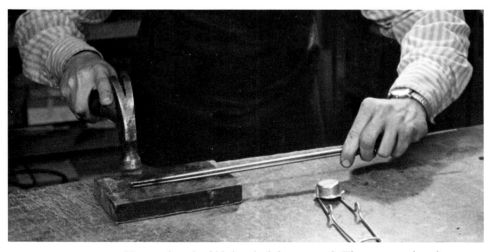

4–19. Hammering the folded end of the truss rod. The arms are kept in alignment while the fold is flattened.

Step 2—Threading the Rod

The longer arm is now threaded with a 10-32 N.F. thread die (these can be purchased in hardware stores). Threading proceeds as follows: With a fine-tooth mill file, chamfer the end of the long arm into a flattened cone shape. Place the filed end vertically in a vise (gently flex the shorter arm out of the way). A small vise-grip wrench clamped to the longer arm, as shown in Fig. 4-20, will aid in counteracting the twisting of the rod during the subsequent threading procedure. Have a can of light machine oil handy.

Initial mounting and threading of the die onto the rod end will require patience and a steady hand. After the die is mounted and the initial threads cut, back the die out and apply some oil from the can. Rethread the die until it stops, and give it one more turn. Back off the die two turns, and add another drop of oil. Turn the die back down till it stops. Give it another turn, back it off, oil, and back down again until it stops; then one more turn, back off, oil, and so on. Continue until 1¼ inches of thread appears. Threading the rod without backing off periodically will result in a poor-quality thread.

Step 3—Fabricating the Cap

The truss-rod cap is fabricated from a short segment of

¾ × ³⁄₁₆-inch-thick steel bar. Fabricating the cap consists simply of drilling two holes lined up vertically, as shown in Fig. 4-16. Note that the top hole is drilled very close to the top edge of the cap. An elongated portion of the cap is left below the holes—this extra material will facilitate prying out the rod in the unlikely event of a truss-rod replacement.

Using a square, scribe a line across the bar stock. Measure and mark two cross lines for the drill centers. Strike the centers with a hammer and a center punch to provide an accurate starting point for the drill. Clamp the bar stock in the vise and drill the holes as described in Fig. 4-16. Protect your drill bits: Apply light machine oil at intervals to keep the temperature down. Finally, hacksaw the drilled bar stock to a final width of ½ inch. File all surfaces smooth and chamfer all edges. Wipe the surfaces down with a light coat of wax or oil.

4–20. *Threading the long arm of the truss rod.*

THE ADJUSTING NUT

The best type of adjusting nut for this job is a ¾-inch-long brass hex connector, known also as a *threaded spacer.* Greater threading force can be exerted on the truss rod with the hex connector than with an ordinary 10–32 N.F. nut. Brass is chosen to ensure that the adjusting nut will never strip the threads on the embedded rod. Do not use a standard steel nut: if the hex connector is hard to find, several brass nuts soldered together while threaded on the rod will serve.

Step 4—Wrapping the Rod

A ½-inch width of gummed metal tape is now tightly wrapped diagonally, as shown in Fig. 4-27. The tape will keep the two rod arms tightly bound together for proper operation of the truss rod.

PROCEDURE: STEEL-STRING ONLY— CUTTING OUT THE TRUSS ROD SLOT AND THE NECK TENON

We now make several important cuts in the assembled neck blank.

First, we must excavate a slot for the truss rod precisely down the center of the shaft. This slot starts under the nut location and runs the full length of the shaft, exiting at its end.

The precise depth and width of the slot is significant; if the amount of wood left under the slot is insufficient, it may crack and ruin the neck. The width of the slot must provide clearance for the truss rod: forcing the rod into a too-tight slot will push the walls of the slot apart and distort the neck. If the rod fits too loosely, it will rattle when you play its resonant frequency on the strings.

After the truss rod slot is excavated, we must cut the end of the neck blank to the shape of a tenon that will later fit into a mortise in the guitar's headblock. Although the neck tenon is best cut on a table saw, we have provided a hand-tool procedure for this step.

TOOLS
portable electric router with parallel guide attachment
hardwood extension bar for the parallel guide attachment
3/16-inch round-bottom mortising bit, 1/4-inch flute
vise
flat mill file
dovetail saw
two bar clamps, at least 6-inch openings
sharp pencil
machinist's square
straightedge

Step 1—Marking the Neck Blank

With the aid of the square, carry the third line (neck/body junction line), which was drawn across the shaft, down both side faces of the heel-block and connect the lines accurately across the bottom.

Now draft the lines denoting the tenon at the end of the neck blank. The tenon is 3/4-inch wide, so mark a set of double lines, each parallel to and 3/8-inch away from the centerline. Start behind the neck/body junction line on top of the shaft; then carry them down the end of the neck blank and end them at the neck/body junction line at the bottom of the heelblock.

Finally, on the end of the neck blank, draft the lines that represent the 3/16(wide)- × 1/2(deep)-inch truss-rod slot. The neck-blank end should look like Fig. 4-21.

4-21. *Marking the end of the steel-string neck blank.*

Step 2—Routing the Slot

Do not attempt to excavate the slot with hand tools. Instead, use a portable electric router with a parallel guide. You will also need a ³⁄₁₆-inch round-bottom mortising bit with a ½-inch flute length to cut the ½-inch-deep slot.

Place the neck blank in the vise by clamping it *very tightly* by the block (Fig. 4-22). Place the router and guide on the shaft, pressing the guide against the side of the shaft. Adjust the guide so that the bit can travel precisely down the centerline. The marks previously drawn on the rear end of the block are helpful to make this adjustment. Tighten the adjusting screws securely. Retract the bit and slide the router down the length of the shaft with the motor off. The guide should not strike the vise or hang up in any way.

Rout the slot in several passes, making the first cut no deeper than ⅛ inch. Lower the bit progressively to a final ½-inch-deep cut. Stop the slot precisely at the start of the headstock slant.

You must now widen the slot slightly to accommodate the wrapped truss rod. This can best be accomplished by applying strips of masking tape on the guide bar, one strip at a time, and rerouting the slot until it accepts the truss rod with only a little resistance.

Note that the folded rod may flare slightly at its bend, possibly hanging it up in the slot. To avoid this, simply file the flared portions with a flat mill file.

Step 3—Cutting the Tenon

HAND-TOOL TECHNIQUE

A dovetail saw, sharp and well set, is ideal for this purpose. Clamp the neck blank to the edge of the table with the headstock pointing toward the floor and the heelblock facing up. Saw down slightly to the outside of the two tenon lines drawn on the end of the block until the kerfs reach about ¹⁄₃₂ inch beyond the neck/body junction lines crossing the top of the shaft and bottom of the block. Unclamp the neck blank and remove.

Next, clamp the shaft down on its side to make the cross-grain cuts, which expose the cheeks of the tenon. These cuts must be sawn tightly to the drafted lines, without

4–22. *Routing the truss rod slot. A ³⁄₁₆-inch veining bit leaves a round-bottom slot. A straight wooden extension is screwed to the guide and then held securely against the workpiece during the routing operation.*

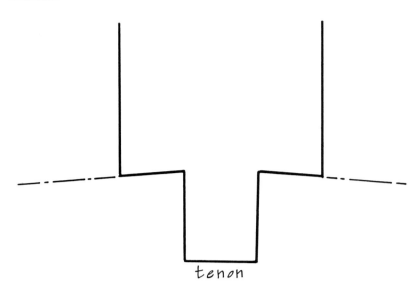

tenon

4–23. *Undercutting the end-grain face of the heel helps achieve a tight seam between the neck and body.*

4–24. *Table sawing the tenon cheeks.*

obliterating them. Slant the cut slightly, as in Fig. 4-23.

Slow, deliberate, full-length saw strokes are best. If a dull, poorly set saw has caused the kerf to wander, you may have to file or rasp selectively (or shave with a chisel if you can sharpen it well enough to cut end-grain cleanly) to true the end-grain surfaces and make them equal on both sides of the tenon. Making these surfaces equal to each other and flat is more important than achieving a tight correspondence to the penciled guidelines, since final adjustments can be made later.

TABLE SAW TECHNIQUE

To make the tenon cuts accurately, all neck-blank and block surfaces must be strictly square to each other. The circular saw blade must also be precisely squared to the table and to the miter fence.

Place the neck blank on end against the miter fence with its shaft pointing upwards, as in Fig. 4-24. Raise the blade to cut a precise $^{15}/_{16}$-inch depth. Make the two tenon cuts tightly to the pencil lines that were previously drafted on the shaft.

For the cross-grain cuts that expose the tenon, raise the blade just high enough to intersect the kerf of the previous cuts. Now tip the blade 5 degrees and start the cut $^{1}/_{32}$ inch away from the neck/body junction line on the block faces, as shown in Fig. 4-25. Hold the neck-blank shaft against the miter fence for the first cut, then flip the blank over, and this time, hold the bottom of the block against the miter fence for the second cut (Fig. 4-26).

A sheet of fine sandpaper double-faced taped to the miter fence will "grab" the workpiece and prevent slipping.

4–25. Cutting out the tenon on the table saw (steel-string).

4–26. Removing the tenon cheeks. The saw blade is angled very slightly to produce a slight undercut.

PROCEDURE: STEEL STRING ONLY— TRUSS ROD INSTALLATION

A strip of ebony, rosewood, or maple, called the spline, is now carefully dimensioned to fill the remaining space above the truss rod in the slot (Fig. 4-27). The function of the spline is to lock the truss rod tightly into the slot. Without it, the rod would bear directly on the fingerboard, possibly prying it off the shaft or cracking it. To perform this function, a high-quality glue joint between the spline and the slot walls is important. This is ensured by the correct fit of the spline into the slot.

A too-tight fit will not only wipe the glue from the surfaces when it is inserted into the slot, but may also wedge the slot walls apart, possibly distorting the shaft in the process. Too much clearance will result in a thick, weak glue joint.

TOOLS
scraper
block plane
cam clamps

MATERIALS
spline (see Step 1)

SUPPLIES
AR glue

Step 1—Fitting the Spline

Start with a strip $\frac{7}{32} \times \frac{1}{4}$ inches in cross section, long enough to span the distance from the headstock slant to the end of the tenon. Lay the strip flat on the table. Holding a sharp scraper blade between the thumb and two fingers of one hand, gradually reduce the thickness of the spline, scrap-

4–27. *Truss-rod installation. The folded rod is wrapped with metal tape to distribute the bending load. The hardwood spline spreads the forces underneath the fingerboard and must be well fit. The cap clears the tenon end by about $\frac{1}{16}$ inch.*

ing from its center to its ends. Be methodical and apply even pressure, checking for fit often. Chamfer the corners of the spline to keep it from jamming in the slot. Continue until the spline pushes in with light finger pressure.

Step 2—Inserting the Rod and Gluing in the Spline

The truss rod itself is not glued into the slot. Insert the rod into the slot. *Warning: Make sure the longer (threaded) arm is against the bottom of the slot.* Its adjusting nut must be loose. Make sure the rod is fully driven down to the bottom by pressing down along its length with a screwdriver. Apply glue to the spline and press it into the slot, wiggling it up and down and lengthwise to transfer the glue to the slot wall. Press the spline down firmly; if it wants to float up again, keep it pressed down with two or three cam clamps, using very light clamping pressure. Now apply at least three cam clamps across the shaft, with the cams thrown for light pressure.

When the glue is leather hard, pick off the excess with a stick. Allow forty-five minutes for drying time.

Plane the spline down flush with a small block plane after removing the clamps. Plane until only a fine stub remains on top of the surface. The remainder is scraped down flush with a scraper blade. Be careful not to scoop out the shaft surface while scraping, but do not allow any portion of the spline to protrude lest it obstruct the fingerboard when it is glued.

PROCEDURE: APPLYING HEADSTOCK VENEER

The headstock veneer enhances the rigidity of the headstock and increases the scarf joint's resistance to torque and shock.

The headstock can be faced with a single 1/16-inch hardwood veneer, or with a sandwich consisting of the 1/16-inch veneer and one or more 1/40-inch veneers underneath. The single 1/16-inch veneer is most common on steel-string guitars, while the veneer sandwich is usually seen on classical guitars. These designs, however, are interchangeable. The student is advised to adhere to the common forms on the guitar being built from this book, but the choice is purely a matter of taste. One important functional consideration, however, must be kept in mind: The tuning machinery must fit the final total thickness of the laid-up headstock. The steel-string headstock must not be allowed to thicken to the point that the tuning-machine grommet nut will not begin to thread down into its housing. Conversely, the classical headstock must not be thinner than the width of the tuning-machine mounting plate.

Any sound piece of rose-wood, ebony, or other hardwood, 1/16 inch thick, will serve for the face veneer. It can also be sliced from a narrower, thicker piece and bookmatched, creating a symmetrical effect. Some builders try to match the veneer to the back and side wood; others seek particularly dramatic grain patterns. If an inlay is planned, we usually choose an evenly colored piece that will not compete with the inlay design.

The traditional sequence for the veneer sandwich on the headpiece of the classical guitar is a dark 1/40-inch veneer glued to the mahogany headstock, followed by a light 1/40-inch veneer and finally the dark 1/16-inch face veneer. This sequence, of course, can be varied according to taste.

The following procedure is divided into two sections: a freehand technique for applying the single face veneer, and a system for the veneer sandwich that employs position pins to keep the individual veneers from sliding around during application. If the single veneer is used, on the steel-string guitar it can be trimmed at an angle at one end to abut the nut. If the sandwich is used, the veneers may shift minutely even with the position pins, so we dispense with angling the nut end of the veneer. On the classical guitar, we do not angle the nut end in either case because the precise location of the fingerboard will be contingent upon a number of factors that are difficult to predict with absolute precision. Thus, the classical veneer is left untrimmed on its leading edge until the fingerboard is glued in place, at which time the veneer or veneer sandwich is cut back to receive the nut.

Before beginning this procedure, turn to Figs. 4-38 and 4-39 and make a headpiece template by tracing the appropriate diagram and transferring the tracing to a piece of cardboard or other sturdy material.

SINGLE VENEER, FREE-HAND CLAMPING TECHNIQUE

TOOLS
six 4-inch clamps

IMPLEMENTS
¾(to 1) × 3 × 6¾-inch (SS) or × 7¾-inch (CL) caul
3 × 6 thin caul

SUPPLIES
AR or PVA glue

MATERIALS
hardwood veneer, 1/16(to 3/32) × 3 × 6¾ inches (SS) or 7¾ inches (CL)

Step 1—Trimming the Veneer

The veneer must be precisely the same width as the headstock. If it is not, trace the headstock width on it and trim with a plane.

Steel-string only: Angle the end-grain of the veneer where it will abut the nut, as in Fig. 4-28. Stroke that edge on the sanding board while holding the piece at the angle shown in the diagram. (Hold it up against an angled backing block if you cannot do it freehand.)

TABLE-SAW TECHNIQUE

The veneer end can be trimmed on the table saw with a well-squared miter fence

using a fine-tooth plywood blade. This is done *after* the veneer is glued, a bit overlong, to the headstock. Make a pencil mark on the side of the shaft where the headstock angle begins. Place the neck blank upside down against the miter fence. Under the shaft, place a long ⅛-inch-thick wooden spacer slat. Elevate the blade until it *just* skins the shaft surface. Turn the saw on and trim the veneer end at the pencil mark.

Step 2—Gluing the Veneer

Tape the thin caul to the underside of the headpiece, for protection from clamp marks. Clamp the neck blank in the vise so that the headstock is level. Apply a moderate amount of PVA or AR glue to the underside of the veneer. Make sure the beveled end (if

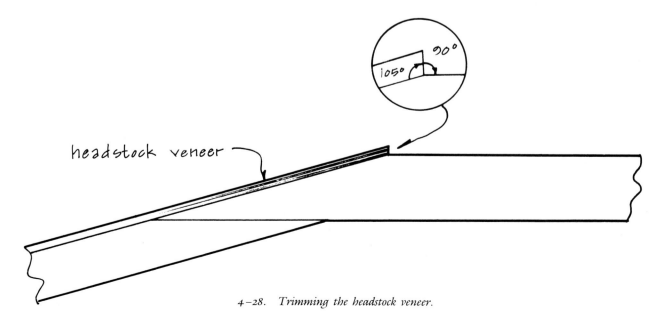

4-28. *Trimming the headstock veneer.*

any) is toward the nut, and place the veneer on the headstock. Move it around slightly until it begins to grab. Align the nut end of the veneer in place where the headstock angle begins. Place the thick caul on top so that it covers the veneer but does not overlap the nut end and hide it from view. Place the first C-clamp in the very center of the headstock. The point is to tighten the clamp progressively and adjust the caul and the veneer (both of which may want to wander slightly) until they all

sit square and accurately. The clamp can be untightened and readjusted, and the pieces shifted around until this is accomplished. Do not tighten down this clamp all the way just yet.

Add four more clamps in a rectangular arrangement. Tighten them gradually, alternating one and another. When they are completely tightened, loosen the center clamp and slide it to one side. Add another clamp opposite and tighten both down. (See Fig. 4-29.)

4-29. *Clamping the headstock veneer. Because the veneer or veneer sandwich covers a broad area, it requires a thick caul and several clamps. The clamp handles are staggered to avoid crowding. Note the thin caul protecting the underside of the headstock.*

VENEER SANDWICH POSITION-PIN CLAMPING TECHNIQUE

TOOLS
five or six C-clamps
hand drill and bits

IMPLEMENTS
$\frac{3}{4}$(to 1) × 3 × 6$\frac{3}{4}$-inch (SS) or 7$\frac{3}{4}$-inch (CL) caul
3 × 6 × $\frac{1}{4}$-inch (or less) caul
headpiece template

SUPPLIES
two wire brads, about $\frac{1}{16}$ inch in diameter
AR or PVA glue

MATERIALS
hardwood veneer, $\frac{1}{16}$(to $\frac{3}{32}$) × 3 × 6$\frac{3}{4}$ inches (SS) or 7$\frac{3}{4}$ inches (CL)
two hardwood veneers (one light, such as maple; one dark, such as rosewood), $\frac{1}{40}$ × 3 × 6$\frac{3}{4}$ inches (SS) or 7$\frac{3}{4}$ inches (CL)

Step 1—Locating the Position Pins

Draft the template onto the face veneer with a yellow pencil. Make two marks for the position pins outside the boundaries of the headpiece outline and diagonally opposite one another.

Place the neck blank in a vise and tighten securely. Mount the dark $\frac{1}{40}$-inch veneer, the light $\frac{1}{40}$-inch veneer, and the $\frac{1}{16}$-inch face veneer on the headstock. Line them up evenly to the headstock edges and at the line where the neck begins to angle backwards. Tape the sandwich down securely in preparation for drilling the position pin holes. Using a bit corresponding closely to the diameter of your wire brads, drill at the two marks through the veneers and about ¼ inch into the headstock underneath. Press the brads in with a finger; if they wobble, use larger brads.

Step 2—Drilling Out the Caul

You must drill through the ¾- to 1-inch caul with a ⅛- to ¼-inch bit in order to accommodate the positioning brads, which will be left in place during the actual gluing operation. Use the brads to mark the caul by pressing it down on their heads. Then drill through at the two resulting dimples (Fig. 4-30).

Step 3—Gluing Down the Sandwich

Pull out the brads and remove the veneers. Tape the thin, flat caul to the underside of the headstock to protect its show face from clamp marks. Lay out the three veneers in their proper orientation.

We recommend the following gluing sequence to avoid curling of the ¼₀-inch veneers. Begin the operation by applying glue to one face of the ¹⁄₁₆-inch veneer, making sure to cover the whole piece. Set

it down on the bench (show face down, of course). Take the dark ¼₀-inch veneer and apply glue to one face. Place the light ¼₀-inch veneer on the gluing surface of the ¹⁄₁₆-inch face veneer, and then add the dark ¼₀-inch veneer's glue side to the light ¼₀-inch veneer. Line up the predrilled holes and push the brads through the veneers. Apply glue to the headstock face and press the sandwich down onto it, locating the brads in the holes already drilled in the headstock. Tap the brads down

lightly but firmly enough to secure them. Place the caul over the brads onto the headpiece, and clamp with six C-clamps, tightening gradually all around. Leave clamped for about an hour.

4-30. *Headstock-veneer sandwich ready for gluing. Position-pin holes are drilled through the veneers into the waste area of the headstock. The caul is drilled out to fit over the pins during the gluing operation.*

HISTORICAL HEADPIECES

From the earliest days of the guitar's history until about 1680, guitar necks typically retained a uniform width from the neck/body joint to the end of the peg head. This design can be seen on all early surviving four-course guitars. By the 1680s, however, peg-head edges began to flare very slightly (Fig. 4-31), and by the early 1700s more dramatic tapering became evident in the peg head's outline, coinciding with the advent of the tapered fingerboard (Fig. 4-32).

The flaring peg head reached its zenith in Spain on the six-course guitar. By the early 1700s and continuing over the following century, Spanish peg heads grew very large, tapering vigorously (as in Fig. 4-33). Some were almost as long as the shafts on which they were mounted!

The change to six single strings occurred elsewhere in Europe around the turn of the eighteenth century. Coincidental with the change, a new "look" in peg heads became the vogue: it took the form of the figure-eight peg head (Fig. 4-34). This rounded shape retained its popularity in France and Italy up until the mid-1800s, when geared tuning

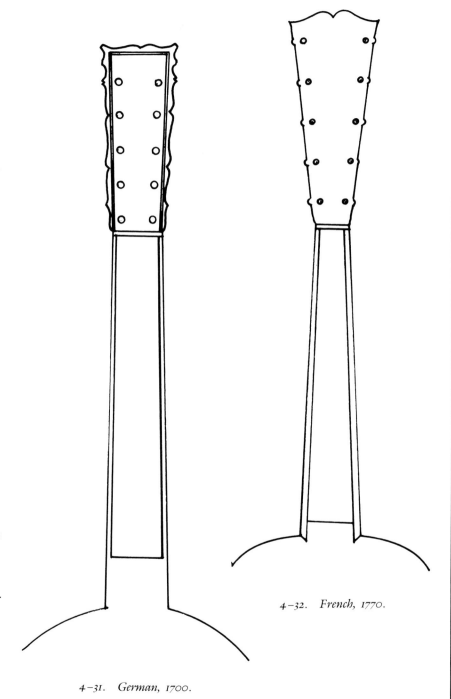

4–31. German, 1700.

4–32. French, 1770.

machinery appeared on the scene and made rear-mounted friction pegs and the figure-eight peg head obsolete.

One of the first luthiers to redesign the headpiece for tuning machines (the term "peg head" no longer being appropriate) was the great Louis Panormo. An early Panormo headpiece of striking design can be seen in Fig. 4-35. Later, Antonio de Torres' design (Fig. 4-36) became the archetype of the modern classical headpiece. Several notable builders, such as Hauser, Velazquez, and Romanillos, symbolize their debt to Torres by duplicating Torres' crest on their own instruments.

When C. F. Martin first started building guitars in this country in 1833, he adopted the headpiece design used at Johann George Staufer's studio in Vienna, where he had previously worked. His early headpiece had an elongated, rounded shape that curled to one side, reminiscent of a Turkish slipper. The slipper-shaped headpiece was soon dropped in favor of the more popular style in the America of his day: the simple slab ending with a severe, straight cutoff at the top.

The traditional American steel-string headpiece has changed very little since then. Although arch-top guitarmakers revived the cult of individualized elegance on their headpieces, American steel-string folk guitars typically retain the slab's understated, austere simplicity of form.

Figure 4-37 illustrates the traditional V-joint connection between the headpiece and the shaft. It appears on early guitar headpieces (dating back as far as the 1500s) and was used on most fretted string instruments until the scarf joint began to gain prominence in the early 1800s. The V-joint has all but vanished today, the high strength of modern synthetic glues rendering it obsolete. A small number of luthiers still use it, however, preferring it for its technical challenge and aesthetic value.

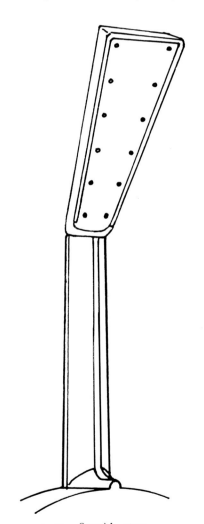

4–33. *Spanish, 1800.*

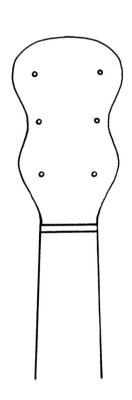

4–34. *Figure-eight headpiece.*

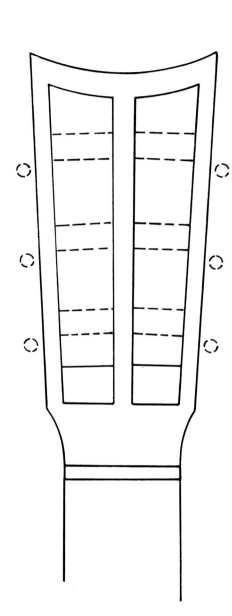

4–35. *Headpiece by Louis Panormo, early 1800s.*

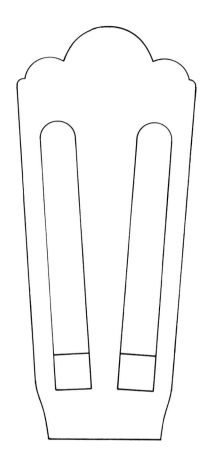

4–36. *Torres headpiece, 1863.*

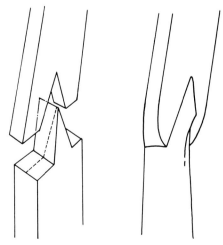

4–37. *V-joint (at headpiece).*

PROCEDURE: CUTTING OUT THE HEADPIECE OUTLINE

When the headstock with its face veneer or veneer sandwich is trimmed to its final outline, we begin to refer to it as a headpiece. The template diagrams provided in this book are simple designs recom-

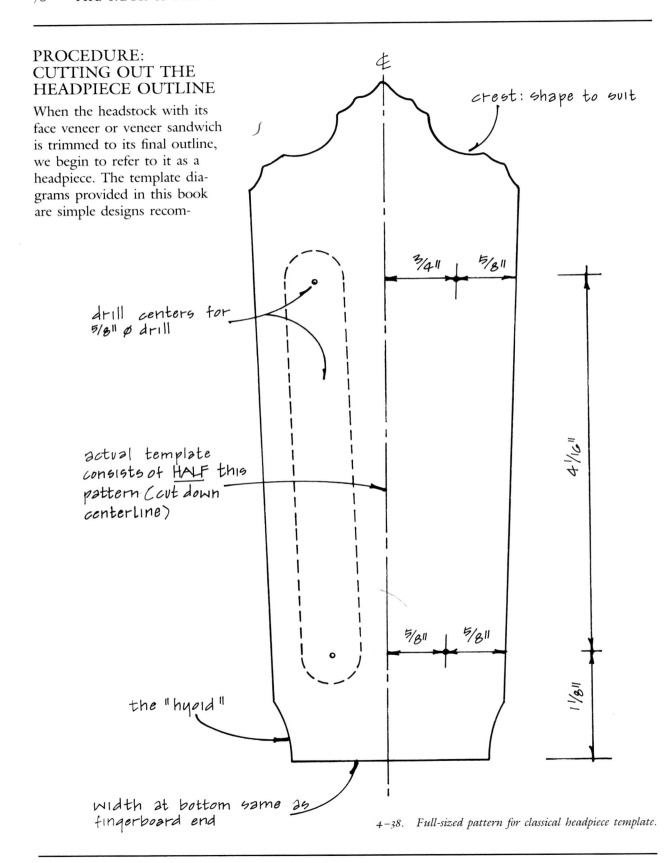

crest: shape to suit

3/4"   5/8"

drill centers for 5/8" ø drill

actual template consists of HALF this pattern (cut down centerline)

4 1/16"

5/8"   5/8"

1 1/8"

the "hyoid"

width at bottom same as fingerboard end

4–38. *Full-sized pattern for classical headpiece template.*

mended for the student. The builder, of course, is free to use a different crest design or a different outline altogether.

The workmanship displayed in the refinement of the classical-guitar headpiece is the luthier's trademark, providing an opportunity for personalization of the instrument. The build-

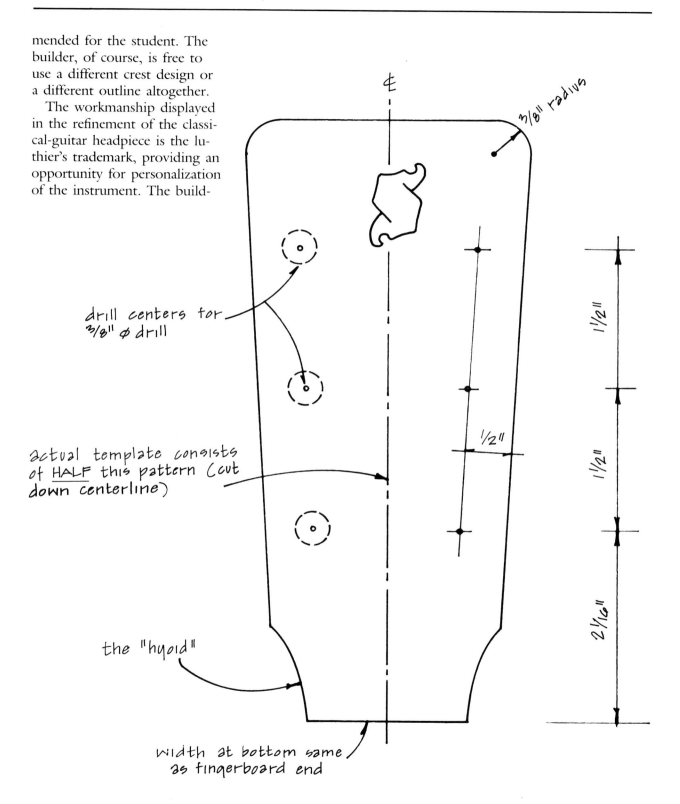

3/8" radius

drill centers for
3/8" ⌀ drill

actual template consists
of HALF this pattern (cut
down centerline)

the "hyoid"

width at bottom same
as fingerboard end

1 1/2"

1/2"

1 1/2"

2 1/16"

4-39. *Full-sized pattern for steel-string headpiece template.*

er's personality, in fact, sometimes appears startlingly manifest in the choice of headpiece design.

For the beginner, execution of the classical guitar headpiece crest can be one of the most challenging steps on the guitar. We note, therefore, that it is not absolutely necessary to finish the classical headpiece crest at this stage. The edges of the headpiece must be trimmed in order to drill for the tuning machines, but the student should feel free to postpone finishing the crest until after having gained experience by doing other procedures.

TOOLS
ruler
awl
backsaw (SS only)
coping saw
square
block plane
assorted files
yellow pencil

SUPPLIES
sandpaper

Step 1—Laying Out the Headpiece

If you have previously drawn the headpiece outline on the face veneer, scrape it off. Draw a centerline down the length of the face veneer continuous with the neckshaft centerline. Using the headpiece template laid on each side of the centerline, draw the headpiece outline on the veneer

with a needle-sharp yellow pencil.

Transfer the drill centers from the template to the face veneer by pressing through the template into the veneer with an awl. Make the awl marks as deep as possible.

Step 2—Sawing the Outline

Steel-string crest only: Trim the top of the headpiece right to the drafted line with a fine-tooth backsaw or on the table saw. If you are cutting with a backsaw, make sure the cut is as close to the line and as square to the headstock face as possible. Start just beside the drafted line on the veneer, with the headstock clamped flat (the shaft will overhang

the edge of the bench). Your starting strokes should be made very slowly, using two fingers of your free hand as a guide against which the saw blade is pressed. If you are unsure of your ability to make this cut accurately, try clamping a squared guide block of wood right up to the line, using that as a stop to ensure a square cut.

If you have a table saw, use a fine-tooth plywood or finishing blade, pressing the veneered face down to the table and the headstock edge against the miter fence.

Steel-string and classical—sides of the headpiece: Using a coping saw (Fig. 4-40) or a bandsaw, cut along the sides of the headpiece outline, leaving no less than 1/16 inch excess. Con-

4-40. *Sawing the headpiece outline. The blade must be kept absolutely square to the face veneer.*

tinue the cut a little beyond the headpiece into the shaft and then rapidly swing it away, exiting about where the first fret will be located and leaving the remainder of the shaft untapered.

Classical crest: Resting the square on the face veneer, transfer the points at which the crest begins down the edges to the back of the headstock. Use these reference points and the headpiece template to draft the crest on the back of the headstock. With the coping saw, cut away the excess at the top of the headpiece, leaving a bare ¹⁄₁₆ inch to remove with a file.

Step 3—Truing the Edges of the Headpiece

Using a block plane, carefully trim the edges of the headpiece to the layout lines (see Fig. 4-41). Check frequently with the square to ensure that the edges remain square to the face of the headpiece; also check to see that the edges are straight.

4-41. Truing the headpiece edge. The sawn edge is planed to the layout line.

4-42. Carving the crest.

Step 4—Finishing the Crest

Both the steel-string and classical crests must be carved precisely to their outlines with files and sandpaper (Fig. 4-42). Keep the edge vertical and as square as possible; try not to round it at all. When using a file, take special care not to chip away a corner.

(Using very fine cutting files reduces chipping.)

File marks can be removed and rounded areas flattened with a freshly sharpened scraper shaving across the end-grain. A very fine cutting round "file" can be made by wrapping a piece of sandpaper around a pencil or similar object.

A NOTE ON TUNING MACHINES

There is an incredibly wide range of quality among the tuning machines available for steel-string and classical guitars. A few things to look for in judging quality:

All guitar tuning machines have a worm-and-cog mechanism that translates the rotation of the button (the piece you turn) into rotation of a roller around which the string winds. The key to smooth operation and long life is a good mating between the cog and worm for both size and spacing. If you have a chance to try out a set of machines before you buy them, make two tests. First, note whether there is slop in the gears when you turn the button—that is, whether the button turns a bit before the roller starts to turn. Second, check for slop by wiggling the post to which the button is attached. The best machines will be tight in all directions, yet will turn smoothly.

On classical guitar machines, look at the cogs (gears). Good machines always have concave-cut gears. Gears cut straight across will wear out very quickly. The rollers should be nylon rather than brittle plastic. Ideally the posts should go all the way through the buttons and lock on the ends. The plating (on the plates) should be smooth; it should not be pitted or peeling.

Better steel-string machines always have sealed gear mechanisms to hold in grease, which reduces wear caused by high-tension strings. There should be a screw in the button to allow periodic adjustment to take up excessive internal clearances produced by wear. Look at the metal finish under the plating—it should be smooth rather than grainy or lumpy.

PROCEDURE: DRILLING THE STEEL-STRING HEADPIECE

TOOLS
hand-held drill or drill press
3/8-inch drill bit
awl

After being puncture-marked with an awl according to the locations on the full-sized headpiece template, the steel-string headpiece must be drilled through to accommodate its rear-mounted tuning

4-43. Drilling tuning-machine holes for the steel-string headpiece. We use a self-centering brad-point bit that secures itself in the awl mark, making clamping unnecessary. Using a standard bit necessitates clamping.

machinery. This step can be done on a drill press, or with a hand-held drill and a little help from a friend.

Three-eighths inch is the standard hole size for the shaft housings of most popular high-quality enclosed tuning machines. If your own tuning machines are different, check the shaft diameter and select the appropriate drill size for a good fit.

With a self-centering brad-point bit, the headpiece can be held flat to the drill press table with hand pressure, as shown in Fig. 4-43. If you are using the more common conical-tipped drill bit, you may have to clamp the workpiece to keep it from wandering. When drilling with a hand drill, have a friend stand to one side to sight for perpendicularity as you drill.

PROCEDURE: DRILLING AND SLOTTING THE CLASSICAL HEADPIECE

Once you have finished the outline of the classical guitar headpiece, you are ready to lay out and drill the tuning machine holes and to cut out the slots. When laying out the tuning machine holes, it is important to be aware that the spacing between the rollers of classical guitar tuning machines can be inconsistent. The spacing may not conform exactly

to the dimension provided by the manufacturer or the supplier. Sometimes a spacing that is actually metric is described in inch measurements to the closest $1/32$ inch. This is inadequate for a really close fit. We have also had the experience of trying to fit classical machines on which the spacing from one roller to the next was inconsistent on a single plate!

To avoid vexing problems in fitting the machines, then, the best and simplest method of laying out the tuning machine holes is to disassemble the machines and use the plates themselves to draft the holes. Once you have done it a few times, it takes only a few minutes and is well worth the effort. If you shy away from taking apart small mechanisms, however, you must at least carefully measure the distance between the centers of the roller screws on both plates.

Some instruction manuals suggest that the classical guitar tuning machine holes are difficult to drill accurately without a drill press. In our view, however, the hand technique is easier and more reliable and accurate than the power-tool technique. We use a doweling jig and hand drill (or hand-held electric drill) and with but a few minutes' work achieve perfect results every time. Although in a production shop a drill-press jig for this procedure would be appropriate, we do not think it is worth the effort for a hand-builder because the doweling-

jig method is so easy and reliable.

Stanley Tools makes a simple, accurate, compact, and inexpensive unit that uses interchangeable guides, an important feature for our purposes, as will be seen below.

TOOLS
calipers
hand drill or hand-held
   electric drill
drill bit (see Step 1)
doweling jig
bit brace and ⅝-inch auger
   bit
coping saw
wide chisel
square
pencil
ruler
files

SUPPLIES
masking tape
sandpaper

MATERIALS
set of tuning machines (see
   A Note on Tuning
   Machines, page 74)

Step 1—Selecting a Drill Bit and Doweling Guide

With calipers, measure the diameter of your rollers. A certain amount of clearance is necessary for smooth operation of the machines, even if the holes are perfectly aligned. Minimum clearance is .010 inch; less than that may result in binding and squeaking when the rollers turn. Maximum clearance is .030 inch; more than that will cause the rollers to rack under string tension, dramatically shortening the life of the machines. Optimal clearance is about .010 to .020 inch.

If the diameter of your tuning machine rollers plus a clearance factor of .010 to .030 inch corresponds to one of the guides that come with the doweling jig, proceed to Step 2. If not, refer to the sidebar on drill guides, page 80).

Step 2—Drafting the Tuning-machine Holes

Clamp the neckshaft firmly in a vise. Measure along the headpiece edge 3⅛ inches from the point where the headstock begins to angle backward and, with a square resting on the face veneer,

draft line *M* as shown in Fig. 4-44. Mark a centerpoint exactly halfway down line *M*.

To determine which tuning machine plate goes on which side of the headpiece, a simple rule of thumb is that the gears are always *forward* (toward the nut) in relation to the posts. Select the correct plate for the side on which you are working. Either disassemble the mechanism (put all the little screws and whatnot into an envelope), or carefully measure the roller screws on center. Using either the plates or your measurements, find the other two roller locations and draft lines O_1 and O_2 as shown. Mark the midpoints of lines O_1 and O_2 and connect them. If that line does not pass through the midpoint of line

M, measure all three midpoints and redraft them. Repeat for the other side of the headpiece.

Step 3—Flagging the Bit

Mount the doweling jig on the headpiece at line *M* per the instructions that come with the tool and as shown in Fig. 4-45. Before putting the bit into the drill, slide it into the guide, allowing it to rest on the side of the headpiece. Note where the bit emerges from the guide. Measure from that point up the bit a distance equal to the length of your tuning machine rollers plus ³⁄₁₆ inch, and mark it there with a piece of masking tape. This will indicate where to stop drilling (Fig. 4-45).

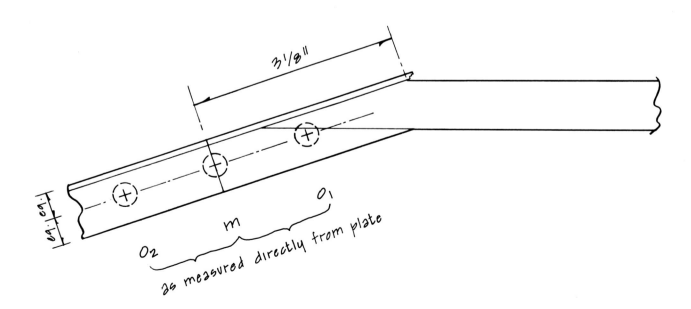

4-44. *Tuning machine roller layout.*

4-45. Drilling the classical tuning machine holes with a doweling jig and a custom-made drill guide.

Step 4—Drilling the Holes

Test the alignment of the doweling jig by just twisting the point of the bit against the side of the headpiece at line *M*. If you are not exactly on the midpoint of line *M,* adjust the doweling jig as necessary. When satisfied with your alignment, proceed to drill, stopping when the tape marker reaches the top of the guide.

Move the doweling jig to line O_1. Make a test cut to check alignment. *Do not* make any vertical adjustment along line O_1, however, even if the bit does not hit the midpoint; once the first hole has been drilled, your sole concern (besides the spacing) is to keep the holes in a straight line—which is ensured by the jig, if used properly. If the holes come out slightly high or slightly low on the side of the headpiece, it is not a problem as long as the plate does not overlap the edge. Drill out the second hole; then move the jig and drill the third hole at line O_2.

Remove the doweling jig and test the machines for fit. They may not slide in easily, even if you have drilled accurately; but as long as they go in without heavy resistance or distortion, you may proceed to the other side. Slight resistance at this point will disappear when the slots are cut out. Even a seemingly badly misdrilled hole may turn out to need only a little reaming after the slots are cut. (Of course, if a hole is completely off, it will have to be plugged and redrilled.)

Note: If the worm-gear assemblies on your tuning machines are riveted from the backs of the plates, you must drill shallow relief holes to accommodate the rivets. Press the machines into the roller holes and against the side of the headpiece, leaving dimples where the rivets are located. Drill about ⅛ inch deep with an appropriate bit at each mark to provide the necessary relief. The classical machines used on the guitar in this book do not have rivets, so the headpiece pictured does not have relief holes.

Step 5—Drilling End Holes for the Slots

The slots in our design are cut by drilling two ⅝-inch holes and removing a ⅝-inch swath of material between them. The drill centers should already be on the face veneer, transferred from the template.

Use a ⅝-inch auger bit and a bit brace for this step. The sharper the auger bit, the more square and smooth will be its penetration and the cleaner will be the hole walls. (A ⅝-inch spade bit mounted in an electric drill works well also.) Drill through the four holes with a piece of waste stock underneath the headpiece to avoid tearing out when the drill bit emerges.

When the holes are finished, connect them on both the face and back of the headpiece with tangent layout lines scored with a razor knife held against a straightedge. These score

lines will precisely denote the boundaries of the slots.

Step 6—Rough-cutting the Slot

Clamp the neck firmly in the vise. Disconnect one end of a coping-saw blade from its catch in the saw frame, pass the blade through one of the four holes, and reconnect it. Saw along inside one layout line to the opposite hole, leaving a full ⅟₁₆-inch excess to the line (Fig. 4-46). If you can simply turn the saw around and cut back to the first hole on the parallel layout line, do so; otherwise, back the saw up in the first cut to the original hole and make the second cut

in the same direction as the first. Disconnect the blade and repeat for the other slot.

Step 7—Finishing the Slots

You must create a flat, smooth surface between the layout lines on the front and back of the headpiece. Work with a chisel from both faces toward the middle, creating a slight peak on the wall of the slot; then gradually pare down the peak until the surface is flat (Fig. 4-47). We discourage the use of a file or rasp here because file marks are difficult to sand off without distorting the slot. When working with the chisel, however, be *very* sensitive to grain direction. Remove fine slivers and change direction as necessary. Tearing out caused by careless chiseling will leave a visible scar.

The slot walls should be just tangential to the ⅝-inch holes. The rounded ends of the slots should be left untouched. The nut ends of the slots will be ramped at a later time (Fig. 4-48).

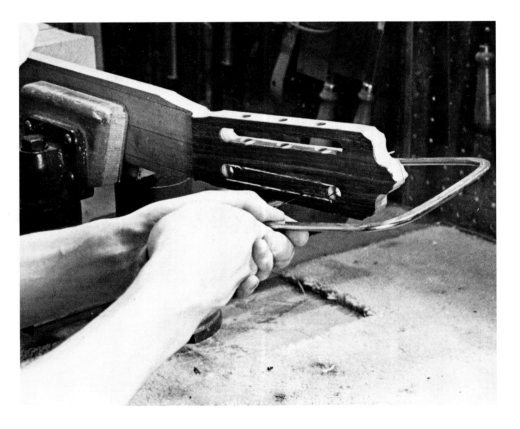

4-46. Sawing the classical headpiece slots. The layout lines are drawn in yellow pencil for visibility. This cut can also be made with a keyhole saw.

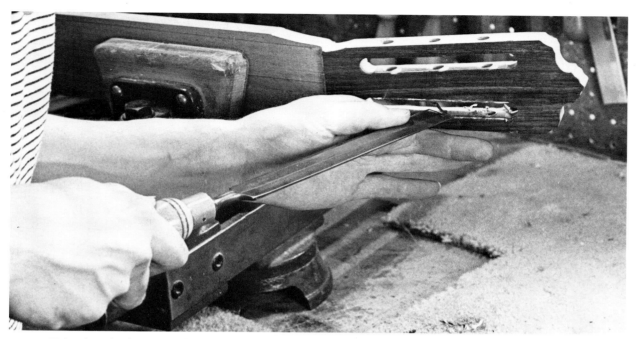

4-47. *Trimming the classical headpiece slots.*

4-48. *The classical headpiece. The leading end of the slots will be ramped at a later stage of construction.*

ON DRILL GUIDES FOR CLASSICAL TUNING MACHINES

Doweling jigs do not provide infinite drill guide adjustment; as a rule, the guides supplied with the jig take drill bits in $\frac{1}{16}$-inch increments. If the dimensions of your tuning machine rollers plus proper (.010- to .030-inch) clearance do not correspond to one of the guides provided with your doweling jig, you have two choices: either use the next larger size guide (resigning yourself to premature tuning machine wear), or make yourself a correctly dimensioned guide to fit the doweling jig.

Making your own guide is actually much easier than it sounds. All that is necessary is a short piece of pipe or metal tubing (about the same length as your factory-supplied doweling jig guides) with an inside diameter slightly smaller than the diameter of the correct bit for drilling your tuning machine holes. The piece of pipe is simply locked in a vise and reamed out by drilling through with the correct bit. For example, we had tuning machine rollers that measured 10 mm (about .396 inch). We wanted to use a $\frac{13}{32}$-inch (about .408-inch) drill bit, so we picked up a piece of $\frac{3}{8}$-inch (.3875-inch) inside-diameter pipe and drilled it out with the $\frac{13}{32}$-inch bit. It worked perfectly.

Note: The walls of the pipe must, of course, be thick enough to allow removal of some metal, but not so thick that the pipe will not fit in the doweling jig. Iron pipe will last longest, but if you do not have a drill press, forget it—use brass, copper, bronze, or lead. Whatever material you choose, the drill must travel straight through the pipe—or very nearly so—in order to yield a useful guide. You might have to try a couple of times to get it right.

PROCEDURE: CARVING THE HEEL

TOOLS
pencil
compass or French curve
razor knife
coping saw or bandsaw
wide chisel
skew knife (violinmaker's knife)
fine wood rasp
scraper blade

SUPPLIES
stiff paper (SS only)
#120-grit garnet sandpaper

Step 1—Tracing the Heel-cap Outline and Heel-curve Outline

Refer to Fig. 4-49 and trace the heel cap for your guitar on a small piece of heavy paper. Symmetry is assured if you make a small template of *half* the heel cap, then align its longer edge with the centerline that was drawn previously on the bottom of the heelblock. Trace its contour on both sides of the centerline to complete the heel-cap outline. Also, draw two parallel lines at either side of the heel cap, as shown. These lines will serve as the heel-cap carving limit during the first heel-carving step. Next, refer to Fig. 4-50 and transfer the appropriate heel-curve outline onto both heelblock side faces, using a compass or a French curve.

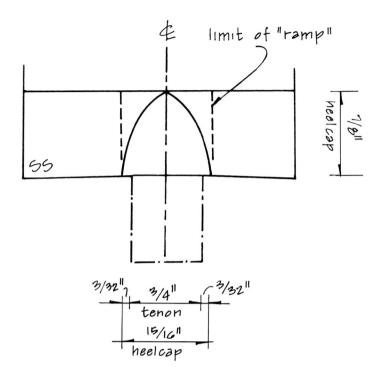

limit of "ramp"

heelcap 7/8"

SS

3/32" 3/4" 3/32"
tenon
15/16"
heelcap

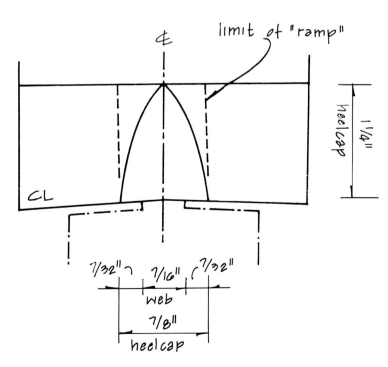

limit of "ramp"

heelcap 1¼"

CL

7/32" 7/16" 7/32"
web
7/8"
heelcap

4–49. *Heel-cap layout (steel-string and classical), full-sized.*

Step 2—Sawing the Heel Profile

The bulk of the heelblock that lies in front of the heel profile must now be cut away with a coping saw or bandsaw. To use a coping saw, clamp the neckshaft to the table, upside down, with the heelblock facing upward. Place the headstock off the edge of the table to avoid crushing the projecting portion of the headstock veneer. Use a clamping caul to avoid marring the back of the shaft.

You will now be looking at the bottom of the heel. Cut down toward the shaft, making your entering cut just $\frac{1}{16}$ inch ahead of the heel-cap profile.

For best results with the coping saw, grasp the handle with both hands, place one foot in front of the other, and bend your knees slightly. Keeping your elbows near your sides, saw down the lines with slow, deliberate strokes, letting the blade do all the work. Twist the handle as you saw to follow the curved portion of the line. The kerf exits just shy (about $\frac{1}{16}$ inch) of the shaft, leaving a small step as shown in Fig. 4-50.

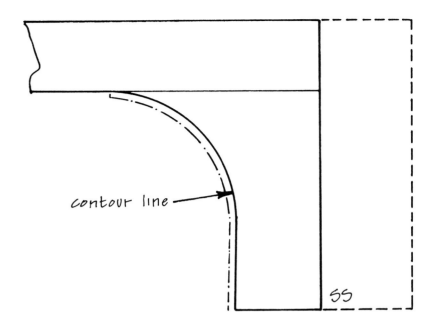

The width of the heelblock must be reduced to the width of the fingerboard by sawing, planing, or chiseling. Remove an equal thickness of material from the entire area of each face. Do not come closer than ⅛ inch from the actual fingerboard line. The reduced portion extends about 4 to 5 inches from the end of the neck blank.

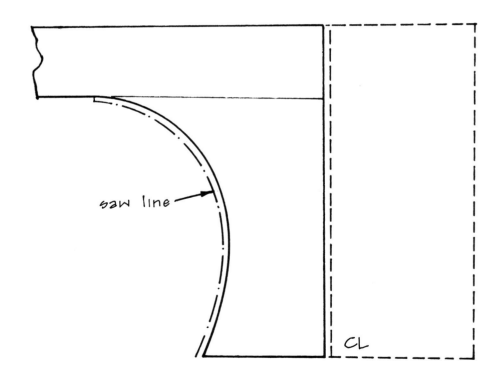

4–50. *Heel-curve outlines (steel-string and classical), full-sized.*

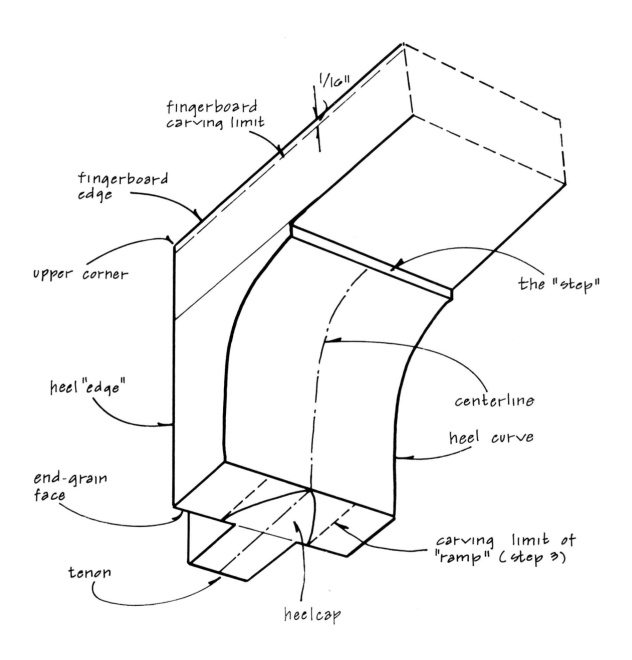

fingerboard
carving limit

1/16"

fingerboard
edge

upper corner

the "step"

heel "edge"

centerline

heel curve

end-grain
face

carving limit of
"ramp" (step 3)

tenon

heelcap

4-51a. *Initial stage of steel-string heel (before carving).*

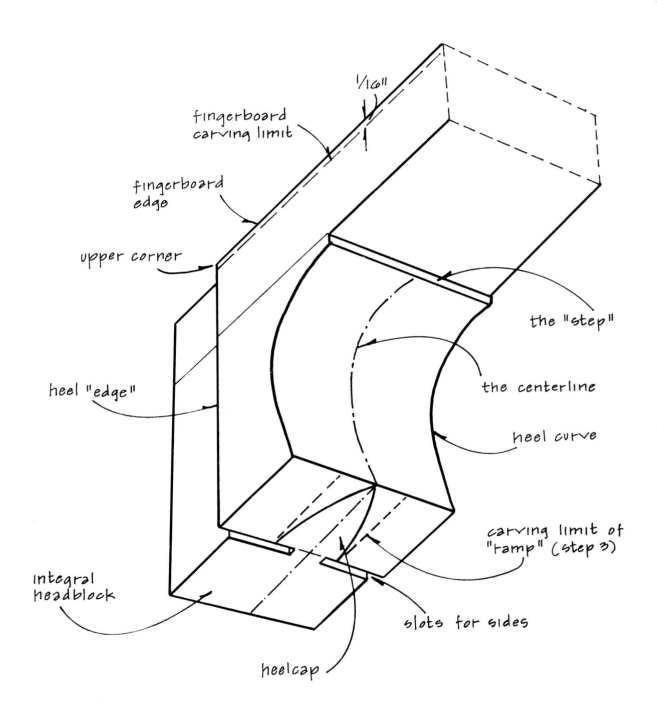

fingerboard
carving limit

1/16"

fingerboard
edge

upper corner

the "step"

heel "edge"

the centerline

heel curve

integral
headblock

carving limit of
"ramp" (step 3)

slots for sides

heelcap

4–51b. Initial stage of classical heel (before carving).

Step 3—Ramping the Heel

The heel should now look like that in Fig. 4-51a or 4-51b. Study the names of the important features of the heel. We will hereafter use these terms during the heel carving steps, as well as in other procedures in this book. Now examine Fig. 4-52a or 4-52b.

Clamp the neck on edge to the table or in a tabletop vise. Using a wide chisel, shave a flat, inclined plane from the fingerboard limit line to the heel cap limit line. Hold the chisel at the desired angle and chisel the stock away across the grain, removing only as much each time as will leave a smooth surface for the next stroke (Fig. 4-53a). As you

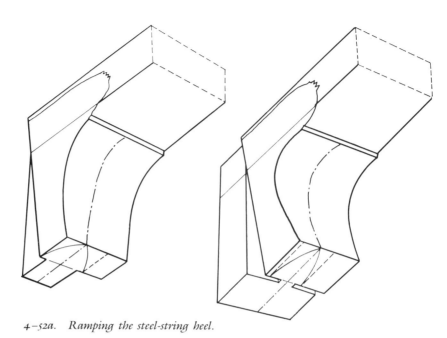

4—52a. Ramping the steel-string heel.

4—52b. Ramping the classical heel.

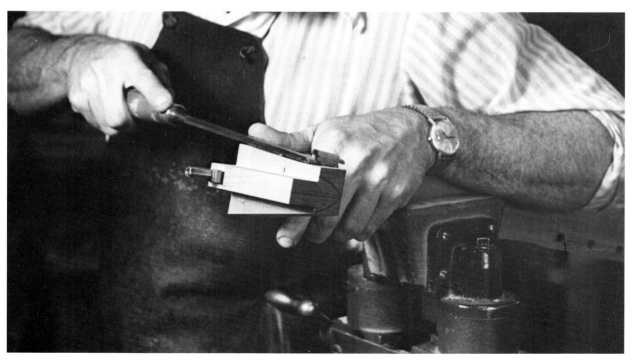

4—53a. Ramping the steel-string heel. The chisel should enter from both directions to avoid chipping out.

approach the heel cap limit line, reverse direction, carving *up* the ramp to avoid chipping out the bottom of the heel, as shown in Fig. 4-53b. A fine-surfaced, angled plane should result. Repeat this process in mirror image on the other side of the heel. Do not proceed to the next step until both ramps are identical.

Step 4—Concaving the Ramp

The flat ramps are now hollowed into an in-curved shape by scooping them with the chisel (see Fig. 4-54a or 4-54b). (*Steel-string only:* Examine Fig. 4-55.) The chisel is held flat side up and belly side against the wood. Note that lifting the handle while push-

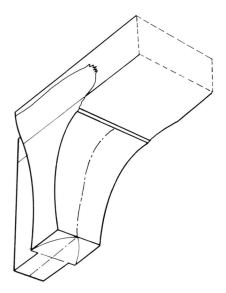

4–54a. *Concaving the ramps (steel-string).*

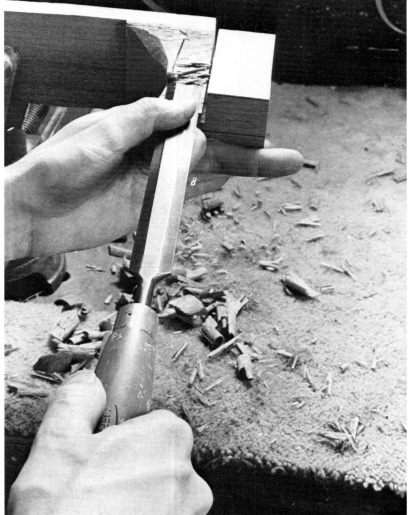

4–53b. *Ramping the classical heel. Note that the paring chisel is held somewhat like a pool cue, with one hand acting as a "bridge" for the blade.*

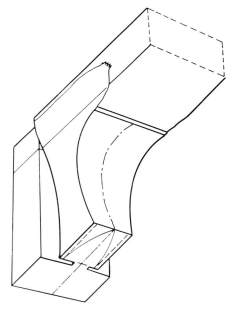

4–54b. *Concaving the ramps (classical).*

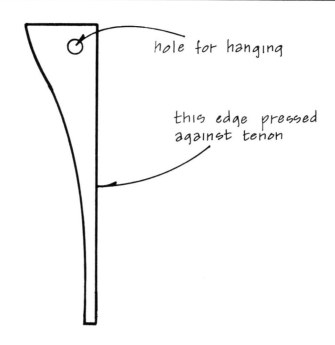

4–56. *Full-sized pattern for concaving template (steel-string).*

4–55. *Symmetry will be improved by marking the end-grain face of the steel-string neck with a curved template. (See Fig. 4–56).*

ing up the ramp causes the chisel to dig in and take a deeper bite. Lowering the handle will allow the chisel to scoop a thinner shaving. Adjust the handle height as necessary to remove smooth, even-sized shaving curls, producing a hollowed curve as indicated in Fig. 4-57. Do not proceed until both cheeks of the heel are carved to a similar curve.

4–57. *Concaving the ramp. The chisel, held belly-side down, takes fine shavings.*

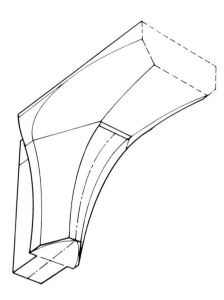

4–58a. *Carving the primary facet (steel-string).*

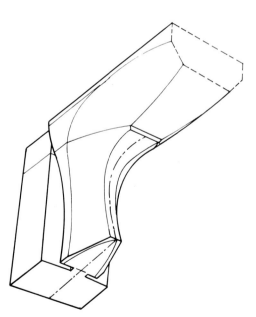

4–58b. *Carving the primary facet (classical).*

Step 5—Carving the Primary Facet

We now begin the initial step in carving a graceful transition between the horizontal shaft and the vertical heel. A large facet is cut, starting at the heel cap outline, traveling up the heel, swooping around and into the shaft as shown in Figs. 4-58a and 4-58b, and exiting as shown in Fig. 4-59.

The smoothness and continuity of this facet cut will determine in great measure the final appearance of the finished heel. Take care to remove material with light, full-length strokes, rather than short gouges. The student must strive to remove progressively only as much material with each pass as will leave a smooth surface for the next pass, lest the curved facet become a random, lumpy form. (If lumps or creases occur, you may fall back on the wood rasp to even out the lumpy surface before proceeding to make the next, deeper facet cuts with the chisel.)

The chisel is held belly down, as we have said, except to make the initial entry cuts into the heel at the heel cap area; here it is pushed flat side down into the facet for an inch or so into the heel, then flipped over onto its belly to carry the facet around towards the shaft. (*Classical only:* See Fig. 4-60.)

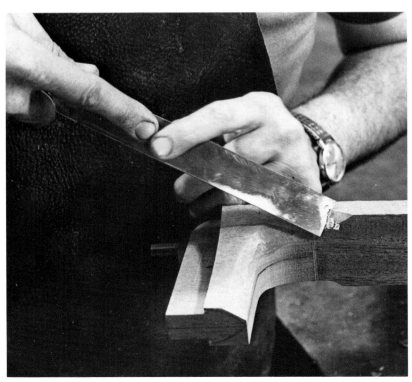

4–59. *Exiting from the primary facet in the steel-string heel.*

If the chisel exits prematurely or pops out during the stroke as you travel around the curve, try to reenter the cut where you left off, always with the purpose of leaving behind a smooth sweep for the next, deeper facet cut. If you chronically stop the chisel midstroke in the same spot along its travel, a nasty crease will develop that will interrupt the smooth transition and will be difficult to remove. If you must stop along the facet stroke, stop in a different spot each time.

Duplicate the major facet on the other side of the heel. Do not proceed until both are as similar and symmetrical as possible (Fig. 4-61).

4–60. *Using the skew (violinmaker's) knife to carve the facet on the classical heel. This tool is necessary because the headblock limits mobility with a chisel. The knife is designed to make a "rolling" cut, and the handle is elongated to facilitate a two-hand grip, as shown here.*

4–61. *Steel-string heel, both sides primary faceted. Note that the ramp stops short of the edge adjacent to the fingerboard.*

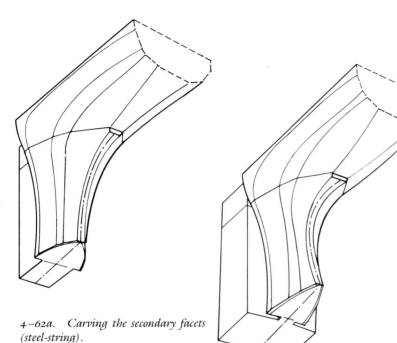

4–62a. *Carving the secondary facets (steel-string)*.

4–62b. *Carving the secondary facets (classical)*.

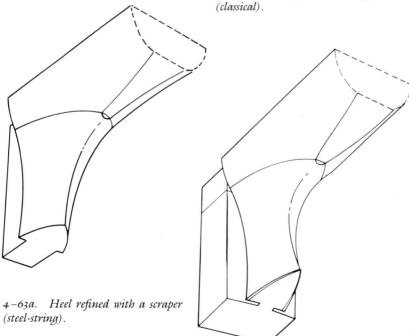

4–63a. *Heel refined with a scraper (steel-string)*.

4–63b. *Heel refined with a scraper (classical)*.

Step 6—Carving the Secondary Facets

The primary facet is now broken into smaller, or secondary, facets as the heel approaches its final contour (Figs. 4-62a and 4-62b). From here on be sensitive to grain direction, particularly at the shaft. If tearing or splitting begins as you enter the shaft, reverse the direction of the chisel cut.

Step 7—Refining the Carved Heel

Examine Figs. 4-63a and 4-63b. All lumps, creases, and facet lines must be shaved away with the skew knife (Fig. 4-64), and finally with a finely burred scraper (Fig. 4-65). Work the heel surfaces to a sharp crease down the centerline with the scraper, working the crease until it is straight and sharp for most of its length. Remove all tool marks with #120-grit garnet sandpaper. The heel should appear like one of those in Fig. 4-66.

4-64. *Using a skew chisel to remove lumps and tool facets.*

4-65. *Refining the heel with a scraper.*

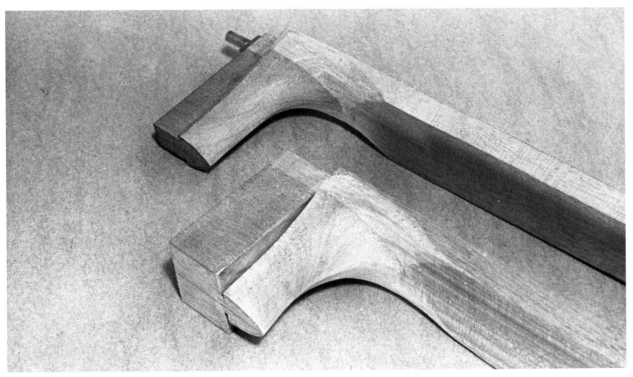

4-66. *The rough carved heels. Note the different profiles for the steel-string and the classical.*

CHAPTER 5

PLATE MATERIALS AND TONE-WOOD SELECTION

The major components of the soundbox—the soundboard (also called the *top* or *table*), sides (also called *ribs*), and back—begin as bookmatched pairs of rough-sawn wood slices, typically about 3/16 inch thick.

The three pairs are edge-jointed, and the top and back are joined into single bookmatched plates prior to planing and scraping to final thickness. (The back can be made from more than two pieces if timber wide enough to make up a two-piece back is unavailable.)

Bookmatched pairs, rather than single wide pieces, have for centuries been the norm for guitar backs and sides. It is obviously far easier to obtain quarter-sawn tone wood sections half the width of the instrument than it is to obtain them full width, but this is not the only reason for making plates out of bookmatched pairs. By bookmatching, the

The Plates

builder imparts a natural symmetry to the instrument, both visually and acoustically. The plates tend to be more uniform and homogeneous in structure, and the effects of changes in bracing weight and design are more predictable. It also becomes possible to make the plate specifically more rigid toward its center or toward its outer boundaries if so desired, simply by choosing one common edge or the other for joining.

Soundboard Materials

Guitar soundboards traditionally are made from softwood (coniferous) trees. The softwoods most commonly found on production and handbuilt instruments are spruce, cedar, and redwood.

Several varieties of spruce are or have been popular: Alpine spruce (*Picea excelsa;* also commonly known as European spruce, Bavarian spruce, German spruce, and German silver spruce), which is found throughout Alpine Europe; Sitka spruce (*Picea sitchensis;*

also sometimes called Alaskan spruce), which grows along the northwestern coast of North America from California to Alaska; Engelmann spruce (*Picea engelmannii*), which grows primarily at high altitudes in the Rocky Mountain region of the United States and Canada; and Eastern white spruce (*Picea glauca*), which grows principally in the Great Lakes states and New England.

Of these, Alpine spruce is usually the most highly prized. It has been the soundboard material of choice in Europe and elsewhere for centuries. The forests have been heavily logged, however, and mature trees are in short supply. It is thus expensive and sometimes difficult to obtain.

Sitka spruce is currently the most widely used soundboard material for production steel-string guitars. Most steel-string (and some classical) handbuilders also use it extensively, for it is much more readily available and less expensive than European spruce, although it is nonetheless a superb soundboard material.

Eastern white spruce closely resembles Alpine spruce; although it was once commonly used on production steel-string guitars, it is no longer widely available in quarter-sawn widths sufficient for guitar soundboards. Engelmann spruce, which also resembles Alpine spruce in appearance, is not as strong as other spruces but is suitable for all types of guitars if handled properly.

In the last twenty years or so, Western red cedar (*Thuja plicata*) has gained a wide following as soundboard material, particularly for classical guitars. It grows in the Pacific Northwest and along the Canadian Pacific coast to Alaska. Because it is neither as strong nor as durable as spruce, cedar is not widely used on steel-string guitars. Even on the classical guitar, the life expectancy of a cedar top is far shorter than a spruce top. Its principal advantage seems to be its relatively short break-in period: A cedar soundboard will reach its peak when the instrument is still relatively new, while a spruce top will require more time to mature. Cedar is also significantly more stable than spruce, and thus is less subject to shrinkage cracks.

Redwood (*Sequoia sempervirens*) has recently begun to achieve popularity among builders on the West Coast. As a soundboard material, it has properties similar to Western red cedar and, like cedar and Sitka spruce, is presently still abundant because of the huge quantity of timber available in single trees.

Soundboard Selection

Of all the guitar's parts, the soundboard (or top) plays far and away the most significant role in tone generation. Proper selection of top wood thus is essential to the luthier's art.

Looking through a stack of tops, the beginner will notice only gross and obvious differences. Marks of quality often are mistaken for defects, and vice-versa. Accomplished builders, however, rely on a variety of senses to evaluate top wood, and with experience decide which features actually will affect the instrument's ultimate sound, structural integrity, and appearance.

Needless to say, your senses will be sharpened over an extended period of time, but if you have a stack of tops available to choose from, you will learn a great deal right away. In the process of flexing and tapping, you will find that some pieces feel as rigid as glass, while others can be bent almost into a cylinder. Some

have a noticeable bell-like ring when tapped; others sound like cardboard. You will soon observe a correspondence between these features. In any event, the selection criteria enumerated below are provided only as basic points of reference. What remains of the learning process is contact with the material, for which there is no substitute.

VERTICAL GRAIN

The first step in top selection is examination of the end-grain. In our experience, the more vertical the end-grain, the stronger the top will be both laterally and longitudinally in relation to its weight. As an approximate rule of thumb, a top should be no more than 20 degrees off the vertical for at least two-thirds of its width in order to be minimally acceptable, and no part of the top that will fall within the template should be more than 40 degrees off.

CROSS-GRAIN STIFFNESS

Of the observable effects produced by quarter-sawing, that which is most significant to tonal response of both the top and the finished instrument is lateral stiffness. Stiffness across the grain typically allows the builder to work the top thinner without making its response flabby. (A thinner plate has less inertial mass to move when stimulated by the strings' vibrations.) This is not to say, however, that the stiffest top available is always the

best for the guitar you are building. For medium- and small-box steel-string guitars, we recommend topwood that is only moderately stiff, although good quarter remains a desirable and important feature.

SILK

You will notice that where the piece is perfectly quarter-sawn a silky, luminescent, cross-grain pattern frequently appears. These are the medullary rays, running perpendicular to the annual rings. Since the rays provide lateral strength, where the rays appear more strikingly, the top will usually be stiffer. Because of this, tops that display well-developed silk are usually highly prized. The rays are also thought by some builders to improve tonal quality by providing a cross-linkage between the longitudinal fibers.

GRAIN

Fineness, evenness, and straightness of grain are frequently accorded great significance to the quality of top wood. In our experience, however, these are primarily cosmetic features, although very wide, grossly uneven, badly angled, or severely swirled grain should be avoided. Fineness (or closeness) of grain may have a marginal effect on longitudinal strength, but it is not a reliable indicator thereof. It is of no particular significance at all to lateral strength, which, as we have seen, is controlled by other factors. Evenness and straightness of grain are generally matters of personal preference. Little wiggles and occasional swirls are sometimes actually preferred by luthiers for the character they impart to a top. One very interesting feature you may see are "bear claws"—very tight wiggles that are sometimes heavily distributed over the whole top. This characteristic is highly coveted by many violinmakers and other bowed-instrument makers; guitar builders variously prize or disdain top wood in which it appears.

COLOR

Color is of cosmetic importance only. As a rule, uniformity of color is sought. Builders who tint their tops can often get excellent quality wood at a lower price simply because of uneven color.

SEASONING

Many luthiers, especially builders of bowed instruments, are particularly enamored of soundboard wood that has been aged for many years. While our experience confirms that top wood that has been seasoned for several years is both more stable than and acoustically superior to top wood that has been only recently dried to equilibrium moisture content, we have perceived no specific evidence of

superior acoustic qualities in wood that is very old.

Guitar tops that are well seasoned usually display marked end-grain shrinkage. This creates a fuzzy, almost mummified effect, which is a good indicator to look for during selection. If the wood feels distinctly cooler than the surrounding atmosphere, beware: It may not yet even be fully dried, much less seasoned.

SHORT-GRAIN OR RUN-OUT

The orientation of the sawn piece in relation to the axis of the tree is one of the most commonly overlooked structural features of soundboard woods. If lumber is not cut parallel to the tree axis, or if the tree grows with a twist ("corkscrews"), the longitudinal fibers will run off the face of the board (Fig. 5-1). A guitar plate with parallel fibers running its length will be lon-

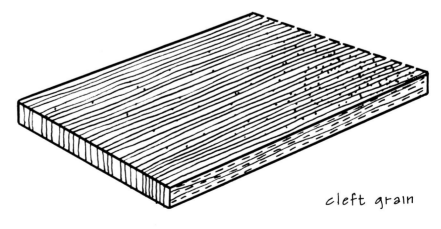

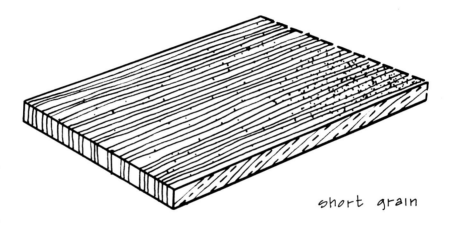

5-1. Fiber orientation in softwood edge-grain tissue is ordinarily invisible. The two pieces may appear identical, but the short-grain piece is much weaker.

gitudinally stronger than one with short, angled fibers coming up out of its surface. Runout or short-grain is extremely difficult to spot in top wood, even for the expert. The only way to avoid or minimize it with any certainty is to obtain soundboard material sawn from split billets. A split will invariably run along the tree's growth axis, and billets split from soundboard-length pieces bucked from the log will be too short to manifest any appreciable twist.

Splitting has the further advantage of ensuring a perfectly quartered face for resawing. This happens because the split occurs along the medullary rays, which, as we have noted, run perpendicular to the annual rings.

We certainly do not suggest that a top must have every quality enumerated above in order to be usable. A multitude of factors other than the quality of the raw top material affect the quality of the final product, and the use of "better" soundboard material does not guarantee a good result. The accomplished builder can achieve excellent results by varying construction of the soundboard to allow for particular characteristics or to compensate for their absence.

Back and Side Materials

The timbers for the back and sides are typically hardwoods, although historically solid pine and pine laminates have been used. The varieties of hardwood most frequently seen on modern guitars are rosewood, mahogany and related woods, and maple. Cypress from Spain and Italy is the traditional material for flamenco guitars; in North America, however, Alaskan yellow cedar (sometimes called Canadian cypress) is often substituted for the European varieties.

Of all species, by far the most highly prized is Brazilian rosewood (*Dalbergia nigra*), which grows primarily in the coastal forests of the state of Bahia, in Brazil. Also called jacaranda and Rio rosewood, Brazilian rosewood has been an important timber of commerce since it was first discovered by European explorers centuries ago. It is easily the most beautiful and exotic of all tropical hardwoods; the finest pieces display almost kaleidoscopic color and interlacing grain patterns that can be awe inspiring.

For the guitarmaker's purposes, however, the characteristic that makes Brazilian rosewood so highly regarded is its extraordinary resonance. This can be most directly observed in applications other than on guitars; many Latin American percussion instruments are made from Brazilian rosewood because of the loud report it produces when struck. The intensity and velocity of its vibrations when acoustically stimulated thus make it the ideal material for the soundbox of the acoustic guitar.

Second to Brazilian rosewood, and for the past fifteen years or so the most common variety used for high-quality guitar backs and sides, is East Indian rosewood (*Dalbergia latifolia*). Although not quite as dense or hard as Brazilian rosewood, it is nonetheless a very heavy, hard, and strong timber. It also does not display the same intensity of color or figure, yet it is highly regarded as a decorative wood. Acoustically, East Indian rosewood is fairly close to Brazilian in resonant properties. Some luthiers, in fact, prefer the sound they can obtain with East Indian rosewood to that of Brazilian rosewood.

Other species sometimes used include Honduras, Madagascar and Madras rosewoods, and Cocobolo and Kingwood, also of the genus *Dalbergia*.

American mahogany (*Swietenia macrophylla*) is widely used on both handbuilt and mass-produced instruments. It is strong, stable, and relatively lightweight. It takes a finish very well, and it is very easy to work. We emphatically recommend that beginners build their first guitars from mahogany, both because of its stability and working characteristics and because of its ready availability.

Other varieties of mahogany used for backs and sides are African mahogany (*Khaya*, spp.) and Cuban mahogany (*Swietenia mahoganii*). Both of these are somewhat denser than American mahogany. The African varieties tend to have pronounced ribbon figure due to heavy grain interlock; this can cause difficulties during bending and scraping operations. Cuban mahogany is actually preferred over Honduras by some builders because of its harder temper.

Several varieties of maple have been used on acoustic guitars over the years. North American rock maple (*Acer saccharum*) is the species most commonly seen, while soft maple and European maple are sometimes used by handbuilders in this country. The most sought-after pieces of maple are those that display a curly, or fiddleback, figure.

Many other exotic and domestic hardwoods can be used for the guitar body, such as padouk (also called vermillion), black walnut (both plain and figured), and pearwood (traditionally used on lutes). Koa, related to mahogany, is currently enjoying a resurgence of popularity.

Virtually any straight-grained hardwood *could* be used for guitar backs and sides, but many of these would present difficulties in bending or working to the thicknesses required for instrument building. We thus recommend that the student select from one of the more commonly used materials listed above, and not waste a lot of time experimenting with unknown materials.

Back and Side Selection

Selection for the back does not entail quite the same structural considerations as selection for the top, but most of the quality indicators are similar. Vertical, straight-grain pieces are generally preferred for strength and stability. Run-out is undesirable, but not critically so, and it is easy to spot by looking at the side grain of the piece. We have seen some fine instruments made with flat-sawn and even core-cut materials for the back, but we disapprove of such practices. If cracks or splits occur, they will wander at bizarre angles through the piece, making reinforcement difficult and gluing sometimes impossible. Also, wild grain and knots should be avoided. Although apparently sound, they may cause damage to the guitar's finish because of uneven shrinkage.

Aesthetically, straight-grain is our preference, but highly figured quarter-sawn materials can be the most pleasing of all. Choosing for this factor is obviously a matter of taste. One very desirable feature to seek is a good match between back and sides.

The structural considerations for side selection are somewhat different from those for either the back or top. Withstanding the stresses placed upon the finished instrument is not a significant problem for the sides. Rather, the material must be selected for its bending properties. Straight, vertical-grain material is optimal for bending. Many of the grain configurations that would be acceptable on the back should be rejected for the sides. Waves and swirls even in well-quartered material are potential bending problems. Severe run-out must be categorically avoided.

PROCEDURE: JOINTING THE PLATES

After selecting the pieces of wood that will be used for the top and back of the guitar, the next step is to cut their corresponding bookmatch edges straight and true (jointing) in preparation for gluing them together into full plates (joining). The bookmatched edges of the side slats are also jointed to prepare them for subsequent assembly to the top (obviously, they will not be joined).

For a jointed seam to be flawless, its mating edges must be correctly bookmatched, parallel to the grain and dead straight. Before gluing, the seam must pass a test called candling, in which it is closely scrutinized for light seepage in front of a bright light source. After gluing, the result will be an invisible seam that will not fail under ordinary circumstances.

During the actual jointing sequence, the plates are stacked

together and their common edge planed straight. Stacking them cancels out minor deviations when they are flipped open and joined (Fig. 5-2). The plates are kept from shifting while being planed by placing them in a simple open fixture called a shooting board. The term originates from the fact that the plane is "shot" across the edges while lying on its side.

The edges can also be jointed with a portable electric router or on a power jointer.

Machines of this sort can quickly cut a joint of adequate quality and are thus attractive to production guitarmakers. However, the quality of a jointed seam produced by a skilled worker using a sharp plane is superior to a machine-jointed seam.

Jointing with sandpaper, a practice recommended in other texts, is not recommended here since sandpaper produces a minutely grooved, torn surface that is unsuitable for this critical seam.

TOOLS
hand plane, freshly sharpened (a small block plane can be used, but a longer one, such as a No. 3 or 4 smoothing plane, is best, provided its sole is known to be flat)

MATERIALS
bookmatched soundboard, back, and side sets (see text)

IMPLEMENTS
shooting board, constructed as in Step 1 (perform Steps 1 through 5 with your soundboard plates; Steps 6 and 7 apply to the back and side plates)
bright light source, such as an unshaded lamp, a candle, or a bright window (a fluorescent light fixture placed on a table and covered with a sheet of plate glass makes an ideal light table for this purpose)

Step 1—Making a Shooting Board

The basic shooting board (Fig. 5-3) consists of no more than a flat board, or other platform, with a raised lip nailed or screwed against two of its adjacent sides. The fixture is clamped securely to the table. The platform is narrower by a small amount than the plate halves, thus exposing the stacked plates' common edge to the plane. During its use the plates are inserted into the crook formed by the raised

Jointing plate halves individually

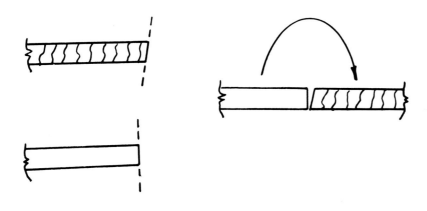

Jointing plate halves together

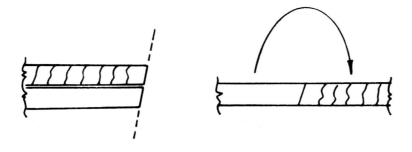

5–2. *Jointing plate halves together helps achieve a tighter seam.*

stops of the device. The plates are held down firmly with the fingers of one hand while the plane is laid on its side and "shot" across the edges with the other hand. The fixture is fairly foolproof provided:

(1) the surface on which the plane rides is not rough or warped, which will cause the plane to make a random cut;
(2) the edges of the plates correspond well with the stops on the board; otherwise they will not return precisely to their original orientation after each removal for candling;
(3) the plates lie obediently flat on top of each other and on the platform.

In our shop, we use a more elaborate shooting board that provides a smooth-faced runway for the plane, two metal pins sticking up from the platform that fit into holes drilled into the waste areas of the plates (a substitute for the raised stops), and finally, a removable pressure bar near the mating edges, which holds them flat while they are planed (Fig. 5-4).

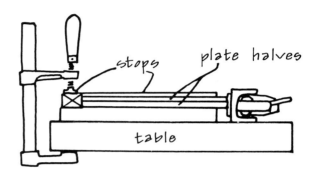

5–3. *Basic shooting board.*

5–4. *Jointing with a smoothing plane on a refined shooting board.*

Step 2—Getting Ready

Verify the bookmatch of your set of plates. Choose the edges to be jointed and mark them clearly. Drawing the soundboard-template outline provides an unmistakable reminder of that choice.

It is traditional to put the tightest grain in the center, along either side of the center seam. We feel this is less important than having the *stiffest* portion in the center (tightness of grain and stiffness do not always coincide; see Soundboard Selection, page 94)

The edges to be jointed must be parallel to the face grain of the plates. If not, or if there is any discoloration or flaw to be avoided near the selected seam edge, trace a line with a pencil and straightedge inboard from the edge, as necessary (is there enough width left for your template?) and with a plane or bandsaw cut the waste area away to the line.

The edges opposite the seam must be approximately straight and the ends of the plates square so that the plates will not shift against the stops on the shooting board. Trim the edges straight and square the ends as required.

Place the plates on the shooting board, pressing them down and against the stops with one hand. The other hand will manipulate the plane, which is placed on its side with its sole against the exposed edges.

Step 3—Adjusting the Plane

Retract the blade fully, and shoot. Extract the blade by a tiny amount and shoot again. Continue alternately extracting the blade and shooting until a fine wood powder appears in the plane pocket. Do not adjust the plane any further.

Step 4—Shooting the Edge

Continue shooting until fine curls appear. Continue until a single full-length double-curl appears. If no curls appear after 10-12 strokes, resharpen the blade. If curls still do not appear, extract the blade a bit more and continue.

Step 5—Candling

Remove the plates and "candle" them by holding them carefully together and scrutinizing the seam closely in front of a bright light source (Fig. 5-5). If light can be seen through the seam, return the plates to the shooting board, stacked in their original orientation, and continue as before. If the next candling test reveals a worsening trend, devise a

5-5. Checking the jointed edge. The seam is inspected by holding the two halves of the plate up to a window and looking for light passing through.

strategy that favors high spots with selective planing or with selective pressure on the plane during each stroke.

It is best to manage a perfect seam along the entire length of the soundboard plates. However, since the most crucial portion of the seam lies below the soundhole, you may choose to allow small imperfections in the area where the seam will be cut away at the soundhole or where the seam is hidden under the fingerboard.

Step 6—Jointing the Back Plates

This step is identical to Steps 2 through 5 except for the fact that, since we are planing hardwood, you can adjust your plane for a slightly deeper cut and gain speed without sacrificing accuracy.

Step 7—Jointing the Side Plates

The bookmatched edges of the sides must be jointed so they will sit accurately on the soundboard. They need not pass the candling test, however, as long as the common edges are straight. It is sufficient to mark the location of the desired finished edge on the side with a long straightedge and pencil, clamp the piece flat on the table with the edge overhanging, and plane freehand to the line. More or less can be removed from one or both plates to "balance" the

figure or to ensure that some predominant or outstanding grain feature shared by both plates appears in approximately the same location on their surfaces.

Step 8—Dimensioning the Side Plates

Trim the sides to a consistent width (SS: 4 inches; CL: 3¾ inches). The trimmed edge is left a bit rough to easily distinguish it from the jointed edge.

PROCEDURE: JOINING TOP AND BACK

The soundboard glue seam requires only light to moderate pressure for proper closure, because the top material is soft and because clamping pressure is focused by the narrowness of the jointed edge. The back requires only slightly more pressure. Builders of carved-top instruments of the violin family sometimes merely rub the jointed edges together and leave them to dry with no pressure at all. Although this is impractical with the wide, floppy plates that make up the guitar top, it illustrates the lack of necessity for heavy clamping forces.

The craftsman's chief concern when effecting this joint is maintaining the alignment of the jointed edges while the plates are pressed together. If the proper amount of side

pressure is used, however, a moderate weight should suffice to hold the plate halves down on a flat surface, which will ensure correct alignment. If the jointed edges want to pop up, even when moderately weighted, or if the plates buckle at all, the clamping pressure is far greater than necessary.

The necessity of executing this unusual joint has been the mother of an astonishing variety of inventions, contraptions, and specialized rigs, all developed for the purpose. We, however, use a very simple and ancient joining technique that requires an absolute minimum of tooling and virtually no experience to master.

Our simple fixture for this procedure is made in Step 1, below. Steps 2, 3, and 4 refer to joining the top. Step 5 covers joining the back.

IMPLEMENTS
joining board (see Step 1); have a couple of extra scrap blocks handy

SUPPLIES
AR or PVA glue

Step 1—Making a Joining Board

This need not be an implement made specially for guitar-building; it can be fashioned from odds and ends that you have on hand. It entails one piece of plywood, particle board, or other smooth, rigid material, about 20 × 24 inches; a piece of 2 × 4 about 24 inches long; a few scrap blocks; and three small hardwood wedges. The wedges taper from about ⅛ to ¼ inch and should be about ¼ inch high so that they protrude slightly above the plate (Fig. 5-6).

The board must be raised off the work table so that clamps can reach underneath it. If you have some right-angle bar clamps (as shown in the photo), they will support the board themselves during joining. Alternatively, you may glue, screw, or nail supporting blocks underneath the board.

Step 2—Positioning the Blocks

Clamp the 2 × 4 to the edge of the joining board as shown in the photo. Place the left half of the plate against the 2 × 4 with the jointed edge toward the middle of the board. (The edge butting the 2 × 4 must be reasonably straight.)

Slip a piece of newspaper about six inches wide under the length of the jointed edge to avoid gluing the plate to the joining board. (Do not use waxed paper, as it will inhibit the drying process.) Place the right half down with its jointed edge flush to the jointed edge of the left half. Position the three blocks along the outer edge of the right half, leaving a bare ³⁄₁₆-inch clearance between the edge and each block. Clamp the blocks securely, and check the wedges for fit. They should tighten when inserted about halfway; if they do not, readjust the blocks.

Step 3—Applying Glue and Pressure

Remove the wedges and place them near the blocks. Carefully apply a bead of glue to the right side of the plate along the full length of its jointed edge. Smooth the glue with one clean finger so that

5-6. *The joining board. Wedges tapped in between the plate and the blocks provide clamping pressure.*

the entire edge is soaked. (*Note*: If glue drips down the face of the plate, wipe it off but do not spread it back on the jointed edge, as it may be contaminated with dust or other foreign matter. Use more glue from the bottle if necessary.) Place the right side down adjacent to the blocks, and then carefully slide the glued edge into contact with the dry left-side edge. Gently slide the seam back and forth once or twice to ensure that the glue spreads evenly on both edges. Holding the seam down with one hand, insert the three wedges between the outside edge and the blocks. Inspect the seam carefully to ensure that one edge has not ridden up away from the joining board at any point. Still holding the seam down with one hand, take the hammer and *very gently* tap the wedges in a little further. With an extra scrap block, tap along both sides of the seam to ensure that both halves of the plate are flush to the joining board. Still holding the seam down, tap the wedges in a bit further, and then lay a weight (a clamp, for instance) gently across the seam to keep it from buckling up.

Step 4—Removal

After about thirty minutes, the glue should be thoroughly set. To remove the plate from the joining board, it is important that the wedges be popped out before the seam is

unweighted. Once the wedges are released, you may remove the plate from the board. Peel the newspaper off the underside of the seam and lean the plate against a wall, allowing air to contact both faces, for at least another thirty minutes before flexing or working the top.

Step 5—Joining the Back

Steel-string builders planning to use a wide decorative marquetry strip as a centerseam inlay should simply repeat Steps 2, 3, and 4 with the back. A channel will be routed later for insertion of the wide marquetry strip when the back is constructed, in Chapter 10. We do not recommend gluing wide marquetry strips *between* the plates because the structural integrity of marquetry strips may be unreliable.

Classical builders, and steel-string builders planning to use a centerseam decoration consisting simply of a contrasting veneer strip or sandwich, must lay in the strip between the halves while joining. Apply glue to *both* jointed edges before inserting the veneer strip. Otherwise, Steps 2, 3, and 4 are performed as above.

PROCEDURE: PLANING THE PLATES TO THICKNESS

The decisions involved in planing the plates to thickness, especially the soundboard, are essential to the guitar's tone. The experienced luthier calls upon a refined sensitivity to determine the "weight" of all the guitar's plates relative to each other and relative to the design and function of the particular instrument.

As the plates are thinned, they undergo more than just visually perceivable dimensional changes, for fundamental changes in their acoustic anatomy occur simultaneously. This is a fact that the cabinetmaker ignores, but is essential to the guitarmaker's pursuit.

While alternately planing and tapping the soundboard, we note that its "ring" drops in pitch. As we remove material from the face of the sheet we are causing both a rapid diminution of its stiffness and resilience and a fundamental and irreversible change in its acoustic response. We have "loosened" the plate, lowering the pitch as well as lengthening the duration of its fundamental (or predominant) frequency, as elicited by tapping. We have also increased the variety and prominence of a "halo" of accompanying sounds. This "halo" is the lower energy spectrum of the overtone series characteristic of the plate at a given size and thickness. The fundamental continues to drop in pitch until a threshold is crossed and the clear ring disappears as a distinct entity. All that can be distinguished now is a jumble of apparently disorganized sounds, none as loud or as distinct as the original fundamental. Crossing that threshold results in a change in response described by some builders as "dispersing" or "quenching" the fundamental. Planing much further kills the resilience of the plate, making it both acoustically and structurally useless as a soundboard.

The novice should simply attempt to reduce a top to a specified thickness, tapping all along and becoming acquainted with the tools, the way the wood is worked, and how the voice and feel of the wood changes.

Soundboard thicknesses on fine classical guitars generally range from two to three millimeters (about .080 to .120 inch). This rather broad range illustrates the fact that soundboard materials vary widely in mechanical characteristics and, of course, that luthiers vary widely in their construction techniques and designs. For the guitar being built from this book, we recommend a final thickness of about .10 to .11 inch (7/64 inch or a bit less) for spruce and .11 to .12 inch (7/64 inch or a bit more) for cedar.

Steel-string tops range between .10 and .125 inch, depending on plate size and material stiffness. Tops on particularly large guitars can go as thick as .130 inch; on very small guitars, down to as thin as .095 inch. Beginners should aim for 1/8 inch on the soundboard for the steel-string guitar built from this book.

Classical back thicknesses vary between .085 and .095 inch in our shop, with the softer varieties (such as mahogany) toward the thicker end of the scale and the harder (such as rosewood) toward the thinner. The beginner should strive to achieve an even 3/32 inch, aiming for just a hair less on harder plates.

Steel-string backs on full-sized guitars in our shop vary from .110 inch in mahogany to .100 inch for rosewood. Dimensions for smaller steel-string guitars are equivalent to classical thicknesses. The beginner should strive to achieve an even 7/64 inch, again aiming for just a hair less on harder plates.

We thin our sides, regardless of material, to .085 inch on steel-string guitars and .080 inch on classical guitars. These dimensions are between 5/64 and 3/32 inch, which is the range we recommend on student instruments.

The novice will soon find that planing rosewood, mahogany, or maple presents challenges that are distinct from those presented by spruce. Hard, highly figured wood such as that typically used for backs and sides requires finer plane-blade settings and often a keener edge for equivalent results. Beginners would be prudent to practice first on cheap lumberyard variety hardwood slats before proceeding on their tonewood plates. Note that some luthier supply houses offer plates machine-sanded to your specified thickness.

Finally, bear in mind that the softwoods used for soundboards are extremely vulnerable to punctures and deep scratches caused by careless handling. Whisk or blow off the work surface religiously before laying the soundboard down to avoid embossing hard particles into the soft wood.

TOOLS
template
smoothing plane with two
   cutters (see below), or
   two smoothing planes
outside caliper
vernier caliper
scraper blade
straightedge
two bar clamps

IMPLEMENTS
small sanding board
large cork-lined caul, about
   3/4 × 4 × 4 inches
smooth particle board or
   birch plywood workboard,
   20 × 24 inches

Step 1—Cutting Out the Soundboard

Place the template against the centerseam, taking care to exclude any gross defects in the soundboard (check both faces!), and draw the template on the soundboard. Flip the template over to the adjacent half, and repeat. The soundboard will be cut out oversized, about ⅜ to ½ inch outside the template outline.

The soundboard can be cut out quickly on a bandsaw with a narrow (¼- to ⅜-inch) blade (Fig. 5-7). A hand-held coping saw will serve equally well and cut almost as quickly. Use the finest-tooth blade you can obtain. Holding the tool in one hand (teeth pointing down), rotate the workpiece into the blade with the other. Pump up and down quickly while feed-

ing *slowly*. Operate the tool with as little of the soundboard extending over the edge of the workboard as possible, to minimize the danger of breakage in the event that the tool jams. You may have to pivot the blade in its frame several times to keep the frame from interfering with the progress of the cut.

Retrieve the off-cuts and store them away for future use: There is no better source of matching material for repairing the plates, should that become necessary in the future.

Step 2—Cleaning the Faces

In order to select the outside, or show, face properly, it may be necessary to first shave a fresh surface onto both. This is just a cleaning and leveling step performed in anticipation of the actual planing procedure; it also allows you to assess the state of sharpness and adjustment of the plane and scraper, as well as the direction of grain run-out.

Clamp the workboard to the table, then clamp one end of the soundboard plate to the

5-7. *Bandsawing the soundboard out of the joined plate. The off-cuts are saved for parts and, if necessary, future crack repairs.*

workboard using a large protective caul or pad (cork- or leather-lined), which safely disperses the clamping pressure.

When planing a bookmatched plate, it is important to be aware that the run-out, if any, reverses itself from one side of the centerseam to the other (Fig. 5-8). Thus, planing and scraping against the run-out will raise a nap (or chip-out), a tendency that reverses direction on the two sides of the plate. This effect is less pronounced when planing diagonally to the grain and is absent when planing cross-grain. For best results when planing parallel to the grain, the luthier must remain aware of the direction of the run-out and plane accordingly.

Until such time as you gain sufficient confidence, your plane blade should always be adjusted to cut a fine shaving, in order to allow you more tries before reaching your goal. If you are unable to cut a fine shaving with your plane, the problem may be with your plane. Look for a warped sole, a dull blade, or poor adjustment.

If the adjacent halves are smooth and level to start with, it may only be necessary to scrape off all the dirt, fuzz, and crayon marks to reveal the surface. However, if the halves are skewed, stepped, deeply grooved by saw marks, or otherwise chewed up, planing

will be necessary. Advance the plane evenly across the surface, overlapping as little as possible. Do not repeat a stroke in the same spot, even if the plane has just barely nicked the surface. Resist the temptation to extend the blade further, unless it produces absolutely no effect. Remember, if you let the plane do its own job, it will nick the high points first before attacking the valleys. Transferring hand pressure from front to back on the plane during the stroke helps to even the action of the plane. If the adjacent surfaces are stepped (as may be the case if the halves are unequal in thickness), approach the thicker half exclusively, hook-

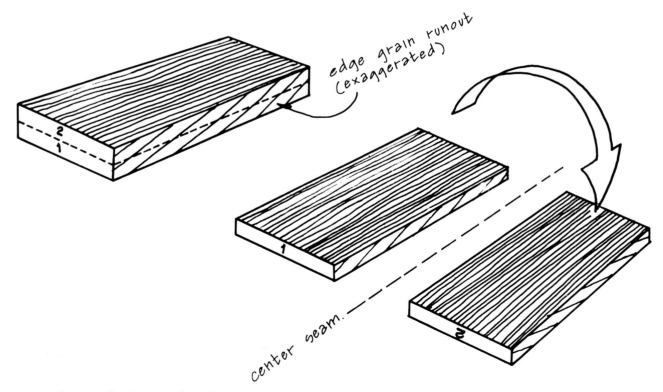

5–8. *Run-out direction in bookmatched plates.*

ing the blade onto the lip each time until the surfaces are approximately equal. Then, plane across the full width of the plate.

Scrape the plane marks off, following the grain (*with* the run-out to achieve the best surface). The plates should display bright, new surfaces on both sides.

Shine a bright light on the surfaces and scrutinize them, making mental note of all the irregularities and discolorations that may exist. Remember that certain areas of the soundboard will eventually be hidden from view by the fingerboard, bridge, pickguard, soundhole, and binding. Take a census and pick the face with the fewest exposed imperfections. Smooth out irregularities left by the plane and scraper by stroking that face with the small sanding board until the overall surface is reasonably level. Mark that face "show" or "out," turn it over so it lies against the workboard, and proceed to the next step.

Step 3—Planing the Soundboard to the Specified Thickness

Because the material can be reduced by the plane so easily, distracted, haphazard planing can quickly cause areas of the soundboard to thin out excessively. Uneven thinning can be prevented by following a strictly methodical planing technique. The surface is worked in one direction, then another, is rotated, and then worked again. It is then scraped flat and checked with measuring tools. This sequence is repeated over and again. You must bring the top down in even, slow stages until the desired results emerge. You

may develop your own personal sequence as long as it is thorough and methodical and you stick to it.

Toothing, which aids visualization, is indispensable to the beginner luthier. It is done with a toothing blade in the plane. The toothing blade is nothing more than a standard blade into which small triangular notches about 1/16 inch deep have been filed, about 1/4 inch apart (Fig. 5-9). This will leave an even track, or comb, of spaced furrows on the wood surface, which are in turn planed away with a single swipe of another plane fitted with a standard blade. (See Fig. 5-10.)

5-9. The toothing blade.

5-10. Thinning the soundboard. The plane blade is notched to produce a furrowed surface, which is later cleaned with a regular smoothing blade. Note that the plane is held at an angle to the cutting stroke for smoother action.

Measure the edge with the vernier caliper for a base dimension. Take an average from several readings around the soundboard. Also, take the opportunity to tap the board. You will likely hear a tight, restrained, high-pitched note of relatively short duration, with few accompanying overtones. Keep tapping often as you progress through the sequence, listening for changes (Fig. 5-11). Ideally, the workboard should be clamped to the end of a narrow table so that the soundboard fixed to it can be approached from three sides. The following suggested sequence is keyed to Figs. 5-12a through j.

Place the square cork-lined caul at the bottom center of the soundboard and clamp it firmly (clamp handles *down*) to the end of the workboard. Set the toothing plane so that, with an easy stroke, it leaves a clearly grooved track, but not so deep that it snags or grabs the surface. Start your stroke diagonally from right to left (as shown in Fig. 5-12a). Starting from the top of the soundboard, work progressively down, with as little overlap as possible, and stop when the clamps interfere with your stroke.

In order to complete the pattern unencumbered, rotate the soundboard 180 degrees and reclamp, picking up the pattern with the toothing plane where you left off (Fig. 5-12b). As before, avoid overlaps. Continue till the grooved pattern covers the entire area of the soundboard.

Commence to *remove* the grooved pattern by planing diagonally to the right (opposite the original strokes) with the smoothing plane (Fig. 5-12c). The blade should be set so that it cuts deep enough to remove the grooves but not so deep as to cause a rough or difficult stroke. As before, avoid overlaps. Go over the skipped areas only if they have been neglected. Do not go over them if the plane chooses to miss them. Continue to "erase" the grooves until the clamps interfere.

As before, to continue the new pattern unencumbered, rotate the soundboard 180 degrees, reclamp, and continue the diagonal-right strokes until the original grooved pattern disappears (Fig. 5-12d).

Repeat the previous sequence but start the toothing plane strokes diagonally to the right instead of diagonally to the left.

Before proceeding further,

5–11. Tapping the soundboard during planing. Doing this at frequent intervals provides a sense of the acoustic changes that take place as the plate is progressively thinned.

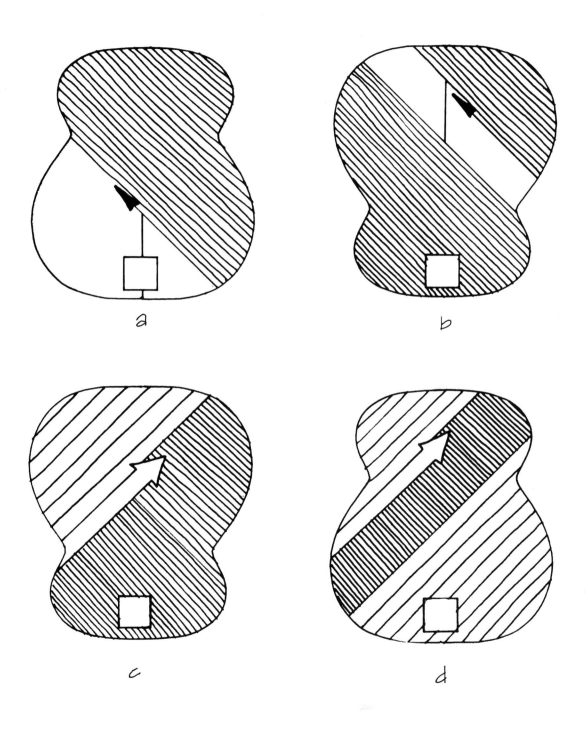

5–12a, b, c, and d.   Toothing and smoothing plane action.

check your progress. With a good backlight, run a straight-edge across the surface (run it diagonally, longitudinally, *and* transversally), reading the line of light that shows between the edge and the surface. You are looking for gross trends, such as large hollows or hills, rather than local deviations (the constantly reversing technique is designed to overcome these trends). Now examine the soundboard edges. Note their consistency. If a section or sections are coming down faster or slower, resulting in thin or thick segments, note them mentally (or on the surface with a pencil) for special emphasis or purposeful neglect later. Measure the thickness of the edge with the vernier caliper as far in and at as many locations around the edge as possible. The average reading will give you an idea of how much material came off during the first removal sequence and, therefore, how close you would come to the specified thickness if you simply repeated the sequence.

If your technique has been consistent, you should have had a favorable straightedge reading. If so, it would appear that your technique is adequate to repeat the foregoing sequence until you approach finished thickness. If you have, instead, planed some serious hollows or slopes into your soundboard, it would be helpful to vary the sequence as follows to prevent these negative trends from progressing:

With the soundboard clamped at the bottom, plane parallel to the grain with the toothing plane. There will be an area left untouched due to the clamps (Fig. 5-12e); in order to complete the longitudinal groove pattern, rotate the soundboard 180 degrees, reclamp, and carefully groove the untouched area with the toothing plane, overlapping as little as possible (Fig. 5-12f).

Rotate the soundboard 90 degrees and place the clamps and caul to one side of the waist, as shown in Fig. 5-12g. Remove the longitudinal grooves with transversal strokes of the smoothing plane. If you get a rough or torn surface, it may be time to resharpen. Otherwise readjust for a finer cut. Continue planing until the clamps interfere. Rotate the soundboard 180 degrees, reclamp as in Fig. 5-12h, and continue the transversal strokes until the grooves are eliminated. Rotate the soundboard 90 degrees and reclamp off center, as shown in Fig. 5-12i. With the smoothing plane, stroke longitudinally *with* the run-out for best results. Rotate and reclamp as in Fig. 5-12j, or as necessary to achieve the best surface.

Recheck with a straightedge and vernier caliper. If you are not yet close to your goal, repeat the foregoing sequences as often as necessary to approach the final dimension. The last 1/64 inch or so should be left for the scraper (Fig. 5-13).

The scraper can be used to advantage in conjunction with an outside caliper. If the caliper is set at an opening a tiny bit larger than the desired finished thickness of the soundboard, it will indicate where the board is at finished thickness by clearing or where it is too thick by stopping. The thicker areas are then scraped selectively until the caliper clears. If the plate is too thick everywhere, so as to prohibit the entry of the caliper from any direction (yet you know by measurement that you are close), you can scrape the entire board down evenly by duplicating the foregoing sequences (using the scraper instead of the plane), until you can gain entry with the outside caliper; then scrape selectively until you are satisfied.

Smooth out irregularities in the surface with the small sanding board (following the grain) until a clean, uniform surface is achieved.

As a final note, although we generally aim for uniformity, do not be overly concerned if you do not achieve a mathematically flat surface on your early or even subsequent tries. There is no certainty that a perfectly uniform soundboard yields the best acoustic results.

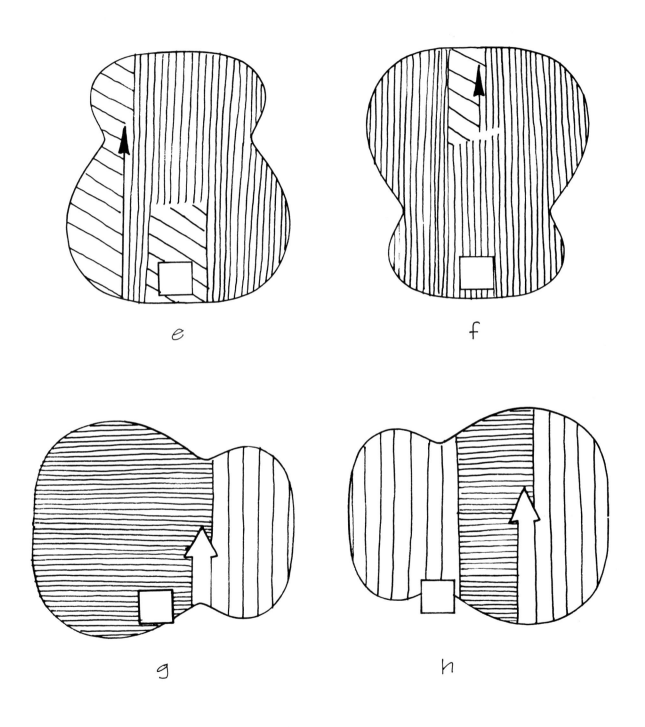

5–12e, f, g, and h. *Further toothing and smoothing plane action.*

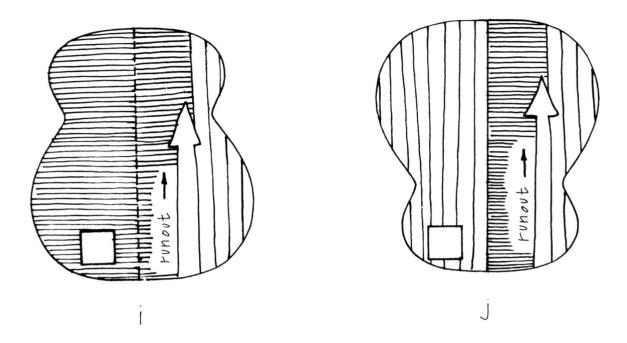

5–12i and j.   Wind-up toothing and smoothing plane action.

5–13.   Scraping to remove plane marks.

Step 4—Planing the Back

The sequence of steps for planing the back is essentially identical to Steps 1, 2, and 3 in this procedure. We recommend, however, that all plane strokes be made diagonally to the grain (Figs. 5-12a through 5-12d). If you are getting large chipouts or deep splintering, you should put your work aside and spend whatever time necessary to sharpen and adjust the plane properly. Alternatively, use a scraper plane—a device that looks like a cross between a plane and a spokeshave and uses a scraper blade as a cutter.

Step 5—Planing the Sides

When planing the sides, chipping or gouging is a more serious problem than before, especially as you approach the finished thickness, since the side will be subsequently submitted to the stresses of bending.

Start by shaving the surfaces clean from saw marks and the like. Select the best face as the show face and then plane the opposite face. Clamp one end; plane toward and then past the other end, starting from the middle each time. Rotate the workpiece 180 degrees and re-

clamp, then repeat. Alternate the smoothing and toothing blades as before, but you may find diagonal or transversal strokes counterproductive—stick to straight longitudinal strokes instead. If you have approached within $\frac{1}{32}$ inch of final thickness without digging or chipping, do not press your luck: bring it down the rest of the way with the scraper.

There will be a natural tendency to thin out the edges, so favor the middle by applying a firm torquing force to the handle toward the center as you make your stroke.

CHAPTER 6

The soundhole rosette has always been the luthier's main decorative focus. But like many other "decorative" details on the instrument, the rosette has a practical as well as an ornamental rationale. The soundhole edge has always been regarded as a weak area on the guitar top because it is composed of alternating edge- and end-grain. The rosette reinforces the area, acting as a belt to strap together and protect the exposed fiber ends.

HISTORICAL NOTES ON THE ROSETTE

Several soundhole decoration techniques have been used throughout the evolution of the guitar, including soundboard piercing, parchment roses, incrustation, and mosaic marquetry. Of these, all but the last are considered historical techniques that are inappropriate on any modern guitar. Builders of reproductions of Renaissance, baroque, and romantic-era guitars (as well as modern lutemakers), however,

6–1. A repeating floral motif on a mosaic-marquetry rosette.

The Soundhole Rosette

continue to use the historical decorations.

The designs of pierced roses and mosaic marquetry recall the Islamic and Semitic origins of both lutes and guitars. Much of Spain's cultural underpinnings were Islamic, the Moors having ruled Spain for almost a thousand years. The pierced rose evolved from simple geometric symbolism to a more decorative ornamentation, usually embellished into tightly plaited wickerwork.

During the baroque period and into the 1800s the parchment rose was popular. These were multilayer pierced-parchment constructions attached to the soundhole edge and receding into the cavity in tightening circular platforms, sometimes in as many as ten layers. The surfaces were finely pierced, and construction ended with a central, shredded-parchment pompom growing upward from the base of the lowest level. These decorations were often built up from thin parchment strips cut like paper doilies, then wetted and wrapped around the perimeters of progressively smaller

wooden discs, which acted like molds. They were then dried, removed, and glued at the ends, and then glued along a central axis to progressively smaller parchment platforms, also pierced and circular.

The parchment-rose technique was often accompanied with and, in fact, during the 1800s was supplanted by the incrustation of decorative shell cutouts laid into a trough filled with colored gum mastic. Numerous guitars from the early 1800s display these incrustations of shell in mastic around the soundhole and around the edges of the soundboard. Mosaic-marquetry rosettes did not become universally accepted on classical guitars till the early 1900s. It was about that time that the marquetry work of Manuel Ramirez (and his successors) firmly established the marquetry rosette as the traditional classical form (Figs. 6-2 and 6-3).

It can be said that the pearl soundhole ring, seen on very early C.F. Martin gut- and steel-string guitars, was a decorative evolution of the early

shell-incrusted mastic soundhole rosettes made in Europe and Spain for hundreds of years before. Soundhole decoration on early American guitars was extremely sparse until Martin began introducing colored purfling and herringbone rosettes on his guitars. Many of his decorative schemes were subsequently adopted as traditional steel-string motifs.

ROSETTE MATERIALS

Rosettes for both steel-string and classical guitars are made from combinations of veneer lines and contrasting marquetry or shell inlay. Marquetry on the steel-string is usually a mass-produced strip displaying a herringbone or similar pattern. The marquetry on the classical guitar is typically a mosaic design made up from small sticks or slivers of wood.

Veneer lines can be purchased from luthier-supply houses. Lines are typically available in black or white (usually dyed or undyed holly); some suppliers also

6–2. *Mosaic-marquetry rosette on a guitar built in 1863 by the great Antonio de Torres; restored at Stringfellow Guitars.*

6–3. *Rosette with engraved shell encrusted in mastic.*

carry rosewood (brown) or maple (light blond) strips. Colored veneer lines are occasionally available from suppliers, but it is frequently necessary to buy natural lines and dye them. We suggest liquid aniline dyes of the type used in dyeing leather. It takes about three days of soaking holly or maple strips (up to a thickness of .025 inch) for most colors to thoroughly penetrate.

Veneer line sandwiches (such as black/white/black, rosewood/white/rosewood, and so on) are also available from luthier-supply houses, and these can significantly reduce the complexity of an inlay job. Sometimes, however, they are too stiff to bend for soundhole rings, in which case prebending by the hot-soak method (described in this chapter) is necessary.

Colored veneer line sandwiches must be made up in the luthier's own shop. Contrasting veneers are stacked and glued in sheets (such as two dyed yellow veneers sandwiched around a rosewood veneer), and then resawn into fine strips on the table saw.

The 1/32- or 1/64-inch-square sticks used for building up the mosaic for the classical rosette are extremely difficult to make without veneer manufacturing equipment, and thus should be bought from a luthier supply house. If square sticks are unavailable, it is possible to create a mosaic out of veneer lines instead of sticks, although

this obviously limits the refinement of the design. If sticks are only available in natural colors, they can be dyed as suggested above for veneer lines.

Marquetry strips such as herringbone are available from virtually all luthier suppliers.

PROCEDURE: PREPARING THE MOSAIC LOG FOR THE CLASSICAL ROSETTE

To the uninitiated observer, creating the mosaic inlay appears to require intensely close effort and extraordinary finesse. In reality, its preparation is quite simple and requires only a modicum of manual dexterity. As such it is a marvelous exercise for any woodworker who may be interested in learning how to produce an impressive and artistically complex form of marquetry with little or no experience.

The mosaic pattern consists of tiles which are cross section slices of a "log" built up from fine slivers of wood. The desired pattern is usually first laid out in grid form on a piece of graph paper, and then slivers of different colors or species are glued up in rows to correspond to the rows of the pattern. The rows are then glued together to yield a log with the preplanned cross section, and tiles are sliced off the log in sufficient number to extend

side-by-side in a band around the soundhole.

The fineness of the slivers is the primary determinant of how complex the design can be. Commercially available precut slivers are most commonly 1/32 inch square in cross section. A tile 5/16 inch in width and 5/16 inch in height will thus consist of ten by ten, i.e., one hundred, slivers. Reducing the slivers to 1/64 inch square, the size we like to use for detailed patterns, increases the density of a similar-sized pattern to twenty by twenty, or four hundred, slivers. For the beginner, however, we emphatically recommend the larger squares and a simple geometric design.

Modern classical guitars typically have rosettes about 3/4 to 1 inch in width. The precise proportion of the mosaic to the rosette as a whole is purely a matter of taste, but as a rough rule of thumb we recommend that the mosaic be about one-third the width of the rosette. (Some rosettes, of course, have inner and outer mosaic bands as well as a central pattern; in such cases the proportions will naturally be altered.) Thus, the height of the tiles will ordinarily be in a range of about 1/4 inch to just under 3/8 inch. The width of the tiles is limited by the curvature of the mosaic band; if the tiles are too wide, the design will be distorted or obliterated when the tops and bottoms of the tiles are rounded and the edges are tapered to fit around the circle. We ordinarily try to avoid making the tiles wider than their height.

For the guitar built from this book we suggest a modest design such as that shown in Fig. 6-4. It consists of nine rows, each with eight ⅟₃₂-inch slivers, with a final log dimension of ⁹⁄₃₂ inch high by ¼ inch wide. At that dimension, the tile would be appropriate for a rosette width of ¹³⁄₁₆ to ¹⁵⁄₁₆ inch. The student should feel free, however, to vary the design according to taste. A book of needlepoint designs is an excellent source.

TOOLS
two thin 6-inch straightedges, such as rulers or scraper blades
small square
razor saw
two small C-clamps

SUPPLIES
PVA (white) glue
graph paper
waxed paper

MATERIALS
sufficient ⅟₃₂-inch-square slivers to make up a 6-inch log
various scrap blocks

Step 1—Layout

Sketch your chosen design freehand and then transfer it to grid form on graph paper, or copy the design suggested in this book. Plot out the number of squares of each color or species you plan to use. Break off enough 6-inch lengths to make up your pattern and separate them into piles for the rows.

Step 2—Gluing Up the Rows

Take the pile representing the first row and arrange the slivers to correspond to the first row of your design. Hold them between a thumb and forefinger and smooth them out with your other thumb and forefinger. Drip a bead of glue along the row and work it in between the slivers by alternately fanning and smoothing (Fig. 6-5). Transfer the

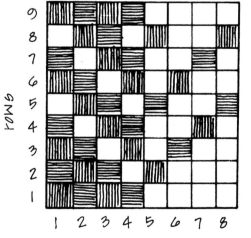

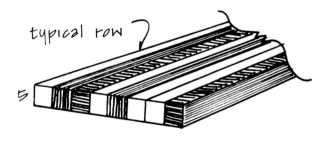

typical row

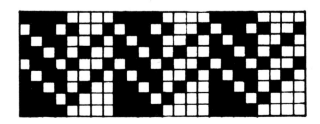

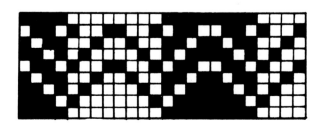

6–4. *Mosaic-marquetry, recommended pattern and designs.*

row to the other hand and work glue into the end you were previously holding. Place the row down on a piece of waxed paper. Slide two 6-inch straightedges up to the edges of the row and gently press the slivers together (Fig. 6-6). Press only enough to squeeze out excess glue; too much pressure will cause the row to buckle and fly apart. You must hold down the row and the straightedges while applying side pressure. This can be a little tricky, but you will improve quickly with practice.

Hold the row under pressure for one to two minutes; this is sufficient for the glue to set up enough to hold the row together. Set the piece of waxed paper aside and begin the next row with a fresh piece. After five to ten minutes, you can peel the waxed paper off the first row and then set the row somewhere to dry thoroughly (undisturbed) for at least thirty minutes. Repeat this process for all the rows. (Start with clean fingers each time.)

Step 3—Cleaning Up the Rows

When the glue is fairly hard you must lay each row on a flat surface and gently scrape off the excess. Do not dig too deeply in any one spot, but rather use long, smooth strokes with the scraper blade held level in one hand. Be especially gentle when cleaning the edges, lest you tear the outer slivers away from the row.

Step 4—Gluing Up the Log

The rows must be glued together in the order required by the design. This step is simple enough in theory but requires

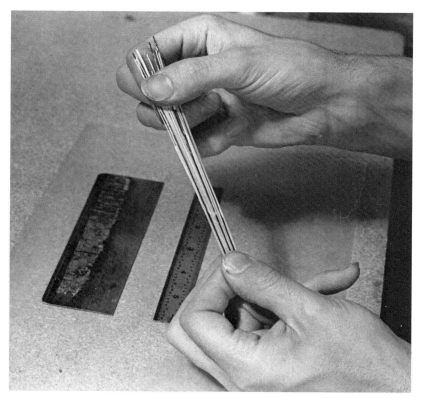

6–5. *Working glue between the slivers of a row for the mosaic log.*

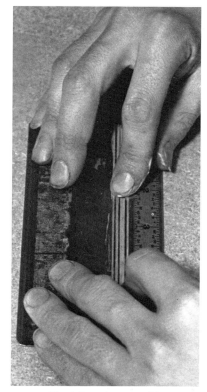

6–6. *Clamping the row with two 6-inch straightedges. The straightedges and the row must be held down carefully while being pressed together.*

special care to ensure rectangular cross sections of uniform dimension. You must avoid side-to-side slippage, which will distort the design, and uneven pressure, which can produce a log of uneven height. We use a Plexiglas jig, but with care you can do the job with two smooth blocks of wood about 6 inches long and slightly wider than the log width.

Apply a bead of glue to the first row (Fig. 6-7) and smear it, covering the whole surface. Place the second row on top of the first and smooth it down. Then apply glue and smear, repeating the process until all the rows are glued. Work quickly. Do not apply glue to the top face of the last row. Smooth the edges of the log so that the rows line up properly, and press gently to squeeze glue from between them. Lay the log on its side on a piece of waxed paper and, using two small C-clamps as shown in Fig. 6-8, squeeze the log between the two blocks. Check continuously to ensure alignment; use another flat block, as in the diagram, to press the rows down flat. Clamp the blocks gently at first and, as the glue sets, apply more pressure. Tighten only until the rows all come into intimate contact with one another; excessive clamping pressure will distort the cross section of the log. Because uneven clamping pressure will vary the vertical dimension of the log, you must measure for

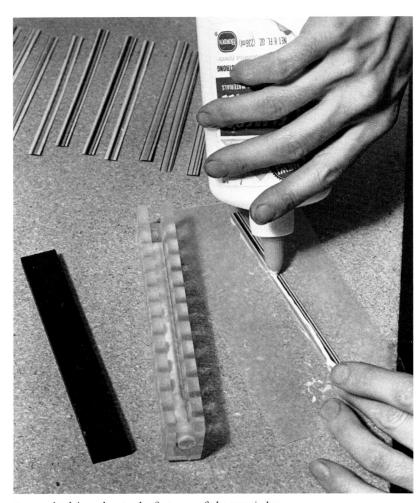

6–7. *Applying glue to the first row of the mosaic log.*

significant variation and adjust clamping pressure accordingly.

Peel away the waxed paper and let dry for at least one hour. When you remove the clamps the blocks may be stuck to the log, but you should be able to knock them off without damaging the outer rows. The log should be rigid before proceeding to the next step; if it is not, allow it to dry longer.

Step 5—Cleaning Up and Tapering the Log

Scrape the sides of the log to remove excess glue, just as with the rows. If the upper and lower faces are rough with glue, clean them as well, but do not scrape away the wood.

Note the taper required for the tiles, as shown in Fig. 6-10a. The log as a whole can be tapered by stroking it on the sanding board. Work

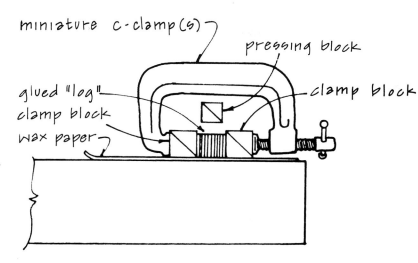

miniature c-clamp(s)

pressing block

glued "log"
clamp block
clamp block
wax paper

6-8. *Assembling the marquetry "log."*

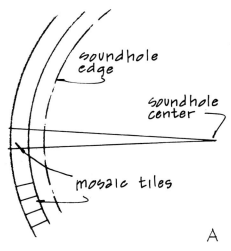

soundhole edge

soundhole center

mosaic tiles

A

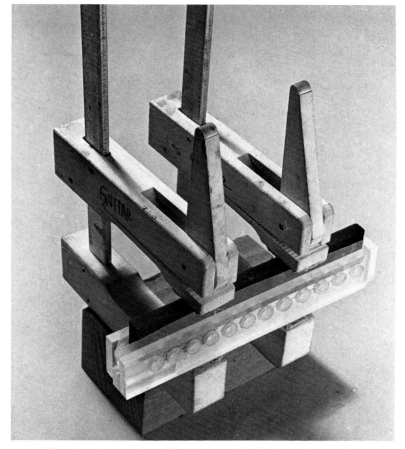

6-9. *Clamping the rows in a Plexiglas jig. The jig keeps the rows horizontally aligned while permitting glue to evacuate through holes drilled along the side. Note waxed paper wrapped around the clamping block.*

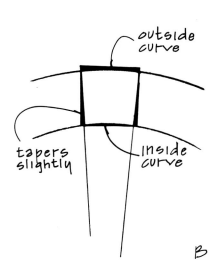

outside curve

tapers slightly

inside curve

B

6-10a and b. *Determining the shape of the tiles; A is full sized, B is magnified.*

6–11. *A simple miter box for cutting mosaic tiles. Inside the slot is a stop placed ¹⁄₁₆ inch past the razor-saw kerf.*

6–12. *Cutting tiles on a table saw using a fine-toothed blade rim ground to about .020 inch to reduce waste. The stop is a section of a razor-knife blade tapped into the facing clamped to the miter fence. Note the special saw table insert, which leaves no gap into which the small pieces could fall.*

slowly and carefully; better to err on the side of too little taper rather than too much, because you will be checking the taper when preparing for installation and can always remove a bit more material from individual tiles at that time.

To make the outside curve as shown in Fig. 6-10b, stroke the corners of the log gently on the sanding board. The inside curve is not executed until the tiles are already cut.

Step 6—Cutting the Tiles

This requires nothing more than a slot in a piece of wood in which the log will fit snugly so that it can be sliced without tearing apart. This jig can be made on a table saw in a few

seconds, or with a handsaw and chisel (Fig. 6-11). Alternatively, you can glue up a slotted jig from three separate pieces.

When you have made the slotted piece, make a square, vertical cut into it with a razor saw. Use the small square to guide the cut down past the bottom of the slot. If the cut is either unsquare or off the vertical, move over a little and try it again until it is right. Then install a stop ¹⁄₁₆ inch past the cut.

Slide the log into the slot until it butts against the stop. Cut down through with the razor saw, retract the log, and pick out the piece. The end of the log will be uneven, so discard the first few pieces until

you begin getting complete tiles. Continue until the whole log is cut up. (A 6-inch log will yield more than enough ¹⁄₁₆-inch tiles, but now is the time to cut them all. You may need more than you expect, anyway.)

We cut these tiles on a table saw with an ultrafine blade (Fig. 6-12).

Step 7—The Inside Curve

To do the inside curve, find a bottle with about the same diameter as the mosaic ring and wrap it with a piece of #120-grit sandpaper. Gently sand each tile (a few strokes should be sufficient) to approximate the inside curve, as shown in Fig. 6-10b.

MASS-PRODUCING MOSAIC LOGS AND ROSETTES

The system described in the procedure on preparing the mosaic log is inefficient for the professional luthier because of the amount of time required to make rosette logs individually.

Some builders turn to store-bought rosettes; others submit a custom design to a manufacturer and have a production run made up. If the quantity is sufficient, the cost of a private production run will be comparable to mass-produced designs. An in-between alternative, however, is small-scale mass production in the luthier's own shop. This can be limited to production of mosaic logs only or, for the very ambitious, can involve production of completed rosettes.

We mass-produce mosaic logs, making enough for about fifteen guitars at one time. Because we use ordinary veneers, we can buy the necessary supplies almost anywhere at about one-tenth the cost of precut sticks. We happen to have a thickness sander that will accurately reduce a standard $\frac{1}{28}$- or $\frac{1}{40}$-inch veneer to $\frac{1}{64}$ inch for very fine patterns, but $\frac{1}{40}$-inch veneer is perfectly all right to use as is.

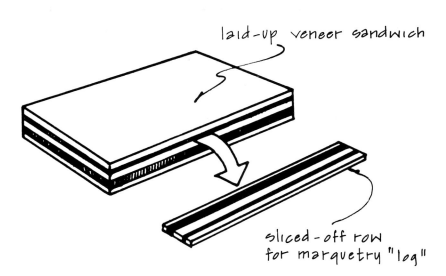

laid-up veneer sandwich

sliced-off row for marquetry "log"

6-13. *Mass production of rows for the making of multiple marquetry "logs."*

6-14. *Identical rosette logs can be produced with a small-scale mass-production technique. The rows on the right were sliced off veneer sandwiches.*

Our system differs from the single-log sequence in but one major respect: instead of gluing up a row of slivers as the first step, we glue up a stack of veneers, the edge of which displays the pattern of a completed row. One stack is made for each row of the de-sign. The stacks are then sliced on the table saw with a fine 6-inch plywood blade rim-ground to about an .020-inch kerf. The slices are passed through the thickness sander for uniformity. One slice from each stack, glued together in proper sequence, yields a log.

PROCEDURE: LAYING OUT THE ROSETTE

The classic soundhole must be positioned so that it will just breach the nineteenth fret; the top of the steel-string soundhole lies ⅛ inch below the imaginary twenty-first fret. Refer to Chapter 3 to calculate the correct distance from the fourteenth fret to the twenty-first fret (SS) or the twelfth fret to the nineteenth fret (CL).

TOOLS
ruler
pencil
compass

Step 1—Finding the Soundhole Center

Using a soft pencil, lightly draw a line on the centerseam of the outside face of the soundboard. Placing your template along that line, draw the outline of the guitar.

Steel-string: Measure from the top of the outline, and mark the distance from the fourteenth to the twenty-first fret plus 2⅛ inches. This will be the centerpoint of the 2-inch radius (4-inch diameter) soundhole.

Classical: Measure from the top of the outline and mark the distance from the twelfth to the nineteenth fret plus 1⅝ inches. This will be the centerpoint of the soundhole; since the soundhole radius is 1¹¹⁄₁₆ inches (3⅜-inch diameter), the soundhole will just break through the nineteenth fret.

Step 2—Drawing Concentric Circles

Steel-string: Spread a compass to a radius of 2 inches, press its centerpoint into the centerpoint of the soundhole, and draw the soundhole outline. Expand the compass to 2⅛ inches and draw the inside circumference of the ring. Expanding the compass successively, draw five more circles with radii 2¼ inches, 2⅜ inches, 2⅝ inches, 2¾ inches, and 2⅞ inches.

Classical: Spread a compass to a radius of 1¹¹⁄₁₆ inches. Press its centerpoint to the centerpoint of the soundhole, and draw the soundhole outline. Expand the compass to 1¹³⁄₁₆ inches and draw the inside circumference of the rosette ring. Refer to the mosaic tiles to determine the total width of your rosette (see discussion on mosaic design, pages 115–18). Add that measurement to 1¹³⁄₁₆ inches, and spread the compass to the resulting dimension (e.g., for a ⅞-inch rosette width, the outer circumference will be 1¹³⁄₁₆ inches plus ⅞ inch, or 2¹¹⁄₁₆ inches). Trace the outer circle on the soundboard.

PROCEDURE: EXCAVATING THE ROSETTE CHANNEL(S)

In the following procedure we describe a technique involving the use of a portable electric router, which is suitable for both the steel-string and classical rosette channels. For classical builders who wish to minimize power-tool use or prefer for any other reason not to use the router, we present a very simple and elegant hand technique in step-by-step form.

Both techniques require a workboard that consists of a sheet of plywood or other rigid material approximately 18 × 22 inches (use the joining board if you wish), with part of a nail protruding to be used as a pivot pin for circle cutting. The soundhole center on the soundboard must be drilled out with a bit that matches the diameter of the nail so that the soundboard can be mounted on the workboard.

In the hand technique, a homemade circle cutter pivots around the nail and scribes the inside and outside perimeters of the classical-guitar rosette channel. The material in between is then removed with a chisel. In the router technique, the pivot pin secures a point on the router base that defines a radius from the cutter. The principal advantage of using the router, and the reason we recommend it for the classical as well as the steel-string rings, is that the tool that defines the perimeters of the channel also removes the material in between at a uniform depth.

As will become obvious during the following steps, the soundboard must fit snugly on the workboard pivot for best results. We have had success using a 4d finishing nail for the pivot pin and a #49 machinist's bit for the center hole (both measure .073 inch, so the fit is *very* snug), but nails vary from one lot to another and not everybody has a complete set of machinist's bits. Thus, you must experiment with bits and nails until you find a good match somewhere between ¹⁄₁₆ (.060) inch and ⁵⁄₆₄ (.078) inch. If the drill bit is slightly larger (.005 inch at the most) than the nail, it is close enough.

PORTABLE ELECTRIC ROUTER TECHNIQUE

TOOLS
portable electric router
¼-inch and ⅛-inch straight router bits (SS), or ¼-inch straight router bit (CL)
wire cutter
hand drill
small drill bit (see above)
6-inch ruler
scraper blade
assorted cam clamps

IMPLEMENTS
workboard (see above)

SUPPLIES
finishing nail
scrap of sandpaper

Step 1—Mounting the Soundboard on the Workboard

Draw the soundboard outline on the workboard. Locate approximately the soundhole center and tap in the nail you have found to match with one of your drill bits. When the

nail is solidly embedded, snip off the head with a wire cutter, leaving about ¼ inch protruding from the board. Sand off the burr left by the cutter.

Using the matching bit, drill through the centerpoint of the soundhole as marked on the soundboard. Press the soundboard down on the workboard with the nail through the hole. The nail should protrude no less than ⅛ inch.

Step 2—Drilling Out the Router Base

The base must be drilled out at marked intervals from its theoretical center with the same bit used to drill the soundhole centerpoint in the guitar top (Fig. 6-15). Because an increment of ⅛ inch in radius will yield an increment of ¼ inch in diameter, we drill two rows of ⅛-inch-spaced holes: One defines diameters that fall on the quarter-inch and the other defines diameters that fall on the eighth-inch. This produces ¹⁄₁₆-inch radius increments, enhancing the versatility of the technique.

Step 3—Routing the Outer Channels

The most important technical aspect of this step is its geometry, which, although simple enough in theory, can be confusing in practical application. The inside and outside radius of a cut will vary according to the bit used. Thus, for example, a hole drilled in the router base 2 inches from

the center will cut a circle with a theoretical radius of 2 inches and a theoretical diameter of 4 inches. Using a ¼-inch router bit, however, the inside radius of the resulting channel will be reduced by half the diameter of the bit to 1⅞ inches, and the outside radius will be increased to 2⅛ inches; the inside and outside diameters will be 3¾ inches and 4¼ inches respectively. When computing the radii for concentric rings or for the inner and outer perimeters of a channel, these variables must be carefully plotted out. The best and simplest way to achieve accurate results, however, is always to make test cuts in the area that will be covered by the fingerboard and note their relationships to the marked layout lines.

For the single wide channel (traditional on the classical guitar and sometimes used on the steel-string), the inner and outer perimeters should be ex-

6–15. *Router base drilled with pivot holes for cutting circular channels. The two rows permit ¹⁄₁₆-inch radius increments.*

cavated first with a ¼-inch or smaller straight bit, and the area in between then removed. The steel-string design in this book calls for three rings ⅛ inch apart. The outer and inner rings will be ⅛ inch wide and the middle ring ¼ inch wide. Thus, begin with the ⅛-inch bit for the inner and outer concentric rings.

With the top mounted on the pivot pin, secure its edges to the workboard with four cam clamps. The workboard will thus be lifted off the workbench, but the four clamps will provide adequate stability.

Adjust the bit flush to the base so it will not protrude enough to actually cut. Do not plug in the router. Choose a locating hole in the base that, when the diameter of the bit is taken into consideration, will produce a cut with an *inside* diameter corresponding to the innermost rosette layout line. (Remember that the smallest circle in the layout denotes the *soundhole* perimeter, not the rosette ring.) For the inside perimeter of the classical channel, the *inside* radius of the resulting cut must be 1¹³⁄₁₆ inches; for the inner ring on the steel-string rosette, the *inside* radius must be 2⅛ inches. Mount the router on the pivot and visually double check the location of the *inside* edge of the bit against your layout.

Remove the router from the soundboard and adjust the depth of cut by laying a scraper blade on edge across

the base plate to observe the bit's protrusion. Set the depth of cut at ¹⁄₁₆ inch. Return the router to the soundboard, using the same locator hole as before and keeping the protruding bit confined to the area that will be concealed by the fingerboard. Visually check again to see that the inside radius is correct. Make sure the router is turned off, and then plug it in.

Holding the router firmly on the pivot pin (anticipate a kick when it starts) and supporting its weight so that the bit is not pressing into the top, turn it on. Lower the bit gently into the concealed part of the ring and then shut off the router. Remove it from the soundboard and check what you have done. This is your last chance to change the radius or depth of cut. When you are satisfied that it is correct, replace the router in the same spot and, again holding it firmly on the pivot, turn it on. Slowly and smoothly bring the cutter around in a full circle. Reverse the direction for one swing around to remove fuzz left behind by the initial cut. Do not stop the cutting motion or shut off the router anywhere but in the concealed area.

For the outer concentric ring or the outside perimeter cut of the wide channel, repeat the above operation but use the *outside* edge of the bit (that is, the cut) against *outside* circumference of the layout lines.

Step 4—Cutting the Middle Channel

Steel-string: The middle ring is cut exactly as were the inner and outer rings, except that we must replace the ⅛-inch bit with a ¼-inch bit. Use either the inside or the outside circle of the middle ring as a guide against which to align the corresponding edge of the bit.

Classical: For the classical rosette, the remainder of the channel can be excavated simply by moving the radius in and out within the perimeters without adjusting the depth of cut (Fig. 6-16).

HAND TECHNIQUE (SINGLE, WIDE CHANNEL ONLY)

TOOLS
ice cream bar stick
razor knife blade
chisel

IMPLEMENTS
workboard

6–16. *Cutting the rosette channel. The router is mounted on a pivot pin protruding from the workboard underneath through the soundboard at the soundhole center.*

Step 1—Mounting the Soundboard on the Workboard

Same as Step 1 of the portable electric router technique, page 125.

Step 2—Making a Circle Cutter

Our favorite application of this technique employs an ordinary ice cream bar stick and a razor knife blade. Drill through one end of the stick with the same bit used in the previous step. Measure from the center of that hole 1¹³/₁₆ inches and press the razor-knife blade through at that point, perpendicular to the grain of the stick. The tip of the blade should protrude no more than ¹/₃₂ inch.

Step 3—Cutting the Circles

Align the stick so that the tip of the blade will enter the top under the area that will be concealed by the fingerboard. Press the drilled end down on the pivot. Hold the pivot end with one index finger and hold the cutting end firmly, as shown in Fig. 6-17. Make a small test cut in the fingerboard area to get a feel for the cutting action, and also to double check your radius; then proceed around the circle. Press the point in a little further and cut again, repeating until the blade glides without resistance while protruding a full ¹/₁₆ inch. Then move the blade, pressing it through the stick at the outer radius of your rosette, and repeat the above step.

Step 4—Removing the Channel

Using a well-sharpened chisel (½-inch is ideal), flat side down, begin removing fine shavings from between the concentric-circle cuts. Avoid striking the vertical walls of the channel with the chisel. It is risky and unnecessary to shave right up to the lines; shaving to within about ¹/₁₆ inch will pull the remaining material away from the circle cut, at least until you are well below the soundboard surface.

Continue until the floor of the channel is almost ¹/₁₆ inch deep all around. Check your progress by running the edge of a ruler or scraper over the channel and observing the gap as the channel deepens. Also, hold the soundboard up to the light. More opaque

6–17. A simple hand method for cutting the rosette channel. The material between the circles is removed with a chisel.

6–18. Checking the rosette channel for even depth. Shallow areas are less translucent.

patches in the channel will denote where the cut is shallow (Fig. 6-18).

Finish the floor of the channel with the chisel turned belly down. Make the final shavings very carefully, as the wood remaining underneath is only a little over $\frac{1}{32}$ inch thick. If you have difficulty being precise in your depth, *DO NOT go too deeply;* err on the side of shallowness. One tip that may be useful for the less secure: Make one or more additional concentric cuts inside the inner and outer perimeters of the channel, with the circle cutter adjusted to cut $\frac{1}{16}$ inch deep. Then use these marks as depth guides as you remove material.

TECHNICAL NOTE ON CLASSICAL ROSETTE ASSEMBLY

Once the mosaic is prepared, the marquetry band is customarily completed in one of two ways: either in a sequence that calls for assembly on a workboard, followed by installation of the completed rosette into an excavated circular channel in the soundboard; or in a single procedure that involves assembly of the rosette *in* the excavated channel. With the latter method, the rosette never exists as a free-standing unit. Both methods can be used successfully by experienced luthiers, but we prefer the latter.

Assembling the rosette on a workboard typically involves a laborious process of wrapping the lines of the rosette around a disc and gluing them in place one at a time. The mosaic is laid around the inside band of lines and held in place by a continued sequence of outside lines. Tacks are usually used to hold the first band outside the mosaic and are gradually moved around the circle as the tiles are butted together.

In our view, assembling the rosette in the soundboard while it is being glued in place is decidedly superior for the purpose of achieving a tight-fitting and perfectly round rosette. A pressure fit is assured by the simple fact that the final design can be dry tested for snugness in the excavated channel. Irregularities in the tiles will be corrected somewhat by pressure fitting, and roundness is assured by the inside and outside perimeters of the circular channel. The time required for the operation is but a fraction of the time required for assembly of the rosette by itself with subsequent installation.

PROCEDURE: INLAYING THE CLASSICAL ROSETTE

The following procedure is simple and straightforward, but it can turn into a glue-sodden nightmare if preparation is inadequate. The fitting process that precedes assembly is crucial to a smooth and successful installation. In addition, several caveats are in order.

The lines that make up the bands inside and outside the mosaic must be of uniform *width*, so that they will all have the same *height* in the channel. Any variation in width creates the risk that some lines will not sit flush to the bottom of the channel when being glued in. If this occurs, those lines may be scraped away to nothing when the rosette is leveled after installation.

The *thickness* of the strips should not exceed $\frac{1}{16}$ inch. For harder species such as rosewood, even at that thickness it may be necessary to soak the strip in hot water for about a minute just before installation. This undesirably complicates the process, so we suggest that the beginner stay with ordinary veneer thicknesses (up to $\frac{1}{28}$ inch).

The lines immediately adjacent to the mosaic tiles must be a material at least as hard as the material used to make up the tiles. When the tile is slid in between the bands, the strips with which it comes into contact must be sufficiently durable to resist shredding and tearing, even when soaked with glue. Flimsy veneer material may fall apart under the pressure of a snug fit. Even if hard material is used, it should not be thinner than .020 inch (standard 1/40-inch veneer is .025 inch).

Grain run-off in the individual lines can result in breakage during assembly. Although broken lines can be repaired, they always complicate the installation and should be avoided if at all possible. Flex the lines before beginning assembly and replace any that display a tendency to split or fray when flexed.

TOOLS
water cup
small screwdriver
razor knife
block plane
scraper blade
ruler
pencil
chisel
end nipper

MATERIALS
sufficient veneer lines (about 18 inches long) to make up two identical bands, each 1/4 to 5/16 inch in width
mosaic tiles
thin scrap of hardwood

SUPPLIES
PVA (white) glue
masking tape
paper towels

Step 1—Fitting the Bands and Tiles into the Channel

Choose an aesthetically satisfying arrangement of veneer lines to make up the bands inside and outside the mosaic tiles. The two bands should *mirror*, rather than repeat one another. The sum of the two band widths added to the length of the tiles should be almost as wide as the channel. Take one of the bands arranged in proper sequence and tape it together gently but firmly about 3 inches from the end with a small piece of masking tape. Wrap the tape around only once. Repeat with the other band (Fig. 6-19). Place one band against the inner perimeter of the channel and the other band against the outer perimeter. Take a mosaic tile and slide it between the two bands. The tile will appear to press the bands against the walls of the channel, but you must squeeze all the bands against one wall of the channel to determine actual clearance. Under pressure, there should be a 1/64- to 1/32-inch gap to allow for swelling of the lines when they are soaked with glue. If the gap is greater than 1/32 inch, add a line or lines; if it is less than 1/64 inch, remove a line or lines. If you have lines of varying thicknesses, you can make very fine band width adjustments without destroying the symmetry between the two bands. If you have lines of only one thickness, you may be forced to add or subtract a line from only one band to achieve a proper fit. If so, place the extra line on the inside band, preferably on the inner perimeter (closest to the soundhole) of the channel.

Step 2—Getting Ready

Lay out the tiles just as they will appear in the rosette, so that you can pick them up and insert them with a minimum of manipulation when gluing begins (Fig. 6-19). Have the

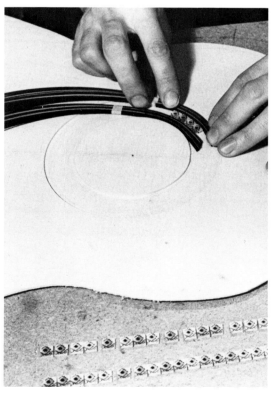

6-19. Dry-fitting rosette bands in the rosette channel.

glue bottle, water cup, paper towels, and other tools close at hand. The bands should be taped as in Step 1; if you have added or removed lines when fitting, be sure to retape before proceeding. Get yourself comfortable with the guitar top horizontally in front of you. We prefer to do this operation sitting down. Do a dry insertion run with five to eight tiles, as in Fig. 6-19, to final-check for proper fit.

Important: Now is the time to check the taper of your tiles. When you insert five to eight tiles in a row you will see rather clearly if you have tapered too much or too little. If either, you must retaper each tile individually. One or two light strokes on a sanding block will significantly change the taper, so work as carefully and consistently as you can. Do them all now; the extra time invested will significantly improve your result. (It will also encourage you to taper the log accurately the next time around.)

Step 3—Assembly

During the following process you need not feel hurried, as there is little danger of the glue drying too quickly. Remain aware, however, that dawdling may result in excessive swelling of the lines and consequent difficulties.

Starting at the top of the channel about ½ inch from the centerline, cover 3 inches of the floor of the channel (work-ing counterclockwise if you are right-handed) with a heavy film of glue. Do not fill up the whole channel with glue, but completely coat the bottom. Take the inside band, fan the first inch or so slightly, and work glue in between the lines. Closing the fanned lines, place the band on the inside of the channel. Repeat with the other band, placing it on the outside of the channel. After the first inch, the assembly process will draw sufficient glue between the lines to make further fanning unnecessary. Pressing the bands against their respective channel walls with the fingers of one hand, take a tile with the other hand, dip it into the water cup for a couple of seconds, shake off excess water thoroughly, and then slide it in between the bands. (*Important:* Once you begin inserting tiles, you must check constantly to be sure that all the lines are within the walls of the channel and that no tile has slid underneath a line immediately adjacent to it.) Also, check to see that the lines are flush to the bottom of the channel. Continue the process with a second tile and then a third. Use the flat edge of the screwdriver to press each tile completely into place. After you have positioned three tiles, carefully remove the masking tape from the bands. A drop or two of water will dissolve the adhesive, allowing the tape to come off easily. After progressing about 2 inches with the tiles, coat an-other 2 inches of the channel with glue, smearing it under the bands, and insert more tiles. Continue around the circle in this way until you return to the area under the fingerboard. Occasionally stop to rinse and dry your fingers. As you progress, scrutinize your work frequently to make sure none of the tiles has been inserted upside down or backwards. If you have to remove a tile for any reason, use the knife carefully to separate the tile, and then push it out with the screwdriver.

When you still have about 2 inches of tiles to go, clip off the excess of the lines (leaving about a 1-inch gap between the beginning and the end) with the end nipper. If you wait until the very end you may have difficulty clipping the lines without disrupting the last tiles.

When you are done, wipe up wet glue and heavy moisture with a paper towel and survey your work. Do not be alarmed by the rosette's rough appearance. If all tiles are positioned snugly and correctly and all the lines are within the channel, the rosette will emerge dramatically when it is cleaned up. Take the butt end of the razor-knife handle and go around the mosaic ring, pressing the tiles down flush in any place they might be loose or buckled (Fig. 6-20). Do the same with the bands if it appears necessary. Cover the rosette with a flat weight and leave it overnight.

Step 4—Clean-up

This is one of the most exciting and rewarding steps on the whole guitar. Aside from the thrill of seeing the rosette emerge like a diamond from the rough, the process yields a fascinating array of debris—ringlets laminated from multicolored veneers, translucent curlicues displaying mosaic patterns, and so forth. In order to experience all this, however, you must have a well-sharpened block plane to work with. A dull plane will not only make the job more difficult, but it also may damage the rosette by chipping or tearing instead of shaving.

Work with a circular motion, keeping the plane flat on the raised surface of the bands (Fig. 6-21). *Do not* tip the plane toward the outside of the rosette, lest you gouge the top. Continue until you are almost flush; then go to the scraper to finish the job. With both the plane and the scraper, take care not to tug on the rough ends of the ring. They are usually not as securely embedded as the rest of the inlay. If necessary, leave them a little high for now, as you can finish surfacing the area after Step 5.

We do not recommend the use of abrasives for this step because of the danger of grinding particles of the hard rosette material into the soft soundboard. If you have extreme difficulty with the plane, however, you can switch to the small sanding board until the rosette is nearly flush, and then use the scraper to finish. Avoid touching the spruce with the sanding block. When scraping flush, keep the scraper as flat as possible to avoid hollowing out the softer top material around the rosette.

Step 5—Filling the Gap Between the Ring Ends

With the razor knife held against a ruler, scribe lines delineating a "keystone" at the top of the ring. The object here is to remove only as much of the ring ends as is necessary to achieve a clean cross section. Using a sharp chisel, carefully shave away the portion of the ring ends within the keystone area (Fig. 6-22).

Cut a scrap of wood about 1/16 to 3/32 inch thick to the size and shape of the cleared-out area. It need not fit perfectly, but the neater the better. Spread a little glue in the channel and clamp the piece in

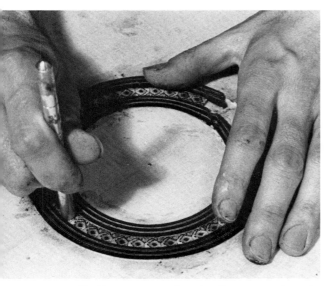

6-20. *Checking to ensure that the tiles are seated on the floor of the channel by pressing with the butt end of a razor-knife handle.*

6-21. *Planing the bands. The block plane must be well sharpened. When the bands and the mosaic are almost flush to the soundboard surface, a sharp scraper finishes the job.*

6–22. *Trimming the ends of the band to form a keystone-shaped cavity into which a hardwood piece is inlayed to close the channel.*

place. When it is dry, shave it and the top of the rosette flush. This little insert improves the gluing surface for the fingerboard and, more importantly, prevents tearing of the soundboard if the fingerboard ever needs to be removed. (See Figs. 6-23 and 6-24.)

When you are done and the rosette face of the soundboard is clean, lightly redraw a visible line down the centerseam.

6–23. *The finished rosette with the soundhole cut out. The keystone-shaped inlay will be concealed by the fingerboard on the finished guitar.*

6–24. *Detail of the finished rosette.*

PROCEDURE: STEEL-STRING ONLY— PREPARING AND INLAYING PURFLING ROSETTE MATERIALS

The primary consideration in planning rosette ring inlays is their fit into the routed grooves. Proper fit is crucial for a neat, attractive result. If the ring components must be pressed in tightly to fit the groove, they will resist entry when wetted with glue; the result may be broken lines and a botched job. Conversely, if the ring components do not take up enough space in the groove, they may, at first, spread out in the slot and give the initial appearance of a successful fit. Later gaps will inevitably appear as the glue dries thoroughly and shrinks, revealing precisely where the clearance was excessive.

Ideally, the components of the ring should slide in snugly but effortlessly—and then be checked to see if there is any perceptible side-to-side play, a condition that betrays excessive clearance. Given available router-bit sizes and accessible inlay materials, beginners may have to be resigned to less than ideal ring-inlay clearances. As their stock of tools, skills, and sources increases, so will the accuracy of their results. We use a fly-cutter with precision-ground bits to create rings of any desired width (Fig. 6-25).

Our design calls for three separate rings that are concentric to the soundhole. This is the scheme most commonly found on steel-string guitars. Some students may have chosen a different number of rings, with inlays different from those described here. In that event, they may have to extrapolate from the information below and make their own calculations as necessary.

The inner and outer rings of the trio will be ⅛ inch wide and will contain a "ribbon" of black and white lines arranged in a black-white-black-black-white-black (BWBBWB) pattern. Each channel will be cut with a ⅛-inch (.125-inch) router bit. Proper clearance for a ⅛-inch slot is .005 inch. Thus, our choice is either to inlay six separate black and white lines, .020-inch each, into the channel (adding up to .120 inch) or to inlay two BWB veneer-line sandwiches, .060-inch each, into the channel (also adding up to .120

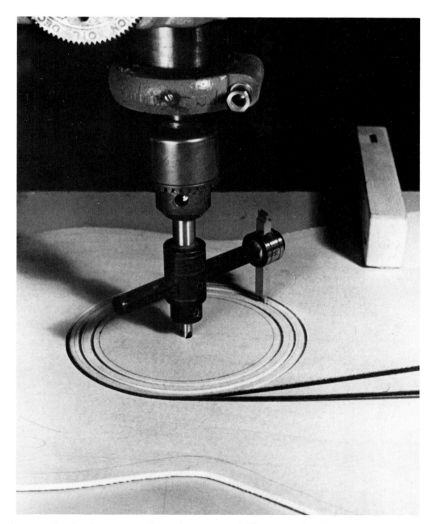

6-25. *Steel-string rosette channels cut on a drill press with a fly-cutter.*

inch). The two BWB sand-wiches are easier to manipulate than the six individual lines, but depending on their quality and composition, the BWB sandwiches may split if in-serted in a ring channel of too small a radius. They may have to be hot-soaked and prebent, an added step (see below).

The middle ring will be ¼ inch wide and consist of BWB/contrasting inlay/BWB. The contrasting inlay may consist of one of the following:

(1) a ribbon of colored lines (see notes on Rosette Ma-terials, page 115);

(2) a prebent length of mar-quetry purfling, such as "herringbone" (see below, as well as notes on Ro-sette Materials); or

(3) a ring of shell elements, sawn from wafer-thin blanks of mother-of-pearl or abalone.

Since the black and white lines will add up to .120 inch, an added contrasting inlay .120 inch wide will give us a satisfactory amount of clear-ance in the channel for glue.

The following procedure de-scribes the preparation and in-lay of veneer purfling lines and marquetry purfling strips inlaid into the three steel-string soundhole-rosette chan-nels. Immediately following it, the reader will find a more ad-vanced procedure describing the preparation and inlay of shell segments into the middle channel.

TOOLS
router
small wooden or metal push tool (scribe, stick, screwdriver)
scraper blade
felt block
end nipper

IMPLEMENTS
hot plate and saucepan
sheet-metal tray or trough (such as a 30-inch metal planter)
clock or stopwatch

SUPPLIES
PVA glue
paper towels
#120-grit garnet sandpaper

Step 1—Prebending Inlays by the Hot-soak Method

If your ring-inlay materials (veneer lines, sandwiches, and marquetry purfling strips) are too wide or too brittle to con-form to the desired rosette ring slot without breaking, they can be molded to shape as follows:

Fill a small saucepan with water and set to boil. Take a scrap piece of hardwood and, using a router (see Excavating the Rosette Channel, page 124), cut a circular groove identical in size, diameter, and depth to its corresponding in-lay channel in the soundboard. This will serve as a "mold." (We do not use the actual in-lay channels to avoid damag-ing them during the procedure).

As soon as the water starts to boil, pour it into a tray and drop in the inlay material. Soak for forty-five to ninety seconds (depending on the material's hardness and thick-ness). Towel up the excess moisture. Insert one end of the softened strip into the groove and draw it around the curve by holding the free end with one hand while helping it into the slot with the other. If the material has not softened sufficiently to comply, throw it in for another short bath. Avoid curling the strip too tightly or kinking it in any way and avoid quick or jerky movements since it may still pop apart. With an end-nipper tool at hand, estimate the strip's finished length as you approach the starting point. Clip it and push the end in. Let dry thoroughly. When re-moved, the strip will hold its shape sufficiently to enter the slot in the soundboard easily.

Marquetry purfling strips, such as herringbone, are avail-able in 1-mm and 2-mm thick-nesses. For this book we use the 2-mm strips for the ro-sette. Like the veneer lines, these can also be hot-soaked and prebent, as above. Soak them for ninety seconds. You may discover that herringbone and other diagonal-design mar-quetry strips bend much better with the diagonals pointing in one direction and resist bend-ing with the diagonals point-ing the other way. If your strips resist and start to delam-inate, try starting from the op-posite end.

Step 2—Inserting Rosette-ring Inlays

You should have at the ready all your veneer lines and veneer-line sandwiches. Also at hand are the contrasting center-ring inlays: the hot-soaked marquetry purfling strip just removed from its mold, or a band of colored veneer lines. Have handy a bottle of PVA glue and a push tool, such as a wooden stick or a pointed scribe.

Start with the inner and outer rings. Apply glue to the bottom of the slot over the full length of the groove. A thin, even bead is best: intermittent blobs can be spread out by carefully inserting the push tool into the slot and running it around the circumference once or twice. Starting at the soundboard centerline above the soundhole, insert the lines into the slot over a short distance. If the clearance is a bit tight, simply continue to insert the rings into the circular slot in a quick, steady movement. If the clearance is a bit loose, take the time to coat one or several of the lines with glue to help take up some of the room. Do not worry about excessive glue squeeze-out, since it can be cleaned up later. (*Important:* Avoid letting any glue slop into the adjacent empty ring slots.) Repeat the process with the other ring. It is very important to make sure that the inner-ring inlay starts and stops precisely at the centerseam above the soundhole,

since the fingerboard end will eventually stop precisely at that point and will hide the junction only if it is located at the centerseam (Fig. 6-26).

After gluing each inlay, go back around its length, tamping down firmly until seating is complete and "floating" stops. Take care not to slip and poke the soundboard with the push tool.

The center-ring inlay procedure is essentially the same, with the added caveat that the excessive use of glue may cause difficulty with the seating and accommodation of all the strips. It is a common beginner's problem to find that one or more thin veneer lines have disappeared after the rosette has been scraped flush. This results either from lines float-

ing too high off the floor of the ring channel or twisting *under* the contrasting inlay. Working clean by using glue sparingly allows you to discover these problems before they develop.

Step 3—Clean-up

The glued inlays must be absolutely dry before proceeding to level them flush.

Start with a scraper blade, freshly sharpened to a fine-burred edge. Avoid scraping directly across the grain of the soundboard by keeping the scraper at an oblique angle to the grain as you follow the curvature of the rings with your strokes. The oblique orientation causes the blade to slice across, rather than butt

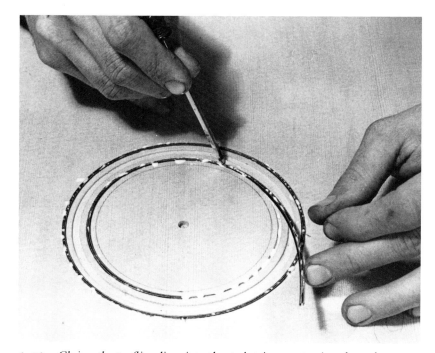

6-26. *Gluing the purfling lines into the steel-string rosette-ring channels.*

directly into, the inlay materials. When the entire surface is level, sand in the same direction as the grain with #120-grit garnet paper wrapped around a felt block until the surface is pristine. Blow off the surface. Light scraping as a finish step will clear away any tinted material that may have dusted onto the spruce.

ALTERNATE PROCEDURE: STEEL-STRING ONLY— PREPARING AND INLAYING SHELL ROSETTE MATERIALS INTO THE CENTER RING

The following procedure (Fig. 6-27) provides the information needed for cutting and inlaying curved shell segments into the center of the middle ring of the three-ring steel-string soundhole rosette. The middle ring will consist of a circle of 1/8-inch-wide shell segments bordered on both sides by 1/16-inch ribbons of black-white-black veneer-line strips. The shell is cut from 1/16-inch (.060-inch) wafers of mother-of-pearl or abalone, which can be purchased from luthier-supply houses. The inner contour of each curved segment is first ground into the wafer's edge by pressing it against a spinning sanding drum of the proper diameter. The outer contour is sawed out with a jeweler's saw and then filed to

accurate shape. We also provide a description for a refined segment cutter (see sidebar), which allows us to accurately grind the outer as well as inner contour on the same sand-

ing drum. A detailed description of how the wafers are cut into decorative shapes and inlaid, as well as a discussion of pearl edge purfling techniques, can be found in Chapter 11.

6–27. Abalone shell, genus haliotis. *Shown are the complete shell, a surfaced fragment, several wafers ground to 1/16-inch thick, and several segments for a pearl soundhole ring.*

TOOLS

electric drill or drill press
sanding drum (see Step 1
     below)
curved miter box (see Step 4
     below)
compass: two needle points
     installed in jaws
jeweler's saw frame
jeweler's saw blades 2/0 and
     4/0
vise
fine flat miniature file
medium sanding board
¼-inch drill bit
miniature backsaw or razor
     saw
push tool: wood or metal
     (scribe, stick, screwdriver)
bandsaw or router

SUPPLIES

particle mask
PVA (white) glue
double-faced tape
#100-grit garnet sandpaper
paper towel

MATERIALS

.060-inch pearl or abalone-
     wafer blanks (about ten
     are required, depending
     on size and quality)
¾-inch plywood piece, 5
     inches square
¼-inch steel bolts, 5 inches
     long, with lockwasher and
     nut

IMPLEMENTS

vacuum cleaner

Step 1—Making a
Sanding Drum

Start with a 5-inch square of
¾-inch plywood. Drill a ¼
inch hole in the middle. It
must be sawn or circle-routed

6–28. *Grinding the inner curve of the soundhole-ring segments. The vacuum nozzle on the left collects the toxic pearl dust particles.*

(see page 278) into a disc that
is 4⅞ inches in diameter, equal
to the inner diameter of the
pearl ring. The disc can be cut
out on a bandsaw by fixing a
pivot through the hole 2⁷⁄₁₆
inches from the blade and rotating the piece into the blade.
Send a long ¼-inch bolt
through the middle of the
blank and snug it tight with a
lockwasher and a ¼-inch nut.

Insert the bolt in the chuck
of an electric drill or drill
press. Line the curved edge of
the disc with double-faced
tape.

Adhere a long ¾-inch-wide
strip of #100-grit garnet sandpaper around the disc's curved

edge. Trim its ends so they
meet along a diagonal rather
than a vertical line. The strips
of sandpaper can be pulled off
and replaced as they wear out.

Step 2—Grinding the
Inner Curve

Obtain four or five ¹⁄₁₆-inch
(.060-inch) wafers of abalone
or mother-of-pearl. The sanding drum should be rotating at
a slow speed. Push the square
blanks slowly and squarely into
the spinning abrasive edge of
the drum (Fig. 6-28). Avoid
heat buildup by feeding the
wafer only as fast as the abrasive can grind it away.

Warning: Pearl dust is reputed to be a toxic material. Always cut pearl wearing a particle mask.

Step 3—Marking and Cutting the Pearl

With compass points set at ⅛-inch radius (the width of the segment), hook one point on the curved edge of the wafer. Draw across the pearl surface with the compass, scratching a curved line parallel to the ground edge. Clamp the pearl blank into a vise with the curved edge up and curved scratch line showing.

With your dust-particle mask on your face, approach the work about eye level. With your jeweler's saw, cut down the line using slow, long strokes (Fig. 6-29). Hold the saw level with the jaws of the vise. Cut as close as possible to the original scratch line without obliterating it. File the sawn edge down to the scratch line with a fine-tooth miniature file, taking care to keep the filed edge perpendicular to the segment's face. Cut enough segments this way to circle the center rosette channel one and a half times.

Step 4—Trimming the Ends

The ends of the segments must be trimmed so they butt tightly against each other. For this purpose, a tiny miter box with a curved slot is made: Duplicate a segment of the pearl ring channel on a piece of hardwood scrap (rout it a tiny bit deeper than the channel in the soundboard). Cut out a rectangular piece of the scrap containing a 2-inch-long segment of the slot (Fig. 6-30). Tighten the miter box into the vise and cut a fine kerf down the middle, across the slot, with a razor saw. The kerf need not be perfectly perpendicular to the floor of the slot. As long as the segments are all fed into the slot from the same direction and you inlay the segments the same side up as they were cut, everything will fit together tightly in the end.

Saw down the original kerf and through the pearl segments with long, slow strokes and little down-pressure. Take this opportunity to trim away imperfections that may be

6-29. *Sawing the outside curve of the soundhole-ring segments. The outside curve is trued with a fine file.*

6-30. *Cutting the pearl segments on a miniature miter box.*

found on the segments, such as holes, chips, and thinned-out areas.

Line up all the pieces and insert them all dry into the center slot, accompanied by the black and white lines. If any pair does not butt tightly together, there is likely to be a bump or nib on one or both ends. File the problem away and recheck. Remove all the pieces and line them up neatly in preparation for the gluing step that follows.

Step 5—Inlaying the Pearl Segments

Do a dry run first with all the components. All the components should enter the center channel readily, with just barely perceptible side-to-side movement. Having hand-filed the segments, you may find some too tight, some loose. Excessive tightness can be reduced by touching each oversize pearl segment momentarily to the spinning sanding drum. For some pieces you may have to resign yourself to a loose fit. Very slightly thinned white glue provides reduced viscosity for tighter fits. AR glue, with its higher solids content, works best for looser fits.

A pointed metal push tool helps position or remove segments as needed. A blunt "finger" of softwood will be useful to tamp down all the components.

Apply the glue over a short distance and arrange the lines,

starting at the top, so that the first segment will fit between them (Fig. 6-31). If your fit is good, it is necessary to apply glue only to the floor of the slot. However, try to coat the floor thinly and evenly. When pushing the adjacent segments into their proper places, previous pieces may "float" up slightly and must be tamped down firmly as often as necessary.

Insert each new piece diagonally with the fingers and then guide it in with the push tool until it seats, with the lines accommodated comfortably beside. Then push the segment to meet the last one installed. Glue may squirt out as the two end faces meet, obscuring the seam. Wipe away with a finger to verify a closed seam. Push again until the seam closes tight.

Apply the glue, one quadrant at a time, and insert all the segments. Continue wiping up excess glue with a paper towel and tamping down all the pieces till they all lie flat and securely. A small, heavy weight covering the rosette will keep the soundboard from bulging until all dries.

Step 6—Cleaning Up

Let dry for several hours, preferably overnight. Since the center ring is pearl, the rosette must be made level with #80-grit sandpaper mounted on the small sanding board. It is imperative to frequently vacuum the built-up

6-31. *Inserting the pearl segments. The pieces are pressed into the slot with the purfling lines carefully seated on either side. Adjacent segments are butted tightly as they are inserted between the lines.*

debris before it can get ground into the spruce. The pearl will come down flush fairly quickly. Rather than risk scratching the soundboard too deeply with the sanding board, finish cleaning up with #100-grit garnet on a small wooden block, vacuuming as you go. Do not sand without a backing block of some sort: the spruce will come down faster, leaving the pearl raised up above the surface. Light scraping will remove whatever debris has been worked into the surface.

A REFINED SEGMENT CUTTER

The outside curve as well as the inside curve of each pearl segment can be cut on the same sanding drum with a pivoting segment vise, as shown in Fig. 6-32. The segment vise rotates around a pivot in a small platform that is clamped to the drill-press table. The platform is cut away to hug the sanding drum closely.

The segment first has its interior curve ground directly against the drum and has been cut to size with a jeweler's saw as described in Steps 2 and 3 above. The rough-cut segment is secured in the segment vise which is placed on the pivot, and the segment is thus rotated into the spinning abrasive drum (Fig. 6-33).

The width of the finished piece can be accurately adjusted by moving the platform closer to or further from the drum when clamping it down to the drill-press table. Lower or raise the chuck as needed to expose fresh abrasive.

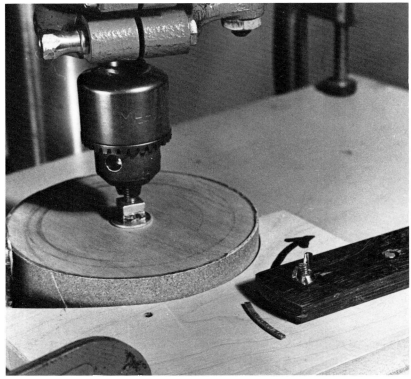

6–32. *A device for shaping the outside radius of the soundhole pearl segments. The pivoting vise holds the segment while it is being sanded. The vacuum shroud has been removed to show detail.*

6–33. *A refined pearl-segment shaper.*

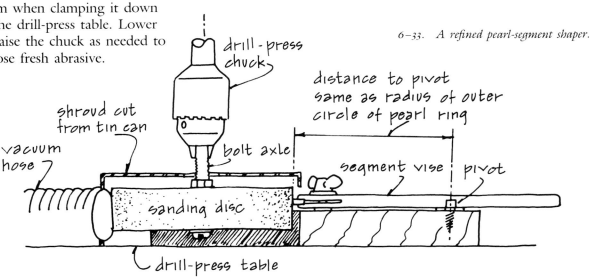

PROCEDURE: CUTTING OUT THE SOUNDHOLE

The two methods shown in the rosette channel excavation procedure are both useful for cutting out the soundhole. The ice cream bar stick technique, which was presented as an alternative for the classical builder only, is the more foolproof of the two; those students who used it for the rosette channel should use it again for cutting out the soundhole. Steel-string builders and classical builders who used the router can also make and use this simple circle cutter by referring to the appropriate procedure, or can again use the router.

ICE CREAM BAR STICK TECHNIQUE

Set the top back on the workboard used for cutting the rosette channel(s) and clamp it as before. Set the ice cream bar stick cutter to a radius of 2 inches (SS) or $1^{11}/_{16}$ inches (CL). Cut exactly as described in the channel-excavation procedure, but instead of stopping at a depth of $1/_{16}$ inch, continue to push the blade through the stick until the soundhole pops out.

ROUTER TECHNIQUE

Set the top back on the workboard used for cutting the rosette channel(s). The top *must* be immobilized during this step, so *clamp it securely.* The *outside* edge of the router bit must touch the soundhole layout line. With the router off and the bit retracted, determine the correct base-plate hole for the bit you are using.

There is no waste area to hide errors this time around, but we begin at the top of the soundhole anyway. Hold the router down firmly with the bit still retracted, and turn it on. Carefully release the depth-of-cut lock and slowly lower the bit until it just tickles the soundboard, and then retract the bit and lock it. Shut off the motor but leave the router in place. Look in to see where the cut began. This is the very last chance to see if you are adjacent to the soundhole layout line with the *outer* edge of the cut. If you are not, find the correct base-plate hole and repeat this process.

When you have the correct hole and the cut is properly aligned, turn on the router. Carefully unlock the depth adjustment and lower the bit. When the bit just touches the soundboard, note the position of the depth gauge. Very gradually proceed into the soundboard until the depth gauge indicates a $5/_{32}$-inch (SS) or $1/_8$-inch (CL) depth of cut. Very carefully lock the depth adjuster and then slowly begin sweeping around without stopping until the bit completes the circle. Then shut off the router and remove it.

This operation will, of course, leave a shallow channel in the workboard, but that will not affect its future use.

We also use a fly-cutter for this procedure (Fig. 6-34).

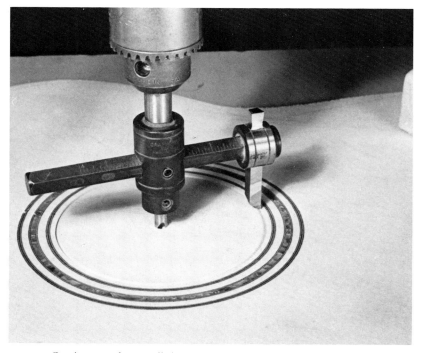

6-34. Cutting out the soundhole with a fly-cutter.

CHAPTER 7

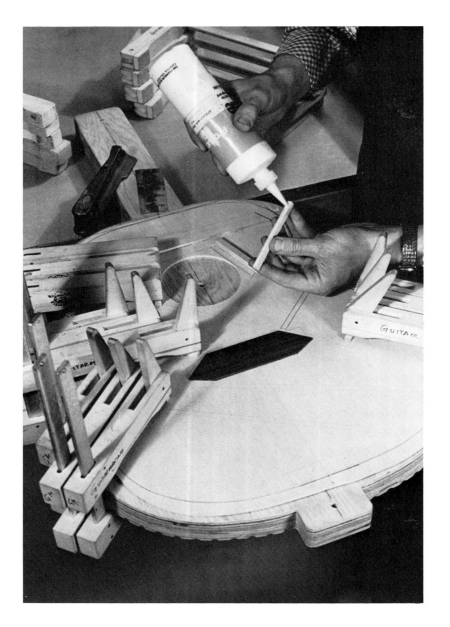

Although construction of the acoustic guitar principally involves cabinetmaking techniques, its design considerations are primarily architectural. Nowhere is this more evident than in the design of the soundboard. In order to remain acoustically responsive to the relatively nominal energy imparted by a plucked (as compared to a bowed) string, the tone-generating plate (soundboard) is usually made from a thin sheet of softwood; yet it must be sufficiently rigid to resist, with minimal distortion, substantial levels of tension, torsion, and shear stresses continually exerted over a very long period of time. The thin plate, therefore, must be trussed (reinforced) with a variety of struts (braces), which impart the rigidity necessary for long-term structural stability.

In bracing the soundboard, however, the luthier's parallel concern is to avoid serious impairment of the plate's ability to respond to the string signal. The required balance between structure and tone is achieved by maximizing the efficiency of

Soundboard Bracing

the bracing system. The evolution of efficient brace designs has been essential to the development of modern classical and steel-string guitars.

Resolving structural engineering problems does not, however, end the inquiry. For the serious luthier, in fact, it is only the beginning. Within the range of structurally efficient designs, there are an infinite number of variables that can dramatically affect the quality and quantity of an instrument's tonal response. As is seen in the historical discussions that follow, the systems presently recognized as structurally efficient for both classical and steel-string guitars were synthesized early in the latter half of the nineteenth century. Yet myriad design experiments within those established frameworks have marked the work of virtually all of the great makers since that time. By varying brace designs (among other things), each builder has sought to produce a sound that conformed to his concept of the ideal. Even after having achieved world-wide acclaim, many famous

makers have continued to work with new patterns and proportions.

The student's objective, then, is first to develop an appreciation of the instrument's structural requirements, and then gradually to learn how to control the variables that affect volume and tone. The process is complicated by the fact that a given combination of placement, dimension, and weight that proves highly successful with one set of materials may fail with another. For this reason, and because the soundboard bracing pattern cannot be divorced from other elements of the guitar's integrity, the designs of great builders cannot be simply extracted and recast as formulas for success. They are, however, invaluable as educational tools and, at the least, should serve as points of departure for the evolving craftsperson. In keeping with this notion, we have chosen traditional designs for the guitars built according to the step-by-step procedures that follow.

CLASSICAL BRACING DESIGN

The now familiar system of "fan" bracing on the classical guitar, found in rudimentary form on instruments dating as far back as 1650, was first significantly refined on the six-course (double-strung) guitar, an instrument widely produced in Spain during the latter part of the eighteenth century and the early part of the nineteenth century. The six-string (as opposed to six-course) guitar actually developed outside Spain in several other countries in the latter part of the eighteenth century. The use of fan bracing on the six-string guitar appears to have been initially adapted from the Spanish six-course guitar by Louis Panormo (Fig. 7-1), a London-based builder noted for his work from the 1820s through the 1840s. His work was seminal and astonishingly ahead of its time in the development of fan-bracing systems; it included symmetrical patterns similar to designs that evolved in the latter half of the nineteenth century, and asymmetri-

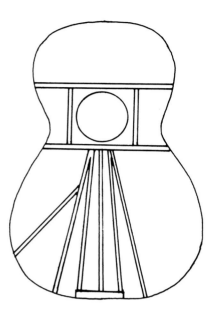

7–1. Early fan bracing: Panormo, 1823 (after R.E. Brune).

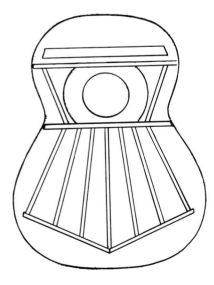

7–2. Torres's bracing pattern (from guitar built in 1863).

cal patterns that foreshadowed designs which were not seen again until the twentieth century.

Development of modern classical guitar bracing design, however, is attributed to a Spaniard, the great Antonio de Torres. Torres' system consisted of seven symmetrical braces fanning out from a focal point frequently, though not always, located at the twelfth fret, and two braces arranged in a V pattern at the lower end of the soundboard (Fig. 7-2). His system was emulated by the great builders of the Madrid school—José and Manuel Ramirez, Santos Hernandez, Domingo Esteso, and Marcelo Barbero, to name but a few; and outside Madrid by the likes of Ignatio Fleta, in Barcelona, and the great Hermann Hauser, of Munich.

To this day, many luthiers produce great instruments using Torres' basic design intact, and virtually all aspiring classical guitar builders use it as a point of departure. Variations on his design that have evolved in the twentieth century are innumerable, but the basic architectural concepts have remained the same in all but a few highly experimental cases.

The most notable variations (Fig. 7-3) on Torres' work have entailed increasingly complex and beefed-up structures, a phenomenon that has accompanied expansion of the soundbox since Torres' day in response to a demand for louder instruments to fill larger halls. Much of the design emphasis has been placed on mechanisms that seek to "stiffen the treble side" of the soundboard in an effort to boost high-frequency response, balancing the naturally in-

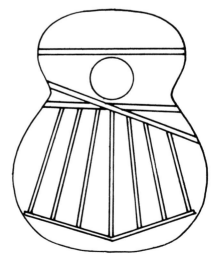

7–3. Asymmetrical variations of the classical soundboard.

creased bass response of the expanded soundbox. Some builders slant the lower cross strut down toward the treble side of the soundboard; others add a third major member at a diagonal to the lower cross strut. It is unclear, however, whether these features do in fact produce qualitative changes that cannot be duplicated simply by varying the weight of the materials in the basic design.

Another major direction that has become popular with traditionalists and innovators alike is the use of a thin pad notched into the fan braces underneath the area of the bridge. This feature is seen on the classical guitar built from the procedures in this book. Some builders use a transverse strut notched *over* the fan braces, instead of a flat pad. All of these systems are designed to produce an increase in cross-grain stiffness and stability in the area of the bridge.

The classical guitar built in this book also employs increased reinforcement of the area under the end of the fingerboard. We use both a transverse bar and a transverse graft to prevent splitting caused by the dissimilar expansion and contraction rates of the hardwood fingerboard and the softwood top, and to increase resistance to the shear stresses that tend to force that section of the soundboard downward toward the soundhole.

Many builders, including

Torres himself, have used a variety of soundhole-rosette reinforcements. The most common variation from the basic design is a circular or rectangular pad through which the soundhole itself must be drilled.

When run cross-grain, these pads (or doughnuts, as they sometimes are called) impart a plywoodlike stiffening effect to the soundhole area.

Unfortunately, it is extremely difficult to prove a concrete causal relationship between any specific design modification and tonal improvement. Our observations have led us to a conclusion that some readers may find surprising: Specific elements of brace design, in and of themselves, are not all that important! One has only to look at the myriad designs employed on great guitars to recognize that there is no design secret that will unlock the door to world-class consistency. A great maker will probably build a great guitar no matter what brace design is used. What the great builders have in common is the ability to integrate the proportionate weight and stiffnesses of all the parts relative to one another and relative to the volume of the soundbox and the scale length. The brace design, in short, can only be as successful as the whole of which it is a part.

STEEL-STRING-GUITAR BRACING DESIGN

The X-bracing system, first developed and introduced at the C.F. Martin guitar company, has been universally accepted by virtually every maker of the steel-string folk guitar. According to the remembrances of C. F. Martin III, it was the family patriarch C. F. Martin who, between 1840 and 1845, originated the X-brace shortly after moving to Nazareth, Pennsylvania. Seeking to improve his product, he experimented with and created a series of X-braced gut-string guitars that eventually became standard production items, supplanting the modified fan bracing and ladder systems with which he was familiar.

The X-brace gut-string sound, however, was not universally accepted. In response to a growing new market for the brighter, louder sound of wire strings, the company began to experiment with the substitution of wire for gut on X-braced guitars sometime around World War I. The results were so promising that by 1917 the Martin Company offered wire strings as an option on all the guitar models in their catalog. The appearance of these hybrids was an auspicious event in guitar history. The combination of wire strings with a bracing pattern first conceived seventy years earlier for use with gut worked so well that, by 1927, the situation had reversed: Wire-strung guitars had become the standard Martin-catalog items and gut had become the available option. It was to be the beginning of the American (and worldwide) love affair with the steel-string guitar. The brilliance, balance, and power of the X-braced steel-string folk guitar caused it to become the ascendant American form.

As it has evolved to the present day, the modern X-brace system consists of the following:

(1) two crossed, interlocked bars extending across the major portion of the soundboard's surface area (the X-brace);

(2) a flat, hardwood graft or "patch" extending between the lower arms of the interlocked bars, located precisely under the bridge;

(3) one or two canted bars supporting the area between the bridge patch and the bottom of the soundboard (the "lower face braces");

(4) a massive transversal brace (the "upper face brace") above the soundhole, spanning the upper bout of the soundboard;

(5) several miniature bars or "finger" braces supporting the areas between the X-brace and the edges of the soundboard;

(6) reinforcement of the soundhole, consisting of either a series of small braces or individual flat grafts; and

(7) a transversal reinforcement supporting the open area between the headblock and the upper face brace, consisting of either a long brace or a flat graft.

The two angled and converging bars of the X receive and diffuse twisting loads originating at the bridge. This torsional load is diverted, or dumped, by the X across the soundhole area and onto the area above it. These forces act along the length of the brace arms by twisting them around their own axes. Loads originating at the bridge are also dumped outward toward the rim of the sides. The major portion is, however, accepted by the massive upper face brace via the upper arms of the X and via the soundhole braces. The finger braces transmit their share of the load to the rim and, like the soundhole braces, they work to keep the stressed area of the soundboard under control, preventing it from distorting under load.

The upper arms of the X must closely approach the ends of the upper face brace so they can effectively bridge the naturally weak area at the soundhole. The lower arms must necessarily intersect the bridge so that the stresses can be

transferred directly. Considerable soundboard distortion will occur if the X misses the bridge altogether.

Despite the fact that several other factors such as scale length, soundbox volume, soundboard selection, and soundboard thickness exert a greater impact on the acoustic result than does the precise placement of the braces within the pattern, the splay of the X is still considered carefully in the context of the entire design concept. For example (viewing the X as if it were a scissor), we tend to "open" the arms of the X on small guitars to loosen the soundboard. Conversely, we "close" the arms of the X on large guitars to tighten the soundboard, seeking to balance the instrument's response.

To touch briefly upon the functions of the other members in the system:

The bridge patch provides a stable platform for the bridge and enhances its hold on the soundboard. The patch diffuses stresses and provides a hard-wearing surface for the ball-ends of the wire strings.

The lower face braces determine to a large extent the degree of flexibility of the soundboard area below the bridge. Their purpose is not to protect that region against any and all distortion, but rather to allow maximum compliance to resonance while limiting the amount of bulging caused by the forces exerted on the bridge. The flexibility of the region can be controlled by the angle and by the stiffness of these braces.

The upper transversal graft acts to bind the soundboard together under where the fingerboard is glued. This is important since the denser material of the fingerboard shrinks and swells at its own rate. The graft also counteracts the forces originating at the headpiece, which tend to push the fingerboard down toward the soundhole. The shearing forces on the soundboard along the edges of the fingerboard are considerable, and guitars with inadequate support in this crucial area may develop serious fractures.

The area of the soundboard around the upper transversal graft has popularly been considered acoustically inactive. On the contrary, studies have shown that the area is particularly active in the production of many high-frequency resonances. Indeed, some knowledgeable luthiers increase the stiffness in this region when enlarging the soundbox in an effort, they say, to bring about a more favorable treble balance.

PROCEDURE: PREPARING THE BRACE BLANKS

Spruce for guitar braces is usually sold in billets, usually around 2 × 3 × 22 inches. Ordinarily the billets are randomly sawn down to size from larger planks, in which case the grain may suffer some run-out along its length and may or may not be vertical. Thus, they may have to be further processed to extract high-quality brace blanks, as the discussion below describes. You may be fortunate enough to obtain straight, vertical-grain billets if you have been allowed to select them from a large pile. Processing will then be simplified and waste will be minimized.

In any case, you will obtain the stiffest and easiest-carving braces if you cleave or split the billet first (Fig. 7-4). The split face is surfaced and the billet is resawn to dimension. Resawing is easily done with power tools. By hand, you can extract brace blanks from the split slab by splitting it further into smaller (yet slightly oversized) blanks and then planing each of them to finish dimension.

When selecting billets, discard any pieces that betray sworls or display changes in grain or texture: these will not split well and will result in a very low yield of usable stock.

7-4. *A split billet of spruce. The cleft face follows the axis of the tree's growth, ensuring that the braces do not have invisible grain run-out.*

7–5. *Splitting braces. The froe is driven into the billet at right angles to the end-grain to split off a slab. The split slab is then sawn or split to brace size and then planed into a brace blank.*

7–6. *Splitting brace-sized pieces off a split slab with a mallet and chisel.*

Although you can extract all the braces you need for your guitar from one billet, you should obtain several in case splitting does not go well.

TOOLS
splitting froe (as below)
hammer
wooden mallet
large chisel
straightedge
pencil
ruler
sanding board
optional: belt sander

MATERIALS
one or more spruce billets
　(see above)

The froe: A simple splitting froe can easily be made from a 12-inch length of ³⁄₁₆ × ³⁄₄-inch (or similar size) cold rolled-steel bar, ground on a belt sander to an edge (Fig. 7-5). As the wooden billet gets reduced in size, a chisel becomes more convenient for splitting (Fig. 7-6).

Step 1—Splitting and Dimensioning the Brace Blanks

The brace block should be cut down to the length of your longest brace (SS: 18 inches; CL: 12 inches).

Place the billet upright on the most rigid, unyielding surface you can find (right over a table leg, for example). Place the froe on the upright end of the block, perfectly square to the end-grain. Cleave the billet approximately in half with several vigorous whacks with a hammer. If you succeeded in entering precisely square to the grain *and* have entered from the best end (there usually is one better entry end), the billet will cleave asunder with a pop. If not, try from the opposite end. Mark the better end for subsequent entries.

The two cleft surfaces can now be planed flat and braces sawn off by machine. You may choose, however, to keep re-

ducing the stock into braces by further splitting.

Split one of the cleft halves again, parallel to the original split face, creating a slab thick enough for your tallest brace (SS: ⅞ inch; CL: ¾ inch). With the mallet and chisel,

split your two longest braces (SS: X-brace arms; CL: upper and lower cross struts) off the slab by splitting *between* grain lines at ⁷⁄₁₆-inch separations (Fig. 7-7a).

Cut down the remaining portion of your slab to the length of your next longest

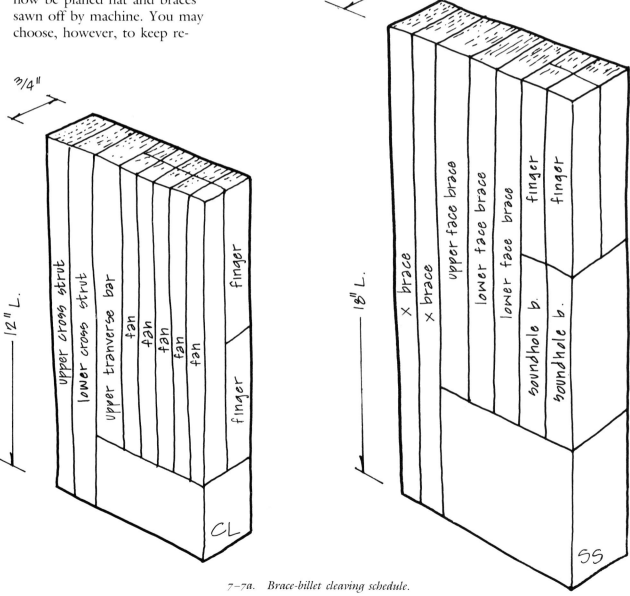

7–7a. Brace-billet cleaving schedule.

braces (SS: 12 inches; CL: 10 inches). Now split these braces off the slab along the grain, as above. (SS: upper face brace [⁵⁄₈-inch blank width], two lower face braces [³⁄₈-inch blank width]; CL: upper transversal bar [³⁄₈-inch blank width], fan braces and finger braces [split the rest of the stock into five ⁵⁄₁₆-inch slabs. These will be cross-split into ten ⁵⁄₁₆ × ³⁄₈-inch brace blanks].)

Steel-string only: Cut the remaining slab down to 5 inches in length. Split two soundhole braces (³⁄₈-inch blank width) and four finger braces (⁵⁄₁₆-inch blank width, finally split to ⁵⁄₁₆ × ⁵⁄₁₆ inches) off the slab.

Step 2—Planing to Dimension

Braces that are large in cross section can be held securely and planed in the leather-lined jaws of a vise. The more fragile lengths can be held firmly and safely on the tabletop, mounted on a length of double-faced masking tape. After one surface is leveled by the plane, the workpiece can be carefully paddled unstuck with the help of a table knife, turned over, and re-adhered for finishing up. Refer to Figure 7-7b for dimensions.

Since the braces will be radically reshaped after they are glued by the soundboard, it is not crucial to achieve flawless accuracy in the dimensioning steps, just as long as at least

one face—the face that will be glued to the soundboard—is true and square to the end-grain lines.

Step 3—Preparing the Flat Grafts

The grafts can be cut to size from the off-cuts of the soundboard. (We keep a scrap bin filled with damaged or otherwise rejected soundboard plates, which we recycle into grafts.)

Plane the scrap material to the dimensions shown (Fig. 7-7b). At least one face must be trued flat for gluing. If you cannot achieve this with the plane, stroke the blank against the sanding board until the entire surface is textured with sanding scratches.

Step 4—Making an Arch Template

The curved braces (SS: upper face brace, two lower face braces, X-brace arms; CL: lower cross strut only) have one curved edge that is glued to the soundboard, thus coaxing the flexible plate into a gently domed shape.

The edge of the brace is curved by planing or grinding to a curved line traced with the aid of an arch template. A ⅛-inch slat of hardwood will serve. To mark the template for curving, strain a length of thin metal rod (rod with a square cross section is best) between three pushpins. The distance between the

outer pins is equal to the desired template length. The offset between the center and the ends of the template is determined by placing the center pushpin as shown in Fig. 7-8. You can curve the edge of the template to the curved mark by planing to the line with a block plane and finishing off with pendulumlike strokes on the sanding board. With a file, put a small V-notch at the center, or highest point, of the curve. Templates useful for the arched braces on the guitars made from this book are steel-string: ⅛-inch offset, 18-inch span (all soundboard braces); ¼-inch offset, 16-inch span (all back braces); classical: ¹⁄₁₆-inch offset, 12-inch span (#1 back brace); ¹⁄₁₆-inch offset, 10-inch span (#2 back brace and soundboard lower cross strut); ⅛-inch offset, 10-inch span (#3 back brace); ⅛-inch offset, 15-inch span (#4 back brace).

Step 5—Arching the Braces

Lay the template on the side of the brace, placing the template center notch on the middle of the brace right up to the trued edge of the brace. Make sure the offset is similar on both ends, and trace the curve with a sharp pencil point. (*Steel-string only:* Do not arch the X-braces until *after* completing Step 6 in the steel-string bracing procedure. *Lower face braces:* Displacement goes from zero at one end to

1/4"
1/4"
fb
(4)

3/8"
5/16"
shb
(2)

1/2"
1/4"
lfb
(2)

5/8"
1/2"
ufb
(1)

3/4"
5/16"
xb
(2)

1/8"
7/8"
utvgft
(1) 12" L.

SS

CL

1/4"
3/16"
fnb
(9)

1/4"
3/16"
fgb
(2)

1/2"
5/16"
utvb
(1)

5/8"
5/16"
u,lcs
(2)

1/16"
1 1/4"
pad (1) 8" L

1/8"
1 1/4"
ros. gft
(2) 4" L

1/8"
1"
utvgft (1)
5 1/2" L

7–7b. Schedule of final finished brace-blank cross sections.

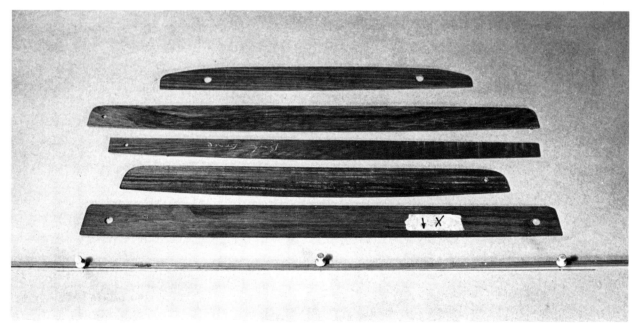

7–8. Brace-arching templates. A fair curve is drafted by straining a length of metal rod between three pushpins.

a full ¹⁄₁₆ inch at the other end.)

The quickest, easiest way to arch a brace is to grind the curved surface perpendicular to the faces of the brace with belt or disc sander with a fixed, squared fence (Fig. 7-9).

If you are not mechanized, you must rely on a sharp block plane and some attentive concentration. Fix the brace in a padded jaw vise, with the edge to be arched facing up. Set your block plane to a coarse cut. As you approach the curved template line, you must retract the blade for a progressively finer cut. You might be able to avoid tipping the surface by holding the plane between the thumbs of both hands and working directly *over* the brace rather than from

one side. Concentrate your gaze into the plane pocket, watching the curl intently. As long as the curl comes off full-width, you are maintaining the original perpendicularity of the surface. If a half-curl comes off, you are favoring that side of the brace (keep a small square handy to check the quality of your work). To correct, you must favor the *opposite* side, following with a balanced full-width curl. An erratic or random result betrays a dull or poorly adjusted plane. You may have to average irregularities left by the plane with a few pendulumlike strokes on the sanding board. Do your best, but bear in mind that you are not likely to get perfectly hand-arched braces on your first guitar.

7–9. Arching a brace on a belt sander. The brace is kept square to the belt by pressing it against a squared fence. Unless a very fine sanding belt is used, the sanding scratches must be reduced on a fine-grit sanding board or eliminated with a plane.

PROCEDURE: LAYING OUT THE BRACING PATTERN

The following marking procedures provide mechanical instructions that will yield a full-sized layout on the soundboard. If the student has difficulty visualizing any of the instructions, we suggest reference to the scale drawings (Figs. 7-10a & 7-10b).

TOOLS
plastic drafting triangle
ruler
ball-point pen
soft pencil (sharp)

IMPLEMENTS
template

All students must draw a light but visible pencil line down the centerseam of the soundboard. Using a pen for indelibility, draw the guitar outline with the template, taking care to line it up precisely on the centerseam. (*Important:* The distance from the top of the soundhole to the top of the outline must be *identical* to that distance on the rosette side.)

Classical Bracing Layout

The first two braces marked will be the upper and lower cross struts. Using the plastic square, draw lines perpendicular to the centerseam ¼ inch above and ¼ inch below the soundhole. Then draw lines parallel to each of these, ⁵⁄₁₆ inch above the upper line and ⁵⁄₁₆ inch below the lower line.

These depict the width of the cross struts.

To denote the fan-brace locations, we now use as an initial reference the lower parallel line for the lower cross strut. Mark on that line, at intervals of 1¼ inches, three dots on both sides of the centerseam (that is, at 1¼ inches, 2½ inches, and 3¾ inches from the seam).

Next, measure 1½ inches up the centerseam from the bottom of the outline, and make a dot. Using the ruler, find a point on the guitar outline that is 7 inches from that dot and draw a line connecting the two points. Repeat for the other side. These lines denote the bottom V of the bracing pattern. Measuring from the centerseam on each leg of the bottom V, mark dots at intervals of 2 inches. Connecting the six dots on the lower cross strut with the six dots on the bottom V completes the fan-brace layout.

The rosette grafts are laid out by drawing lines tangential to the soundhole and square to the cross struts, and then drawing parallel lines 1 inch from each tangent. To denote the finger braces, mark a dot on the upper parallel line of the lower cross strut ¾ inch from the outer edge of each rosette graft. Then mark a dot on the lower parallel line of the upper cross strut 1½ inches from the outer edges of the rosette grafts, and connect the dots.

Measure 1¼ inches up along the centerseam from the upper cross strut and draw a line perpendicular to the seam. Draw a parallel line 5⁄16 inch further up. These lines denote the upper transverse bar.

Next, draw two vertical lines connecting the upper transverse bar with the upper cross strut, each 2½ inches from the centerseam. These lines indicate the boundaries of the upper transverse graft.

To locate the transverse bridge pad, mark from the top of the outline down the centerseam the distance from the twelfth fret to the saddle. For a 25.6-inch scale, that will be 12.8 inches plus .10 inch compensation, or 12.9 inches. Draw a line perpendicular to the centerseam at that point, and then parallel lines ¼ inch above and 1 inch below. The pad will actually be shaped as shown in Fig. 7-10 (scale drawings), but it will be positioned using the horizontal lines 1¼ inches apart.

Finally, draw a line perpendicular to the centerseam tangent to the top of the outline. This will be a guideline for cutting off the top of the soundboard squarely.

Steel-string Bracing Layout

The template outline and centerline have been marked on the undersurface of the soundboard. Refer to Fig. 7-10 (scale drawings) while reading the following steps.

The *headblock* is represented by a 2 × 2½-inch rectangle, which is located at the upper center of the template outline. Draft the rectangle so that it is bisected by the soundboard centerline. The top line of the rectangle must be set back 3⁄32 inch from the template outline (the thickness of the sides) and accurately perpendicular to the centerline. The accuracy of this line is vital, since we will align the actual headblock to it when it is glued to the soundboard. If the headblock is crooked, the neck will be also.

The *bridge* outline must be drafted on the undersurface of the soundboard. Refer to Chapter 15 to make a bridge outline template, and locate its outline as shown in the layout drawing in Chapter 3.

The *upper face brace* is just above the soundhole. Its closest edge is ¼ inch above the soundhole rim. Draw two parallel lines ½ inch apart, perpendicular to the centerline. Extend the lines till they reach the template outline.

The *upper face graft* is between the headblock and the upper face brace. Draw two parallel lines ⅞ inch apart, perpendicular to the centerline. Center them in the space allotted. Connect the ends with angled lines as shown.

The *X-brace* is represented by two sets of two parallel lines 5⁄16 inch apart, which cross at the centerline. You may copy the splay of the X-brace from the diagram, paying particular attention to the distance between the ends of

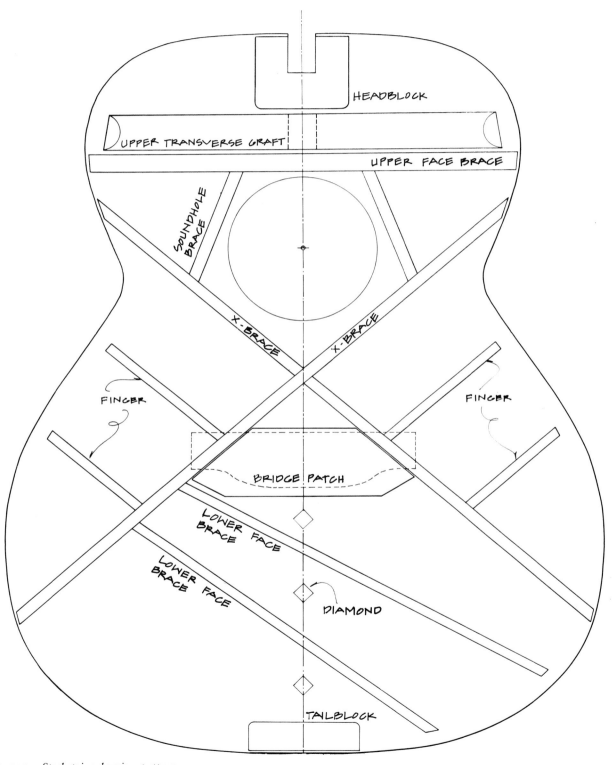

7–10a. Steel-string bracing pattern.

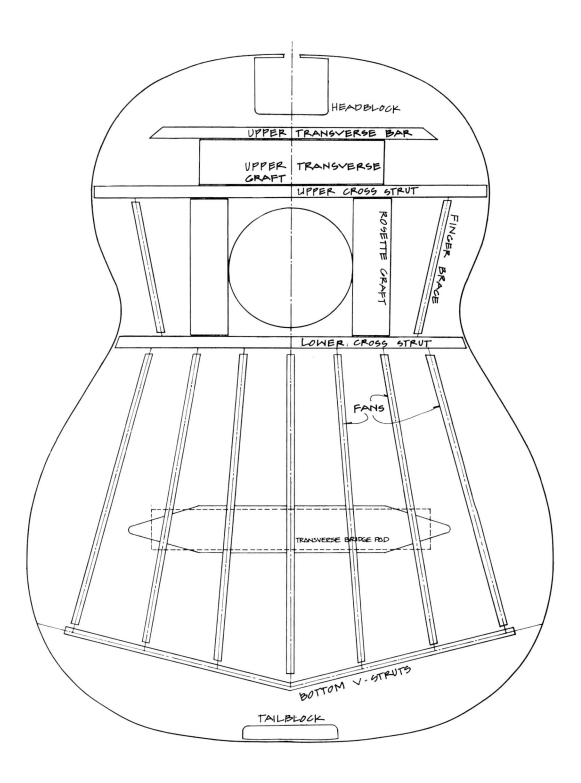

7–10b. Classical bracing pattern.

the upper arms and the ends of the upper face brace, as well as where the lower arms cross the bridge. The *bridge patch* lies between the two bottom legs of the X, immediately under the bridge. Its size and location are determined by drafting a line perpendicular to the centerline ⅛ inch above the front edge of the bridge and another, parallel to the first, which lies ¼ inch below the back edge of the bridge. These two lines are extended until they meet the arms of the X-brace. The ends of the bottom line of the bridge patch are "clipped" at both ends, as seen in the diagram.

The *lower face braces* are represented by two sets of two parallel lines ¼ inch apart. Our preference is to have them converge toward the treble half of the soundboard, the topmost set starting right below the bridge patch. They both end ⅜ inch from the template outline. Splay them as you choose, or make them parallel as they are on C.F. Martin guitars. Alternatively, you may choose to space and separate them precisely as in the diagram, which is how they are placed on the guitar made in this book.

The *finger braces* are represented by four sets of two parallel lines ¼ inch apart. They start right from the lower arms of the X-brace and end ⅜ inch from the template outline. They run parallel to the upper X-brace arms, and are spaced as shown in the diagram. Note

that they divide the open spaces allotted for them into approximately equal areas.

The *soundhole braces*, represented by double parallel lines 5/16 inch apart, are placed at either side of the soundhole. They angle toward each other slightly, converging at an imaginary point on the centerline somewhere above the soundhole. They should come no closer to the soundhole edge than 3/16 inch. We normally slant them so that they leave as little unsupported soundboard area adjacent to the soundhole as possible.

The *tailblock* is represented by a 3 × ¾-inch rectangle, bisected by the centerline and set back from the template outline by 3/32 inch. The bottom line must be strictly perpendicular to the centerline because, like the headblock, it will guide the actual tailblock when it is glued. If it is crooked, an odd lump will appear at the bottom of the guitar.

TECHNICAL NOTES ON BRACING THE SOUNDBOARD

Clamping

As a general rule, clamping soundboard braces requires relatively light clamping pressure. Gentle pressure is particularly important when gluing classical fans, for example. Somewhat exceptional to the general rule, however, are operations

involving flat grafts. Heavy pressure is not required, but it must be sufficient to ensure that all parts of the wide area to be glued come in contact with the soundboard plate.

Flat grafts, therefore, must be glued using a rigid caul between the graft and the clamps in order to distribute clamping pressure. But even with a caul, an array of clamps is necessary to ensure that the pressure is adequately spread. The caul used should be close in length and width to the graft itself, but it must be slightly smaller in all directions to permit accurate location of the graft during gluing.

Braces that are high and stiff can usually be glued without cauls. The natural rigidity of the brace blank will adequately distribute clamping pressure. Lighter braces such as fans and fingers can be glued either with or without cauls, but we recommend the use of cauls when possible. Fewer clamps are required with a caul in place, allowing greater control over clamping pressure; also, the tendency of the clamps to twist the brace will be reduced if a caul is used.

Twisting is also minimized by clamping from more than one direction. Sometimes the pulling action of the clamps can be used advantageously, as we will note in the procedures, but ordinarily it must be avoided, especially with the more flexible braces.

Clamping the braces can be done on the assembly workboard, against a rigid backing board, or against a flexible backing slat (usually a smooth piece of hardwood 1 to 2 inches wide and about 3/16 inch thick), as required. The grafts should always be clamped with a rigid backing to ensure the spread of clamping pressure. *Flat-bottom* braces can be glued with any of the above methods. *Curved-bottom* braces *must* be clamped with a flexible backing for the obvious reason that some flex is required to follow the curve.

When clamping with the flexible backing slat, you must be *very* certain that the slat is properly positioned under the brace being glued. If the slat is misaligned, the soundboard plate may be scissored under pressure between the slat and the brace, resulting in a disastrous fracture. If necessary, the slat can be held in place with masking tape. You must also make sure that the clamps are properly aligned on the backing slat, lest one of them slip off and do similar damage.

As a final note, we recommend that cauls be made carefully and accurately for each operation in which they are necessary. We have seen many gluing operations go awry simply because the clamping caul was misshapen, too large, or too small.

Humidity

In our discussion of the properties of wood as an instrument-making material in Chapter 2, we gave substantial attention to environmental considerations. These become critical when bracing the soundboard, for after braces are applied, the wide, flat plate can no longer freely react to moisture changes in the atmosphere. If the top is braced in a relatively humid environment that then becomes relatively dry, the braces will inhibit and distort the normal parameters of shrinkage that would otherwise occur. The plate will simply proceed to shrink in whatever direction the resistance is least, often causing bizarre warpage and sometimes straightening or even concaving otherwise convex braces.

Thus, it is essential that the environment be reasonably controlled during and after bracing. It helps to do all the bracing on the soundboard in a compact period of time, such as over a weekend, and to progress to assembly of the soundbox as soon as possible after bracing. If you have difficulty controlling your workshop environment, we suggest that you leave curved-bottom braces uncarved until you are ready for assembly.

Gluing

When applying glue, you must spread a sufficient amount on the brace to wet the gluing surface thoroughly.

Do not, however, flood the surface with glue, as the brace will swim around excessively during clamping. All braces and grafts must be held in place with finger pressure until the glue starts to set and the piece stops sliding. The ideal amount of glue will provide a minute amount of squeeze-out on both sides of the brace along its entire length but will grab within a few seconds under finger pressure. When the glue begins to hold, clamps can be applied, starting in the middle of the brace and working outward.

Unless otherwise noted, setting time for gluing braces is thirty minutes for either yellow or white glue at 70°F and forty to fifty-five percent humidity; with higher relative humidity or lower temperature, clamping time will be longer.

Carving and Sanding

The braces must be carved in stages rather than after all are glued in place because the position of some will obstruct the carving of others. Thus, for example, the classical fan braces should be carved before the bottom V and lower cross strut are glued; the steel-string finger braces should be carved before the X-brace is glued.

When carving away significant amounts of material, extreme sensitivity to grain direction is crucial. Using split brace wood minimizes problems, but if you cut into a brace and notice that the wood wants to tear instead of shave, stop and go from the other direction. If you ever happen to mangle a brace, note that you can always carve it off completely, scrape the surface, and glue on a new brace blank.

Feathering the brace ends (carving down to nothing), required for all fan and finger braces, must be done very carefully, lest you nick or gouge the soundboard plate. Using a slicing motion (rather than simply pushing the chisel) sometimes helps. If necessary, switch to a ¼-inch chisel to do the last bit of shaving.

After each stage of preliminary carving, the braces should be coarsely sanded (with #100- or #120-grit garnet sandpaper) to remove chisel marks. Fine sanding (with #220-grit) occurs after final graduation (after all the braces are glued in place and rough-carved), with the exception of the flat grafts, which should be fine-sanded at the preliminary stage. When either coarse or fine sanding, it is important to avoid making grooves in the soundboard adjacent to the braces. Placing a thin sheet of plastic or metal next to the brace when sanding will prevent this.

Glue squeeze-out must be cleaned up before carving is begun. Small beads are easiest to remove when crystal hard; larger beads should be removed when leather hard to avoid tearing the soundboard

material. In any case, never smear the glue when it is still wet, as this will make it impossible to remove the excess without taking soundboard material as well.

PROCEDURE— BRACING THE CLASSICAL SOUNDBOARD

TOOLS
clamps, as specified
razor saw
straightedge (metal or
    wood)
chisels
glue chisel
pencil

IMPLEMENTS
flat backing board
clamping slats
assembly board
cauls, as required

SUPPLIES
PVA glue
sandpaper

MATERIALS
soundboard and dimen-
    sioned brace blanks

Step 1—Gluing Down the Flat Grafts

After the rosette is installed, the soundhole cut out, and the top marked for bracing, the rosette area of the top should be reinforced as soon as possible and before the top is handled for any other operation. Thus, the rosette grafts should be glued first, followed by the transverse bridge pad and the

upper transverse graft. Before gluing, trim the grafts to the precise lengths necessary to fit your layout.

The grafts are glued down using rigid cauls, each slightly smaller than the graft over which it is clamped.

Apply a moderate amount of glue to one of the rosette grafts and place it in position on the soundboard. Press down on the graft with your fingers until the glue begins to grab. Using a cam clamp, apply clamping pressure gently. If the graft moves under the initial pressure, realign it and try again. If it appears that the graft is being dragged by the clamp, check under the workboard to see that the clamp is not racked in any way. Maneuver the clamp from underneath to align the graft. When the graft is aligned properly and not moving, apply the other clamps, still watching for movement. When the graft is stable, tighten the clamps. Repeat for the other graft.

The bridge pad and the upper transverse graft are applied in the same way. Cut the bridge pad to length and shape as in Fig. 7-10 before gluing; make sure that it is centered (from side to side) when clamped (see Fig. 7-11).

When all the grafts are glued down and the clamps have been removed, clean up the squeeze-out with the glue chisel. Sand the grafts with #120-grit garnet and finish with #220. *Do not* round the edges of any of the grafts.

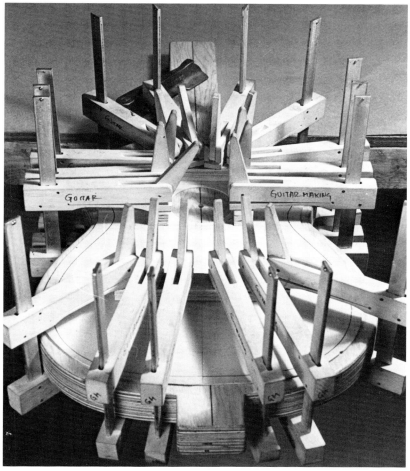

7–11. *Gluing the flat grafts on the classical soundboard with cam clamps. If fewer clamps are available, the grafts can, of course, be glued one at a time.*

7–12. *Gluing a fan brace on the classical soundboard with cam clamps and a slotted caul. The rigidity of the caul minimizes the twisting action of the clamps.*

Step 2—Gluing Down the Fans and Finger Braces

Cauls for the fans should be the same length as their respective braces; thus, four cauls will do the job for seven symmetrical fans. The cauls should be a little wider than the fans themselves. If you have a table saw, you can make the cauls easier to use by cutting in each a shallow slot the width of the fan brace (Fig. 7-12).

The middle five fans must be notched to fit over the bridge pad. To accomplish this, cut each brace to its proper length, lay it on the pad in its proper alignment, and mark on both sides where the notches will fall. Saw slightly inside your marks, angling the cuts to match the angle of the notch in relation to the pad. Using a chisel, shave about ¹⁄₃₂ inch deep between the saw cuts. Check each fan for fit on the pad and expand the notch lengthwise until it is just right. Then gradually deepen the notch until, with gentle pressure, the brace touches the soundboard on both sides of the pad while still fitting snugly on the pad itself.

When all the fans are ready, begin the gluing operation with the middle fan. When gluing, always be certain that the trued edge is down. Apply a bead of glue to the fan and smear it so that the gluing surface is thoroughly wetted. Locate the fan on its layout line and press down with the fingers until the glue starts to grab. Clamp carefully, watching for slippage. Start with very gentle pressure; when all the clamps are in place and the brace is set, increase the pressure only very slightly. Glue all seven fans down and then cut to length, position, and glue down the small finger braces on either side of the rosette grafts (Fig. 7-13). Do not glue the bottom V-braces in place just yet.

Step 3—Carving the Fans

This job is done best with a long-bladed (paring) chisel, but an ordinary butt chisel will do. The chisel must, however, be very sharp.

The objective is simply to convert the cross section of each brace from a rectangle to a parabolic shape (to "peak") and to carve the ends down to a feather edge. The exact profile and cross section of each brace eventually becomes an element of each luthier's particular design, but for the beginner it is sufficient simply to peak and feather (see Figs. 7-14 and 7-15).

Leave the middle three fans close to full height. The outer fans should be shaved down a bit lower. Peak and feather the finger braces too, leaving them at full height (Fig. 7-16).

Sand off the chisel marks with #120-grit garnet, but do not final sand with #220-grit just yet.

Step 4—Gluing and Carving the Bottom V-Braces

Cut the braces for the bottom V roughly to length but leave them overlong. The two braces must butt closely together while following the layout lines exactly.

Measure the angle of the V on your top with a protractor and transfer it to a piece of scrap. You can cut the butt end of one brace and then the other with that layout as a guide, but the simplest way to get a perfect joint there is to overlap the two pieces at the proper angle and then cut through both of them at once with a razor saw. Any variation from square in the cut will be mirrored in the two pieces so that they will butt without a gap. When the ends butt accurately, cut the braces to final length.

7–13 *Classical fan and finger braces glued and ready for carving.*

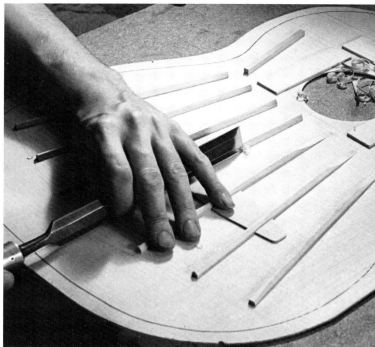

7–14 and 7–15. *Peaking and feathering the fan braces. Note that the chisel is held like a pool cue, with one hand acting as a "bridge" to steady it.*

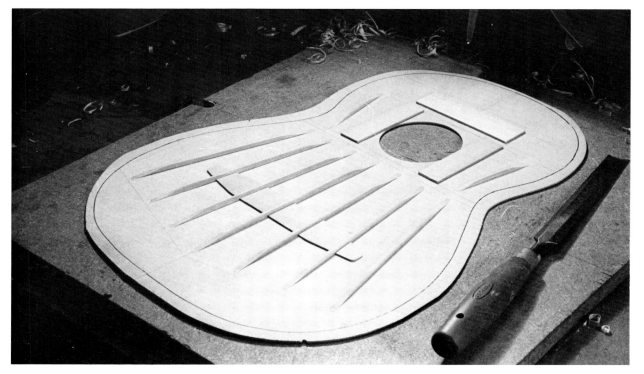

7–16. *The fan and finger braces carved.*

The legs of the V should both be glued at once, without cauls. Get a little glue on the butting ends and try to keep them in contact while clamping.

Carve the V in the same way as the fans, feathering the ends but leaving the legs and their junction point at full height. Sand with #120-grit garnet.

Step 5—Gluing and Carving the Upper Cross Strut and Upper Transverse Bar

The upper transverse bar should fit snugly against the upper transverse graft. A neat way to accomplish this is to use the pulling action of the clamps. Start with a clamp through the soundhole in the middle of the brace and continue clamping outward. As you approach the brace ends, reverse the direction from which the clamps extend.

The upper cross strut should extend beyond the edges of the template when initially glued in place. Shave back the rosette grafts if you need a little extra room between them and the upper transverse graft. Clamp from both directions (Fig. 7-17).

Clean up the glue squeeze-out on these two braces and then peak the upper transverse bar at a height of ⅜ to ⁷⁄₁₆ inch and the upper cross strut at about ⁹⁄₁₆ inch. Carve the ends of the upper transverse bar to about ⅛ inch from the soundboard; they need not be feathered. The ends of the upper cross strut should be scalloped as in Fig. 7-20 rather than cut straight down all the way. Carve the ends straight down to about ⅜ inch (starting the descent about 2 inches from the outline) and then flip the chisel over to take a sweeping cut, which flattens out as it runs off the brace. Leave the ends about ³⁄₁₆ to ¼ inch high.

7-17. Clamping the upper cross strut.

Step 6—Gluing and Carving the Lower Cross Strut

This brace was slightly arched in the procedure on preparing the braces, so it must be glued using a semi-rigid backing slat instead of the workboard. (See Technical Notes on Bracing the Soundboard, page 156).

The first clamp should be in the center of the brace. Clamp down from the headblock end of the soundboard to pull the brace against the rosette grafts. The brace ends may be clamped from the other direction (see Fig. 7-18).

When dry, clean up the glue squeeze-out and carve in the same manner as the upper cross strut. Note, however, that because this brace is arched, the soundboard will no longer be flat. When cleaning the squeeze-out, take special care not to dig into the soundboard, for the chisel may have a tendency to dive into the concave surface. When both cleaning up and carving, do not press on the top in such a way as to force it to flatten out, lest you fracture the fragile plate or pop the brace ends. Peak the lower cross strut at a height of 9/16 inch at its midpoint.

Step 7—Cutting Back the Brace Ends

The ends of the two cross struts must be cut back to allow the sides to fit inside the template line. Cut through the brace ends with a razor saw 3/32 inch from and parallel to the line at each end. Use the tip or the heel of the saw for the last bit to avoid cutting into the soundboard.

Shave away the excess with a chisel. Do not try to take too much at once. Work cross-grain only, except perhaps to remove the last few shavings, for which you can cut toward the brace. Clean the surface with a scraper, but try not to obliterate more than an inch or so of the outline.

Step 8—Making the Tangential Cut at the Top of the Outline

During the marking procedure, we drew a line perpendicular to the centerseam, exactly tangential to the top of the outline. Using a straightedge as a guide, saw through

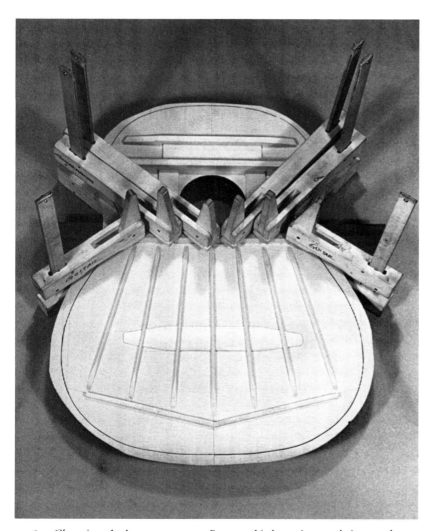

7–18. *Clamping the lower cross strut. Because this brace is curved, it must be clamped with a flexible slat.*

7-19. *Making the tangential cut at the top of the soundboard outline, using a hardwood block as a saw guide.*

the soundboard with a dovetail saw *adjacent* to and *inside* the tangent line (Fig. 7-19).

Step 9—Final Graduation

Like thinning the soundboard, final graduation of the braces (Fig. 7-20) is a step that invokes and ultimately tests the luthier's mastery of the medium. As such, its successful execution cannot be reduced to a mechanical formula, but rather must be learned over the course of building many instruments. We strive for a familiar combination of resilience and tap response that is difficult, if not impossible, to describe in words alone.

The beginner should strive primarily to leave the soundboard braces smooth, clean, and free of debris or glue squeeze-out in corners and crevices. Finish sand with #220-grit garnet, and round any exposed sharp corners of the grafts.

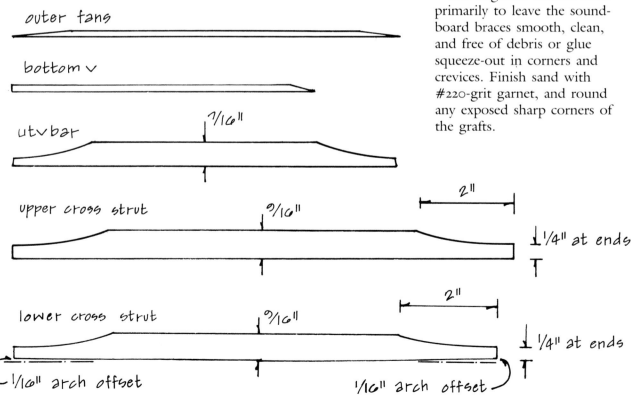

7-20. *Classical brace shapes (soundboard).*

PROCEDURE: BRACING THE STEEL-STRING SOUNDBOARD

TOOLS
block plane
plastic square
small metal straightedge
sanding board
razor saw
razor knife
clamps, as specified
dovetail saw
glue chisel
rattail file or curved rasp
felt sanding block
chisel
6-inch ruler
pencil
flat metal spatula or joint
   knife (see Step 2)
flat mill file

IMPLEMENTS
flat backing board
assembly board
backing slats
cauls, as required

MATERIALS
soundboard and dimen-
   sioned brace blanks
rosewood or maple bridge
   patch blank (see Step 1)
two or three ⅛-inch spruce
   pieces, ⅜ inch square
two strips of linen fabric,
   about ¾ × ⅜ inch

SUPPLIES
AR glue
#100-, #120-, and #220-
   grit garnet sandpaper
masking tape

Step 1—Making the Bridge Patch

The bridge patch begins as a small sheet of straight-grained rosewood or maple about 2 inches wide by 6½ inches long and about ³⁄₃₂ inch thick. It should be made from clear, unflawed material, preferably quarter-sawn, with its grain oriented parallel to its longest dimension. The bridge patch must be cut from the blank so that its outline is exactly the same as the outline drafted on the soundboard.

First, draft the patch outline onto the blank with a sharp pencil. Visibility can be improved on dark wood by following the line with a cut made with a razor knife against a small straightedge. With the small block plane, trim the parallel edges of the blank down to the line. Next, trim the angled ends of the blank down to the line by cutting them off with a small razor saw. (*Save the cutoff pieces*—they will be useful later.) On these angled ends, strive to achieve a straight edge that is square to the face of the blank. You can make fine adjustments to the angle by stroking on the sanding board. In the process, the patch may end up sitting a tiny bit closer to the junction of the X-brace, but this is acceptable.

Clip the bottom corners of the patch, as shown in Fig. 7-21. Round off all the sharp corner edges except those that will butt up against the X-brace arms or those actually touching the soundboard. Sand the faces of the bridge patch with #220-grit garnet

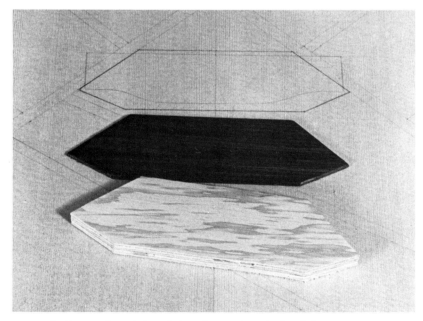

7–21. Bridge patch and shaped clamping caul ready for gluing.

and blow off all the sanding dust in preparation for the next gluing operation.

Step 2—Gluing the Bridge Patch

The patch must be glued accurately in its allotted place on the soundboard. This is a bit tricky: working against you will be the tendency of the piece to shift while the clamps are being placed. This can be caused by the use of excessive amounts of glue, the use of bent or beat-up clamps, or careless placement of same. If after gluing you find that the patch has shifted or crept significantly away from the outline on the soundboard, the patch must be removed, either by prying with a flat metal spatula (if only recently set) or by prying with the spatula after carefully heating the patch with an iron (if set and dry).

Cut a clamping caul from a ½-inch-thick piece of plywood or flat hardwood. Use the finished bridge patch as a template and trace its outline on the caul blank. Cut within the traced outline to yield a slightly smaller, yet similar-shaped caul.

Place a flat backing board under the soundboard (Fig. 7-22). Apply glue to the undersurface of the patch in moderate amount—just enough to wet the entire surface. Wipe back the edges with a finger to reduce the squeeze-out. Press the patch in place firmly against the soundboard with the fingers until it starts to grab.

Place the caul directly over the bridge patch.

Apply the first clamp through the soundhole and onto the middle of the caul. Tighten the clamp lightly. Make sure the clamp is not skewed or angled when tightening or it will forcefully drag the glued piece in an effort to right itself. Maneuver the clamp from underneath to realign the patch to its desired place if it starts to creep. Tighten down some more. If

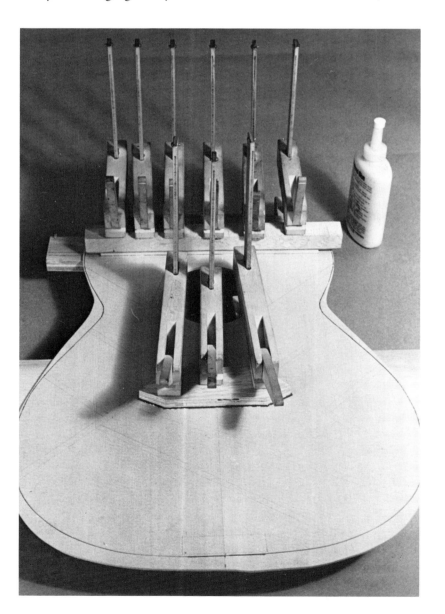

7-22. *Clamping bridge patch and upper transverse graft with rigid backing boards underneath.*

it appears stable and well aligned, add two more clamps through the soundhole and tighten them bit by bit, checking and repositioning as you go until the clamps are very tight. If glue squeeze-out has obscured your lines, quickly remove it with a pointed stick. If you must move the piece at this stage, you might still be able to loosen the clamps just enough to free the patch and forcefully realign it.

After about thirty minutes, remove all clamps. Do not stress or disturb the workpiece for at least an hour.

Step 3—Preparing, Gluing, and Shaping the Upper Transversal Graft

Start with the graft blank cut during the procedure Pre-paring the Brace Blanks (page 147). Using a razor saw, trim the ends to the angle and length shown on the soundboard.

A long, straight caul, cut from $1/2$-inch plywood, $7/8$ inch wide and about as long as the graft (angle its ends if it overhangs), will spread the clamping force. Apply the clamps from the center outward, as shown in Fig. 7-22.

After the glue dries, shape the top surface of the graft into a curved cross section with lengthwise strokes using a block plane held at a successively varying angle with each stroke. Try to achieve a symmetrical rather than a lopsided cross section that is constant throughout the graft's length.

Next, bevel the blunt ends as shown in Fig. 7-23. A slanting, slicing movement with the chisel will yield the best results.

Finally, sand off all facets and cutter marks with a piece of #120-grit garnet sandpaper wrapped around a small felt block. Follow with #220-grit for a smooth final result.

Important: Clearance notch— To allow clearance later for the truss rod wrench, a deep clearance notch must be cut across the center of the graft precisely over the centerline of the soundboard. The notch must be at least $1/2$ inch wide and must cut through most of the thickness of the graft, leaving only a thin web actually spanning the centerline. Round its edges with a rattail file or curved rasp. Follow with coarse, then fine, grits of sandpaper.

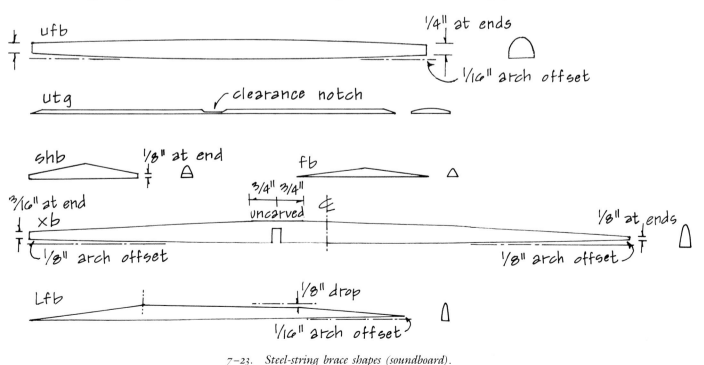

7-23. *Steel-string brace shapes (soundboard).*

Step 4—Gluing the Flat (Finger and Soundhole) Braces

Cut the four finger braces down to length with a razor saw from the ¼ × ¼-inch blanks. Angle each end slightly to correspond to the slanted X-brace and template lines on the soundboard.

Set up the assembly workboard. It should be clamped or bolted so that it fully projects over the end of the work table.

Since the area of the actual "footprint" of the brace is so small, use just the lightest clamping pressure, lest you drive the brace into the soundboard. Apply enough glue to just wet the surface of the brace. Make sure the trued face is down. Hold it down firmly in place for about ten seconds and apply the clamps as shown in Fig. 7-24.

The soundhole brace blanks, ⁵⁄₁₆ inch wide by about ⅜ inch tall, should be cut a bit *longer* than the length allotted for them between the X-brace and upper face brace.

Glue and clamp as shown in Fig. 7-24. Make sure the overlong ends overlap into X-brace and upper face brace territory. They will be trimmed back as described below.

Step 5—Shaping the Flat Braces

RAMP THE FINGER BRACES

Chisel a ramp from the top-middle of the blank down to both ends as shown in Fig. 7-25. Shave down to a small stub at the ends with your initial strokes, then feather the stubs away with a controlled, slicing motion of your chisel. Try not to stab the soundboard.

7–24. *Soundhole and finger braces glued with cam clamps.*

7–25. *Ramping the finger braces. Straight ramps are cut with progressively lengthened strokes, starting from the ends and working toward the middle of the brace.*

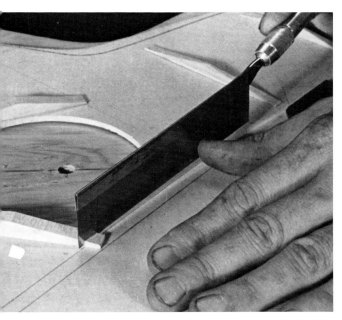

7–26. *Trimming the ends of the soundhole braces. Rather than being feathered, the ends of the soundhole braces butt against the X-brace to improve the transfer of stresses to the upper face brace.*

7–27. *Shaving the finger braces into a pyramidal shape. Note the shallow chisel angle.*

RAMP AND TRIM THE SOUNDHOLE BRACES

Since the soundhole braces must receive and transmit loads between the X-brace and the upper face brace, it is best not to feather their ends, as we did on the finger braces. Instead, we leave ⅛ inch end stubs that will later butt up snugly to their neighbors.

Measure and mark on the soundhole brace ⅛ inch up from the soundboard at the locations where it intersects the lines drawn for the X-brace and upper face brace. Now chisel and ramp the brace precisely as you did the finger braces, but go no closer to the soundboard than the measured marks.

Trim the ends back with a razor saw so the brace stops short precisely at the intersections with the X- and upper face brace outlines (Fig. 7-26). Guide the course of the saw with your thumb and forefinger.

To avoid marring when you approach the soundboard, change your stroke so that you utilize only the last ½ inch or so of the saw blade. Run the tip of the blade through the kerf to make sure the last few fibers are severed right down to the soundboard surface.

Pop the overhanging stubs off the soundboard by gently levering them with the chisel. Make sure that no debris of wood fibers or glue trespasses into adjacent brace territory.

The trimmed ends should be square to the soundboard surface. If they are not, file them upright with a fine-tooth flat mill file. (Our file has a smooth ground and polished edge so it will not groove the soundboard during the step.) It is all right if, in doing so, the ends shorten a tiny bit.

SCULPT THE FLAT BRACES

Carve the vertical walls of all the flat braces so that a pyramidal shape results, as in Fig. 7-27. Starting at the top, a progressively larger triangular facet should appear as you chisel with the blade held at a constant angle. Stop when you reach the center point of the rise, then repeat on the opposite face.

Sand all faces with #120-, then #220-grit sandpaper. Finally, sand all sharp edges lightly with #220-grit sandpaper.

Step 6—Cutting the X-Brace Lap Joint

The two arms of the X-brace meet and are secured together where they cross by a lap joint. The lap joint consists of notches accurately cut into each brace arm, which allows them to interlock at a predetermined angle. For structural and acoustic purposes, it is best that the fit of the two arms in the joint be as snug as possible. The notch should be cut so the precise angle originally drafted on the soundboard is faithfully duplicated between the braces.

MARK ALL THE INTERSECTIONS

Erase the X-brace intersection lines from the soundboard. Take out the first 18-inch brace blank. Place it on the soundboard, trued edge down, so that it butts against the angled edge of the bridge patch and one of the soundhole brace ends while overlapping the template line at both ends. Mark "top" on the top surface of the brace and "D" for "down-notch." This will avoid a mix-up with its partner. Holding the down-notch brace arm firmly against its two stops (check the overlaps), trace two new lines on the soundboard at the intersection. Put that brace aside and place the second 18-inch brace blank on the opposite brace location on the soundboard. Mark this one "up" for up-notch and "top" on its top surface. Hold it firmly against its own two stops and mark its location precisely on the soundboard to complete an accurate cross-hatch of the intersection.

MARK THE NOTCH LINES ON THE FIRST BRACE

Remove the second brace and return the first one to its original location, "top" up, tight against its stops. The brace crosses over the hatch lines intersecting them at a total of four points. With great care, mark these four points onto the brace, as shown in Fig. 7-28a. Now, mark the second brace in the same way.

On the first brace, carefully transfer the four marked points over and around the corners and accurately connect the points with two straight lines, as in Fig. 7-28b.

Starting from the four original points, mark four lines on the brace sides, squared to the "down" edge. Do not carry these four lines clear across the brace, but instead stop them short at about two-thirds of the brace's full height. These squared lines plus the connecting oblique lines will serve as guides for sawing the notch cuts. Mark the second brace also, but carry the squared lines completely *across* the brace.

SAWING THE CUTS

A sharp razor saw works best for sawing the notch cuts. Make the cuts carefully into the brace, keeping the kerf about 1/64 inch to the inside of the squared lines (Fig. 7-29). The kerf should stop a hair past halfway through the height of the brace. Pop out the wood between the kerfs with a 1/4-inch chisel, yielding a notch just a tiny bit tighter than it should be. Our purposely overtight lap joint is progressively "relieved" and its angle corrected with a file. The technique relies on the natural compressibility of the soft spruce.

Replace the second, unnotched brace in its proper home on the soundboard. Try mounting the notch of the first onto the "top" edge of the second, just where the guidelines say it belongs. If it does not mount, you must file back the "walls" of the notch—closer to the squared guidelines (use a small mill file)—until the notch *just* starts to mount the second brace. Alternately file and check. Stop filing when, with firm pressure (and a little bit of wood compression), the notch on the first brace mounts the second brace at the proper place. If the notch enters part way and jams, chances are one or both notch walls converge slightly (check the walls

7–28a and b. Marking one X-brace arm for notching the lap joint.

against the squared guidelines). Correct by favoring the proud part of the wall with the file.

As soon as a *tight* but positive mount has been achieved, compare the angle of the locked braces with the desired angle on the soundboard. Sight with your eyeball right over the braces to assess the match. It should be very close. If it is not, file more material off the notch walls selectively to try to angle the notch a bit so that the X-brace arms rotate into the desired position. At the same time, this will bring about a slight loosening of the fit of the brace in the notch. A little bit of filing goes a long way (Fig. 7-30).

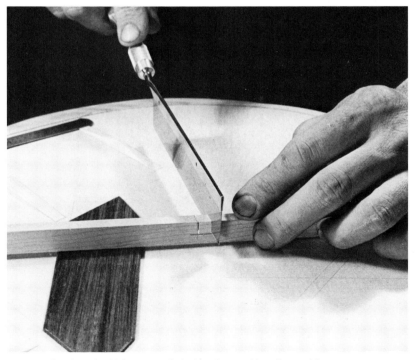

7–29. Cutting the X-brace notch inside the marking lines with a razor saw.

7–30. *Relieving the X-brace notch to achieve a good fit and the correct angle. The* **X** *marked on the brace indicates in which direction to favor the filing strokes.*

Now mark the second brace where the notched brace contacts it. This will provide the oblique guidelines for the "up" notch (Fig. 7-31). Proceed to notch the second brace using the same sequence as in notching the first.

Sometimes, twisting the braces as they enter and chamfering the notch edges slightly help the parts go together. If the braces jam together, pull them apart *very* carefully. They are liable to split, since they are *very fragile* until glued down.

The two "down" edges that are to be glued to the soundboard must be level with one another when interlocked. Make sure the braces do not inadvertently interlock backwards (see Fig. 7-32).

7–31. *Marking the second arm of the X-brace, using the first arm as a guide.*

7–32. *Checking the X-brace for fit. Once interlocked, the X-brace arms must comfortably abut the soundhole braces and bridge patch.*

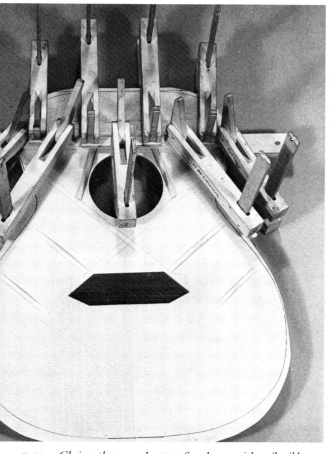

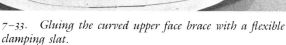

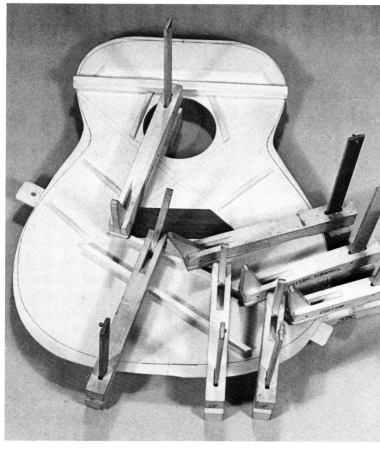

7–33. *Gluing the curved upper face brace with a flexible clamping slat.*

7–34. *Gluing the lower face braces.*

The arms must now be pulled apart and the "down" edges arched as described in the previous procedure, Preparing the Brace Blanks.

Step 7—Gluing the Upper and Lower Face Braces

The single upper and the two lower face braces have already been dimensioned and arched in the procedure Preparing the Brace Blanks. Refer to the gluing tips immediately below as well as to the techni-cal notes in this chapter for additional clamping and carving suggestions.

UPPER FACE BRACE

Tape a backing slat to the soundboard's show face, right under the location of the upper face brace.

Apply a generous bead of glue to the curved edge of the brace and spread it with a clean finger. Align the brace and place the first clamp through the soundhole and onto the middle of the brace. Apply the clamps from the center outward, as shown in Fig. 7-33. Manipulate the clamps so the brace pushes firmly against the stub ends of the two soundhole braces.

LOWER FACE BRACES

Remove the clamping slat by pulling the tape off very slowly to avoid pulling up splinters. Replace it under the location of the short lower face brace, then under the longer brace, as they are glued in turn to the soundboard. The clamps are placed in an alternating fashion (Fig. 7-34) whenever possible to balance the clamping forces. The clamps can be removed after thirty minutes.

Step 8—Carving and Shaping the Upper and Lower Face Braces

LOWER FACE BRACES

Both braces will be ramped with the chisel, starting from a point that is in from each end by one-third of the brace's length. This leaves a flat plateau in the center, which is then tipped with flat strokes with a block plane so that it slopes down toward the template line. The highest point of the longer brace measures ½ inch from the soundboard. The highest point of the shorter brace is ⅜ inch from the soundboard (see Fig. 7-23).

Both braces are now sculpted with the chisel and sandpaper into a graceful, rounded shape with a parabolic cross section.

UPPER FACE BRACE

The upper face brace is planed in a curve from its maximum height in the middle to ¼ inch at both ends. The cross section will be parabolic, like the other braces, except it will be a thick, bulky parabola rather than a slender, elongated one. Final-shape and smooth with #100- and #120-grit garnet sandpaper.

Step 9—Gluing and Shaping the X-Brace

Tape the clamping slat to the soundboard under where the first glued X arm (the up-notch arm) is to lie. Do a dry run to select the clamps that will give the proper reach.

Interlock the two X-brace arms in their proper orientation. Apply a bead of yellow glue over the full length of the curved edge of the up-notch brace *only*. Do not get any glue on the down-notch brace or in the notch crevices. With a clean finger, spread the glue evenly, covering the entire brace surface and removing the excess. Wipe back the edges to lessen the amount of squeeze-out. Place the interlocked braces in place on the soundboard, and begin clamping with a short cam clamp reaching through the soundhole to the intersection. This first clamp is important, since it must pin the intersection down at the precise spot where the four arms comfortably abut the edges of the bridge patch and the ends of the soundhole braces. When everything seems aligned and stable, snug down the cam on the clamp.

Apply the rest of the clamps from the center out toward the ends of the brace. Before tightening down each clamp, push the brace against its stop. Manipulate the clamp closest to the stop in such a way that it drags the brace tightly against the stop. The other clamps should be upright and

balanced so they do not bend the free end of the brace. You may have to unclamp and re-clamp to coax the brace to its rightful place, so do not throw the cams fully until everything sits just like you want it.

After about forty-five minutes, remove the clamps and ease out the unglued down-notch brace. Reposition the clamping slat under where the down-notch brace is to be glued. Repeat the previous gluing steps on the down-notch brace, but with one addition: Wipe a thin film of glue on the notch walls of the lap-joint before clamping. Leave clamped for one hour.

The four arms are block-planed to a long, fair curve from their greatest height at the apex down to ³⁄₁₆ inch at the ends of the two upper arms and down to ⅛ inch at the ends of the two lower arms. The silhouette of the long arms shows them dropping slowly until they pass the bridge area, then dropping more quickly to the ⅛-inch ends. When planing the curve, start with short strokes at the end of the brace and follow with progressively lengthening strokes. The upright walls will be sculpted with the chisel so they form a parabolic cross section that is continuous down the full length of the brace. The apex area is not sculpted but left rectangular for ¾ inch in each direction.

Step 10—Final Graduation

After all the braces are shaped, the luthier makes further refinements as necessary to adjust the flexibility and resonance of the total system toward a familiar standard. We consider our steel-string soundboards ready for assembly when the resonances emitted by tapping are balanced; that is, when no strong fundamental note exists to overpower the accompanying chorus of partials. This we achieve by selective removal of material from the sides, rather than the tops of the X-brace arms and lower face braces. The brace's height is reduced only as a last resort, such as when the braces have been thinned and a strong fundamental resonance still persists. We stop just short of "loosening" the top all the way however: The last amount is left for the final soundboard scraping and smoothing steps that occur just before the finish is to be applied to the soundbox.

Clean and smooth all the soundboard undersurfaces with #220-grit garnet sandpaper.

Step 11—Gluing on the Centerseam Diamonds

Although we do not expect the centerseam to fail under normal conditions, we dread the prospect of a future centerseam repair since it is a particularly tricky and difficult operation due to the many braces that cross underneath. Therefore, for good measure, we support the longest lengths of unsupported seam with a small wooden stitch with its grain running *across* the centerseam; it is called a "diamond" (Fig. 7-35). The diamondlike, pyramidal shape results from trimming away all of its excess mass, leaving only the barest amount to perform its support function adequately.

Small (⅜-inch) square pieces of spruce about ⅛ inch thick are glued to the centerseam. Press the glued diamond in place with your thumb for about ninety seconds. It can be trimmed with a chisel and sanded smooth about twenty-five minutes later.

Step 12—The Linen Patch

The linen patch bridges the otherwise weaker up-notch arm of the X-brace. The apex of the X-brace is secured by applying two small crisscrossing strips of thin but tightly woven fabric that are saturated in glue. The strips, about ¾ inch long by ⅜ inch wide, are draped over the openings between the braces, forming an X of their own. Pat them against the walls and top of the junction with fingers moistened so they will not stick to the strips.

Step 13—Sawing Off the Top of the Soundboard

With a straight-edged piece of wood as a guide, saw a line tangent to the template line and approximately perpendicular to the centerline, using a dovetail saw as shown in Fig. 7-19.

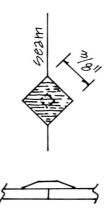

7–35. *Soundboard seam reinforcing "diamond."*

CHAPTER 8

Wood in its natural state is elastic to a degree. When bent within its limits, it will return to its original shape when released. If bent further, some permanent deformation will occur. Additional stressing will fracture the piece, soonest on the stretched convex face. When wood is treated with heat and moisture, however, it will become semi-plastic; its compressibility (and somewhat less so, its stretching ability) is substantially increased.

When the wood is bent, there is a theoretical line, called the neutral axis, along which no change in length occurs. In untreated wood, this axis is situated midway between the concave and convex surfaces; that is, as much wood is stretching above the line as is compressing below it. When the wood is treated with heat and moisture, the axis moves toward the convex surface because of increased compressibility. Much more wood is now compressing below the axis than is stretching above it. The convex face thus requires relatively little stretching; this fact allows the wood

Side Bending

to take a tighter bend before fracturing.

After bending with heat and moisture, the material must be held in restraint to prevent residual stresses from causing the piece to open out and return approximately to its original shape. "Setting" in the desired shape can be accomplished by drying and cooling the bent section while holding it in tension, a reversal of the heating and moistening process by which it was made semi-plastic.

Some timbers must be heat and moisture treated very carefully. Over-wetted curly maple may fracture at each figure when bent. Certain slats of mahogany, especially ribbon-striped and particularly dense or coarse-textured specimens, pucker or collapse easily if not expertly bent.

Ideally, straight-grained, clear material should be selected for bending, especially where the bend is most severe. Planes of weakness resulting from defects will cause fracturing even before straining has begun. Wood from near the core of the tree should be avoided. Builders should be wary of slats cut from trees with severely off-center cores, since they may contain tension wood that will distort when being wetted or dried.

In general, most of the temperate-zone hardwoods such as beech, maple, oak, and ash bend the easiest. Unfortunately, many of the tropical hardwoods used on good guitars are considered ill-suited for bending. Luthiers, therefore, must overcome this obstacle with skill and perseverence.

Over the centuries, guitarmakers have traditionally bent sides by pressing the wetted slats over the hot surface of an oval metal pipe placed like a chimney over a metal box containing hot charcoal. The subsequent development of electrical resistance coil heating and bottled gas has resulted in several modern variations on the theme. Modern hot pipes (also called "bending irons") vary widely: construction, heat sources, temperature controls, shapes, and sizes reveal the priorities and ingenuity of the builder. The choice of heat source (either electricity or gas) generally determines the type of pipe that can be used and the availability of different shapes and sizes. (See Figs. 8-1 and 8-2.)

To use electricity as a heat source, a ceramic heating-coil element (preferably cylindrical, rather than conical) is screwed to a heat resistant ceramic socket that has been mounted on an insulated backing board (Fig. 8-2). An on/off switch mounted on the top edge of the backboard will allow rudimentary heat control. More sophisticated temperature control can be obtained with the use of either a rheostat or a thermostat.

Gas pipes are simpler, since they require no temperature control device; a nozzle valve provides all the variable heat control that is necessary. The source of the gas flame can be a hardware store variety propane torch. The torch enters the backboard through a large hole that opens into the interior of the pipe. Several drilled holes or hacksaw cuts must be made into the pipe to allow air to flow into the torch noz-

8–1. *Gas-heated bending pipes, ovalled and round. The smaller diameters are used for tight bends. The baffles wedged in the mounted pipes prevent excessive heat loss.*

8–2. *Electrically heated bending pipe. The mounting board is protected with sheet asbestos. The pipe is shaped as an irregular oval to provide several bending radii.*

zle. The replaceable bottle is held in a cradle behind the backboard (See Fig. 8-1).

While gas heat has the advantage of a "built-in" temperature control, it also has a disadvantage. With a single flame source, the heat must be diffused by a thick-walled pipe to prevent the possibility of a "hot spot" on the iron which could burn the wood during bending. An electric heating element does not create this problem; it thus permits the use of thin-walled pipe such as steel conduit. This provides a measure of flexibility for the builder, as is seen below.

The simplest and cheapest bending iron is a thick-walled 3-inch diameter steel pipe segment about seven inches long, threaded on one end and screwed onto a 3-inch pipe flange that provides holes for mounting onto a backboard. The round cross section is adequate, but not ideal, since it contacts the side only along a thin line, rather than over a broad surface. For this reason, an oval pipe is better for most bends. Thick-walled pipe, however, is relatively difficult to squeeze into an oval shape. It requires a powerful mechanism such as a hydraulic press, or a

combination of pressure and high temperature heating. (We took ours to a scrap metal yard and had the crane operator drop the magnet onto it from a few inches up.) By contrast, thin-walled pipe can be pressed to an oval in a large vise. It also can be handled in relatively large diameters (e.g. 5 or 6 inches), where thick-walled pipe would become unwieldy.

With either conduit or thick-walled pipe, the oval cylinder can be sawn with a hacksaw on one end to produce two protruding tabs that can be heated with a torch, folded back at right angles to the pipe, and drilled through to become mounting brackets. A sheet-metal lid is used to enclose the opposite end of the pipe. The baffle retains heat and shields the operator. An electric pipe can have a tightly shut baffle, but a gas pipe must have a partially open baffle.

The student can begin by using either a gas or an electric pipe, simply choosing the one that is more convenient to make.

Our choice to bend sides over a hot pipe rather than in a bending mold allows us to use many different guitar templates. The expense of learning can be minimized by practicing with slats of any locally available hardwood rather than with mahogany or rosewood. Several hours of practice should give the beginner confidence to bend the actual sides that will go on the guitar.

SIDE-BENDING PROCEDURE

You will probably find bending guitar sides on a hot pipe the most challenging of all the techniques in this book. For this reason we urge that you read the whole chapter carefully and study the illustrations before attempting the procedure.

The hot-pipe-bending technique requires you to rally all of your senses and focus them on the experience: feeling the wood relax under your hands when it reaches the right temperature, listening for straining fibers and the popping of water on the hot iron, smelling the aroma of hot wood and sometimes the stench of burning wood, watching the graceful curve emerge while you match it to your template, even tasting the bitterness of disappointment if your impatience or inexperience causes a fracture on a fine set of sides!

You must master the wood by being sensitive to its natural limits. In few other woodworking experiences do you so directly *work* the wood with your bare hands. Before beginning, gently flex and probe the entire surface of each side blank. A small end-check may cause the whole blank to split dramatically when flexed during bending.

Study the template. Your success at capturing its outline in the bent wood depends on your familiarity with it. The two types of curves found most commonly are fair curves (sections of a circle) and accented curves. An accented curve is one that seems to have the force of a point straining to push it outward. A fair curve has no accent. Mentally subdividing the template into straight line segments, fair curves, and accented curves will help you during bending (Fig. 8-3).

Step 1—Preparation

Lay the sides out on your workbench, jointed edges together, show faces up. Mark with contrasting crayon as in Fig. 8-4 to denote an upper and lower bout on each. Remember that the sides *mirror* one another: It is very easy to forget the relationship of the bouts to the jointed edge and

8–3. *Templates can be subdivided into straight-line segments (S), sections of a circle (R indicates a radius to an imaginary center), and accented curves (ACC.).*

thus wind up bending two left or two right sides.

Fix your template to the workbench with clamps or double-faced tape or have a line showing the template outline drawn on the workbench or on a sheet of paper taped to the bench. The position of the template, along with the crayon reference marks, will remind you which way you are bending. The jointed edge will always be down, but one side will have the upper bout facing to your left while the other side will have the upper bout facing to your right, re-

distinguishing crayon marks

upper upper

jointed edges

rough - sawn edges

lower lower

8-4. *Marking the sides before bending.*

quiring an inversion of the template.

The sides can be soaked in any watertight container in which they can be laid flat. A 36-inch window planter makes an ideal soaking trough, but a bathtub with a couple of inches of water in it will work just as well. You may need to put a weight on the side while it soaks to keep it from floating on the surface.

Immersion time will vary slightly with side blank thickness, but for the usual range (.080 to .090 inch), ten to fifteen minutes in scalding tap water will suffice for rosewood. Mahogany and maple can soak for five to ten minutes. Soak one side and then bend it before soaking the other side.

Remove all encumbrances and place the bending iron and template conveniently close to one another. You will be bending and taking the piece off the pipe at intervals for comparison with your template.

Begin heating the pipe and checking its temperature. A good test for correct heat is to

sprinkle a few drops of water on the pipe. If they sit calmly or boil on the surface, the pipe is too cold. If the drops hop about, sizzling loudly, it is hot enough. If they instantly pop or vaporize, the pipe is too hot. If you find yourself burning the wood despite extreme care, it may be that your iron is too hot; if the wood does not respond to steady bending pressure, the iron may be too cold.

Step 2—Bending

Every builder has a personalized way of manipulating the wet side on the hot iron to get it to bend and remain bent. Basically, however, the process always involves feeding the side across the iron with one hand and applying bending pressure with the other (Fig. 8-5). The slower the feed and the greater the bending pressure, the tighter will be the curves. The hand applying bending pressure determines the angle at which the side leaves the pipe, and this too determines the curvature (Fig. 8-6).

The side can be advanced in short, hopping increments, rarely stopping in one place. Shorter and faster hops combined with a slow feed will produce tight curves, while longer, slower hops combined with a faster feed will produce broad, gentle curves. Or the luthier can begin by rolling the side over the pipe, pausing

8-5. *The initial bend. The side is advanced with one hand while bending pressure is applied with the other.*

8-7. *Bending pressure can be applied with one hand directly over the pipe, "wrapping" the side around it. We sometimes wear a work glove to protect the hand on top of the iron.*

momentarily to let it heat up and soften, applying pressure, moving, pausing, applying pressure, and so on, until the bend is steady and even.

In either case, it is necessary to have a sense of the wood giving under your hand in order to bend effectively. The closer your hands are to the point you are bending, the more control you have. We sometimes work with the bending hand "wrapping" the side right around the oval iron (see Fig. 8-7). Occasionally we use a cotton work glove on the bending hand if the side gets too hot to handle.

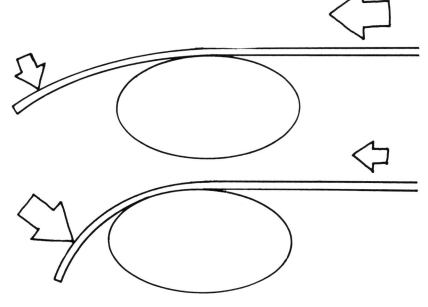

8-6. *The amount of pressure and the rate of feed determine the tightness of the curve.*

During the process, you are feeling for a change in the springiness of the material as heat is applied. As you advance the blank over the top surface of the oval pipe, the rate of feed must be matched to the rate at which the wood absorbs enough heat to become plastic—to "relax." You should attempt to feel this change in stiffness, for it is at this point that the best bending occurs. If you are not sensitive to this change, you may be applying pressure ineffectively. At best, the side will simply not take the bend; at worst, the side may crack. Gentle pressure at first will give you an idea of when and if the wood is going to relax in order to bend. You will feel it when it happens.

Pay attention to the heat of the iron. You must be listening very carefully at all times for any slight tearing sound which would indicate that the fibers are beginning to part. At the same time, be very cautious about leaving the piece on the iron for too long, because it will scorch and eventually burn. Although minor surface scorching is not a problem (it can eventually be scraped out), deep scorching may be permanent.

If you have mentally subdivided the template into simplified steps, deciding when and where to apply pressure is likewise simplified. At the end of each step you should take the piece away from the iron and wave it in the air to cool it and let it set in that position. You must maintain tension or the piece will not hold the desired shape. The pause is critical: The wood is setting at this time and the fibers are returning from a plastic to a rigid state in the new shape. If you relax tension here, the piece will return to a random shape and there will be no bending progress (Fig. 8-8).

It often helps to overbend slightly before moving to the next major section of the side. If, for example, the bend of

8–8. *Holding the side in tension while it cools to "set" the bend.*

8–9. *Checking the bend against a drawn template line.*

8–10. *Bending the waist. After bending the first bout (either upper or lower), making a mark where the waist must lie will help focus the bend in that area.*

the lower bout is brought inside the template at the waist, then when the waist is bent, the slight spring of the lower bout will bring it up to the template line.

Check the outside face of the side against the template line. (See Fig. 8-9.) You must judge the point on the unbent part of the side where a bend is going to begin (Fig. 8-10). Always begin the bend and then check to see that you are in the right spot before continuing. If you have to move a bend, simply change the focus of where you are bending. *At all times you should have a sense of where the focus of your bend must be* in order to duplicate

the template. That is where you must work the wood. By working that area you can gradually tighten the bend.

It takes practice to acquire a sense of where things have to move in order to duplicate the curve of your template at any given spot. This becomes even more critical if you overbend and have to unbend in some area. It can be tricky to spot where the overbend is located. You have to place the side on a template line and allow it to flex past where the overbend occurs (Figs. 8-11 and 8-12). Sometimes the area where the side appears to run off the template is not where you will find the overbend. The over-

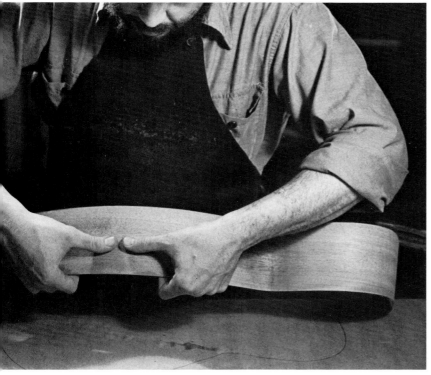

8–11 and 8–12. *Correcting an overbend. The wood can be spread slightly while it is still hot or, if cooled, it can be rocked for a few seconds on the iron at the focus of the overbend.*

bend may be located at one point but not manifest itself until farther along on the template. Eventually you will become sensitive to this. You may unbend an area and find that your focus is not in the proper place. Sometimes you unbend too much; you may, however, think that you have unbent too much when, in fact, you have simply unbent in the wrong spot. This is what practicing side bending is all about: learning to locate the spots. In truth, the feel for bending the wood is not as complex or difficult to master as the sensitivity to where bending pressure should be applied at any given time or where to unbend if you have overbent.

This proposition gains further significance because the more you have to bend and rebend, the more you begin to torture the wood. In the process, you risk severe flat spots, twisting, and possibly folding and kinking. If you make too many mistakes and guess poorly about the places to rectify your errors, the piece will take on a lumpy shape that you will not be able to correct.

Sometimes you may bend properly according to the template but wind up with a flat spot or kink anyway. This can occur if you have paused for too long on the pipe or made a movement too suddenly. It can also occur if you are working on too narrow an area of the iron for the bend you are trying to accomplish. If it does occur, it will be noticeable when the hand is passed over the side of the finished guitar. To remove a flat spot, work the side back and forth as if you had not bent it at all in the area; occasionally you will have to unbend it on either side of the flat and then work a curve gently back in. Removing a kink is similar, except that you will always have to unbend first.

If a few fibers tear or give way, you will probably hear it, and if you are sensitive, you will catch it before it becomes a split. Once you have a small

8–13. *Checking the finished bend against a template. The side must sit within ¹/₁₆ inch of the outline with only the gentlest pressure.*

tear, you must work the area very gently; if it begins to open up, you must stay away from the area entirely. A small split on the inside (such as at the waist) can, after the sides are completely bent, be filled with epoxy and scraped flush. Sometimes moderate tearing of surface fibers on the outside can be repaired by working glue into the fracture and pressing the fibers down with a clamp and a curved caul. Longitudinal cracks on straight-grain material can be closed by gentle clamping with glue and reinforcement from inside with a strip of tightly woven fabric saturated in white glue.

Minor scorching on the outside does not mean that the area can no longer be touched. Let it cool and make sure it is thoroughly wetted before bending again. You may ignore minor scorching on the inside.

The piece should not be assembled onto the instrument until it has had a chance to dry to the appropriate equilibrium moisture content, or EMC. (Overnight should be sufficient.) Because of the thin cross section of the slat, it is fully possible that it may change in shape while it dries. To prevent this, some builders will keep it clamped to a template line on the table until it is used. We simply touch it up dry on the hot pipe just before assembly, if and where its shape has changed.

Practice bending slats of scrap material before attempting to bend your sides. You will discover that the process is far simpler to do than to explain adequately. We have seen dozens of beginners in our courses succeed admirably on the first try.

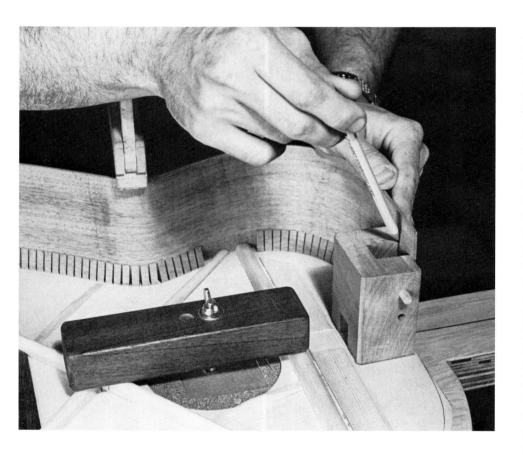

CHAPTER 9

At this stage we will use the parts that have been carefully glued and shaped (or bent) and begin the process of creating the soundbox enclosure. The steel-string soundbox is assembled here as a discrete unit, with the neck to be attached later; the classical guitar, built with a traditional (Spanish) headblock, will be assembled with the neck attached. Because the assembly process involves so many critical and complex procedures, we have divided it into two chapters. In this chapter, Assembly I, the classical neck is joined to the soundboard and the steel-string headblock is made and glued in place. On both guitars, the tailblock is made and glued to the soundboard, the top linings are made and glued to the sides, and the sides are glued in place along the template outline on the soundboard. In the next chapter, Assembly II, the back linings are glued to the sides and the back is braced, fitted to the exposed rim of the sides, and glued in place to enclose the soundbox.

As discussed in Chapter 3,

Assembly I

we do not use molds to assemble our guitars. Although free assembly (our method) may present a greater challenge than does assembly in a mold, we believe that in the long run the student's guitarmaking skills will be enhanced by gaining mastery over this construction technique. The student will soon discover that the ease or difficulty of free assembly is entirely dependent upon the care with which the parts to be assembled have previously been made.

PROCEDURE: CLASSICAL ONLY— GLUING THE SOUNDBOARD TO THE HEADBLOCK

This procedure is very simple and straightforward, but accuracy is crucial and mistakes are common—so read carefully and be certain you know what you are doing before you spread the glue.

The soundboard at this point is fully braced and carved, and the top of the guitar template outline is cut off

square. Centerlines drawn in soft pencil should be visible both on the neckshaft and on the show face of the soundboard.

Before the soundboard can be joined to the neck, a shelf must be cut into the top surface of the headblock to a depth equal to the thickness of the soundboard. When the soundboard is glued to the headblock, it will form a continuous flush surface with the neckshaft onto which the fingerboard will be glued.

The objective of this procedure is to glue the soundboard to the shelf in the headblock while aligning the centerline of the neck to the centerline on the soundboard.

TOOLS
wide chisel and small
   sanding board *or* hand-
   held router
long straightedge
hammer
³⁄₃₂-inch chisel

SUPPLIES
masking tape or double-
   faced tape
two ¾-inch wire brads
AR glue

IMPLEMENTS
caul, 1½ × 2 × (at least) 1
   inch thick

Step 1—Cutting a Shelf into the Top of the Headblock

The depth of this shelf *must* be very close to the thickness of your soundboard. Cutting the shelf very slightly shallow is not a major problem, as the top can be scraped flush to the surface of the shaft when the fingerboard is ready to be glued down. If the shelf is cut too deeply, however, it will have to be built back up with a veneer.

Draft a line around the headblock the same distance from its top surface as the thickness of your soundboard. Work around the block with a chisel, shaving from the edge to form a peak in the middle of the block, and then very carefully shave off the peak until you have a level shelf. (See Fig. 9-1.) Shave back the web between the headblock and the shaft so that the soundboard can rest easily against the back wall of the shelf. The surface must be level, so work slowly and carefully. If necessary, clean it up with a sanding block, but *do not* mar the end-grain face of the heel.

Alternate: This step can also be done with the hand router. Make a few test cuts with a straight bit, ensuring that the depth of cut does not exceed the thickness of your soundboard. Mount the neck blank firmly in the vise and rest the router on the head-block with the bit overhanging the end. *Important:* Work from

the end backward toward the shaft, stopping at the web between the headblock and the heel (Fig. 9-2). Shave back the web with a chisel.

Step 2—Alignment

Clamp the neck in a vise, closing the jaws on the head-block. Lay the long ruler along the centerline of the neckshaft and secure it (just well enough so that it does not slide around) with masking tape or double-faced tape. Slide the soundboard under the ruler until it touches the back wall of the headblock shelf. Align its centerline with the ruler and hold it in place at the headblock. Press a brad into the soundboard over the block and tap it in about halfway. *Do not* let go of the top—it must be supported at one end or the other.

With the brad in place, support the soundboard at the tail with one hand and check the alignment of the centerlines along the edge of the ruler (Fig. 9-3). The two centerlines must both be parallel and adjacent to the ruler edge. If not, pull out the brad and start over.

Step 3—Gluing the Soundboard to the Headblock

Remove the ruler and pull out the first position brad. Apply glue to the heelblock shelf and place the soundboard back onto it. Press the brad back through its hole in the soundboard and into its hole in the headblock shelf. Keep supporting the tail of the soundboard with one hand. Tap the first brad down almost but not quite all the way (leave enough to grab with pliers). Align the centerlines with the ruler again and tap in the second brad about halfway (Fig. 9-4). Check one last time—the ruler should line up within about $1/32$ inch of the center-lines at all points. If you got it right, knock both brads home (add a third if you like) and clamp, using the headblock caul. (See Figure 9-5.) If you did not get it right, pull out the second brad and try again. If you realize at this point that your first brad is in the wrong place, pull it out, clean up the glue with a scraper, and do the whole thing over again.

9–1. Cutting a shelf for the soundboard into the classical guitar headblock.

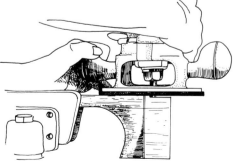

9–2. Using a router to cut the headblock "shelf" (classical only).

9–3. *Checking the alignment of the soundboard centerline to the neckshaft centerline. A few pieces of double-faced tape on the neckshaft help to hold the ruler steady.*

9–4. *Tapping in the second positioning brad.*

9–5. *Clamping the soundboard to the headblock. The caul over the soundboard is about the same dimension as the headblock.*

Step 4—Cleaning Glue Squeeze-out

Remove the clamp after thirty minutes and turn the neck/soundboard assembly upside down on the workboard, securing it through the soundhole with the workboard shoe. (Do not use the paper/cork assembly shim just yet.) With the 3/32-inch chisel or a sliver of wood or other suitable tool, clean up the glue squeeze-out inside the slots. You may need to shine a light directly into the slots to see what is in there. Make sure any glue or debris is removed so that the ends of the sides will slide easily into the slots.

PROCEDURE: STEEL-STRING ONLY— PREPARING AND GLUING THE MORTISED HEADBLOCK

This procedure entails making a headblock with a vertical mortise in it, which will eventually accept the neck tenon. We will also be fabricating a small cutting device here which will shave two blanks into accurate taper pins.

The mortised headblock will be drilled to accept these taper pins. The taper pins will eventually secure the neck tenon tightly to the mortised headblock and thus attach the neck to the soundbox securely, yet will allow future disassembly.

TOOLS
pencil
square
6-inch ruler
dovetail saw or table saw
1/2-inch chisel
rasp
hand drill or drill press
7/32-inch drill bit (preferably with a brad point)
#4 taper machinist's reamer
glue chisel
tool-steel spokeshave blade or scraper blade (see Step 5)

SUPPLIES
#120- and #220-grit garnet sandpaper

MATERIALS
2 × 2½ × 3⅝-inch hardwood block, preferably mahogany
6 × 1½ × 2-inch hardwood block
⅜ × ⅜-inch hardwood lengths; several 4 inches long

Step 1—Cutting the Mortise

The headblock can be a single-piece solid block or it can be a stacked or laminated block, made up of smaller pieces glued together (for grain orientation and dimensions, see Fig. 9-6). In either case, the walls of the block should be well squared to each other.

Saw the headblock down to length, producing in the process a wedge-shaped cutoff segment as the drawing illustrates. Save this segment, since it will facilitate gluing the headblock later on.

Next, mark two parallel lines 3/4 inch apart centered on one of the large faces, denoting where the cuts for the vertical mortise must be. With a dovetail saw, make the two cuts (assisted by additional squared marks on the top and bottom) 1 inch deep into the block. Chisel the waste out between the cuts. Shave or rasp the saw marks off the mortise walls. If you have a table saw, slot the mortise out with successive passes of the circular blade.

Step 2—Sizing the Mortise

Since the headblock mortise and neck tenon are *not* to be eventually glued together, we will aim for an easy fit between the two. Removing material from either the mortise or tenon in a balanced manner with sandpaper, rasp, or chisel will allow a sliding fit between the two. A sloppy, rattling fit, if such occurs, is undesirable since it diminishes the shock resistance of the joint.

Step 3—Notching the Headblock

A gap to allow clearance and access to the truss rod adjusting nut is cut out of the *back wall* of the mortise with several saw cuts. (See Fig.

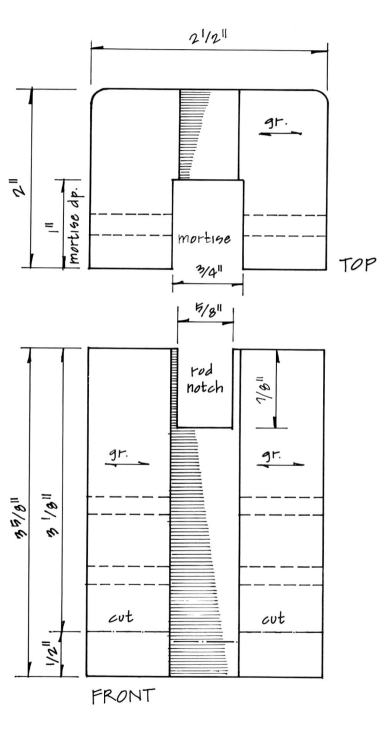

9-6.) The waste portion is chiseled out and its walls are shaved or rasped clean (we cut out the headblock notch with a bandsaw). Finally, round the vertical corners on the unmortised face of the headblock with a plane or rasp. Sand all the exposed surfaces for a neat appearance.

Step 4—Drilling the Headblock

Spot and drill two ⁷⁄₃₂-inch holes clear through the end-grain face of the headblock in the locations shown in Fig. 9-6. A drill press is best for this, since the holes must be drilled squarely to the end-

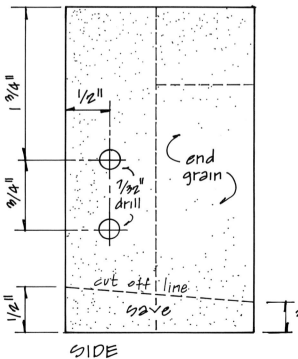

9–6. *The mortised headblock, three views (steel-string).*

grain faces of the headblock. Lacking such a tool, however, you can do an adequate job by spotting accurately on both opposite end-grain faces and, with a hand drill, drilling in from both sides toward the mortise opening; do this rather than trying to drill straight through from one side to the other. You may use a standard $7/32$-inch conical-tip drill bit, but a brad-point bit is best.

Step 5—Making a Taper-pin Cutting Device

In order to produce smooth, accurately tapered pins that will fit into the (later-to-be) tapered holes of the headblock, a taper-pin cutter must first be made.

Start with a hardwood block cut to 6 × $1\frac{1}{2}$ × 2 inches. Drill a $3/16$-inch diameter hole $1\frac{1}{2}$ inches from one end,

through the block's side as shown in Fig. 9-7.

Obtain a #4 taper machinist's reamer, available from tool stores or industrial supply houses. Ream the hole in the block by twisting the reamer until the narrow end of the tool emerges out the opposite end and opens an exit hole just $\frac{1}{4}$ inch in diameter.

One corner of the block is sawn away as shown in Fig.

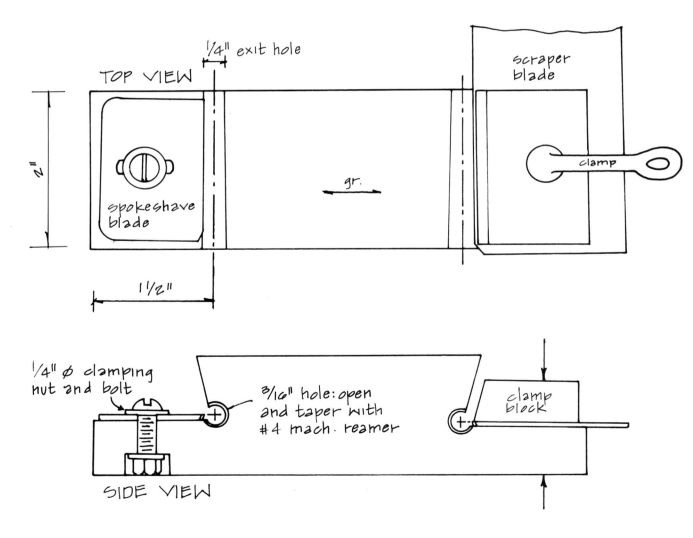

9-7. Taper-pin-cutting device. This diagram shows alternate cutter arrangements.

9-7, resulting in a bed for the cutter blade and an opening for wood chips to escape. Drill a ¼-inch diameter hole in the center of the bed. A clamp bolt that secures the cutter blade will eventually be inserted through this hole.

An ideal cutter blade is a replacement spokeshave blade, available from mail-order tool houses or large hardware stores. The blade works best if ground to a scraper bevel, about 60 degrees. The blade usually comes with a central hole that will allow us to bolt it down to the bed. Alternatively, a scraper blade can also serve as a cutter: the thicker and stiffer, the better. You can secure the scraper to the bed with a clamp and a clamp-block, which keeps it from flexing away from the workpiece as it cuts. Whichever blade you use, the cutter bed must be shaved down or built up with veneer so that the edge of the cutter lines up with the centerline of the reamed hole. To check, extend the cutter blade into the hole and observe if its edge bisects the curved hole wall.

and even-textured. Grind or whittle the first 3 inches into a blunt, elongated cone shape. To adjust the cutter, place the reamer into the hole. Set the blade so it just touches the reamer along its length. Clamp the blade down tightly and remove the reamer. Insert the tip of the conical blank into the hole and twist, exerting only a little inward pressure: The blank should slowly and easily find its way deeper into the hole. If the piece resists entry, whittle the blank down a bit more to help it along. If your fingers get sore, turn the end of the blank with pliers. The first pin should be tested in a reamed hole drilled right into the cutter body (Fig. 9-8). If the pin enters and emerges from the tapered hole with no visible gaps, the pin is fine. If not, readjust the cutter and try again on another blank. When two good, smooth taper pins result, cut them off the blank and into 2-inch lengths in such a way that the narrow end is ¼ inch in diameter. Finally, the ends must be chamfered as shown in Fig. 9-9.

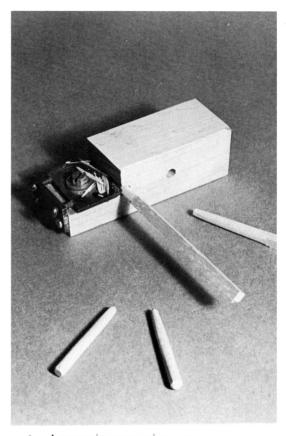

9–8. A taper-pin cutter using a replacement spokeshave blade. The hole in the hardwood block has been reamed to the correct dimension for checking the taper of each pin. This cutter has been improved by the addition of small adjusting screws for the cutter blade.

Step 6—Making the Taper Pins

Start with a 4-inch length of ⅜ × ⅜-inch hardwood. (We usually make the pins out of rosewood and take advantage of its great strength and hardness, but rock maple is an adequate substitute.) The grain of the blank should be straight

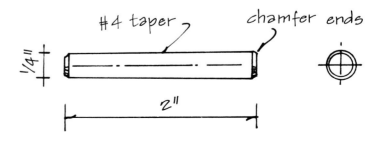

9–9. A typical hardwood taper pin (two are required).

9–10. *Fitting taper pins into the headblock.*

9–11. *Gluing mortised headblock. Note that the tapered piece cut off from the headblock is used to square the clamping caul.*

Step 7—Fitting the Pins into the Headblock

The holes in the headblock must be tapered with the #4 taper reamer in order to accept the two taper pins. The pins must be made to enter, one from each side of the headblock, one above the other and to the proper depth, as follows: Twist the reamer into the hole one or two turns at a time, and keep trying the pins for fit, pushing them in *gently* each time until they just stop. (Since the hole is shaped precisely like the pin, the pin will grab and tighten if pushed in with force. You may then have some trouble extracting it for further reaming.) Stop reaming when the tip of the pin goes about ³⁄₁₆ inch into the second cheek of the mortise. (See Fig. 9-10.)

Mark the pins and block so you will not forget which pin belongs in which hole. Store the pins away safely until they are needed.

Step 8—Gluing the Headblock to the Soundboard

The forwardmost line of the headblock outline has already been drawn precisely square to the soundboard centerline. Secure the soundboard and workboard shoe (but not the cork assembly shim) in place on the assembly workboard and clamp the workboard overhanging the edge of the table. Retrieve the wedge-shaped headblock cutoff segment.

Apply enough glue to the "down" end of the headblock (the end interrupted by the truss rod cutout). Place the glued end down on the soundboard inside its outline. Press it down firmly. Carefully remove the glue squeeze-out with a pointed stick or glue chisel if it obscures the crucial forwardmost line. Place the wedge-shaped cutoff segment back on top of the headblock in its original position: It will provide a flat surface that facilitates clamping. Align the block and apply a single bar clamp as shown in Fig. 9-11. Keep readjusting the clamp and headblock until the headblock sits accurately within the outline. Only moderate pressure is necessary. Wipe away squeeze-out with a glue chisel, and let dry for forty-five minutes.

TECHNICAL NOTE ON TAILBLOCKS

The most commonly used materials for tailblocks (also called end-blocks) are spruce, basswood, and mahogany. For most classicals, spruce or basswood is chosen for its light weight; mahogany is used almost universally on steel-strings. Any of the three, however, can be used on any guitar. We generally use basswood on classicals and mahogany on steel-strings, favoring these two over spruce because of their greater shock resistance.

Grain orientation in tailblocks is a subject of some controversy, but it is our emphatic view that the grain should run horizontally—that is, parallel to the grain of the sides. Running the grain longitudinally (that is, perpendicular to the grain of the sides) provides the advantage of discouraging splits from traveling around the sides in the event of bottom impact (a problem on steel-string guitars having end pins); however, this design has serious shortcomings that, we believe, outweigh its advantage. With the tailblock grain running longitudinally, the soundboard and back must be glued to end-grain, producing an inherently weak joint. Moreover, the end of the tailblock must be planed prior to fitting the back, and planing end-grain is an annoying task that can result in damage to the tailblock or to the sides.

A compromise often found on production steel-string guitars is a cross-grain block into which is inlaid a long-grain splice.

The face of the tailblock that is glued to the sides must conform accurately to the bottom of the outline, which may be either flat or curved. The *interior* face of the tailblock is sometimes rounded, especially on classical guitars, but we use a flat inner face for ease of clamping, rounding the exposed corners only.

Dimensions for tailblock blanks are given in the procedure following.

PROCEDURE: MAKING AND INSTALLING THE TAILBLOCK

For this procedure, the soundboard must be secured to the assembly workboard with the long bolt and shoe. The paper/cork shim made along with the assembly workboard, however, will not be put to use until the next procedure.

TOOLS
small square
cam clamp
sanding board

MATERIALS
tailblock blank, ¾ × 3 × 4 inches (SS), ½ × 2½ × 3¾ inches (CL)

SUPPLIES
AR glue

9-12. *Arching the classical tailblock. Rocking the tailblock while stroking up and down imparts the curve; this stance helps maintain the straightness of the longitudinal plane of the tailblock.*

Step 1—(Classical Only): Arching the Block

This can be done either on a belt sander or on the sanding board. Note that the arch is rather slight; you must check it against the outline frequently as you progress. If you reduce the block below ⅜ inch at its thickest point, you must throw it out and start over. This is one of the few times using the sanding board in which we deliberately use a back-and-forth motion (Fig. 9-12), since, for a change, we are not trying to avoid curving the surface.

When arching the tailblock,

it is critical to keep the curved surface straight in the longitudinal plane. Check with a straightedge as you work, and when the arch is right, check again. Also try to keep the arched face as parallel as possible to the flat (interior) face. Do not worry if it does not come out perfectly parallel, though, because we square the bottom end to the *curved* face of the tailblock only.

Step 2—Marking the Soundboard for Tailblock Position

Use the block to draw a positioning line on the soundboard. The line should be parallel to and ³⁄₃₂ inch from the bottom of the outline, bisected by the centerseam. The classi-

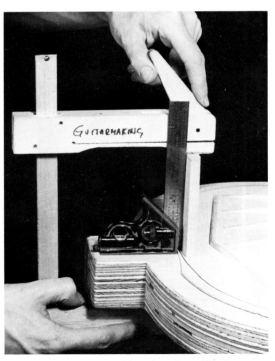

9-13. Clamping the tailblock.

cal block will leave a curved line; the steel-string block will be positioned along a straight line.

After marking, use #100-grit garnet sandpaper to round the vertical corners of the interior face of the block.

Step 3—Squaring the Bottom End

The end of the tailblock that will be glued to the soundboard must be square to the face (the *exterior* face) that will be glued to the sides.

Stand the tailblock on a flat surface and check to see if the exterior face is square to the bottom end. Try both ends; note the better end and mark the opposite end "up."

If the better end is actually square to the exterior face, it is ready to be glued to the soundboard. If not, take the block to the sanding board and work the bottom end with short strokes until the exterior face is square when the tailblock stands on the bottom end.

Just because you have squared the bottom end, it will not necessarily glue down square to the soundboard—with the glue squeezing out all around, you would not notice a slight tipping until it is too late. Thus, we must check with a square while gluing, and use a little maneuver with a cam clamp to ensure that pressure is being applied squarely.

Note: In order to bring the square up to the tailblock, it

may be necessary to remove a small segment of the excess soundboard material at the bottom of the outline. It can either be cut off at a tangent with a dovetail saw or trimmed with successive passes using a razor knife.

Apply glue to the bottom end of the tailblock. Locate the block on the soundboard at the positioning line you drew in Step 2. Apply gentle pressure with a cam clamp and then check with the small square sitting upright on the tail of the workboard. If it is not right, you can adjust the angle by gently manipulating the *bottom* of the cam clamp forward or backward (Fig. 9-13).

When it is right, tighten the clamp and check again. If it is wrong now, loosen the clamp, readjust, and tighten. When it checks out okay with the clamp tightened down, you are done.

PROCEDURE: TRIMMING THE SIDES TO LENGTH

Before the sides are glued to the soundboard, they must be trimmed to length at the head-block and tailblock. On the steel-string guitar this procedure is very simple, because the sides can be clamped at the waist and permitted to overlap the headblock and tailblock for marking prior to trimming. On the classical, the procedure is slightly more complex because the end of the upper bout of each side is stopped by the web between the heel slots; thus, the ends must be nibbled away gradually to ensure a proper fit.

During this procedure, the accuracy of the side bend is put to the test. During marking and trimming, the sides must align to the template outline within 1/16 inch at all points. Since they are flexible, they can be manipulated somewhat with clamps to make them conform to the outline, but if they require forcing into position at this point, many undesirable consequences will follow during the actual assembly procedures. Thus, before beginning this procedure, compare the jointed edges of your sides to the template. If they do not conform to the template with gentle pressure, they can be touched up (dry) on a hot bending pipe.

The paper/cork workboard shim made along with the workboard in Chapter 3 must be installed between the workboard and the soundboard at this point. The shim supports the soundboard edges, which are raised from the workboard by the curvature of one or more soundboard braces. It enables us to put firm downward pressure on the soundboard edges, a necessary part of gluing down the sides, without flattening the soundboard arch or distorting its perimeter. Some builders hollow their workboards to accomplish the same end, but we believe that the

shim is an easier, more foolproof method.

TOOLS
machinist's square
contrasting pencil
dovetail saw
cam clamps

Step 1—Installing the Workboard Shim

Remove the soundboard (and neck, if attached) from the workboard. Place the shim on the workboard, lining up the centerlines and bolt holes of both. Push the bolt through the workboard and the paper backing of the shim.

Important: On the classical, place the additional Masonite neck shim down before reclamping the neck to the workboard. On the steel-string, two small extra pieces of 1/16-inch cork material must be glued to the paper backing along its centerline: one beneath where the upper face brace will lie and one beneath where the apex of the X-brace will lie. These will permit tightening of the wingnut on the shoe without distortion of the soundboard.

Return the soundboard to the workboard and align its centerline to those of the workboard and shim. Secure the soundboard by tightening the wingnut down on the shoe.

Step 2—Trimming the Sides to the Template

Place the template against

the interior face of the bent side and mark where it begins and ends. Draw a guideline across the side at each of these points using the square against the jointed edge. Also mark the side at the waist where the notch in the template falls, and draw an additional line across at that point on the *exterior* face. Repeat with the other side.

On the steel-string, trim the sides to the guidelines with a band saw or dovetail saw. On the classical, the lower bouts can be trimmed to the marking lines, but the upper bouts should be trimmed back 1/8 inch farther from the ends. Draw additional squared guidelines before making these cuts.

Step 3—Classical Only: Trimming the Upper Bout

Take one side to the soundboard, insert the end of the upper bout into the heel slot, and align the mark at the waist on the outline. When inserted into the heel slot, the upper bout will bulge out past the outline (Fig. 9-14). Take note of this bulge and try to estimate exactly how much must be removed for the side to align properly to the outline while still going all the way into the slot. (*Note:* If the fit of the side to the slot is too tight, sand down the side thickness a little at a time until it slides in easily.)

Mark a new trimming guideline on the interior face of the side as far back from

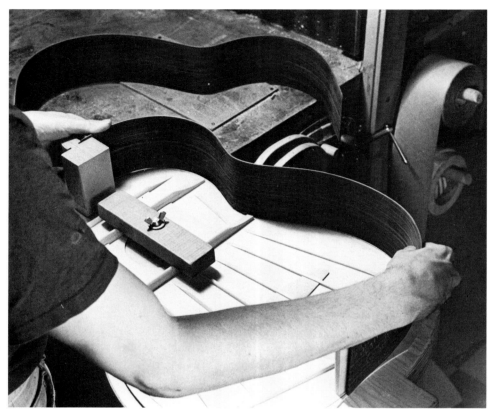

9-14. Fitting the side. The upper bout must be gradually nibbled away until it rests comfortably inside the outline.

make a mark ⅛ inch shy of the soundboard centerline. Remove the side and draw a guideline with a square. Trim both ends back to the guidelines.

CLASSICAL

With the end of the upper bout in the heel slot and the upper bout correctly aligned, clamp the side to the soundboard at the waist. Use a cam clamp with pressure sufficient to hold the side down but not so much that the side is distorted. Then, using one or two cam clamps, align the lower bout to the outline, letting its end overlap the tailblock. Make a mark about ⅛ inch shy of the soundboard centerline. Remove the side, draw a guideline at that mark with a square on the jointed edge, and trim back to the line.

the end as you estimate will need to be removed. Cut off about half that amount with a dovetail saw (we use a belt sander to remove the material), and check the fit again. Continue to nibble away at the end until the upper bout fits properly. Repeat for the other side.

It is important to be aware during this step that a misbent upper bout may produce an illusion of excess length when in fact the trim is correct. Obviously, then, this step cannot be done accurately if the sides do not reasonably match the template.

Step 4—Finish Trimming

STEEL-STRING

Align the mark on the waist of the side to the mark at the waist on the outline, and use a cam clamp with gentle pressure to hold it in place. Align the upper and lower bouts to the outline, using one or two cam clamps for each, letting the upper bout end overlap the headblock and the lower bout end overlap the tailblock. Reach into the headblock mortise with a pencil and draw a guideline on the inner face of the side where it intersects the mortise wall. At the tailblock,

LININGS

Linings are strips of wood that increase the effective thickness of the sides where they meet the soundboard and back. Without the linings, the gluing area of this seam would be inadequate to withstand the strain of string tension and the guitar would eventually pull apart. The linings also keep the guitar's edges together while being routed for purfling and binding, and they lend support and rigidity to the connection between the top and side plates.

The earliest plucked-string instruments antecedent to the guitar used no linings. Sidewall thicknesses were great (about ¼ inch) because the back/side shell was hollowed from a thick plank of wood. The earliest linings were glue-soaked strips of fabric smoothed into the interior corners of the side seams (Fig. 9-15).

Modern linings are applied in three forms: as solid linings, kerfed linings, or individual block linings (lining chips, or *tentellones*).

A solid lining is a long, continuous strip prebent to conform precisely to the side's contour.

A kerfed lining is a continuous strip deeply slotted cross-grain at close intervals, allowing it to conform to the side's contour *without* the need for prebending.

When individual blocks are used instead of continuous strips, the side is secured, unglued, to the soundboard by means of a mold or, in free assembly, with clamps; then, short segments, or chips, sawn off a continuous lining strip are glued in one by one.

The great classical guitar-makers experimented with combinations of these three lining forms. A guitar that we restored, built in 1863 by Antonio de Torres, used spruce tentellones against the top and kerfed-mahogany lining against the back. Hermann Hauser, who so closely emulated Torres, chose nonetheless on some instruments to use solid basswood lining against both the top and back. The configuration most often found on classical guitars is kerfed or chipped linings against the top and solid linings against the back.

Lining materials most often selected on better classical guitars are basswood, spruce, and mahogany. We have also seen Western red cedar and Spanish cedar used as solid lining material on several guitars built by experienced Spanish builders.

Basswood *(Filia americana)* is a light, easy-working material. It is commonly regarded as nonacoustic; that is, its use would serve to isolate rather than couple resonances of adjacent plates. Basswood's cousin, European lime *(Filia vulgaris)* is widely used in Great Britain and Europe. It displays somewhat better bending properties than basswood. Mahogany is denser than basswood and can act as a resonant coupler. It is not commonly used for solid linings because it is not as easily carved; rather, it is preferred for use in preshaped kerfed linings. Spruce is seen most often in the form of tentellones against the soundboard.

Modern steel-string flat-top guitars show less variation than classical guitars in the types of linings they use. Kerfed-mahogany linings of equal size are used in the preponderance of cases, against both the top and the back. Basswood is seen on some older production arch-top guitars. Poplar linings can be found on many cheap, old steel-string guitars.

SIDE-ASSEMBLY PROCEDURES

The following procedures for gluing the sides to the soundboard are essentially identical for the steel-string and the classical guitar. We use a kerfed lining that is glued to the sides before they are glued to the soundboard. As noted in the discussion of linings, however, many great classical guitar builders use individual blocks, or tentellones, glued in one by one to attach the sides to the soundboard.

The major difference between using a continuous lining strip and using individual blocks is relative complexity. To use a kerfed lining, the strip first must be manufac-

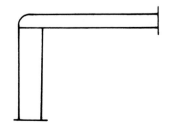
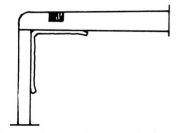

9-15. Details of edge-gluing methods: Medieval and sixteenth-century Orpharion.

tured and glued to the side, and then cut out in the areas where the ends of the major structural braces travel to the template outline. Individual blocks, however, may be simply glued along the junction between the side and the soundboard, skipping over the spaces where the brace ends meet the sides. Also, gluing a lined edge requires deft manipulation of a large number of clamps and cauls, while individual blocks can be glued in a leisurely manner.

The individual-block method, however, is rather te-dious. Although using a continuous lining involves more steps, we have found it a less time-consuming process if lining materials are prepared at one time in sufficient quantities to make several guitars. Because we are practiced in the procedures required for assembly using continuous linings, we have no difficulty with its complexities and can therefore make maximum use of its efficiencies.

We suggest that students read the following kerfed-lining assembly procedures carefully and study the photographs and diagrams. Those in doubt about their ability to execute the assembly of lined sides should return to the following individual-block method as a valid alternative for either the steel-string or the classical guitar.

Individual-block Assembly

Students using this method are assumed to have read all the remaining procedures in this chapter. Before beginning, the sides must be accurately fitted per the foregoing procedure, Trimming the Sides to Length.

The blocks, or chips, can be cut from a lining strip faceted as in Step 1 of the following procedure, Making Kerfed Linings. Simply cut all the way through the lining strip rather than stopping at the web. The blocks should be about ⅜ inch wide. The jointed edge of the side is placed down on the soundboard, aligned at the waist marks, and clamped along the outline as in Fig. 9-16. The side is glued to the tailblock (also to the headblock on the steel-string; on the classical, the upper-bout end is inserted dry into the heel slot) as described in the procedure, Gluing Down the Lined Sides (page 205). AR glue is then applied to each individual block, and it is pressed into the corner and held with one hand for thirty to sixty seconds, with the other hand supporting the side as in the photo.

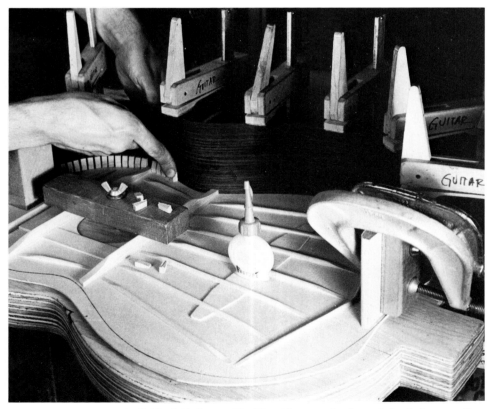

9–16. *Individual block assembly. The sides must be clamped firmly but not distorted by clamping pressure. The bottom jaw of each clamp is manipulated to ensure that the side sits squarely at all points. The blocks are held in place for thirty to sixty seconds.*

When lining blocks are glued all around on both sides, the sides will be securely anchored to the soundboard. To complete this part of the soundbox assembly, turn to page 207, Gluing "Feet" at the Brace Ends, and follow the steps therein.

PROCEDURE: MAKING KERFED LININGS

To make lining strips sufficiently flexible to bend around the edge of a guitar side, they must be partially cut through (kerfed) across the grain at equal intervals. The remaining uncut portion (which holds the flexible strip together) is called the web. The web must be thick enough to maintain the strip's integrity when flexed, but thin enough to permit bending in an unsteamed condition around the small radius curves found on guitar waists. We use a web of about 1/64 inch on our kerfed linings.

The web must be quite uniform in order to equally divide bending stresses at each kerf. If one web is thinner than the others, the strip will fold and pop at that point, rather than taking a continuous curve. Thus we provide a simple system in the hand procedure below that ensures a uniform web by stopping each saw cut at the same depth.

We typically use mahogany linings on steel-string guitars and basswood linings on classical guitars. The material need not be quarter-sawn, but it should be straight-grain and even-textured.

For the following procedure, it is best to use a dovetail saw that cuts about an .035-inch kerf. Most dovetail saws cut kerfs in that range. Kerfs of that size should be spaced about 1/4 inch apart; if you use a finer kerf, the cuts should be a little closer together.

Note: Finished kerfed-lining strips can be obtained from various luthier-supply houses. Students using the following procedure must cut or obtain table-sawn strips of the dimensions listed below.

TOOLS
dovetail saw
scraper blade(s)
block plane
ruler

MATERIALS
(SS): mahogany strip(s), 1/4 × 3/4 inch, to total 128 inches in length (64 inches for top linings and 64 inches for back linings to be used in Chapter 10)
(CL): basswood strip(s), 3/16 × 5/8 inch, to total 56 inches in length

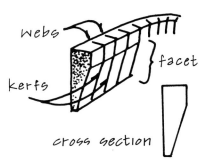

9–17. Modern kerfed lining.

IMPLEMENTS
scrap blocks (see Step 2 below)

SUPPLIES
double-faced tape

Step 1—Cutting the Facet

The kerfed linings will not be rectangular in cross section, but rather will appear as in Fig. 9-17 when finished.

Using double-faced tape, attach the rectangular strip to the workbench. Shave a corner with a block plane, using a long, smooth stroke. When the bevel reaches about 1/8 inch from the bench, tape a long ruler down about 1/2 inch away from the beveled edge. Continue planing at about a 30-degree angle until the corner of the plane meets the edge of the ruler. Use the ruler to guide the plane for a few strokes to make the facet even. Stop when you have about 1/4 inch of unfaceted surface remaining.

Step 2—Cutting the Kerfs

You must fashion a stop block that is about 1/64 inch higher than the maximum depth that your dovetail saw will cut. Any hardwood scrap will do, and you can use scrapers or whatever as shims to adjust the height of the block until it is right. (See Fig. 9-18.)

The strip is laid on the work surface and pressed up against the block. Make a mark or saw cut about ¼ inch away from the block to gauge the spacing of the cuts. Bring the end of the strip out to that mark and cut with the saw flush to the block as shown, until the saw backing stops the cut. Bring the saw down as level as possible. Register the first slot to the spacer mark and cut again. The web left by the cuts should be about ¹⁄₆₄ inch. If it is not right, readjust the height of the block. Continue until the whole strip is kerfed. It should be very flexible when finished.

If you have a radial arm saw, this step can be done with a very fine plywood blade. Simply adjust the saw to cut almost but not quite through, make a spacer mark, and proceed.

9–18. *Making kerfed lining by hand. The guide block is raised or lowered with shims (a scraper blade is used here) so that the saw will stop cutting about ¹⁄₆₄ inch from going through the piece. Note the spacing mark on the cutter platform.*

PROCEDURE: APPLYING KERFED LINING TO SIDES AND PREPARING FOR ASSEMBLY

The kerfing strips are glued to the sides using small spring clamps. Clothespins with stiff springs will do if butted very close together during gluing, but spring clamps (twenty-two to twenty-four ¾-inch clamps will do a side) are much stronger. We think they are worth the investment. If you do not wish to buy a full complement of spring clamps and you do not mind the extra time required, you can buy about a dozen and glue the kerfing in sections. For the solid back lining on the classical, however, you will need to do the whole strip at once.

After the kerfed linings are in place, they will be leveled and then notched out to make room for the brace ends.

TOOLS
spring clamps or clothespins
sanding board
¼-inch chisel
pencil
scraper

MATERIALS
kerfed lining strips totaling about 64 inches (SS) or about 56 inches (CL)

SUPPLIES
AR glue

Step 1—Marking for Kerfed Linings

Position the fitted side on the template line (insert into the heel slot for the classical) and mark where the headblock and tailblock intersect the inner face of the side. These marks will be the boundaries for the kerfed lining.

Step 2—Gluing on the Kerfing

The important thing to remember in this step is that the kerfing must not drop below the edge of the side at any point. It should be as flush to the edge as possible, but it is better to err in favor of leaving the kerfed lining high rather than being in a position where you must remove some of the side to get the lining flush. We jointed a common edge on the sides back in Chapter 5 so that the side would be glued on in a flat plane; that plane must be maintained.

With the foregoing in mind, take a lining strip and apply a film of glue to the flat side (Fig. 9-19). Beginning at the boundary mark on the upper bout, clamp the kerfing onto the side. Work from one end of the strip to the other, keeping it as close to flush as possible but never letting it drop below the side edge (Fig. 9-20). When the first strip is glued, measure a second strip on the lower bout and cut it off where it meets the boundary mark at the tailblock. Then glue it in place, starting at the end of the first strip and working around to the tail. Glue

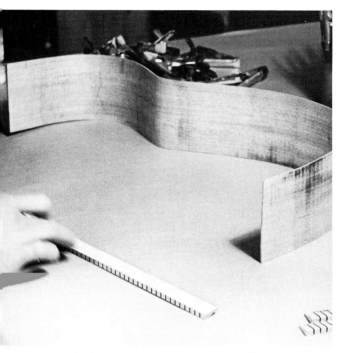

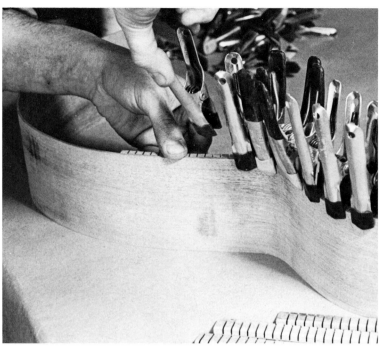

9-19. *Applying glue to kerfed lining strip. Note starting mark on side at headblock location.*

9-20. *Gluing the kerfing with spring clamps. The thumb is used as a guide to keep the strip flush to the edge of the side.*

squeeze-out from below the lining should be cleaned up with the corner of a scraper blade when leather hard.

Step 3—Leveling the Lined Edge

When the glue is hard, remove the spring clamps and knock off large squeeze-out beads from the edge with a glue chisel. If the kerfing is high in spots, plane it down close to the side edge, but try not to remove any side material.

The kerf-lined edge of the side must be leveled on the sanding board. Strive to maintain even pressure all along the edge, sanding with a semicircular motion (Fig. 9-21).

9-21. *Leveling the kerf-lined edge of the side.*

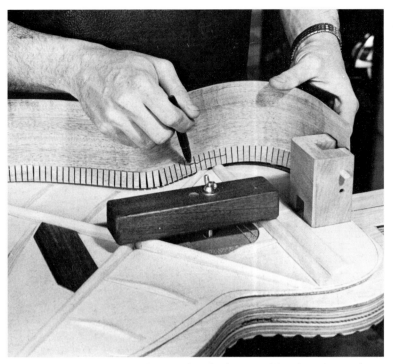

9-22. *Marking kerfing for brace-end locations. These pieces must be removed so that the brace ends can extend out to the sides.*

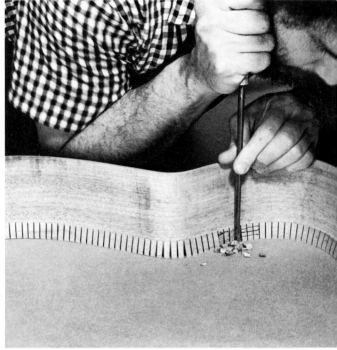

9-23. *Removing marked kerfing blocks. The chisel can be registered flat against the side to shave the last bit.*

Check your progress frequently, continuing until the kerf-lined edge is clean and covered with sanding marks.

Note that the *side* edge is not really an essential gluing surface—it will be routed away during binding anyway. The only reason for observing sanding marks on the side edge is that it is your reference for a flat plane. Once the side edge shows sanding marks in any spot, you must avoid continuing to put pressure on that area. Occasionally check the side on a flat, smooth surface. If the side does not sit flush when held down at its ends, figure out where it is high and sand that area on the board until the flat plane has been restored. As long as the side sits within 1/16 inch of the board all around when the ends are pinned down, you are within specs.

Step 4—Marking the Lining for the Brace Ends

When the lined edge is ready for gluing, return the side to the workboard. Pin it at the headblock and tailblock (on the classical, push it into the heelblock slot), and rest it on the brace ends. Sighting directly over the side, make sure that it follows the outline exactly as it will when it is glued in place, with the side perimeter just inside the template outline.

Note where the brace ends intersect the kerfing, and mark with a pencil those kerfing pieces that are in the way (Fig. 9-22). If the kerfed lining runs into the tailblock or headblock, mark the amount that must be removed from the lining ends as well.

Step 5—Removing the Marked Kerfing Blocks

Take the side to a flat work surface and, using the 1/4-inch chisel, shave away the kerfing blocks that you have marked for removal (Fig. 9-23). Work slowly, taking care not to angle the chisel in such a way that you cut into the side. When most of the kerfing has been removed, clean up the last bit with a scraper, leaving a smooth surface.

Return the side to the soundboard and check for fit. You may have to remove additional kerfing blocks; if you wind up removing more than would have been necessary to accommodate the brace ends, do not worry: You can reglue individual blocks later.

Repeat the entire process on the other side.

PROCEDURE: GLUING DOWN THE LINED SIDES

In this procedure, each lined side of the guitar must be glued to the soundboard and at the tailblock during a single step; the steel-string sides must be glued to the headblock as well. This is conceptually very simple, but in practice it requires careful preparation and thorough familiarity with all the clamps and cauls that must be manipulated in a very short period of time.

Both sides can actually be glued down at once, as we note at the end of the procedure; but to simplify matters for the student, we provide a technique that requires gluing only one side at a time. Because we use clamping bars instead of clamping directly to the side edge (Fig. 9-24), however, both sides must be completely fitted and ready for gluing before the procedure begins. The clamping bars (cut

9-24. *Clamping one side in place. The other side is held approximately in place to provide support for the ends of the clamping bars. Clamping at the tail on the classical requires a slightly concave caul to follow the arch of the tailblock.*

from plywood or 1- × 2-inch scrap) ensure that clamping forces are directed vertically downward regardless of variations in the way the clamps are oriented, reducing the possibility of racking the thin side under pressure. The side that is not being glued supports the ends of the clamping bars, keeping them horizontal.

Clamping the classical-guitar sides to the tailblock requires the use of a special caul. The caul must be slightly concave to follow the arch of the tailblock, and it must be padded

with leather or ⅛-inch sheet cork or neoprene to account for possible irregularities in the arched surface.

TOOLS
four clamping bars: two
    about 14 inches, two
    about 18 inches
six cam clamps
C-clamps: 4 (SS) or 2 (CL)

IMPLEMENTS
cauls, as needed

SUPPLIES
AR glue

Step 1—Final Fitting

The two sides have been lined and the linings have been selectively cut out to receive the brace ends. It is necessary, however, to check the fit under clamping pressure before proceeding to the actual gluing operation. The side that will *not* be glued first must be clamped to the headblock (steel-string) or inserted into its heel slot (classical), and then clamped lightly at the tailblock. The side that *will* be glued first is then aligned at the waist marks and clamped along the outline as shown in Fig. 9-24.

Clamp first at the waist; then clamp the upper bout (and at the headblock on the steel-string); finally, clamp the lower bout and at the tailblock. If the side is well bent, the bouts will follow the outline when secured only at the waist and at head and tail. If the bend is inaccurate, however, the bouts will have to be manipulated to be aligned to the outline while being clamped progressively away from the waist, *before* being secured at the blocks.

When clamping to the tailblock (also the headblock on the steel-string), it is *important* to ensure that the lined edge of the side is pressed down to the soundboard. Clamp lightly onto the block and then clamp down (gently) on the side edge a few inches from the block. When you are certain that the side is down, you can tighten the clamps against the tailblock.

Note the alignment under clamping pressure. It may be necessary to remove additional kerfing blocks at the brace ends to accommodate any shift.

When the side is correctly aligned and clamped, make a clearly visible mark on the tailblock where the side ends, to use as a reference during gluing.

Step 2—Classical Only: Checking for Gap at the Heel Slot

If a gap appears at the slot between the end-grain face of the heel and the exterior face of the side, you may wish to insert one or more paper shims in the slot on the interior face to press the outer face to the heel. The shims should match the dimensions of the slot and should be snug enough to be held in by the side without glue, but not so snug that insertion of the side becomes difficult.

Step 3—Gluing Down One Side

Leave the other side in place to support the clamping bars. *Important:* Run through this step several times without glue to be sure you can perform it comfortably before the actual gluing.

Apply glue to half the tailblock. On the steel-string, glue must also be applied to one-half of the headblock; we do not, however, glue the classical sides into the heel slots.

Apply glue to the lined side edge in a continuous bead. Do not smear it as you ordinarily would, but rather run your finger along the side edge, forming an even bead in the middle of the lining. Try not to drip glue down the side in the areas where the lining has been cut away.

Lower the side straight down on the soundboard outline so that the glue does not smear all over the place. (On the classical, slide the upper-bout end down in the heel slot.) Align the waist marks and clamp with a bar at the waist. Then clamp the upper bout (on the steel-string, clamp at the headblock). Try to keep the tail end from flopping around while you are clamping the upper bout. We sometimes temporarily pin it to the tailblock with a spring clamp. When the upper bout is secure, clamp the lower bout and at the tailblock. Be certain that the side is pressed *down* to the soundboard at the tailblock before tightening the clamps *on* the tailblock.

After about thirty minutes, remove the clamps and bars and gently clean up glue squeeze-out along the kerfed lining.

Step 4—Gluing the Other Side Down

Repeat Steps 1 through 3 with the other side. *Note:*

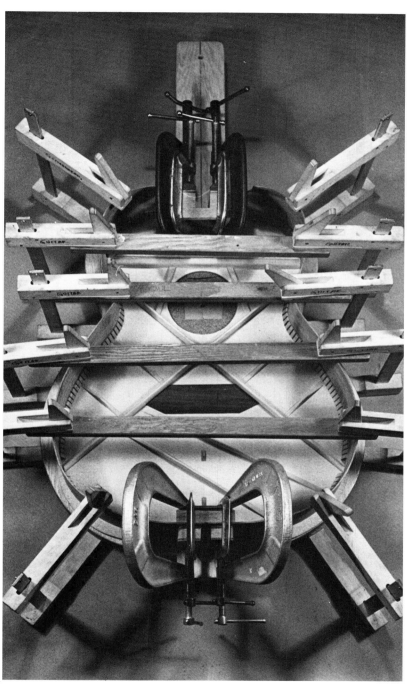

9-25. *Clamping both sides at once.*

Builders who have mastered the one-side-at-a-time assembly procedure can do both sides at once to save time. This requires more clamps and more efficient manipulation; otherwise the sequence is simply doubled at each stage. This is how we assemble our guitars (see Fig. 9-25).

PROCEDURE: GLUING "FEET" AT THE BRACE ENDS

Because of the stresses placed upon the major structural braces, their ends must be reinforced to prevent them from popping loose. Many of the badly caved-in guitar tops we have seen had loose brace ends that could have been prevented by simple reinforcement.

On the steel-string, we simply use extra kerfing blocks to do the job. On the classical, we make up the feet separately, extending them up the sides to provide additional rigidity. The brace ends would be held down adequately by kerfing blocks as on the steel-string, but due to the more delicate construction of the classical guitar, we feel that the strength of the box should be enhanced in the area of maximum stress. The extended feet increase rigidity with only a nominal increase in the mass of the sides.

Step 1—Classical Only: Making Extended Feet

We make the feet from scraps of mahogany or spruce. Cut the blanks to about ⁵⁄₁₆ × ³⁄₁₆ × 2¼ inches and then shape them on a belt sander or on the sanding board to the dimensions in Fig. 9-26. Round the top and the corners that will not be glued to the side, and sand smooth. Take the pieces to the open box and note whether you must concave or convex the gluing surface. A few strokes on sandpaper wrapped around a bottle should be sufficient for concaving; use the sanding board to convex.

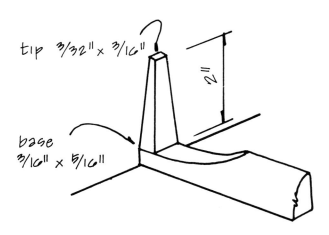

9-26. *Cutting the blanks for classical extended feet.*

9-27. *Gluing extended feet in place at the ends of the cross struts on the classical.*

9–28. Kerfing blocks are used as feet to hold down the ends of the X-brace and the upper face brace.

Step 2—Gluing the Feet in Place

Apply glue to a foot (kerfing blocks for the steel-string), both on the surface that will contact the side and on the bottom where it will contact the brace. Press the foot down on the brace end and against the side, holding it in place until it begins to grab. Apply a cam clamp with the lever outside the guitar. When clamping, try to jockey the clamp so that it pushes the foot down and in rather than pulling up (see Fig. 9-27).

Repeat with the other feet at each location where a brace runs out to the side (six on the steel-string; four on the classical). (See Fig. 9-28.)

CHAPTER 10

Here we will complete construction of the back and, after lining the side edges, fit the back to the linings and glue it down, completing enclosure of the soundbox.

The back is arched laterally by braces that are curved in much the same way that some soundboard braces were curved in Chapter 7. The rim onto which it is glued is arched longitudinally, so that when glued in place the back takes on a domed shape in all directions. Arching the back increases its structural rigidity and thus enhances the structural integrity of the soundbox. Its precise contribution to the instrument's acoustic response is, however, like the acoustic function of the back itself, a subject of much debate.

Whatever may be the back's precise role, it unquestionably interacts significantly with other tone-generating parts of the instrument. Thus, as noted in Chapter 1, the "weight" of the back-bracing system must be reasonably proportionate to other structural and acoustic elements. If the bracing is ill-proportioned, serious problems

Assembly II

with disharmonious sympathetic resonances can result, affecting the clarity of the instrument's response and sometimes even causing bizarre side effects such as peculiar string buzzes and other random noises.

For the guitars built from this book, we provide final back-brace dimensions that fall into a generally acceptable range. As the luthier becomes more sophisticated, however, these dimensions may be adjusted as required from one instrument to the next.

STEEL-STRING ONLY— THE HEADBLOCK FIXTURE

Since the neck will eventually seat against the headblock, we must make sure that the headblock is kept from moving during the final assembly procedures. If it is not, and if after the back is glued on we find that the headblock has tipped away from its correct position, we will encounter serious string-action problems

when we eventually string up the guitar.

Thus, we provide a fixture that locks the headblock rigidly in place throughout the last stages of soundbox assembly. It consists of a block of hardwood shaped and drilled as shown in Fig. 10-1a. A bolt, wingnut, and washer will also be required.

Insert the fixture bolt into the headblock's truss-rod clearance hole from the inside of the guitar shell so that the threaded portion protrudes from its mortise slot. Push the fixture block onto the bolt until the bolt threads project from the hole in the fixture block. Thread the washer, then the wingnut, onto the bolt, and snug the wingnut down so the fixture block presses lightly against the guitar's sides in front of the headblock. The fixture block is clamped down to the workboard, as shown in Fig. 10-1b. Finally, the wingnut is tightened securely to lock the headblock in place. If a tiny gap is present between the guitar and the fixture and it does not easily close when you tighten the wingnut, slip a

cardboard shim into the gap before retightening. If the gap is considerable, try loosening the workboard shoe. Excessive downward pressure exerted by the shoe on the upper face brace can distort the upper soundboard, tipping the headblock radically back from the fixture block. You can restore the tightness of the shoe by replacing the extra shim under the upper face brace with a slightly thicker one.

PROCEDURE: CUTTING THE PRELIMINARY ARCH

The back arch is created by planing and sanding the sides' edges to produce a contoured profile. Most of the contour is shaped into the edge before the back lining is installed. Once the lining is in place, additional material is removed only as necessary to finalize the contour and to produce a smooth, continuous gluing surface.

The preliminary arch is created by maintaining an even side depth from the tailblock

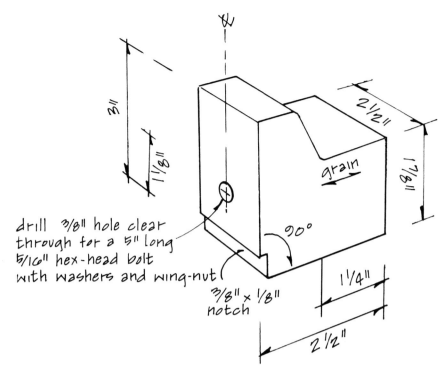

drill ⅜" hole clear
through for a 5" long
5/16" hex-head bolt
with washers and wing-nut

¾" × ⅛"
notch

3"

1⅛"

2½"

1⅞"

90°

grain

1¼"

2½"

10–1a.   Steel-string headblock fixture.

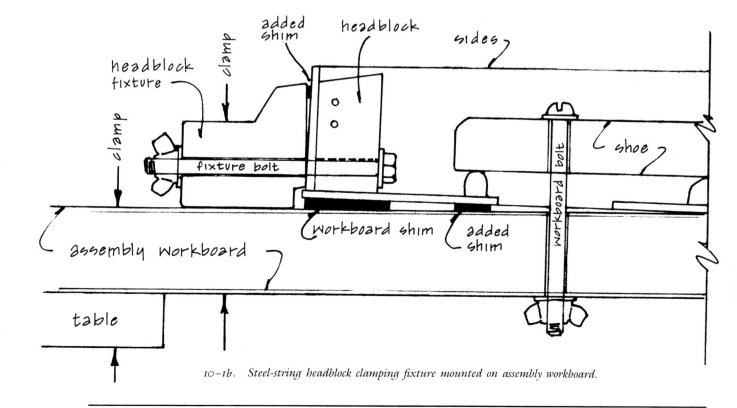

headblock
fixture

clamp

added
shim

headblock

sides

clamp

fixture bolt

shoe

headboard bolt

workboard shim

added
shim

assembly workboard

table

10–1b.   Steel-string headblock clamping fixture mounted on assembly workboard.

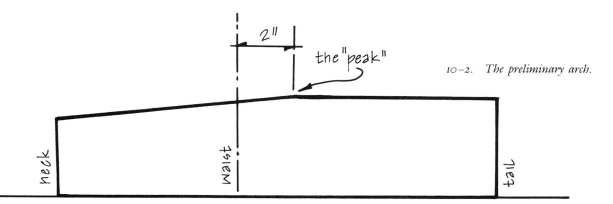

10-2. *The preliminary arch.*

to a point about two inches behind the waist (the *peak*) and then gradually tapering to the heel. As Fig. 10-2 indicates, the preliminary arch is actually a shallow triangle, tilted in such a way that one of its legs remains parallel to the soundboard.

Secure the soundboard edge snugly against the workboard shim with several padded cam

clamps at the tailblock and at the lower bout on both sides. Place the clamps so their bars point toward the floor.

TOOLS
pencil
block plane

SUPPLIES
straight strip of heavy paper, about 12 × 2 inches

IMPLEMENTS
large sanding board

Step 1—Marking for Taper and Planing

The sides and tailblock must be the same height before be-

ginning this step. If the tailblock is slightly high, plane it level with the sides. If the sides are high, plane to the level of the tailblock and then continue that height around on both sides to the peak (about two inches behind the waist).

Using a straight strip of paper as a guide (Fig. 10-3), trace a line on each side from the peak to the side height of the headblock. Plane to the lines, being careful not to plane against the grain direction. Plane strokes should follow the curve of the sides. (See Fig. 10-4).

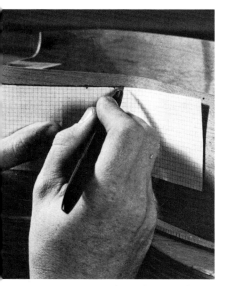

10-3. *Tracing the inclination from the headblock to the high point of the sides (about 2 inches behind the waist).*

10-4. *Planing the preliminary arch.*

Step 2—Smoothing the Initial Contour

The side profile is now divided into two distinct planes. They must be leveled with the sanding board in separate stages. Tip the board forward as in Fig. 10-5 to work the slanted plane, and pull it back level as in Fig. 10-6 to work the level plane. Avoid the peak as much as possible. Let the weight of the sanding board do the work. Continue until sanding scratches are visible along the entire length of the side edges and on the heel-block and tailblock.

When sanding, it is very important to keep the imaginary centerline of the sanding board over the centerline of the soundboard. This will avoid uneven weight distribution of the board, which can result in excessive sanding on one side or the other. Also, when pulling back, as in Fig. 10-6, it is *critical* to support the tailblock with one hand while pulling with the other. Work the slanted plane with push strokes only; work the level plane with pull strokes only.

10–5. *Sanding the inclined forward plane of the preliminary arch. Care must be taken to avoid sanding down the high point of the sides.*

Step 3—Classical Only: Reducing the Peak

The peak must be slightly less angular on the classical guitar because a solid lining with limited flexibility will be glued to the contoured edge. To moderate the peak, rest the sanding board on the slanted plane and pull it all the way back to the tail of the guitar. With the weight of the board on the side edges, one or two full strokes should suffice.

10–6. *Sanding the level rear plane of the preliminary arch. The left hand supports the sides at the tailblock while the board is being pulled backwards. The cam clamps on the soundboard lip prevent the open box from flapping on the workboard.*

PROCEDURE: PREPARING AND INSTALLING BACK LININGS

The linings we use for the seam between the sides and back are ordinarily kerfed on the steel-string and solid on the classical; they are each made from the same species of wood used for the linings against the soundboard.

STEEL-STRING ONLY

TOOLS
razor saw
spring clamps or clothespins

MATERIALS
kerfed lining strips totalling 64 inches

SUPPLIES
AR glue
#120-grit garnet sandpaper

Butt a kerfing strip to the headblock and wrap it around the side. Clip it in place at several locations *without glue,* trying to keep it flush to the edge of the side. When the strip reaches the "peak" it will no longer be possible to keep the strip flush, so mark the strip there, remove it, and cut it short at that spot.

Apply glue to the back of the strip. Holding the strip flush with the thumb and fingers of one hand, apply the clamps along the strip's length, readjusting as may be necessary to keep the strip flush. Do not err toward letting the strip drop *below* the edge of the side. Now trim a second strip so it fits between the tailblock and the end of the first strip. Apply glue to the back of the second strip and clamp it to the side, butting it against the first strip. Repeat on the opposite side.

When the glue squeeze-out below the lining is leather hard, it can be cleaned up with a scraper blade.

Knock the sharp edges off the facets of the linings with #120-grit garnet sandpaper.

CLASSICAL ONLY

The solid linings for the classical must be bent on a hot pipe; maximum feasible thickness is therefore about .15 inch. The blanks must be table-sawn from a billet and sanded smooth on at least one face (very fine saw marks are acceptable).

TOOLS
chisel (hand-tool only)
bending pipe
spring clamps or clothespins and C-clamps

MATERIALS
two basswood strips, .15 × ⅝ × 28 inches

SUPPLIES
AR glue
sandpaper

Step 1—Bending the Lining Strips

This step is essentially the same as the side-bending procedure, but a few additional caveats are in order. The material is thicker here and is thus more difficult to bend around tight curves and more easily broken. Basswood also is more subject to collapse (kinking) than most of the woods we bend. These problems are exacerbated by oversoaking; if the material becomes waterlogged it will not hold a bend and may kink without warning.

Thus, soak the strips for only a few minutes in hot tap water, occasionally rewetting during bending if scorching occurs. When bending the strips, the hands should grip the piece at a greater distance from the pipe than when bending sides (see Fig. 10-7).

10-7. Bending a basswood lining strip over a hot pipe.

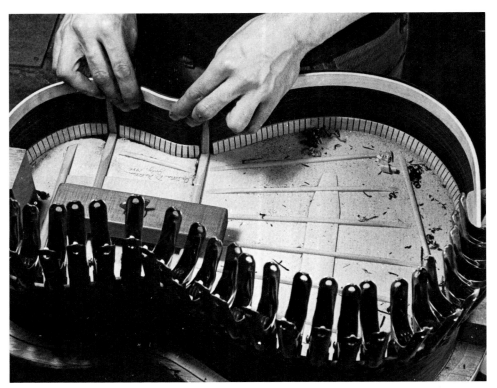

10–8. Fitting a solid basswood lining strip on the classical guitar. The lining must fit the side curve very closely to ensure a good glue seam with spring clamps or clothes pins.

10–9. Beveling the solid lining after it has been glued in place.

Twisting can be avoided and kinking reduced by sliding the piece back and forth over the pipe rather than pausing during the bend. You may wish to bend the waist first. Start on a broad section of the pipe and progress to tighter curves as you gain a feel for the material.

Use the guitar box itself for fitting. Have it handy by the bending pipe so that you can take advantage of the malleability of the strips when they are still hot. Trim the linings approximately to length when the bend is nearly correct; then nibble away at the ends for a close fit.

The linings must fit comfortably, because if excessive pressure is required to glue the linings in place, the sides may be distorted (Fig. 10-8). When you are satisfied with the bend, mark corresponding points at the waist on both the side and the lining for position reference during gluing.

Step 2—Beveling and Gluing, or Vice Versa

The linings must be faceted in cross section, as with the kerfed top linings. If you have a belt sander or a drill press with a sanding-drum attachment, the bent lining strip can be faceted before gluing. If not, it is easier to facet after it is glued in place, using a shallow gouge or a chisel, as in Fig. 10-9.

The solid lining is glued with spring clamps or clothespins, as with the kerfed lining. If you use clothespins, they should have very stiff springs. Small C-clamps may be added in places where the lining resists conforming to the side.

Apply glue to the whole strip. Begin clamping at the waist, using the position reference marks to align. Clamp the upper bout next and then the lower bout. When the glue squeeze-out below the lining is leather hard, remove it with the corner of a scraper blade. When the clamps are removed (after about one hour), facet the lining (if you have not done so already) and sand it smooth with #120-grit garnet sandpaper.

PROCEDURE: FINAL ARCHING

After the lining is in place, the preliminary arch must be refined by additional sanding at the headblock and tailblock. The sanding board is tipped at a greater inclination than before to facet the contour, as shown in Fig. 10-10a. Then, with strokes covering the full length of the contour, the profile is sanded to a continuous curve (as shown in Fig. 10-10b), simultaneously leveling the lined edge for gluing.

TOOLS
glue chisel
chisel or block plane

IMPLEMENTS
sanding board

Step 1—Clean-up and Trimming the Linings

Glue squeeze-out above the lining must be knocked off with a chisel, and if the linings protrude above the sides at any point they must be shaved down flush with either a chisel or a plane. Do not cut into the side edges while shaving down the linings.

Step 2—Sanding the Secondary Facets

The sanding board must be tilted so that it contacts only the regions nearest the headblock and tailblock. Exaggerate the downward pull on the board when working the tailblock area and the forward tilt when working the headblock area.

Because of the exaggerated downward pull, it is especially critical here to support the tailblock with one hand (as shown in Fig. 10-6) when pulling back on the sanding board. Make two reference marks on the sides, one a bare 1/16 inch below the top of the tailblock and one a bare 1/16 inch below the top of the headblock. Sand the ends of the box until the board touches the marks.

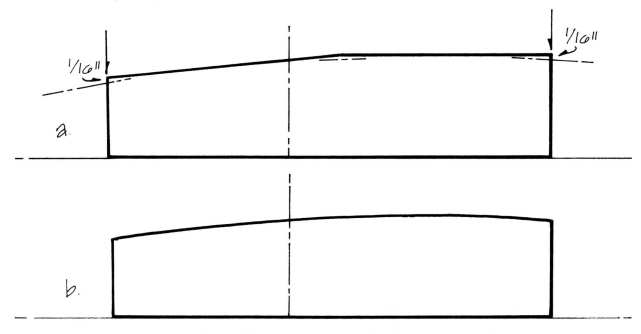

10-10a and b. Refining the preliminary arch with the sanding boards.

Step 3—Final Sanding

The last motion is an overall sanding stroke, accomplished by sanding over the guitar box as shown in Fig. 10-11. Do not let your fingers dangle over the front edge of the board, lest you mash them on the headblock. Try to accentuate your pressure at the ends of the board to work the heel and tail; the weight of the board will work the rest of the arch. This is strictly a refining step; the arch should be well defined by now. Check your results by laying the sanding board on the contoured edge and sighting under it as shown in Fig. 10-12. The points of

10–11. Sanding the final arch. The facets of the preliminary arch are refined with full length strokes until the linings are covered with sanding scratches.

10–12. The quality of the final arch is revealed by "rolling" the sanding board over the arch while observing the points of contact between the board and the contoured edge.

contact should travel evenly up the edge on both sides when the sanding board is "rolled" over the arch. If a contact point widens suddenly, it betrays a flat spot; sand selectively to remove irregularities.

PROCEDURE: MAKING THE BRIDGE BLOCK AND UPPER FACE BRACE CAUL

Bridge Block

Now is the easiest time to make a bridge block. The bridge block, a clamping aid, is placed inside the guitar under the bridge during the bridge-gluing procedure. It is designed to absorb and diffuse the clamping pressure without damaging the delicate spruce understructure or distorting the soundboard in any way.

The bridge block consists of an oblong of ¾-inch plywood, slightly larger than the bridge itself, but not so large that it cannot be easily inserted and retrieved through the soundhole.

Some care must be exercised in the slotting and fitting of the bridge block—if the slots are much larger than need be, the block will not find a single and positive "home" when it is being placed inside the guitar and will wobble about, possibly ending up far from where it must be to do the most good. If the slots are too narrow or too shallow, the block

will, at best, distort the soundboard during bridge clamping or, at worst, crush the braces or even fracture the soundboard.

To fabricate the bridge block properly, place the plywood blank on top of the braces at the bridge location. The bridge must lie entirely within the perimeter of the blank.

Next, mark the block precisely where all the braces emerge from under it, on its front, back, *and* side edges (Fig. 10-13). The marks should accurately denote the width of each brace that crosses under the blank.

Transfer the marks onto the bottom of the block. Connect the marks with a straightedge and a pencil. Clamp the block in a vise, saw down the lines a

bit deeper than the height of the brace, and remove the waste material between the saw cuts with a narrow chisel (Fig. 10-14).

10-13. *Marking the bridge block for fan brace locations.*

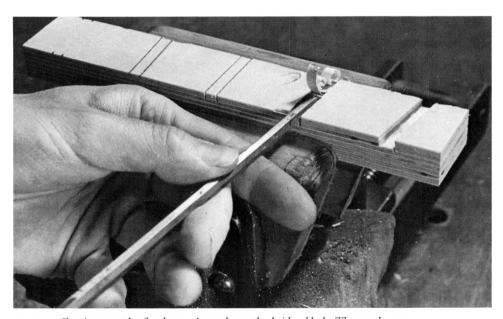

10-14. *Cutting out the fan brace channels on the bridge block. The marks are connected with lines, the lines are sawn down, and the slots are cleared out with a chisel.*

Place the slotted block back on the soundboard. The block should locate in its proper position without pinching or crowding any of the braces.

The block should sit flat without hanging up. If it jams or mounts a brace, you must discover precisely where the trouble is and resolve it by deepen-ing or widening the slots as is necessary.

Steel-string only: Since the steel-string bridge block sits primarily on the bridge patch rather than directly on the soundboard, we must modify the block so it comes into contact with the soundboard in those areas where it does *not* sit on the bridge patch. The areas in question lie under the upper corners of the ends of the bridge.

Retrieve the triangular scraps cut away when the bridge patch was trimmed to shape (we told you to save them, remember?). Since they are exactly the same thickness as the bridge patch, they make perfect bridge block shims. Cut them down and glue them to the corners of the block, as shown in Fig. 10-15.

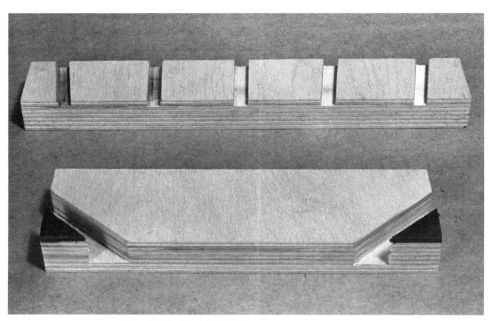

10–15. *The finished bridge blocks.*

Upper Face Brace/Cross Strut Caul

You must make this caul now to support and protect the soundboard later when the fingerboard end is glued down. It must be cut out to clear the upper face brace (or cross strut), resting flush against the soundboard lip at the soundhole and also against the upper transverse graft (see Fig. 10-16).

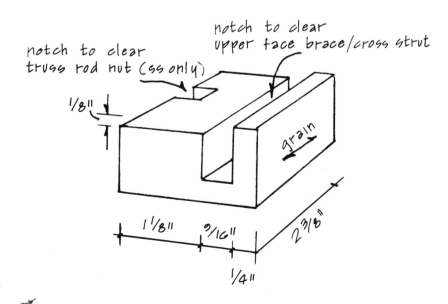

10–16. *The upper face brace/cross strut caul.*

PROCEDURE: INSERTING THE BACK PLATE CENTERSEAM INLAY

This procedure is to be done only by those building the steel-string, but it will be of interest to classical builders also.

It is common practice to insert a stripe of contrasting wood at the seam of adjoining back plates. This stripe can take the form of a single line or several veneer lines placed between the plates when they are joined together with glue, as was done on the classical back plate in Chapter 5. Multi-laminate marquetry strips can also be inserted this way if available in full-height thickness. When the quality or integrity of these strips is suspect, however, or when the strips are not thick enough to be sandwiched in, they must be inlaid into a routed channel on the back surface right over the glued centerseam.

TOOLS
ruler
portable router with circular base-plate
mortising bit (see Step 1 below)
straightedge (a long metal ruler will do)
two C-clamps

MATERIALS
multilaminate marquetry strip at least 21 inches long, any thickness

Step 1—Preparation

Measure the width of the strip(s), and select a mortising router bit that is equal to, or, preferably, smaller in width than the finished inlay channel.

Clamp a thick straightedge securely onto the joined back plate at a distance from its center seam equal to one-half the diameter of the router base-plate. Set the depth of cut to match the thickness of the strip, but in no case deeper than ³⁄₆₄ inch.

Step 2—Routing the Channel

Practice this step on scrap material before attempting it on the back plate. Note which direction of feed produces better results.

Pressing the router's base-plate securely against the straightedge, cut the channel at a slow, steady speed, being particularly careful not to waver at the entrance and exit of the cut (Fig. 10-17). Beware that your hands or the router handles do not strike the hold-down clamps and cause the router to jump.

The strips must fit snugly, with no side-to-side play, for the best result. If the channel is too narrow, a length of masking tape stuck to the contact point on the rim of the base-plate will act as a shim and allow you to widen the channel a tiny bit with another pass. Keep adding tape and routing until the proper clearance of the strip in the channel is achieved. Do not rotate the

10–17.   Routing for marquetry inlay on the steel-string back. The router cuts slightly less than halfway through the back plate.

router as you bear against the straightedge; the base plate may not be perfectly round and will register randomly at different points on its circumference.

Step 3—Gluing the Inlay

Squeeze a narrow bead of glue into the channel. Run your finger down the channel to spread. Insert the strip and run your finger up and down its length for about a half a minute, until the glue grabs. No clamping is necessary. Do not disturb the plate until it is absolutely dry. Scrape flush, as shown in Fig. 10-18. The back inlay, even if slightly off-center, will become the new centerline.

This system will also serve for inlaying straight bits of shell inlay into the back seam. The shell, however, must be

10–18. Scraping the back stripe flush. Care must be taken to avoid scraping a hollow into the back.

ground flush with a file or sanding block.

PROCEDURE: BRACING THE BACK

Tone woods most commonly used for back braces are spruce on the steel-string guitar and mahogany or Spanish cedar on the classical. These can be interchanged, however, depending upon the relative availability of the materials. Back braces need not be split but should at least be quarter-sawn.

The blank sizes given in the tools and materials lists are final dimensions; that is, each brace should be at the full height of the blank (at its deepest point) when glued to the back. This assumes, of course, that the height at the midpoint of the brace has not been reduced during the arching process. Beginners arching by hand should cut their blanks an extra ⅛ inch high to allow for trial and error.

TOOLS
long straightedge
cam clamps, as needed
18-inch clamping bar
block plane
razor saw
¼-inch chisel

SUPPLIES
AR glue
sandpaper

IMPLEMENTS
backing slat

MATERIALS
cross-grain strips, ⅛ × ⅝ (SS) or ½ (CL) inch, to total 18 inches in length
brace blanks:
  SS—two ⁵⁄₁₆ × ⅝ × 14 inches,
    two ½ × ¾ × 18 inches,
  CL—two ⁵⁄₁₆ × ⁹⁄₁₆ × 12 inches
    one ⁵⁄₁₆ × ⁹⁄₁₆ × 13 inches
    one ⁵⁄₁₆ × ⁹⁄₁₆ × 15 inches

Step 1—Making and Installing the Back Graft

The centerseam must be reinforced with cross-grain strips of mahogany or spruce. These pieces can be cut from a thick cutoff scrap (as in Fig. 10-19) or from a thinned piece. Width for the classical graft is ½ inch; for the steel-string, ⅝ inch. The blanks should be about ⅛ inch thick when glued in place.

Draw the outline of the guitar on the underside of the back. Lightly draw the outlines of the braces square to the centerline with a sharp pencil (refer to Fig. 10-20 for brace locations).

10–19. Cutting the back grafts from a plank.

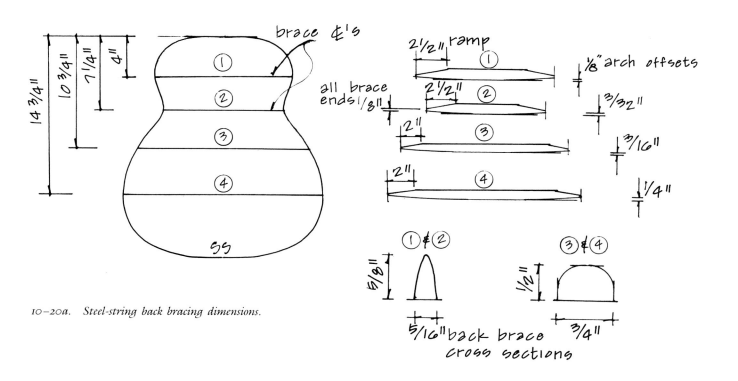

10–20a. Steel-string back bracing dimensions.

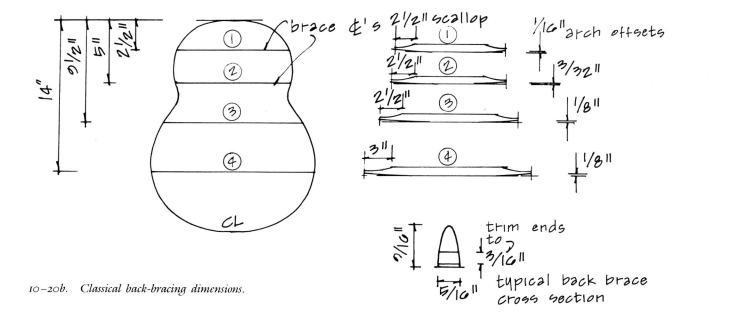

10–20b. Classical back-bracing dimensions.

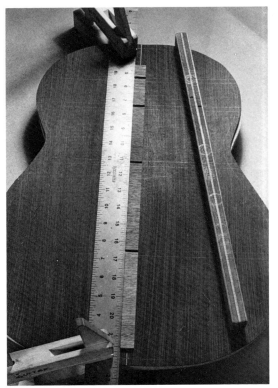

10–21. *The set up for aligning the back grafts. The caul is one of the assembly clamping bars used earlier.*

Clamp a straightedge parallel to the centerseam, at a distance equal to one-half your blank width (see Fig. 10-21). We use the pulling action of the cam clamps to draw the grafts against the straightedge (see Fig. 10-22). A long caul (use an 18-inch side-assembly clamping bar) and a substantial number of clamps are necessary to do the full length at once, but it can be done in sections if you do not have enough clamps. The pieces should overlap the brace outlines slightly so they can be cut back to provide a snug fit for the braces.

Step 2—Planing and Sanding the Graft

The finished thickness of the grafts should be about 3/32 inch (Fig. 10-23). Plane to a gently curved cross section, and sand off tool facets with #120-grit and #220-grit garnet. Lay a sheet of stiff paper alongside the grafts to protect the back when sanding.

Step 3—Arching the Back Braces

The back braces must be arched in the same manner as the arched soundboard braces, using either a plane or a belt sander.

Refer to Fig. 10-20 for the center-to-end deflection of each brace.

Step 4—Fitting the Back Braces

Use the braces themselves as guides for notching out the grafts. Place each brace along its outline on the back and use a razor saw to cut through the graft on one side of the brace (Fig. 10-24). Do not cut into the back with the saw. Move the brace over slightly, just covering the first saw cut, and make the second cut. With a chisel, shave away the graft material where each brace will sit (Fig. 10-25). Try the braces for fit. If necessary, expand the notches by shaving back with the chisel until each brace fits snugly and sits down smoothly on the back.

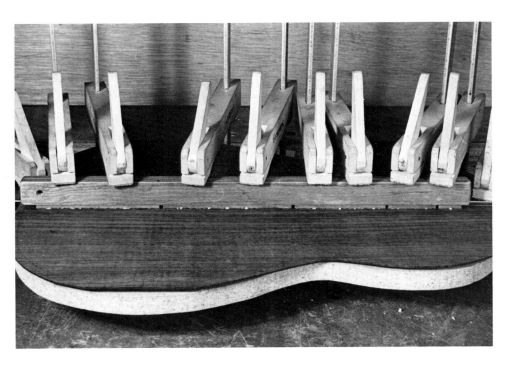

10–22. *Clamping the back grafts. If insufficient clamps are available, the grafts can be glued one at a time.*

10–23. *Planing the back grafts. The plane leaves facets; the grafts are then sanded to a curved cross section.*

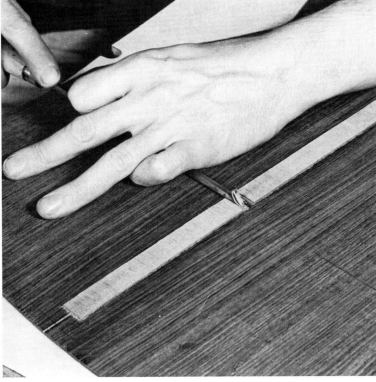

10–24. *Using the brace as a saw guide to notch the back grafts. The braces must fit snugly in between the grafts.*

10–25. *Chiseling out a notch. The notch is widened by carefully shaving back with a chisel until the brace fits snugly.*

10–26. *Making squared positioning reference marks for gluing back braces. The square is registered against the back graft.*

Step 5—Gluing the Back Braces

Sand off or erase the brace outlines drawn on the back. To provide squared positioning references for gluing the braces, place a square against the graft and along each brace, and mark the position of the brace ends in the waste area outside the template line with a contrasting pencil (Fig. 10-26).

When gluing, as always, try to alternate the direction of the clamps. Start from the middle of each brace and work outward, using a backing slat for support underneath (Fig. 10-27). Refer to the marks at the brace ends to ensure that you maintain a square relationship between the braces and the centerline.

Clean up the glue squeeze-out immediately after the clamps are removed, taking special care not to dig into the back with the glue chisel.

10–27. *Gluing the back brace using a clamping slat to follow the brace arch. Note the alternating clamp directions.*

Step 6—Carving the Back Braces

This operation is similar to carving top braces, but the relatively severe curve of the back makes it a little awkward. You may wish to do it on a scrap of pile carpeting. In any event, when carving, do not press on the back in such a way as to fracture it.

If your braces are taller than the finished blank dimensions given at the beginning of the procedure, plane them to their correct height before carving.

The finished cross sections for all the braces are shown in Fig. 10-20. Use a block plane to remove the bulk of the material, as in Fig. 10-28. The brace ends must be carved down as shown in Fig. 10-29.

On the classical, the brace ends should be scalloped rather than ramped straight down. Use the bellied side of the chisel to produce profiles similar to those of the sound-board cross struts.

Sand the chisel marks off with #100-grit or #120-grit garnet and finish with #220. You can protect the back surface while sanding by running a layer or two of masking tape along either side of the brace or by just holding a piece of stiff paper or cardboard on the back against the side of the brace.

10–28. *Peaking the back braces with a plane. The index finger serves as a guide on the top of the brace.*

10–29. *Carving the brace ends. The back is held firmly with the forearm while the chisel is steadied under the hand.*

PROCEDURE: FITTING THE BACK

Fitting the back is a sequence of events that must be followed in a methodical and painstaking manner, since the integrity, appearance, and longevity of the soundbox depend on it.

The ends of all the back braces are let into pockets in the lined edge in such a way that the rim of the back comes to rest on the lined edge, the brace ends bottom securely in the floors of the pockets, and the centerline of the back coincides perfectly with the centerline of the open soundbox.

TOOLS
pencil
plastic drafting triangle
razor saw
¼-inch chisel
wide chisel
block plane
small sanding board
half pencil (see Step 5)

Step 1—Marking a Centerpoint on the Tailblock

The centerline of the soundboard must be transferred to the top of the tailblock to be used for alignment of the back centerseam. Place a plastic drafting triangle against the exterior face of the tailblock, registering it on the lip of the soundboard or, if the lip has been completely sawn away, on the workboard. Position it at the soundboard centerseam and mark where it intersects the top edge of the tailblock.

Step 2—Aligning the Back and Marking for Fitting

Lay the back on the open box with the brace ends overlapping the sides. Align the centerseam to the center mark on the tailblock. Position the back lengthwise so that the bottom of the outline drawn on its underside is aligned at the tailblock to the exterior face of the sides. Secure the back centerseam at the tailblock center mark with one hand and pivot the back so that the seam is centered at the headblock. On the steel-string, align to the midpoint of the mortise; on the classical, align to the point of the heel.

Once the back is aligned, do not let it shift in any way. Holding a pencil in one hand, press down carefully in the center of the back with the other hand. If the back shifts at all, do the alignment over again. If not, proceed to make two sets of marks. One set will be on the brace ends themselves, indicating where they intersect the outer face of the sides (Fig. 10-30); the other marks will be on the sides, indicating the location and width of each brace end, so that the linings can be accurately notched. Mark one side and, without disturbing the back, walk around the guitar and mark the other side. If the back has shifted at all, you must erase all your marks and start over again.

Step 3—Cutting the Back Brace Ends

Each brace end must be cut inside the marks by an amount equal to the thickness of the side. Make the saw cuts parallel to the marks on the brace ends with a razor saw. Try not to cut into the back. Use the tip or heel of the saw blade toward the bottom of the cut. Shave away the waste portion with a chisel or carefully lever off the stub, as shown in Fig. 10-31. Clean up remaining shards with a scraper.

Step 4—Notching Out the Linings

The marks on the sides must be transferred to the linings so that the notches can be located. Use a straightedge to align the notches opposite one another so that the straight-across brace will fit properly (Fig. 10-32).

Cut through the linings on the marks at an angle as in Fig. 10-33. Do not let the saw cut into the side.

Using a chisel, remove enough material between the saw cuts to receive the brace ends. Work slowly, gradually deepening the pockets, until they are almost deep enough

10–30. *Marking the intersection of the brace ends with the lined edge of the side.*

10–31. *Trimming the brace ends. The braces are sawn through where they will meet the sides, and the excess is carved away.*

10–32. *Marking brace positions on the linings. The straight-edge connects the marks on the opposite sides.*

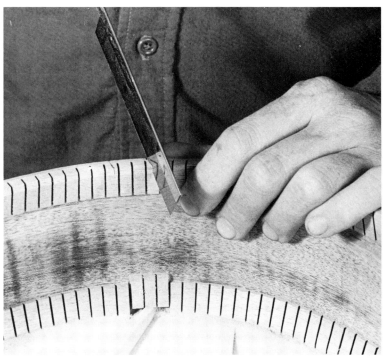

10–33. *Sawing the lining for the brace-end pockets.*

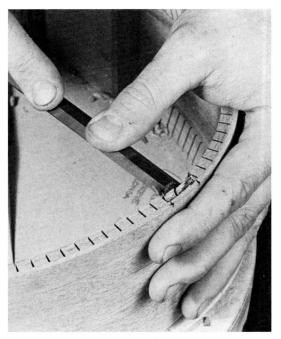

10-34. *Carving out the brace end pockets. Note that the hand supporting the side is out of harm's way.*

for the brace ends to drop in entirely (see Fig. 10-34). Support the side with one hand while holding the chisel with the other. Do not, however, let the supporting hand slide above the side edge, lest you slip with the chisel and cut yourself.

Try the back for fit in the lining. Ideally, the notches will remain exactly the width of the brace ends, but you probably will find that one or more notches must be widened to allow all the brace ends to drop in. If the back is hanging up in one or two spots, appraise the situation before making any further cuts.

Sometimes it appears that one pocket must be widened when, in fact, another is caus-

ing the problem. Sometimes a brace end hangs up on the side because the brace has not been cut back far enough on one end or the other. When deciding where to make additional cuts, remember that the centerseam must remain properly aligned; injudicious cutting may cause it to shift.

When the back fits into all eight notches, gradually deepen them until the back sits flush to the lined edge at all points. It is essential that the back and the lined edge make good contact, so the first priority is to get the back flush all around; however, for maximum support, the brace ends ideally should rest on the floors of the pockets. Try to get the depths just right.

Make sure that the edges of the back at the peak of the arch do not require a lot of pressure to sit flush. Sometimes there will be a little pucker there that can be relieved by widening the outer edges of the pockets for the #2 and #3 braces.

Check each brace end for depth by pressing down directly over it and tapping on the back edge adjacent to the brace end.

Step 5—Trimming the Back Grafts

Grind a pencil lengthwise to a semicircular cross-section. With the brace ends in their pockets, register the pencil against the sides at the tailblock and headblock and mark

the overhang of the back (Fig. 10-35). Remove the back and measure from those marks to determine where the grafts must end so as not to mount either block when the back is glued on. Cut back the grafts accordingly with a razor saw and chisel (Fig. 10-36). Clean up the back surface with a scraper. Bevel the graft ends and sand smooth.

Step 6—Trimming the Overhang of the Back

Sand off or erase the old template outline. Press the back in place with the brace ends in their notches. Lay one arm across it to press it down at the tailblock and headblock, and trace the outline of the sides onto the underside of the back with a sharp contrasting pencil (Fig. 10-37). Remove the back and trim the overhang, cutting *on* the line with a bandsaw or carving with a chisel. If a chisel is used, take extreme care to be conscious of grain direction. A coping saw is inappropriate for this step because of its tendency to chip out when cutting crossgrain on a thin plate.

This step is essential to avoid fractures resulting from clamping pressure on an overhanging section of the thin plate.

Step 7—Removing the Headblock Discontinuity

Because the sanding board is flat, it levels the regions at the

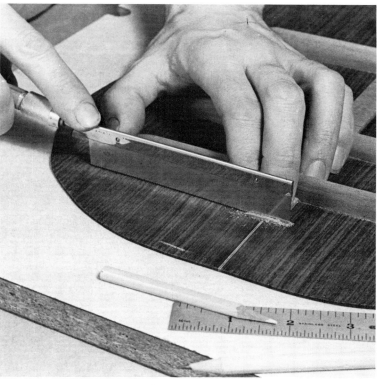

10–35. *Marking the overhang for trimming the back grafts.*

10–36. *Cutting back the grafts. The length of the headblock (or tailblock) is measured from the mark down the centerseam, and the grafts are trimmed so they will end close to, but not mount up on, the blocks.*

headblock and tailblock flat also. The braced back plate is arched laterally, however, so when the back is pressed tightly to those two regions, a discontinuity in the arch will result at both spots. This discontinuity will be manifest when we clamp the back down directly over the headblock and tailblock. An unsightly hollow, or dimple, considerably larger at the headblock than at the tailblock, will result when the back is glued down.

The solution is to remove some more material from the lined edge near the head block so that it drops gently and

10–37. *Marking final back perimeter. When the back is completely seated all around, it is marked as shown and the excess trimmed away.*

10-38. Planing the headblock area to accommodate the rise of the lateral arch imparted by the closest back brace. This avoids a "dimple" over the headblock after the back is glued on.

10-39. Smoothing plane facets with a small sanding board. The leading edge of the headblock is avoided, as it must remain full height.

evenly between the mortise (steel-string) or heel (classical) and the nearest brace pocket. The corresponding amount to be removed at the *tailblock* is much less. Indeed, the amount on the classical is so small that it can be disregarded entirely.

Start by planing across the headblock with a sharp block plane, tipping the sole so it crosses the headblock at a greater angle than the slope of the headblock surface, thus shaving the forward half of the block and missing the rest (Fig. 10-38). Now feather the cut toward the brace pockets with several more strokes of the plane, removing equivalent amounts of material from both sides. Stop the cuts short of the brace pockets.

To check your progress, mount the back on the open soundbox, clamp it down at the tailblock, and, with the spread-out fingers of one hand, wrap the forward edge of the back down over the just-planed area. With your other hand, tap forcefully on the back above the back edge of the headblock. A dull, dead sound means the back is touching the headblock and you have succeeded in removing the discontinuity. A sharp, rattling sound betrays an open space between the back and the headblock; this means that

more planing is needed. Remove the back and repeat the previous planing step. Continue till it passes the tapping test.

Finally, smooth and even out the planed area with curved strokes of the small sanding board (Fig. 10-39). Begin over one brace pocket, curve around and across the headblock, and end over the opposite brace pocket. Several strokes should suffice.

The tipped surface of the headblock has probably been faceted by now. Sand the headblock surface judiciously to transform it into a gentle curve. Keep the tailward edge at its original height.

Several slightly tipped strokes of the plane across the steel-string tailblock should be sufficient to remove the arch discontinuity over that point.

Step 8—Checking Through the Soundhole

Remove the open box from the workboard. Place the back in position with the braces in their pockets and hold it that way while looking through the soundhole. Are the ends of the grafts clearing the heelblock and tailblock? Is the lining flush to the back all around? If you notice anything amiss, now is your last chance to correct it.

When you are satisfied that everything is all right, remove the back and replace the open box on the workboard exactly as it was before.

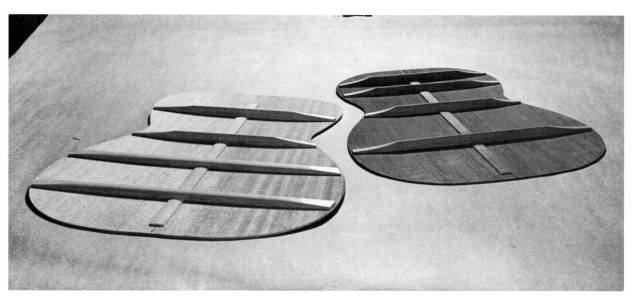

10–40. *Finished backs.*

10–41. *The classical, ready for back assembly.*

PROCEDURE: GLUING THE BACK

The back is glued down using a continuous strip of inner tube about 2 inches wide wound around and around to compress the edge at all points while the glue sets. We call this technique roping.

This is only one of many available techniques for gluing the edge. Some construction systems use elaborate cauls that cover the whole edge at once. Others use a multitude of clamps in order to cover every inch of the outline. In systems where the back is glued on first, it can rest in a hollowed-out form or jig while the sides are clamped onto it. However it is done, the object is to clamp a very long edge of a vaulted plate without causing distortion. Roping is an ancient technique that does an extremely efficient job with little or no investment in tools or fixtures.

To make up the roping strip, take an ordinary car inner tube (not a truck inner tube, as it will be too heavy), and begin cutting a continuous 2-inch strip round and round the perimeter until the whole tube is used up. If you have to make a couple of strips, you can tie them with a square knot.

Step 1—Getting Ready

You will need two cauls, one each with the same cross section as the headblock and tailblock, respectively. For the steel-string headblock caul, use the wedge-shaped cutoff from the headblock itself.

Make sure that the workboard shim is accurately positioned; also, place the wingnut on the bolt through the workboard shoe *underneath* the workboard, rather than on top of the shoe. On the steel-string, also make sure that the extra shim, headblock fixture and bolt, and perimeter clamps are all accurately and securely positioned.

Blow or vacuum out all dust and debris from inside the box, especially in the crevices of the lined edge. If you have not signed the underside of the soundboard, do it now. Did you make a bridge block? If not, do it now.

Finally, make sure that the workboard is very securely clamped to the bench, as you do not want it to flop around when you are pulling on the rubber strip.

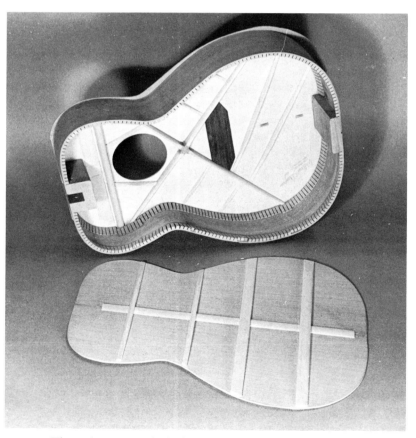

10–42. The steel-string, ready for back assembly.

Step 2—Roping the Back

The sequence for this step is simple, but it must be executed smoothly for best results. Read the following and do the step without glue—a dry run—several times if necessary, to get all the movements down.

Apply a bead of glue around the lining on both sides (Fig. 10-43) and then on the headblock and tailblock. Spread the glue on the headblock and tailblock and then, with one finger, wipe the glue back about ¹⁄₁₆ inch from the edge of each block. Make a V with two fingers and run it around the lined edge as in Fig. 10-44 to form the glue bead into an even trail in the middle of the lining. Get a little glue into each brace end pocket.

Place the back into position with the braces locked into their pockets in the linings. If the back fits a little loosely (rotates) in the pockets, check to see that the centerseam is still lined up before clamping. Clamp gently at the tailblock as in the photos, again checking the alignment of the centerseam. Tighten the clamps and then clamp at the headblock, still checking for untoward movement of the back.

Begin the roping sequence with a single loop of rubber around the waist, knotted underneath the workboard. The

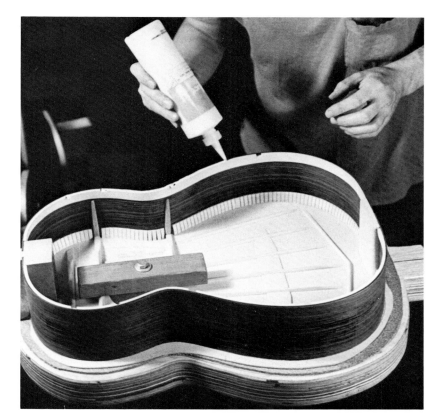

10-43. Applying glue to the lined edge and blocks. A drop or two of glue is left in each brace pocket.

10-44. Forming glue into an even bead on the lined edge.

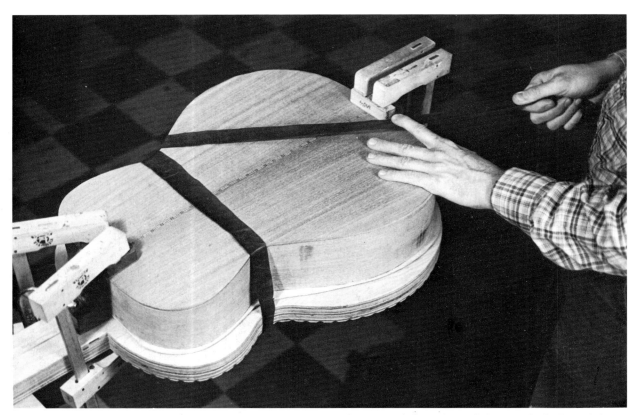

10-45. Beginning the roping sequence. The rubber strip is stretched up around the waist, pulled across the back, and then held as it is stretched down at the tail.

strip is then brought up and stretched in the vertical plane, passed down to the tailblock as in Fig. 10-45, and stretched downward; then underneath the workboard and up again next to the first upward loop; across the back and down next to the first downward loop at the tailblock, as in Fig. 10-46; then back and forth, working around until the other side of the waist is reached. The strip then continues on the upper bout, stretching from the waist diagonally across to the head-block and back as in Fig. 10-47, working around until the whole edge is covered by a

10-46. Continuing the roping sequence. The rubber strip passes round and round on the lower bout until it comes up on the opposite side of the waist from where it began.

double **X** pattern (Fig. 10-48). It is unnecessary to exert a great deal of lateral tension across the back or underneath the workboard—just keep the strip tight—but as you come around each edge pulling up and pulling down, you should stretch the rubber as far as it will go. Do not relax tension on the strip at any time. Keep the rubber strip flat as it goes over the back so that it does not bunch up; do not worry about it underneath the workboard.

Step 3—Removing the Soundbox from the Workboard

After one hour, remove the clamps and cauls. Untie the rubber strip and unwind it from the guitar box. Remove the wingnut from underneath. On the classical, unclamp the neck; do not let the workboard fall. Gently lift the guitar from the workboard. Reach into the soundhole and carefully remove the shoe and any other fixtures. You may have to work the bolt out of the shoe while it is still inside the box in order to get them out. Try not to mar the interior of the soundbox.

10–47. Roping the upper bout. When the X pattern is completed on the lower bout, the strip is brought up at the waist and across the upper bout, pulling down adjacent to the opposite side of the headblock.

10–48. The finished roping sequence creates a double-X pattern. The strip is wrapped around the waist once or twice and then securely knotted.

CHAPTER 11

The verb *purfling* means finishing or decorating the border or edge of a piece of woodwork by means of thin bands of contrasting material (from the Latin *profilum,* meaning *threading forth*); the bands themselves are referred to as *purflings.* The decorative purflings on the guitar that outline the boundaries of the plates are themselves outlined by an edge-banding strip called the *binding.* The binding not only seals the unfinished seams but also protects the edges of the guitar (as well as the delicate purflings) from the daily bumps and knocks to which the guitar is subjected.

The verb *binding* generally denotes the application of both the binding and purfling strips into a precise mortise, called the *staircase* or *ledge,* that is cut into the edge of the guitar box or headstock. Sometimes, steel-string guitar fingerboards are also *bound.* Purfling and binding provide an opportunity to refine the appearance of the instrument and to display the artistic taste and workmanship of the builder.

Binding strips on most

Purfling & Binding

handcrafted guitars are made from maple or rosewood, and sometimes from ebony (Fig. 11-1). Commercially made instruments are usually bound with strips of a flexible white plastic called celluloid and its off-white, artificially-grained variant, ivoroid. Ivoroid is a substitute for binding materials such as ivory and baleen, used in an earlier day but too rare or expensive for modern use. Tortoiseshell, which also bound early instruments, similarly has its modern plastic counterparts.

Decorative purflings can be found bordering the edges of the soundboard, back, and less frequently, the edges of the sides. They may consist of dyed or natural wood-veneer lines, plastic lines, marquetry strips, or shell (abalone or pearl) strips such as in Fig. 11-2.

Antonio de Torres set many of the aesthetic standards that have been passed down to modern classical-guitar hand-builders. He banished the floral carvings, pearl incrustations (Fig. 11-3) and harlequin stripes that were popular in

the mid-1800's, replacing them with a careful linear motif that simply framed all the plates of the instrument, thus allowing no distraction from the inherent beauty of the material. He

used color sparingly and then only to visually pull together the many elements of the instrument. His design sense was truly classic and timeless (Fig. 11-4).

11–1.   *Solid wood bindings and purflings are more difficult to apply and thus are usually seen only on custom handcrafted instruments. This maple guitar with rosewood binding was built at Stringfellow Guitars.*

11–2. *Steel-string guitar built at Stringfellow with abalone purfling. Inlaying the abalone almost doubles the time required to make the guitar.*

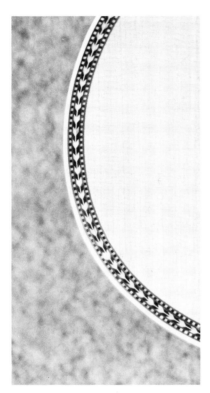

11–3. *Detail of purfling on a French gut-string guitar made in the mid-1800s, probably from the Mirecourt school. Each tiny square and flechette (arrow) is cut from mother-of-pearl and pressed into a field of black mastic.*

11–4. *Guitar built in 1863 by Antonio de Torres, showing coordinated rosette and purfling design. Torres' simple but elegant patterns set the trend for classical guitarmaking, which persists to this day.*

PLANNING AND PREPARING BINDING AND PURFLING

We recommend that the beginner start with a basic binding scheme, increasing the level of complexity in measured stages on subsequent instruments. On your first guitar, use plain binding strips of a species that contrasts with the tone woods of the soundbox: perhaps rosewood binding on mahogany, maple binding on rosewood, rosewood binding on maple, and so forth. The end graft should be of the same species as the binding. Contrasting local hardwoods such as walnut or cherry bindings can be used against maple for an instrument made entirely of local varieties. Purflings should be restricted to veneer lines around the soundboard, back, and back stripe.

A subsequent guitar project might entail the use of simple contrasting binding, as before, but with the addition of marquetry purfling strips. The next level of complexity is the addition of side purfling strips to this scheme, carrying them across the end graft as in Fig. 11-53. The addition of side purflings permits the use of bindings that match the soundbox tone woods; the purfling lines provide the necessary framing contrast.

On a subsequent project, all the above can be attempted, but the end graft can be purfled and mitered to the side purfling. Another advanced project can feature the backstripe purflings mitered into the back purflings. Finally, steel-string builders may eventually be confident enough to try their hand at pearl purfling inlays.

Binding-strip sizes vary from builder to builder. Wood bindings bend easiest if they are no thicker than $3/32$ inch but can vary in width from $3/16$ to $1/4$ inch on the steel-string and from $1/8$ to $3/16$ inch on the classical. Strip lengths should be at least equal to the length of the sides, preferably longer. Selection criteria for straightness of grain and evenness of texture for binding strips are at least as strict as criteria for selecting the side plates.

Binding strips can be obtained in various ways. If your binding is to match the species of your sides, you can produce strips from the long cutoffs that remain when you trim your flat side blanks down to width before bending. Strips can also be cut to width from a third, unmatched or defective side blank, or they can be sawn off a flat-sawn billet that is the same thickness as the strips' desired width (Fig. 11-5a & b).

Laminated bindings are binding strips with purfling lines sandwiched underneath. Side purfling lines should never be applied loose but must be preglued to and pre-

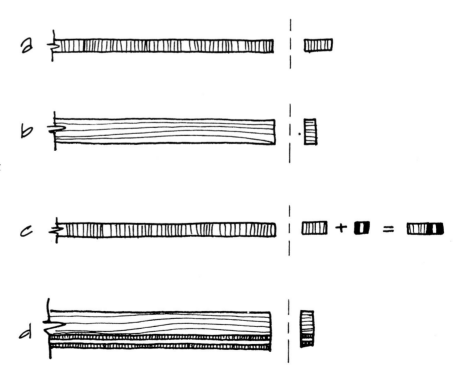

11–5a, b, c, and d.   Cutting plain and laminated binding strips (cross sections).

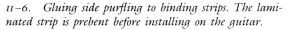

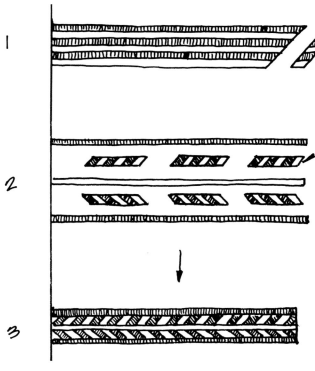

11–6. *Gluing side purfling to binding strips. The laminated strip is prebent before installing on the guitar.*

11–7. *Manufacturing herringbone marquetry for purfling: 1. veneer sandwich cut at diagonals; 2. diagonals sandwiched with outer and inner veneers; and 3. new sandwich sliced into herringbone strips.*

bent with the binding strips. The purfling lines can be glued directly to the bottoms of the binding strips, as shown in Fig. 11-5c, and Fig. 11-6. Alternatively, a laminated sandwich can be laid up and glued, then stripped as shown in Fig. 11-5d.

Purfling veneer lines can be purchased from mail-order luthier-supply houses. They are usually available in several thicknesses, in black or white. Veneer-line sandwiches are also available in BW, BWB, and WBW combinations. Alternatively, ¼₀- or ½₈-inch veneers of holly or maple can

be obtained from woodworking houses and stripped to ³⁄₃₂-inch widths on the table saw with a thin, fine-tooth blade. Additional information on preparing and dying purflings can be found in Chapter 6.

Marquetry strips are available from mail-order luthier- or cabinetmaking-supply houses. The strips you receive are actually slices off an elaborately built-up sandwich (Fig. 11-7). Commonly, marquetry strips can be purchased in thin or thick sizes. The thin strips should be used if they are to be inlaid alone, but the thicker

strips should be used if inlaid while accompanied with other veneer lines.

Marquetry strips do not normally need to be prebent when bound into the ledge since they are being backed with a binding strip that is also being glued in. Simply dropping the strips in hot water for sixty to ninety seconds will soften them sufficiently to conform to the ledge. Do not expect to bend marquetry strips over ⅛ inch wide: These are best kept straight as back-stripe inlay.

PROCEDURE: END GRAFT

We begin the binding and pur-fling process by finishing the seam at the tail of the guitar where the two sides meet. The piece of wood or other mate-rial inserted to finish the seam is called the end graft or bot-tom inlay.

The end graft may have either parallel or tapered edges. We prefer a tapered end graft because it allows a pres-sure fit. Otherwise, the choice is strictly a matter of taste.

TOOLS
chisels (wide and ¼-inch)
clamps, as needed
6-inch ruler
razor knife
block plane
scraper blade

SUPPLIES
AR glue

MATERIALS
hardwood scrap about ³⁄₃₂
    inch thick for end-graft
    (see Step 3, below)

Step 1—Trimming Overhang

The overhang of the sound-board should be trimmed all around to within ⅛ inch of the sides with a chisel (Fig. 11-8) before the end graft is inlaid or the binding-and-pur-fling channels are cut. Special sensitivity to grain direction is required, especially in the waist area. Never carve against the grain, lest you tear away a sec-

11–8. *Carving off the soundboard overhang.*

tion of the soundboard. Carve the edge *flush* to the sides for a few inches on either side of the tail seam. In that area, also carve the rim of the back flush to the sides if it overhangs at all. Avoid cutting into the sides when trimming flush.

This operation can also be done with a router and a flush-cutting bit (Fig. 11-9), leaving the rims flush all around. This should be done with several passes, nibbling closer to flush each time so that the bit does not snag and tear out the soundboard edge.

11–9. *Router with flush-cutting bit. The mortise must be skirted when flush cutting the back edge, but on the soundboard the bit can plow straight in.*

Step 2—Cutting the End-graft Slot

The guitar may be clamped in a tail-up position to work on the end graft. Use the clamping arrangement shown in Fig. 11-10 to hold the guitar. The clamps must be fixed to the guitar's edges only; letting the clamps slide inboard of the edges onto the fragile plates could result in fracture. On the classical, support the neck from underneath with a cushion, a cardboard box, or whatever; do not mar the crest of the headpiece.

The slot should be centered on the centerseams of the top and back. If they are not precisely aligned, average the difference to center the slot. Lay out the widths of the ends of the slot (slightly wider at the soundboard end) by measuring out from the centerline. Connect the layout marks with scribe lines drawn with a razor knife pressed against the 6-inch metal ruler, as in Fig. 11-11. Make several light passes to increase the depth of the scribe lines (heavy pressure will cause the knife to wander). Begin carefully removing material between the scribe lines with a chisel. (See Fig. 11-12.) When you get to the bottom of the scribe marks, use the knife to deepen the scribes, taking care not to let the slot walls creep out of square. Continue to chisel and deepen the scribes until you have cut all the way through the sides and have exposed the tailblock surface. (This step can also be done with a router and jig, as shown in Fig. 11-13.)

Step 3—Making the End Graft

Whether the end graft matches or contrasts with the sides, it should always match the bindings. Sometimes, however, you may wish to choose a strikingly figured piece for decorative purposes.

Draft the taper of your slot on a piece that is slightly thicker than your sides and about twice as long as the depth of your soundbox. At least one face of the piece should be flat and smooth. Cut to within $\frac{1}{16}$ inch of the drafting lines and then begin shaving with a block plane, holding the piece as shown in Fig. 11-14.

When you reach the drafting lines, begin trying the piece for fit in the slot with the smooth face down. If it is loose at the narrow end, you must reduce its taper; if loose at the wide end, increase the taper. As you continue to plane and fit, simply slide the graft further and further into

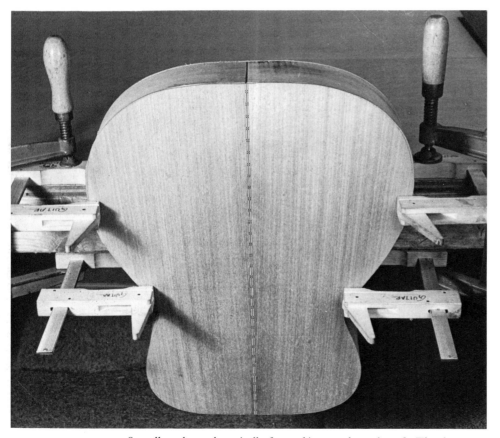

11–10. *Soundbox clamped vertically for working on the end graft. The clamps must hold the soundbox by the edges to avoid cracking the fragile plates.*

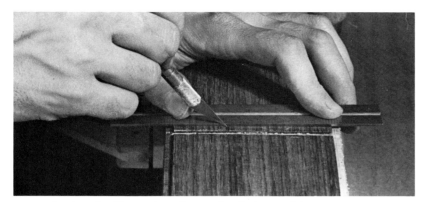

II–II.   Scoring the sides at the tail seam for the bottom inlay.

II–I2.   Chiseling out between the scored lines.

the slot until it is just right. There should be no movement when the piece is jiggled at either end. (*Note:* If you are using purfling lines to border the end graft, they must be inserted with the graft when it is checked for fit. Bunch them on one side for easy handling.)

Step 4—Gluing In the Graft

Cover the bottom of the slot with a moderate film of glue. Place the decorative lines (if any) in their proper sequence against the walls of the slot, working glue between all adjacent surfaces. Slide the graft in while holding the lines to keep them from sliding out. Once the graft is tight, secure it with a couple of gentle taps

II–I3.   End graft routing jig. The fences are adjustable for width and taper.

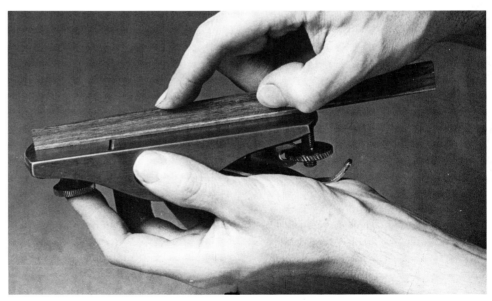

II–I4.   Tapering the end graft with a block plane. The workpiece must be held carefully to avoid planing off a fingernail. Trial-and-error tapering the overlong end graft ensures a wedged pressure fit.

on the wide end. Downward clamping is ordinarily unnecessary, but if you have a long clamp, you may cover the inlay with a caul and clamp from the heel of the guitar. Allow to dry for one hour.

Step 5—Scraping Flush

Carefully cut off the overhang of the graft just inside the top and back surfaces. If the graft is substantially thicker than the sides, plane it almost flush and then scrape it flush; if it protrudes only slightly, just scrape (Fig. 11-15).

11–15. *Scraping the end graft flush. In this photo, a small area around the tail was routed rather than being shaved flush with a chisel, but either method works well.*

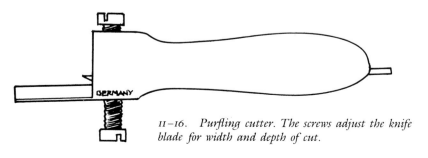

11–16. *Purfling cutter. The screws adjust the knife blade for width and depth of cut.*

PROCEDURE: CUTTING BINDING AND PURFLING LEDGES

This procedure traditionally has been done with a tool called a purfling cutter, shown in Fig. 11-16. Successful use of the purfling cutter relies on several factors: The tool must be well made with accurate, secure adjustments; the cutter blade must be razor sharp and free of burrs or other irregularities; and the tool user must have a steady hand to maintain consistent registry of the tool in order to achieve a uniform cut. This takes some practice.

We have found the hand-held router with edge guide to be so much easier to master than the purfling cutter that we advocate its use for all students. The purfling cutter, however, remains a valuable tool in our shop for specialized purposes. When cutting the binding and purfling ledges on a guitar with a radical back arch, the purfling cutter is essential for evening the ledges in areas where the back arch prevents the router from cutting evenly. This step is specifically required on the steel-string guitar built from this book and is shown in the following procedure. Thus, steel-string builders must have both a router and a purfling cutter; classical builders should wait until the next procedure, Fitting and Gluing the Binding, to decide whether a purfling cutter will be required.

When using the router for this procedure, the bit must be sharp to avoid burning or snagging and tearing. The router must be equipped with an edge guide that has an adjustable pilot wheel. The edge guide shown in Fig. 11-17 is a standard industrial supply part. (*Note:* When routing with an adjustable pilot wheel, it is important to recognize that the bit will cut horizontally shallower or deeper depending upon the orientation of the guide to the workpiece. All test cuts and actual routs must be made at the orientation that produces maximum depth, so that the actual routing depth will match the test depth. To ensure this, the router should be pivoted around the pilot wheel during several passes until the correct—maximum-depth—orientation is achieved.)

We *strongly* suggest the use of ear protection (cotton earplugs will suffice) during the routing operations.

TOOLS
router and straight bit
chisel
purfling cutter (steel-string only)
files (steel-string only)

11–17. Router with laminate edge guide attached. The pilot wheel follows the curve of the side.

Step 1—Routing for Binding

The vertical and horizontal depths of cut for the binding ledge will depend upon the decorative scheme you have planned. If you plan no side purfling or if you plan to use side purfling lines mitered to end-graft purfling lines, set the cutter for the depths of the *binding* strip only. If you plan to use side purfling but do not plan to miter to end-graft purfling lines, set the cutter for the vertical depth of the binding plus the side purfling lines.

Make a test cut in a scrap block. Push the router back and forth in the test cut, pivoting the base-plate around the pilot wheel to ensure that the test cut is to the full depth of the edge-guide setting. Adjust both the bit and the edge guide until a scrap of your actual binding strip (or the strip plus the side purfling lines) fits perfectly. (See Fig. 11-18.)

Make the initial rout on the back edge. The guitar box should be resting face down

on a level, padded surface. Hold the router securely with both hands on the handles. Start at the headblock with the edge guide square to the guitar side. *Important:* On the steel-string, do not let the guide slip into the mortise; on the classical, do not let the bit cut into the heel. Turn on the motor and gently ease the bit into the edge. Travel around the outline slowly but steadily, keeping the guide square to the side. When you return to the other side of the headblock area, again be sure to stop before slipping into the mortise (steel-string) or cutting into the heel (classical). Make one or two more passes, pivoting the base-plate around the pilot wheel as you go.

Routing the soundboard edge is essentially the same, but it requires somewhat more care. A sudden lurch of the router can snag and tear out the soft soundboard material, especially when routing across end-grain. Hold the router firmly and maintain concentration at all times.

11–18. Checking a binding fragment against a test rout in a piece of scrap wood.

To rout the classical sound-board, either support the neck or clamp it in a vise and support the guitar body to hold it level. Note that the neckshaft will interfere with the edge rout; come as close to it as possible, but do not cut into it.

On the steel-string, when routing the soundboard edge it is unnecessary to stop at the mortise as when routing the back. Proceed into the mortise to cut the area of the sound-board over it.

On both instruments, but especially on the classical, be aware that the soundboard may flex under the router base causing the router bit to cut deeper than planned. Hold the router down firmly but keep it level—do not press inattentively into the soundboard while moving around the edge. Make several passes.

Students using side purfling mitered to end-graft purfling must now increase the vertical depth of cut by the thickness of the side purfling. Rout both top and back edges as before, but *do not* cut into the end-graft purfling lines—stop short of the lines leaving little nubs of side wood, as in Fig. 11-27.

Step 2—Steel-string Only: Evening the Routed Ledge with a Chisel

The perpendicular relationship between the router base, the bit, and the pilot wheel, causes the unit to cut deepest into a perfectly square corner.

Where the surface of the back angles up from the sides, the bit thus cuts a shallower ledge than was originally intended. The steel-string (especially our design) has a considerable longitudinal back taper with a considerable transversal arch. The router will thus cut the back ledge with considerable variation in depth; indeed, the ledge virtually disappears in the immediate vicinity of the headblock. Another region with a shallow-ledge problem can often be found between the waist and the widest point of the lower bout. The ledge around most of the rest of the guitar's perimeter will be slightly shallow, but this can be disregarded. When bound, the binding strips will project above the surface of the sides by a small amount but can be easily scraped flush. You will probably find the ledge at its test depth in the vicinity of the tailblock.

The problem is reduced if a router is used with a much smaller base or with a specially made cutter that registers primarily on the side surfaces (such as is utilized in the large factories). Our solution, however, is to follow the routing of each back ledge by final trimming with the purfling cutter.

Adjust the horizontal cutting depth of your purfling cutter to a setting that is about 1/64 to 1/32 inch shallower than the router test cut. The blade of the purfling cutter should be extended from its holder by

only a small amount and should be positioned so that the blade bevel falls in the waste portion of the cut.

With the cutter set as described, press the tool's register bar firmly against the side (use little or no downward pressure on the blade) as you swing it around the upper portion of the bout toward the headblock area (Fig. 11-19). Repeat the score line several times, increasing the downward pressure steadily, taking care that the tool does not rotate around the register bar. A single, deep score line should finally result. With a sharp chisel, carve the vertical wall of the ledge back to the score line, trying to keep it vertical and avoiding the front lip of the ledge (Fig. 11-20). The material should carve away easily, providing you take fine shavings off each time. The inside corner of the ledge should be square and clean of debris. The floor should remain flat.

After the ledge has been deepened on both sides of the mortise, a nub of overhanging back material will remain immediately above the mortise. This nub can be easily sawn away with a razor saw, as shown in Fig. 11-21. The nub is held with the the thumb and forefinger as shown, to provide a guide for the saw blade and to keep its kerf precisely continuous with the rim of the ledge. Chisel the nub away if it hangs on and trim away any projecting material that could interfere with a

11–19. *Scoring a guideline with a purfling cutter to continue the binding ledge across an area missed by the router due to the inclination of the back relative to the sides.*

11–20. *Chiseling the binding ledge to the scored line.*

snug accommodation of the binding strip into the ledge.

A fine-tooth flat mill file with one of its narrow edges ground smooth will serve to even the freshly chiseled surfaces. The smoothly ground edge should glide on the floor of the ledge without chewing up the crucial bottom lip. Trim and file until the binding strip fits well—a minuscule overhang is acceptable.

Repeat this entire procedure in the shallow portion of the ledge found between the waist and the widest point of the lower bout. Avoid any chiseling or filing in the deepest part of the waist, unless absolutely necessary.

11–21. *Sawing off the remaining nub at the mortise using the fingers to guide the saw.*

11–22. *Checking staircase rout for purfling on a piece of scrap. For best results, the binding fragment should be held in place while checking the purfling for fit.*

Step 3—Staircase Routing for Purfling

Adjust the depths of cut for the back purfling ledge (if any). When test cutting on a scrap block, you must begin with your original binding ledge and check the purfling ledge with a scrap of binding in place as well as a scrap of the purfling you plan to use. (See Fig. 11-22.)

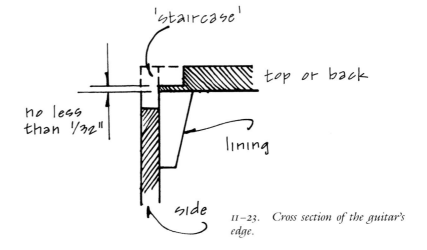

11–23. *Cross section of the guitar's edge.*

11–24. *Routing the purfling ledge. Fuzz left on the routed edge can be shaved clean with a sharp chisel laid flat on the back.*

11–25.   Steel-string soundbox with completed staircase after final ledge trimming.

Purfling ledges should be no more than ¹⁄₁₆ inch deep. All staircase cuts should leave at least ¹⁄₃₂ inch of the plate underneath; for very wide purfling bands, leave at least ³⁄₆₄ inch (Fig. 11-23).

Rout the back staircase, stopping at the heel or skirting the mortise as before. (See Fig. 11-24.) Reset the depths for the soundboard purfling ledge, and again rout as before. (*Note:* The caveat on avoiding lurching movements becomes most critical with the soundboard staircase rout, as

there is no additional material to be removed; a torn-out edge will remain as a flaw from this point on.)

Steel-string only: Repeat the purfling-cutter trimming operation for the back staircase, as necessary. (See Fig. 11-25.)

Step 4—Mitering End-graft Purfling Lines

This step obviously is only for those individuals using side purfling mitered to end-graft purfling lines. The mitering se-

quence is shown in Figs. 11-26 through 11-31. In summary: Begin with the binding rout (Fig. 11-26) and adjust for side purfling, leaving nubs of rosewood as in Fig. 11-27 (this is where you should be as of this step). The nubs are carefully shaved off with the ¼-inch chisel (Fig. 11-28) without disturbing the end-graft purfling lines. (See Fig. 11-29.) Using the chisel perpendicular to the sides as in Fig. 11-30, we trim the ends of the lines at 45 degrees (Fig. 11-31).

11–26. *End graft trimmed to depth of binding.*

11–28. *Trimming the rosewood nubs.*

11–27. *Depth of rout increased for side purfling. Note that the rout stops short of the end graft, leaving rosewood nubs at the four corners.*

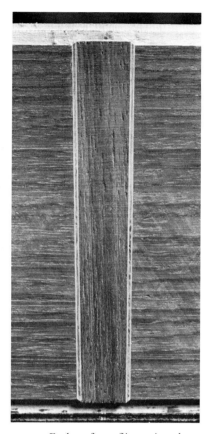

11-29. *Rosewood nubs trimmed.*

11-31. *End-graft purfling mitered.*

11-30. *Mitering the end-graft purfling lines.*

PROCEDURE: FITTING AND GLUING THE BINDING

The binding strips (with or without side purfling attached) must be prebent to fit the guitar's outline. On the classical, the ledges must be sawn through and excavated at the neckshaft and heel where the router was obstructed, and these channels must be accurately trimmed to provide a snug fit for the binding and purfling.

Many luthiers and guitar manufacturers glue in their bindings and purflings by wrapping a long strip of sturdy fabric (such as upholsterer's canvas tape) tightly around the guitar. We use a different method, but the choice is purely a matter of preference. Our method employs doubled-up strips of masking tape (or single strips of nylon-reinforced strapping tape) pulled tightly around the corners, as shown in Fig. 11-32.

Using masking or strapping tape is a somewhat simpler method than wrapping. The tape can be cut into 4- to 5-inch lengths before the gluing begins (about twenty-five doubled pieces for one binding strip), or it can be cut from a heavy dispenser and doubled as needed. (*Note:* When sticky tape is pulled off the soundboard after the binding is in place and the glue is dry, it is important to pull it off diagonally to the grain lines and *with* the direction of grain run-out on the soundboard. Pulling off straight against the run-out may cause soft fibers to be torn from the soundboard.)

In the steps that follow, we fully describe all the trimming and gluing steps for side purfling mitered to end graft purfling lines. All other binding and purfling combinations described in the discussion of planning and preparation are the same but less complex. Readers should extract the

information pertinent to the designs they actually plan to use, and simply ignore the additional mitering instructions if inappropriate.

TOOLS
bending pipe
razor saw
chisels
6-inch ruler

SUPPLIES
masking tape
AR glue

MATERIALS
binding and purfling strips, minimum 32-inch length (SS) or 28-inch length (CL).

Step 1—Bending the Binding Strips

Binding strips without side purfling can be bent individually; to bend binding *with* side purfling attached, we recommend taping two strips together tightly (prior to wetting and bending), as shown in Fig. 11-33, to provide additional support for the fragile purfling lines.

Otherwise, bending binding is very similar to bending sides or lining. When side purfling is attached, the strips must not be soaked—just hold them in hot tap water for half a minute or so, and rewet occasionally if necessary. Plain binding strips may be soaked for a few minutes.

Bend closely to the template and then finish bending each individual strip, using as a

11–32. Gluing the binding with doubled strips of masking tape. The loose strip to the right serves to keep the binding from flopping about while the preceding section is taped.

guide the actual binding ledge in which it will live. The material is reasonably flexible, but it should fit into its ledge with, at most, light pressure. When each strip is fit, mark it for later reference to indicate in which ledge it belongs.

During this fitting step, classical builders should take the opportunity to check for uniformity in the depths of the staircase ledges. In particular, the area around the waist may be shallow; if so, the ledges can be deepened with a purfling cutter and chisel as described in Step 2 of the fore-going procedure, Cutting Binding and Purfling Ledges.

Step 2—Classical Only: Cutting Binding and Purfling Ledges Across Neckshaft and Heel

The staircases must continue across the areas of the soundboard and back that could not be routed because of the obstruction of the neckshaft and heel. A razor saw is used to cut to the bottoms of the binding channels, which are then excavated with the ³⁄₃₂-inch chisel; the purfling ledges are shaved back with the wide chisel.

On the soundboard, connect the ends of the binding rout with a saw cut guided by a short straightedge as in Fig. 11-34. The distance of the cut from the end-grain face of the heel should be slightly *less* than the full thickness of the binding to ensure that the binding strips fit snugly; the channel can be expanded slightly to achieve a close fit using the binding strips themselves for reference.

Shave away the side material in the channels with the ³⁄₃₂-inch chisel, stopping at the web. The ledge should remain level as it enters the heel slots.

Next, take the wide chisel and shave back the purfling ledge so that the staircase continues smoothly into the headblock area. Err on the shy side for now.

Try a binding strip for fit in the channel. If it does not go in, widen the channel slightly by shaving with the wide chisel until the binding strip slides in with little resistance. Then, with the binding strip

11–33. *Bending laminated binding strips. The purfling lines are butted together and the two laminated strips taped tightly to provide support for the fragile lines during bending.*

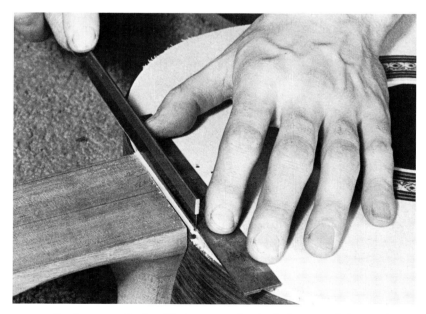

11–34. *Sawing across the headblock area on the classical to extend the soundboard binding ledges into the heel slots.*

11–35. Two saw cuts across the heel area are necessary to connect the back binding ledges.

in its channel, try the purfling lines for fit in the purfling ledge. Widen the ledge as necessary to produce a snug fit. Repeat for the other side.

At the bottom of the heel, make two parallel saw cuts to connect the ends of the binding ledge (see Fig. 11-35). Excavate with the ³⁄₃₂-inch chisel, running the ledge levelly across the heel. (See Fig. 11-36.) Shave back the purfling ledge as in Fig. 11-37, and then expand the binding channel and purfling ledge successively, as on the soundboard side, until the binding and purfling fit snugly. They must slide in rather easily to avoid difficulties during gluing. Again, try to make the staircase flow smoothly into this area to avoid a rough appearance.

Step 3—Trimming the First Binding Strip

This step and the following steps describe the trimming process for binding with side purfling mitered at the end graft. Students using plain binding or side purfling that will not be mitered at the end graft may trim identically, simply ignoring the mitering steps.

Start with a strip on the soundboard. Slip the strip back and forth in the ledge until you locate the point where the waist of the guitar best matches the waist of the bent strip. Tape it securely in place. Run your finger along the strip toward the tail of the guitar, pressing it into the ledge as it will be when glued, and tape it in several places. Mark where it intersects the centerseam of the soundboard and where the side purfling intersects the mitered end-graft purfling, as in Fig. 11-38. Remove the strip and cut through with a razor saw slightly beyond the centerseam mark. Carefully shave the side purfling back to its mark and trim at a 45-degree angle. (See Fig. 11-39.)

Check to see that the purfling ends match angles to form a perfect miter, as in Fig. 11-40. If the miters do not meet perfectly, remove material from the side lines (not the end-graft lines) until they do. Your room for trial and error is less than ⅛ inch. Once you have a proper fit, tape the strip

11–36. Excavating the binding channel between heel and back with a ³⁄₃₂-inch chisel.

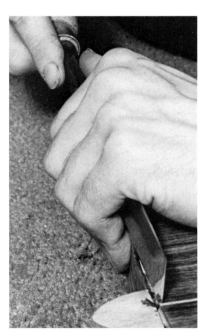

11–37. Continuing the purfling across the heel area by shaving back with a chisel.

at the waist again and in a couple of places toward the tail. The miters should still fit. The waist can move slightly if necessary, but if it has to move ⅛ inch or more due to too many trials at the miter end, you will have to touch up the bend to avoid excessive tension in the area.

Once you have determined that your trim cuts are accurate, tape toward the headblock and mark there about ⅛ inch short of the web between the heel slots on the classical or at the wall of the mortise on the steel-string. Trim to your marks.

II–38. Marking binding and purfling for trimming.

Step 4—Gluing the First Binding Strip

Before applying any glue, it will probably be helpful to tape the binding strip loosely at the waist to support it and keep it from dangling while the first few inches at the tail are being glued.

The cardinal rule to remember when gluing binding and purfling strips in place is that *all* adjoining surfaces must have glue between them. Apply glue to each layer separately if necessary to avoid butting two dry surfaces.

Begin by applying glue to the first few inches of the staircase, starting at the bottom of the centerseam. If you are using several individual soundboard purfling strips, hold them in their proper sequence, apply glue to the first few inches, and fan them out

II–39. Trimming and mitering side purfling on a laminated binding strip.

II–40. Checking the miter for a close fit.

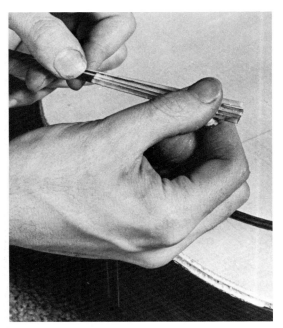

11–41. *Fanning and working the glue between the soundboard purfling lines.*

to work glue between them, as in Fig. 11-41. (If you are using a single veneer, veneer sandwich, or marquetry purfling strip, be certain that its outer edge is covered with glue after it is placed on its ledge.) Lay the purfling band onto its ledge (let it overlap the centerseam slightly) and press the binding strip into place, making sure that the miters mate up. Clean up the initial glue squeeze-out with a wad of paper towel and check to see that the strips are snug and in their proper order and that the miters still meet. Place the first piece of doubled masking tape an inch or so from the end graft, and secure it as shown in Fig. 11-42. (See also Fig. 11-43.) This is your last opportunity to check the perfection of your miter. If it has slipped in any way, remove the first piece of tape and reposition the binding. If it is correct, tape directly over the centerline and miter.

Continue taping around the side, applying glue to the staircase a few inches at a time.

Each time fresh glue is applied, be sure to work it between the lines or coat the outer face of the purfling strip as necessary. (See Fig. 11-44.) Before applying tape to each section, wipe up excess glue with a wad of paper towel, as in Fig. 11-45, simultaneously pressing the binding and purfling strips into place. Make sure they are all touching the floor of the ledges and are not tangled or twisted in any way before taping.

On the classical, when the taping reaches the upper bout, press the remainder of the strips into place without glue and use a scissor or cutting pliers to clip off the purfling where the binding ends. Remove the strips from the slot and finish gluing and taping the upper bout, making certain that the binding is on the floor of its ledge as it enters the heel slot. (See Fig. 11-46.)

On the steel-string, simply continue around the upper bout; finish by clipping the purfling and binding strips just beyond the mortise.

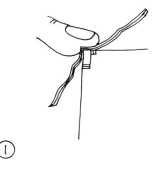

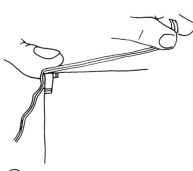

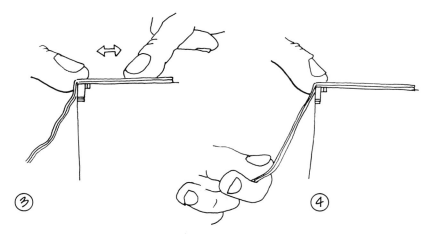

11–42. *Binding, taping sequence.*

11–43. *Applying the first doubled strip of masking tape. We start an inch or so from the beginning of the binding to allow for a final check of the miter position.*

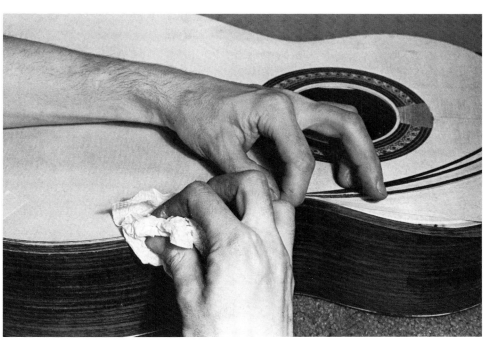

11–45. *Wiping excess glue with a paper towel. This also presses the lines into place and cleans the area to permit a visual check of the alignment of the bindings and purflings before taping.*

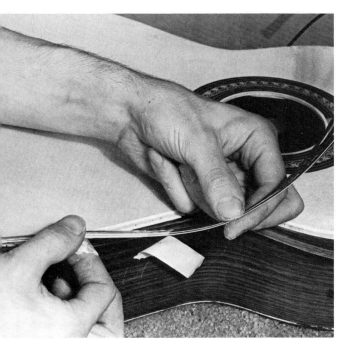

11–44. *Working glue in between the soundboard purfling lines as the binding and purfling are taped around the edge.*

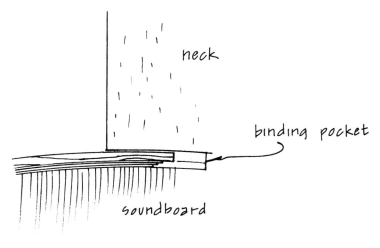

11–46. *Plan view of binding tucked into pocket at the heel slot.*

Step 5—Gluing the Second Binding Strip

The second strip can be glued while the first is drying if you proceed to the back edge diagonally opposite.

The trimming procedures are identical to those in the previous step, except that the upper bout end of the strip should be trimmed slightly (about 1/16 inch) *beyond* the centerseam.

Gluing procedures are also identical, except that when the taping reaches the upper bout and the last section is pressed into place without glue, the binding and purfling must be trimmed *precisely* to end at the centerseam. This is why we leave the binding slightly overlong in the initial trimming. Place a protective scrap on the heel or headblock and shave the strips back with a chisel held vertically, as in Fig. 11-47.

On the classical, when the last section is taped, clean out any glue that might have collected in the channel past the end of the strips.

Step 6—Fitting and Gluing the Third Binding Strip

Remove the tape from the first binding strip, taking special care to peel it off the soundboard diagonally to the grain and with, rather than against, the direction of the run-out. Gently scrape the first few inches at the bottom flush to the soundboard.

Cut into the binding and purfling with a razor saw at the centerseam, as shown in Fig. 11-48. *Do not* let the saw cut into the soundboard or the end graft. Shave away the excess with a chisel, leaving the binding and purfling ends square and smooth as in Fig. 11-49. Try not to remove material from the staircase when cleaning up the ledges.

Trimming the third binding strip is similar to trimming the first binding strip, except that after mitering the side purfling the end of the binding must be shaved back to mate to the end of the first strip. Use the chisel held vertically, as in Fig. 11-50. Check the binding ends for a clean mate after trimming; the purfling miters must remain accurate. (See Fig. 11-51.)

The soundboard purfling ends must also butt cleanly. Trim with a chisel and check for mating on the purfling ledge.

Figures 11-52 and 11-53 show trimming and mating with unmitered side purfling lines.

The gluing procedure is similar to Step 4. Try to keep the soundboard purfling lines mated at the centerseam so that they have the appearance of a continuous band; by adjusting horizontal pressure when taping there, you can ensure correct alignment.

11–47. *Trimming the binding to end at the centerseam of the back. The purfling is clipped off and then trimmed identically.*

11–48. *Cutting through the first binding and purfling strips at the soundboard centerseam to prepare the ends for mating the strips on the opposite side. The saw must not cut into the soundboard or the end graft.*

11–51. *The binding ends must butt snugly while the purfling miters meet accurately.*

11–49. *Binding and purfling ends trimmed squarely. Special care must be taken during trimming to avoid increasing the horizontal depth of the purfling ledge.*

11–52. *Razor saw cut in preparation for trimming binding and unmitered purfling ends.*

11–50. *Trimming back the binding and purfling for mating.*

11–53. *Mating the binding and unmitered purfling ends.*

11–54. Trimming binding and purfling ends to mate at the heel.

Step 7—Fitting and Gluing the Fourth Binding Strip

Fitting and gluing is identical to Step 6, except that as in Step 5, the upper bout ends must be trimmed precisely. This time, however, they must also mate with the previously glued-in strips. Again, check for fit and trim before applying the last stretch of glue (Fig. 11-54). You want to avoid or at least minimize a gap here, but *absolutely no buckling* of the binding is permissible—better to have a tiny gap between the binding ends than a poor glue seam over the last few inches of the binding. Getting it perfect takes practice, so getting it close is very good for the first try.

Step 8—Scraping Bindings Flush

After all glue is dry, remove the tape strips carefully (on the soundboard diagonally *with* the soundboard grain run-out). All excess wood and glue must be scraped flush to the soundboard, back, and sides. (See Fig. 11-55.) Work carefully, constantly monitoring the thickness of the binding strips (Fig. 11-56). If a binding ledge was shallow to begin with, or if a strip was not glued all the way into its ledge in one place or another, it is very easy to wipe out the binding with inattentive scraping. Scrape *with* the grain run-out on the soundboard. Remember that you are working with fine, brittle strips and thin plates.

11–55. Scraping the binding and purfling flush to the plates. On the back, the scraper is held flat and pivoted to avoid tipping or tearing the binding. Scraping across the binding will tear out the fibers.

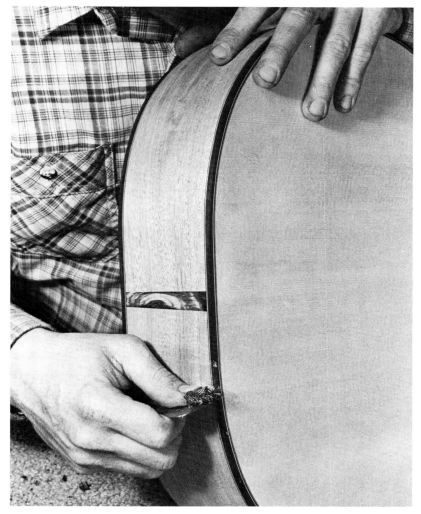

11–56. *Scraping the binding and purfling on the sides. Care must be taken to avoid thinnning the binding excessively.*

Figures 11-57 and 11-58 show the mitered end graft after all the bindings and purflings have been scraped flush to the plates.

11–57 and 11–58. *Mitered end-graft purflings after scraping.*

CHAPTER 12

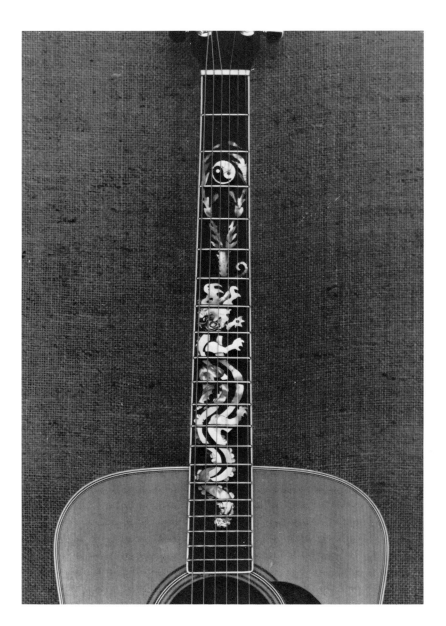

HISTORICAL NOTES

From the earliest days of instrument making, gut-string fretboards evolved distinctly from wire-string fretboards. As early as 1500, the fretboards of such wire-strung instruments as mandolins, citterns, orpharions, and bandoras were separate planks of wood laminated onto the neckshaft and overlapping the soundboard, as on modern guitars (Fig. 12-1). The fretboard on a typical gut-string instrument of the time, however, consisted of a thin veneer that ran flush with the surface of the soundboard (Fig. 12-2). This flush fretboard appeared on most guitars until the early 1800s, at which time a number of British, French, and Viennese guitarmakers borrowed the overlapping fretboard design found on wire-strung instruments for use on gut-string guitars. Although the changeover first appeared as a flush veneer that overlapped the soundboard, this form soon evolved into the thicker, modern fingerboard.

The Fingerboard

The thicker fingerboard raises the strings higher above the soundboard, creating an increased mechanical advantage at the saddle that produces greater tension and sonority. The overlapping fingerboard also provides the guitar neck with greater structural rigidity. Several surviving flush-fingerboard guitars from the transitional period of the early 1800s appear to have been subsequently "modernized" by the addition of an overlapping fingerboard and a taller bridge.

Like overlapping fingerboards, fixed frets were a characteristic unique to early wire-strung instruments. Gut-string instruments such as the viol, the lute, and four-, five-, and six-course guitars, had instead loops of gut cord tied around the neckshaft. This was necessary because early gut strings were not uniform in cross section and musicians needed to adjust the spacing among these movable frets to compensate for tuning problems associated with lumpy strings. Early wire strings were extruded through dies (as are modern wire strings) and thus were far

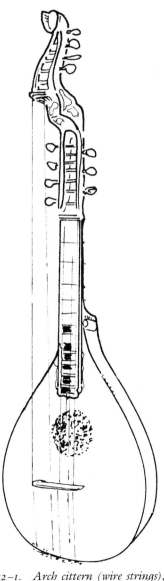

12–1. *Arch cittern (wire strings), circa 1500.*

12–2. *Five-course guitar (gut strings), circa 1600.*

more uniform than gut. Frets made of brass or ivory could therefore be permanently fixed into saw cuts on the fingerboards of wire-strung instruments.

The development of sulfur-treated gut strings and overspun bass strings so greatly reduced gut's inherent tuning problems that tied-on frets eventually became obsolete; hammered-in bar frets were adopted universally by guitarmakers during the transitional period of the early 1800s. These new frets were first made of brass and later of copper alloy; they had a rectangular cross section that was to be used for over a century. Technological advances following World War I brought the now familiar die-rolled T-shaped frets into use; they are still used to this day.

Fingerboard widths have shown considerable variation over the centuries. Early fretboards made during Elizabethan times were extremely wide due to the use of double-string courses. With the widespread advent of single-string courses in the nineteenth century, fingerboards narrowed. This was a period of great resurgence of popular interest in the guitar, and many players fell into the habit of holding the neck of the guitar in the crook of the left thumb. This position made it impossible for the left-hand fingers to stretch across a wide fingerboard. The consequence was that players demanded guitars with still narrower fingerboards.

An associated development was the arched fingerboard, a feature that catered to less capable guitarists who could not hold the index finger straight for a grand barre. This occurred early in the nineteenth century in Europe and was further developed in the United States on guitars built by C.F. Martin I.

Martin was actually making guitars in New York that were unique and very distinct from those made in Europe, presaging the emergence of a truly American style of guitar. The American demand for the greater sonority of steel strings at the beginning of the twentieth century turned the arched, narrow fingerboard into what would become the American standard.

On the classical guitar, however, Antonio de Torres led the return to and standardization of the wider, flatter fingerboard in the latter half of the nineteenth century. Thus, by the early twentieth century, fingerboard design on the two instruments had diverged radically, a distinction that remains generally true today. Styles change, however—we are now seeing a revival of interest in the slightly arched classical fingerboard and in wider steel-string necks.

The final step in the evolution of steel-string fingerboards occurred in the early 1920s. Jazz musicians asked Martin and Gibson for longer necks, and the fourteen-fret-to-the-body neck was created. This form, too, has become standardized.

THE GUITAR'S SCALE

The series of musical intervals playable on the guitar was originally derived from the "scale of nature," the harmonic series. The harmonic series is a set of distinct and simultaneous pitch intervals that make up the sound of a vibrating stretched string or the sound of a thin reed trapped inside a column of moving air.

The first to discover and study the harmonic series was Pythagoras, the Greek scientist of classical antiquity. Pythagoras calculated the appropriate interval sizes for all the notes in the scale from the "perfect" intervals, which he perceived as harmonics occurring naturally in a plucked string. In order to reconcile the natural scale with the arbitrarily conceived diatonic scale used by musicians of his day, however, Pythagoras had to introduce an adjustment in pitch, called the Pythagorean Comma. This was an early effort in scale "tempering."

Over the centuries, many tempering schemes have been created in an attempt to resolve the inconsistencies that occur when music is played in varying keys. Musicians had to choose whether to play upon (and the instrument maker to build) a tempered scale, which shaved or stretched certain intervals in order to allow the playing of music in all keys and along with many other different instruments; or upon an instrument with purer intervals, which resulted in purer harmonies but restricted the player to pieces of music written only in the instrument's key or in related keys.

Since frets cut straight across the entire string field and determine intervals on all the strings simultaneously, builders of fretted string instruments have always had to use an equal-tempered scale, which simply allots equal-sized intervals between all the notes. J.S. Bach precipitated the universal acceptance of the equal-tempered scale with the creation of a series of short, interrelated pieces of music named "The Well-Tempered Clavier," written in all twelve keys and playable on a harpsichord with its strings tuned in equal-sized intervals. Thus, the world came around to using the tempering system that had been used on fretted instruments for centuries.

The equally tempered scale is a series of compromised, and therefore impure, intervals. To the average player, these shaved and stretched intervals are not disturbing in the least. A more knowledgeable musician, however, will discover slight discrepancies identifiable as pitch distortions in even a perfectly tuned guitar. What is gained, however, is a fretboard that offers a compact, overlapping matrix, rich in duplicate fingerings. As a result, complex, multivoiced music can be played in all keys with only four fingers of the left hand.

Deriving Guitar Fret Intervals

A "semitone" is the pitch jump between each of the notes in our musical scale. On the guitar, the scale is divided into twelve equal semitones by proportionally diminishing fret spacings. The spacings are determined by dividing the string length and then, as each fret is located, the remaining string length, by a constant. That constant is derived mathematically.

To do so, a number must first be found which, when divided into the scale length, will increase the string's pitch by one semi-tone. Since the pitch frequency *doubles* at the twelfth fret, that number will be divided *twelve* times to increase the frequency by a factor of two. Thus, the string's pitch will be increased by *one* semitone when the string is shortened by dividing the scale length by the twelfth root of two, which equals 1.0594631.

This means that the scale length will be 1.0594631 times the distance from the first fret to the end of the scale. The relationship of the scale length to the first fret interval is therefore

$$\frac{1.0594631}{.0594631}$$

which equals 17.817152 (rounded off, 17.817).

This constant, when divided into any scale length, will produce the distance from the nut to the first fret and, when successively divided into the remaining scale length, will produce the remaining fret spacing intervals. A series of twelve fret intervals in equal temperament are thus produced.

It is unlikely that many of the early luthiers were familiar with twelfth roots or mind-numbing decimal fractions. Instead, they relied on a far simpler rule, first derived in 1591 by Vicenzo Gallelei. After studying the ancient Pythagorean texts, Gallilei derived the Rule of Eighteen, using the whole number eighteen as the fret constant.

If 18 is used as the fret constant, however, the twelfth fret will end up slightly further away from the saddle than the midpoint of the scale. This is because 18 will make each fret interval about one percent smaller than will 17.817. The net effect produced by using the Rule of Eighteen, then, is that the notes will play progressively flatter up the fingerboard. Interestingly, however, this flattening effect partially counteracts the tightening (sharpening) of the string when pressed to a fret. Thus, the rule provided a rudimentary form of internal compensation to the scale. This is probably why it remained in use for several centuries.

In the modern system, we use the precise mathematical derivation and add a compensation factor (determined when the bridge is located) to the scale length for a more accurate result.

Once we have derived the scale from a given scale length, we can give ourselves a simple shortcut to finding other scales. Dividing the distance from the nut to each fret by the scale length yields a set of decimal constants that, when multiplied in turn by any scale length, will yield the distances from the nut to the frets in that scale. Each decimal is a "fret factor" for that specific interval (Fig. 12-3).

Another traditional method of laying out the fretboard is the geometric construction system described in Fig. 12-4.

	25.4" SCALE		USE FOR ANY SCALE LENGTH		25.6" SCALE	
FRET #	DISTANCE FROM NUT	DISTANCE TO NEAREST $\frac{1}{64}$	FRET FACTORS	FRET #	DISTANCE FROM NUT	DISTANCE TO NEAREST $\frac{1}{64}$
1	1.426	$1\frac{27}{64}$	.056126	1	1.437	$1\frac{7}{16}$
2	2.771	$2\frac{49}{64}$	.109101	2	2.793	$2\frac{51}{64}$
3	4.041	$4\frac{3}{64}$	.159104	3	4.073	$4\frac{5}{64}$
4	5.240	$5\frac{15}{64}$	.206291	4	5.281	$5\frac{9}{32}$
5	6.372	$6\frac{3}{8}$	.250847	5	6.422	$6\frac{27}{64}$
6	7.439	$7\frac{7}{16}$	.292893	6	7.498	$7\frac{1}{2}$
7	8.448	$8\frac{29}{64}$	.332580	7	8.514	$8\frac{33}{64}$
8	9.399	$9\frac{25}{64}$	.370039	8	9.473	$9\frac{15}{32}$
9	10.297	$10\frac{19}{64}$	.405396	9	10.378	$10\frac{3}{8}$
10	11.145	$11\frac{9}{64}$	.438769	10	11.232	$11\frac{15}{64}$
11	11.945	$11\frac{15}{16}$	.470268	11	12.039	$12\frac{3}{64}$
12	12.700	$12\frac{45}{64}$	.500000	12	12.800	$12\frac{51}{64}$
13	13.413	$13\frac{13}{32}$	.528063	13	13.518	$13\frac{33}{64}$
14	14.086	$14\frac{3}{32}$	.554551	14	14.196	$14\frac{13}{64}$
15	14.721	$14\frac{23}{32}$	.579552	15	14.837	$14\frac{27}{32}$
16	15.320	$15\frac{21}{64}$	.603150	16	15.441	$15\frac{7}{16}$
17	15.886	$15\frac{57}{64}$	.625423	17	16.011	$16\frac{1}{64}$
18	16.420	$16\frac{27}{64}$	.646447	18	16.549	$16\frac{35}{64}$
19	16.924	$16\frac{59}{64}$	.666290	19	17.057	$17\frac{1}{16}$
20	17.400	$17\frac{13}{32}$	.685020	20	17.537	$17\frac{17}{32}$
21	17.849	$17\frac{27}{32}$	.702698	21	17.989	$17\frac{63}{64}$

12–3. *Table showing fret distances for the guitars built from this book.*

This is an ancient equal-tempered interval-derivation system that can either be traced on a stick and transferred to the fingerboard or traced on the fingerboard itself. It will work for any scale length, and will produce as many fret intervals as desired. Note: Since the intervals are developed consecutively, a serious danger of compounding errors can result if the compass point is set carelessly or if the lead is not resharpened often.

1
Trace desired scale length full size.

2
At nut end, trace a perpendicular of length, L =
$$\frac{scale\ length}{17.817}$$

3
Connect two points as shown.

4
Drop a compass arc and trace a perpendicular at the point where it bisects the base line, at f_1.

5
Reset the compass to the length of the new perpendicular; then drop a new arc to f_2. Draw a new perpendicular.

6
Repeat for as many fret intervals as desired.

nut f_1 f_2 f_3 f_4 f_5 f_6 f_7 $f_8 \rightarrow$

12–4. Geometric subdivision of the fretboard.

NOTES ON FINGERBOARD MATERIALS

The tone wood that has become universally accepted as the material of choice for the guitar fingerboard is ebony. The hardwoods known as ebony comprise several major species of the genus *Diospyros,* which consists of about two hundred species distributed throughout the world, primarily in tropical forests. *Diospyros* occasionally occurs in temperate climates, especially *Diospyros virginiana,* well known in the United States as persimmon.

The species used for fingerboards are African and East Indian in origin: *D. crassiflora* and *D. piscatoria* from West Africa (generally referred to as gaboon ebony), and *D. melanoxylon* (Indian or Macassar ebony), *D. ebenum* (Ceylon ebony), and *D. marmorate* (Andaman ebony) from India and Southeast Asia. Of the East Indian species, Ceylon ebony is the most dense and uniform in color. The African species are somewhat lighter in weight than Ceylon ebony but are equally hard.

All of the above species are predominantly black, but African ebony tends to have grayish streaks whereas East Indian usually has brownish streaks. Pure black ebony is quite uncommon, especially if the wood is quarter-sawn (as it should be for musical instruments). The streaking runs along the annual rings and hence almost always appears on the quartered face.

The knowledgeable builder will realize that a well-quartered marbled fingerboard is preferable to a jet black flat-sawn fingerboard. To set an example, the classical guitar shown under construction in this book is made with a substantially marbled yet perfectly quartered gaboon-ebony fingerboard. Lightly to moderately streaked wood will generally appear pure black on an instrument after a few months of playing due to absorption of skin oils from the player's hands.

Ebony is often chosen over other fingerboard materials even if it is flat-sawn. Other materials, however, should not be used at all unless quarter-sawn.

Brazilian rosewood (*Dalbergia nigra*) is the most common second choice. Several other members of the genus *Dalbergia* are commonly used; *D. latifolia* (East Indian rosewood), *D. stevensonii* (Honduras rosewood), and *D. melanoxylon* (African blackwood). The last is sometimes fraudulently sold as ebony. Several other species of *Dalbergia* can be used successfully, such as cocobolo and kingwood.

If you receive a fingerboard from a mail-order supply house, examine the billet closely, in a bright light, for checks and splits. After surfacing, examine again closely for hidden defects, especially in the ends and long edges. Small checks found in the waste portion and occasional wormholes are acceptable. (Wormholes can be filled with tinted epoxy.) Sight down the length of the blank for warp, cup, or kinking. A lightly warped fingerboard may be adequate if it will lie flat under slight pressure. If you have a choice, however, pass it by unless it checks out well by other criteria. Kinks will disqualify a fingerboard, as they usually accompany a sworl or a radical change in density and texture within the board.

NOTES ON FRET WIRE AND FRET-SLOT SAWS

The material used for frets on modern steel-string and classical guitars is a cold-rolled wire, in cross section a T shape with a rounded top and studs protruding from either side of the tang (Fig. 12-5). The studs hold the fret in its slot by compression, analogous to the manner in which a nail holds when driven into a piece of wood.

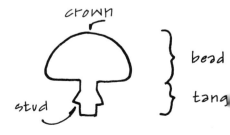

12-5.   Fretwire nomenclature.

Most modern fret wire is made from what is called eighteen percent nickel/silver. The term denotes a common alloy used in many commercial and industrial applications where high corrosion resistance is required and where excellent cold working properties are necessary for fabrication. Eighteen percent nickel/silver is actually a copper alloy, containing eighteen percent nickel and either fifty-five percent copper and twenty-seven percent zinc, or sixty-five percent copper and seventeen percent zinc. Fret wire is made from the latter variety. The alloy contains no silver at all despite the name bestowed by custom. An alloy harder than eighteen percent nickel/silver would yield longer-lasting frets but would quickly wear out the high-speed machinery on which it is formed.

Round wire, typically about .114 inch in diameter, is received by the fret-wire manufacturer in coils weighing up to one hundred fifty pounds. For the largest types of fret wire, the round wire is used full-sized; for smaller types, it is drawn down to smaller diameters. After drawing, there are four cold-rolling operations, using combinations of male and female rolls to produce the cross-section shown in the diagram.

For the builder, the choice of wire is largely determined by the type of instrument being built and, in the case of custom commissions, by the idiosyncrasies of the player's style. A fret of standard width and maximum height will produce a clear, sustaining tone with the least possible effort on the part of the player. But many playing styles, such as lead electric guitar, require a fret profile that is more complementary to a fast, sliding, left-hand attack. Thus, many manufacturers of solid-body and semi-acoustic guitars equip them with low frets with a distinctly flat crown. Wider frets produce a different feel and sometimes are said to give a mellower sound. They are usually found on electric basses, often found on six-string electrics, and occasionally found on acoustic flat-tops, where it is claimed they produce a marginal increase in sustain. Acoustic flat-tops, however, are usually made with standard, or "medium," wire. Classicals are almost invariably made with medium wire.

If a wide variety of fret wires is available, we recommend choosing the smallest tang for new frets to facilitate refretting with progressively larger tangs. The choice of tang size, however, may be limited by preference for a given bead size. Whatever the case, when you have obtained fret wire that most closely approximates your needs, you must acquire or fashion a saw that will cut a kerf of appropriate dimension for your fret wire.

The saw kerf should be .007 to .010 inch smaller than the dimension measured across the studs of the fret wire. This allows for penetration of the studs into the walls of the fret slot sufficient to hold in the fret but not so great that the frets become difficult to hammer in. Excessive stud penetration can result in damage to the fingerboard and can also exert a wedging action on the neck, back-bending it and making accurate leveling of the frets impossible.

The dimension across the studs can be measured with a caliper on a sample piece of wire ground on one end so that no burr interferes with the measurement. This dimension is typically in a range between .032 and .038 inch. Once you have measured (or obtained the dimension from the manufacturer), you can evaluate available saws by crosscutting on a scrap of the same material you plan to use for your fingerboard and checking the width of the kerf with the leaves of a feeler gauge.

Most woodworker supply catalogs will offer one or more dovetail saws. The kerf of these saws is usually in the .030- to .035-inch range, however, so you must reduce the set slightly to achieve a cut in the necessary range for most fret wire. If you can find a saw that cuts a slot of about .025 to .028 inch, you are in luck, as this is the ideal for most readily available fret wires. If the kerf is over .035 inch, you probably will not be able to use the saw for cutting fret slots. If it is .035 inch or under, but too large for the wire you have obtained, the saw set can be reduced slightly by hammering, as follows: Lay the saw blade on a hard metal surface with the spine overhanging so that the blade lies flat. With a regular hammer, tap very gently all along the side of the cutting edge. Try to tap all the teeth with equal force and an equal number of blows. Then turn the blade over and repeat on the other side. Make another test cut and check again with the feeler gauge. By working very gradually, you can keep the set even across the length of the blade. If you try to work too fast, you will wind up with a saw that binds hopelessly when it enters the wood. Note in any case that this is a rough-and-ready technique that will rarely produce results as good as a saw that cuts the correct slot without requiring a change of set.

The slots can also be crosscut on an accurate table saw with a very fine cutting circular blade. A fine-tooth plywood or finishing blade can be rim-ground at a machine shop to the desired dimension.

PROCEDURE: MAKING THE FINGERBOARD

This procedure involves thinning and truing the finger-

board billet, cutting the fret slots, and tapering the fingerboard to its final outline. On the classical, the fingerboard end is also shaped to conform to the soundhole edge.

In order to cut the fret slots, you will need to have obtained your fret wire and a saw that leaves a kerf of the appropriate dimension.

TOOLS
smoothing plane
scraper blade
square
fret-slotting saw
straightedge
razor knife
yellow pencil
drill bit (same diameter as
    brads below; classical
    only)
rasp (classical only)
hammer
assorted clamps

SUPPLIES
double-faced tape
$3/4 \times 1/16$-inch brads
    (classical only)

MATERIALS
fingerboard billet: $5/16 \times 2\frac{1}{2} \times 18\frac{1}{2}$ inch min.
    (SS) or $5/16 \times 2\frac{3}{4} \times 18\frac{1}{2}$ inch min. (CL)

IMPLEMENTS
sanding board
scrap blocks as specified

Step 1—Truing the Gluing Face of the Billet

Scrape both faces of the billet until they are reasonably free of saw marks and debris. Select a show face, and with

double-faced tape attach that face to the work surface.

Scrape (plane, if necessary) the up face until it checks out approximately level with a straightedge. This will be the gluing face, which must be smooth and flat in all directions before it can be glued. Remove the billet from the table and place the gluing face on the sanding board. Distributing pressure evenly, sand the surface flat with either a straight unidirectional stroke, returning it to its starting place each time by lifting it off the sanding board, or with a slow, deliberate circular motion. Stop when the bottom surface is completely covered with sanding scratches from the sanding board.

Step 2—Truing the Edge of the Fingerboard Billet and Trimming the Ends

Your fingerboard billet will need a trued edge in order to mark your fret locations accurately. You must also select one end of the billet to be the nut end and trim it square to the trued edge. This will be your zero stop for fret measurement.

You can true an edge on the sanding board with straight unidirectional strokes. If, however, the fingerboard edges are wavy or very irregular, you must first draft a straight line on one edge and plane down to it. Make sure that the trued edge is square to the face you surfaced in Step 1.

Select a nut end. If the fingerboard has defects that can be cut out by the taper, choose the nut end accordingly.

Mount the square against the trued edge at the nut end and score a line. Clamp the billet to the edge of your workbench. Then clamp a squared scrap block onto the billet, carefully aligning it along the scored line. Pressing the blade against the guide block with your finger, cut through the billet with a dovetail saw.

Trim the opposite end to a length of 18½ inches.

Step 3—Thinning to Dimension

With double-faced tape, attach the gluing face to the work surface. The show face will be planed in order to thin the billet to the dimensions that follow. The finished surface must be flat and smooth, so check frequently with a straightedge while dimensioning. (See Fig. 12-6.)

It may be helpful to draft the recommended dimensions on the edge of the fingerboard before planing.

Steel-string: Plane to a uniform 7/32-inch finished thickness.

Classical: The show face must be tipped relative to the gluing face. The actual thickness of the fingerboard is not as important as the accuracy of the inclination of the show face. We aim for a final thick-

12–6. Planing the fingerboard billet to thickness.

ness at the nut of 9/32 inch, but it can go down to ¼ inch without creating problems. The thickness at the twelfth fret *must*, however, be 1/32 inch less than the thickness at the nut. (The thickness at the soundhole will be approximately 1/64 inch thinner still.) Tapering the fingerboard toward the bridge creates a geometric relationship that provides for correct string action when the saddle is at optimum height (see Chapter 16).

Note: A more sophisticated way of tapering the classical fingerboard is to reduce the thickness by 1/32 inch at the twelfth fret on the *bass* side of the fingerboard only. This results in a more level saddle, as

little or no taper is actually required on the treble side to obtain correct action. (At correct action the treble E string will be 1/32 inch lower—that is, closer to the frets—than the bass E string.) Creating this compound slope while maintaining straight lines under the run of the strings is more difficult than simply tapering evenly across the board. If, however, you favor the bass side when planing the taper (either intentionally or accidentally), you need not make correction.

Step 4—Marking for Slots

Refer to the appropriate table of fret positions (Figure 12-3).

Clamp a block of scrap wood to the bench to act as a zero stop at the nut end. The ruler may be taped either to the fingerboard or to a block that is then clamped to the fingerboard so that the ruler sits vertically, as in Fig. 12-7. In either case, make sure that the ruler and the fingerboard are butted up against the zero stop.

Using the razor knife, cut a clear notch at each fret position. If your rule is engraved, locate the razor-knife point by inserting it into the engraved line and following it down and into the wood. Double check all marks before proceeding. Mark twenty-one fret positions for the steel-string; nineteen fret positions for the classical. Use the square to scribe a clearly visible line across the show face for each notch. (*Note:* At the twenty-first fret position on the steel-string fingerboard, make the scribe line very faint, as it must be sanded off later.)

Step 5—Cutting the Fret Slots

All cuts should be square to the show face and to the trued edge. The slots should be a uniform ⅛-inch deep for the steel-string and ³⁄₃₂-inch deep for the classical guitar. You can make the cuts quickly with the fret saw by simply pressing the saw up to a square mounted at each scribe mark, as in Fig. 12-8. For the less confident, however, accuracy can be assured by using a guide block clamped at each fret position, as in Fig. 12-9.

Students using a table saw for this operation must rub chalk into the notches or draw guidelines for visibility on the edge. (See Fig. 12-10.) The untrued edge of the billet must be trimmed parallel to the trued edge before crosscutting. Check for depth of cut on a scrap.

Steel-string: Instead of cutting a fret slot at the twenty-first fret position, move the saw about ¹⁄₃₂ inch beyond the position mark and cut squarely through the fingerboard.

Step 6—Tapering the Billet to Its Final Outline

Mark a centerline down the length of the fingerboard billet on the show face. It must be absolutely parallel to the trued edge. For the guitars built from this book, the steel-string will be 1¹¹⁄₁₆ inches at the nut and 2⅛ inches at the twelfth fret; the classical will be 2¹⁄₁₆ inches at the nut and 2⁷⁄₁₆ inches at the twelfth fret. Mark one-half of these dimensions on both sides of the centerline with a pencil. Connect the

12–7. Marking the fret locations.

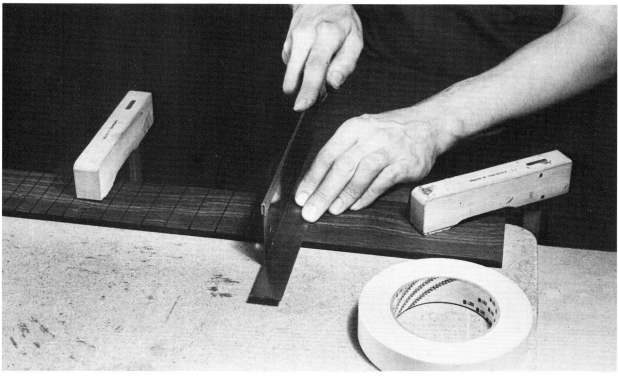

12–8.   *Cutting the fret slots.*

12–9.   *Cutting the fret slots with a guide block. The block is clamped adjacent to each scored line. The height of the block is adjusted with a veneer shim so that the spine of the dovetail saw stops at the correct depth.*

12–10.   *Cutting fret slots on the table saw. Sandpaper is taped to the miter fence to avoid slippage.*

points by scribing with the razor knife. Lock the fingerboard into the vise edge upward and plane to within ⅛ inch of the lines with a coarse setting, noting the grain direction to determine the best direction of your cut. Finish the cut with a fine setting. Repeat on the opposite edge. If necessary, true the edges on the sanding board, being careful not to change the taper or leave the edge out of square to the gluing face.

Step 7—Classical Only: Shaping the Fingerboard End to the Soundhole Contour

Read the following step and then refer to Fingerboard-end Sanding Device (page 278) before choosing your technique for this operation.

Choose a couple of brads

12–11. *Aligning the classical fingerboard. The position pins at the first and eleventh frets are driven into the neckshaft, and the underside of the fingerboard is marked at the soundhole.*

¹⁄₁₆ inch in diameter or smaller and about ¾ inch long. Find a drill bit that corresponds very closely to the diameter of these brads. Clamp the fingerboard to a waste piece and drill through at the first fret and the eleventh fret on the centerline. Try to keep the drill as square as possible going through. The brads should go through these holes easily but should not wobble. Back the brads out so their pointed ends do not protrude below the bottom of the fingerboard. If there is any chipping or roughness on the underside of the fingerboard caused by drilling, clean it up by gently scraping or sanding. Position the tapered fingerboard on the neck of the guitar with the soundhole end protruding over the face and over the soundhole.

You must now locate the fingerboard at three critical

points. First, you will locate it longitudinally by reference to the twelfth fret. The twelfth fret should sit on, or as close as possible to, the intersection of the neck and the body. (The size of the gap at the nut end is not important.) Second, the centerline of the fingerboard should correspond to the centerline of the neck at the nut. Third, the soundhole end is aligned by using one of the concentric rings of the rosette. The outside edges of the nineteenth fret slot should meet the same concentric ring on either side. If it is not possible to get the nut end exactly located at the neckshaft centerline and the soundhole exactly located in relation to the rosette, compromise by averaging the discrepancies at each end.

Once you have located the fingerboard in relation to these three points, hold it in position and drive the two pins through the fingerboard into the neck. The pins should go down a good ³⁄₁₆ inch to ensure solid positioning when the fingerboard is actually being glued. Once you have driven the pins down, check your locations again. (See Fig. 12-11.) If they are correct, you may take a short, sharp yellow or white pencil and reach into the soundhole to scribe a line on the underside of the fingerboard, using the soundhole itself as the template.

Remove the fingerboard from the neck and remove the position pins from the finger-

12–12. Sawing the soundhole outline at the end of the classical fingerboard. The fingerboard and backing are close to the vise jaws to minimize vibration.

board. Remove a portion of the waste by cutting about ⅛ inch from the curved pencil line. Use a piece of scrap for a backing, as in Fig. 12-12. Do not cut into the nineteenth fret slot with the saw. You may have to leave more than ⅛ inch to avoid this. Use a file to trim back, as in Fig. 12-13. Once you have reached the nineteenth fret, put the brads back in the position holes and position the fingerboard on the neck again. Push the brads down with your finger; do not use the hammer. Check your progress; then alternately file and check until you have accurately lined up the fingerboard end with the soundhole. The position pins enable us to return the fingerboard consistently to the same spot.

12–13. Filing to the soundhole contour.

FINGERBOARD-END SANDING DEVICE

This technique gives us a truer curved edge than we are likely to achieve with a file. A ½-inch-thick disk, the same diameter as the soundhole, is faced with #80- or #100-grit garnet sandpaper. A pivoting handle is attached to one face near the rim. The cylinder is drilled through its center, and it pivots on a brad sticking up from a workboard (the sound-hole-rosette workboard will serve this purpose). The curved fingerboard end is fed into the drum with one hand as the handle is turned with the other, as in Fig. 12-14. The disk can also be held by a bolt through its center in a drill-press chuck, as in Fig. 12-15.

In either case, use a shim of scrap wood under the fingerboard to raise it clear of the work surface.

An accurate drum can be made using the router. The router base with pin holes, used in Chapter 6 to excavate the rosette channels, is used once again for this procedure. Drill a hole of the same diameter as the holes in the router base in a piece of ½-inch plywood. Find a brad about 1-inch long that closely approximates the diameter of the hole. Pass the brad through the hole and hammer it into a work surface below. Cut off the brad above the scrap plywood

at about the same height as the depth of the holes in the router base. Locate the router base on the protruding brad so that it will cut a circle of the diameter of the soundhole.

Then make a series of cuts progressively deeper until you pass through the plywood scrap. A strip of sandpaper can be applied using doubled-faced tape.

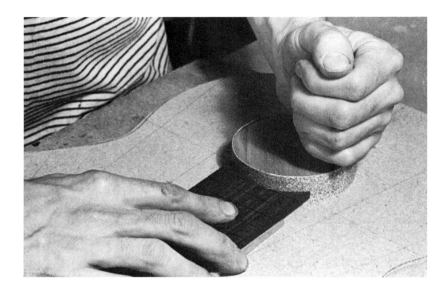

12–14 and 12–15. *Hand and machine fingerboard-end sanding devices.*

PROCEDURE: GLUING THE FINGERBOARD DOWN

You will need a thick clamping caul to prevent the neck from distorting and to spread the pressure when the clamps are applied. To fulfill this function, the fingerboard caul must be made of straight-grain wood (preferably quarter-sawn hardwood) at least ¾-inch thick and meticulously straight (check with a straightedge), and must extend up to the fingerboard edges (use the actual fingerboard as a template). It should extend from the nut to the fifteenth (SS) or nineteenth (CL) fret.

A thin slat is taped under the neckshaft to protect it from the clamps. It must be long enough to span the distance from the headstock angle to the curve of the heel.

White glue is used to glue the fingerboard, since its low temperature release properties will facilitate removal should it become necessary in the future.

STEEL-STRING ONLY

TOOLS
pencil
dull table knife or joint knife
five metal clamps

IMPLEMENTS
fingerboard caul, as specified above
shaft caul

SUPPLIES
PVA glue
masking tape

Step 1—Marking the Fingerboard

Locate the fingerboard on the shaft, aligning the neck and fingerboard centerlines carefully and positioning the fourteenth-fret slot exactly at the right-angle corner atop the heel. About ³⁄₁₆ inch of open space should remain between the headstock veneer and the fingerboard end. Mark a pen line around the fingerboard on the neckshaft, after erasing all previous lines. Also mark the tenon outline on the undersurface of the fingerboard to denote the limit of the glue film.

Step 2—Gluing and Clamping

Apply a moderate amount of glue to the fingerboard, spreading it toward all the edges; stop on the tenon marks under the fifteenth fret.

An overly thick film will both obliterate the neckshaft markings when squeezed out and cause "swimming" of the board. Wipe the glue back from the edges with a finger.

Place the fingerboard on the neck, and press down firmly. Mount the fingerboard caul over the fingerboard. Mount the first clamp about 4 inches from the nut end and snug it down just finger tight. Adjust the clamp, caul, and fingerboard until everything is well aligned. Apply a second clamp four inches from the wide end of the fingerboard caul. Snug it down finger tight and check that the board has not migrated; if necessary, drag it back and realign everything until it sits in its proper place without creeping. Apply three more clamps, finger tight as shown in Fig. 12-16, keeping

12–16. *Clamping the steel-string fingerboard.*

your eye on the alignment of the board. When everything sits correctly, firm down all the clamps bit by bit. Overtightening the clamps too early in the assembly or using bent or worn clamps that exert skewed pressure may make proper alignment impossible.

When all clamps are tight, examine closely for proper alignment. If the glue has set but the board has skewed radically, do not hesitate to remove the clamps now (do not wait until the glue sets completely) and paddle the board off slowly with a dull table knife; scrape the semiset glue off, sand, and try again. Minor misalignments are acceptable, however, since the bridge will eventually be located in rela-

tion to the fingerboard's final placement. After fifteen minutes, remove leather-hard squeeze-out with a glue chisel.

CLASSICAL ONLY

TOOLS
six metal clamps

IMPLEMENTS
fingerboard caul
back caul
shaft caul
upper face brace/cross strut
   caul (see Chapter 10)

SUPPLIES
PVA glue
masking tape

Retrieve the upper face brace (cross strut) caul and insert it in place through the soundhole on the cross strut.

Apply strips of masking tape along the walls of the notch so it will cling to the brace on its own. Insert the position pins into the fingerboard. Mark and drill the fingerboard caul for two ¼-inch clearance holes at the position pin locations. Tape a square, padded caul to the back of the soundbox right over the headblock, adjacent to the heel.

Apply a moderate amount of glue to the undersurface of the fingerboard. Position the fingerboard on the neck and locate the position pins in their holes in the shaft. Push the pins down gently with a finger until you are sure the fingerboard is located where it belongs, and then tap them in a little bit further with the hammer. Apply the clamps as shown in Fig. 12-17. Begin with the C-clamp closest to the heel; tighten only enough to hold the clamp firmly in place. Next, apply the bar clamp over the headblock. Then work toward the nut with the two neckshaft C-clamps, and finally, place the two fingerboard-end C-clamps through the soundhole, mounted on the upper face brace caul. When all clamps are in place, snug them up evenly bit by bit, making sure that none is skewed or overtightened enough to drag the board out of alignment despite the positioning pins. Leave clamped for an hour. Fifteen minutes after gluing, remove leather-hard squeeze-out with a glue chisel. Take special care

12–17.   Clamping the classical fingerboard. The caul is drilled out to accommodate the position pins, which are left in place during gluing.

not to smear the glue squeeze-out on the soundboard adjacent to the fingerboard, or to mar the soundboard in any way. When the large caul is removed, pull out the position pins with pliers.

PROCEDURE: FRETTING

Before the frets are installed, the fingerboard surface must be prepared. The steel-string-guitar fingerboard is arched laterally by a small amount to facilitate the grand barre on medium- and high-tension strings and to facilitate fretting with the thumb. The normal shape of an extended index (or barring) finger is a slight arch, which sets the standard for the proper fingerboard curvature.

The classical fingerboard is commonly flat, but many builders impart a gentle arch at the request of players (we always put a slight arch in our classical fingerboards).

The fingerboard surface must also be dead straight along the run of the strings. The following procedure includes steps for arching and truing.

Fretting can be done with an ordinary carpenter's hammer, but we use a large-headed, short-handled shoemaker's hammer. We polish its domed striking surface carefully and allow no other use for it, lest marks on it be transferred to the frets. Another tool that works well is a plastic-covered "dead-blow"

hammer, available at many hardware suppliers.

Fretting techniques vary widely. On classical guitars, we cut off a short segment of wire for each fret slot (about ¼ inch overlong) and tap in the segments one by one. On the steel-string, we can speed up the process a little: We cut a long segment of wire and, holding one end with one hand, tap in the other end, clip it off flush, then start the new end into the next fret slot, tap it in, cut it off, and so forth. Some builders tap in each fret starting from one end and progressing across its length to the opposite end. Others will hammer in the middle first and work the ends down in turn. You may wish to experiment to choose a sequence that works best for you.

We cut the fret ends flush

to the fingerboard edge with an end nipper (horizontal-jaw wire cutter) ground on its top surface to cut flush.

The neck must be firmly supported during fretting so that it does not recoil in any way when the fret is struck with the hammer. In the following steps we show a variety of support systems. The neck can be held in a vise if the table on which the vise is mounted is sufficiently rigid. It can also be supported with a padded block or a heavy bag filled with sand.

On the steel-string, a special support device must be made for fretting the part of the fingerboard that extends beyond the neck tenon. (See Fig. 12-18.)

On the classical, the part of the fingerboard extending over the soundboard must be fretted using an inertial block, a

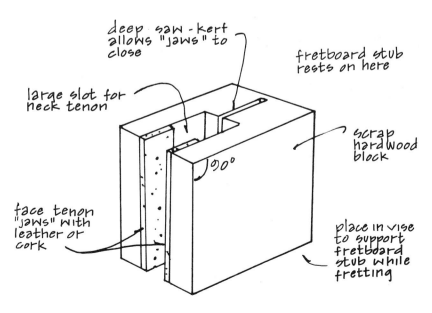

12–18. Steel-string fingerboard end support block.

small heavy chunk of metal that can be pressed against the underside of the soundboard under the fingerboard to focus the energy of the hammer blow. (See Step 4, below.)

When all the frets are installed and clipped flush, they must be ground totally flush to the fingerboard edge using a mill fill. On the classical, this necessitates a mask to protect the soundboard. We use a piece of sheet metal cut out to fit over the fingerboard end and edged with masking tape, as shown in Fig. 12-32.

TOOLS
straightedge
sandpaper plane
long ruler
smoothing plane
fret-slotting saw
fretting hammer
flush-cutting end nipper
triangular file (steel-string
    only)
2- to 3-inch C-clamp
    (classical only)
8- to 10-inch mill file
14-inch mill file (dead
    straight)

MATERIALS
fret wire (minimum of 48
    inches)

FIXTURES
fretting support
inertial block (classical only)
fingerboard end support
    block (steel-string only;
    see Step 2)

SUPPLIES
sandpaper
PVA glue

Step 1—Classical Only: Truing the Surface

Check the surface of the fingerboard with your straightedge. If the fingerboard has gone severely out of true due to the clamping procedure, you will have to plane again. If the fingerboard is still very close to straight at all the string positions, you may finish-smooth it with a sandpaper plane to get it dead straight. (Fig. 12-19.)

Before final smoothing, lay the long ruler on edge on the fingerboard and measure the airspace between the ruler and the soundboard at the eventual location of the saddle. The airspace must be between $3/16$ inch and $1/4$ inch for proper string action at normal saddle height (with our bridge design). If it is greater than $1/4$ inch, increase the slope (forward tilt) of the fingerboard by planing; if less than $3/16$ inch, decrease the slope.

After truing, smooth the fingerboard with #120- and then #220-grit garnet, taking care not to sand irregularities into the surface.

Step 2—Steel-string Only: Arching the Fingerboard

Tighten the truss-rod nut with a wrench until the fingerboard humps in the middle by $1/64$ to $1/32$ inch. Lock the neck securely and horizontally in the vise. The protruding fingerboard end segment must be supported during the arching and fretting steps with the use

12–19. *Truing the fingerboard surface with a sandpaper plane.*

of the fingerboard support block. (Refer to Fig. 12-18.) Clamp the block onto the neck tenon as shown in Fig. 12-20.

The hump must now be planed away, restoring a flat surface to the fingerboard. Several plane strokes across the center, followed with straight strokes with the sandpaper plane, should do the job. Check across the surface with a straightedge to verify. This pretensioning operation is necessary to provide future truss-rod adjustability in both directions.

Adjust the plane to produce fine shavings. Tip the plane just a bit and shoot down the edges with strokes that run the full length of the fingerboard, toward the nut. Your first several shavings will be very tiny since you are, at first, just contacting the corner. Widening facets should soon become visible. Strive to keep them approximately equal on both sides of the centerline. As you take your strokes closer and closer to the centerline, tip the plane less and less until it is flat as you cross the centerline. Resist the temptation to take a deeper cut. If the plane cannot remove thin shavings or skips badly, it is dull or misadjusted. Since all the plane's strokes are converging at the nut, the finished arch will appear to emerge sooner there than at the wide end. Continue planing in converging strokes until the arch at the nut end is approximately $\frac{1}{16}$ inch offset from flat on either side of the

centerline (read the arch against a 6-inch ruler).

You must now change your approach, concentrating your attention at the soundhole end. Tipping your plane more radically than before, make your strokes so they run strictly parallel to the centerline (rather than converging as before).

Since the fingerboard edge is now oblique to the stroke, you will soon run off the edge as the stroke is made. Subsequent strokes, closer to the centerline each time, will contact the surface over a progressively longer distance. As you approach the centerline, the attitude of the plane should follow the arch. Try to keep both halves of the fingerboard worked symmetrically. The final long strokes should run off the edge about halfway up the fingerboard. When you are finished, the fingerboard edge will appear to thin progressively toward the soundhole end by a small amount, about $\frac{1}{32}$ to $\frac{1}{16}$ inch.

Read the surface against the straightedge. Focus your attention between the first and fourteenth frets. A slight dip from the fourteenth fret to the end of the fingerboard may be ignored; a small rise can be planed off in short strokes. The straightedge must be aligned with the run of the strings for a useful reading to take place. Do not skew the straightedge across the arch, for it will always read a hump in the middle. Place a well-lit

piece of white cardboard behind the fingerboard to facilitate an accurate reading with the straightedge. If localized high spots appear, scrape them with short strokes and read again. Gross irregularities should be removed by selective planing. Beginners sometimes feel at this point that they are "chasing" a hump all over the fingerboard. If this happens to you, clean up the surface with the sandpaper plane, applying several full-length, deliberate strokes, tipping it as you did the metal plane. (*Note:* The fingerboard edge should remain sharp. Avoid any rounding or radiusing. If this should occur, you are tipping the plane too radically.) Recheck and work the surface till it reads flat longitudinally and is symmetrically arched laterally. Sand the surface with long, unidirectional strokes with the sandpaper wrapped around a felt block. Start with #120-grit garnet and proceed to #220.

The fingerboard ready for fretting is shown in Fig. 12-20.

Step 3—Deepening the Slots

If in either of the previous steps you have reduced the depth of any slot to less than $\frac{3}{32}$ inch at the ends, you must deepen it to ensure that the fret does not bottom out. Keep the saw square to the surface. If it jams, run it through a piece of beeswax or paraffin.

On the classical, the split nineteenth fret slot must be widened very slightly so that the two fret segments can be pressed in rather than hammered. Run the saw up and down in the slot a few times, letting the set of the teeth grind away a bit of the slot walls. For this operation, and for any slot past the body joint that may require deepening, the soundboard should be masked.

Step 4—Installing Frets

All fret slots must be free of debris before beginning this step. Each fret must be struck with firm, "dead" blows that do not bounce or recoil; the fewer the blows, the better—more than four or five is usu-ally too many. The hammer should never be raised more than a few inches from the fret before striking. Frets can easily be squashed or dented by ex-cessive force.

Before each fret is hammered in, place a dot of PVA glue on your index finger and run the tang across the dot to pick up a bead along the bottom, as in Fig 12-22. By filling in small gaps around the studs, the glue helps to prevent loosening of the fret. When trimming the ends of the frets, press the open jaws of the end nipper against the fingerboard edge and slowly close it onto the fret while pushing the tool firmly into the edge. After the cut is certain, remove the tool *downward,* lest a snag cause tearing out of the fret. Each time you clip fret ends, clean up glue squeeze-out, if any, with a lightly moistened paper towel.

If a fret seats improperly (see Fig. 12-21) and cannot be corrected with further tapping, you may have to remove it. Use the flushground end nipper gingerly to rock the fret up out of the slot. Do not yank it out! If large wood flakes pull up, glue them down. Clean out debris with the slotting saw and then try again, moving the studs over slightly.

Steel-string: Run the corner of a triangular file down the length of each fret slot, chamfering it slightly to reduce chipout during future fret removal. Take a length of fret wire and manipulate it into a curve that approximates the fingerboard curve. Remove debris from the tang with a fingernail. Apply glue to the tang and hold the wire with one hand so that the tang enters straight into the slot. The first blow is crucial, determining whether the fret enters correctly (Fig. 12-23). Examine the fingerboard after the first blow. Any marks or dents in the wood or on the frets betray a tendency to tip the hammer as it comes down. Adjust your stroke as necessary and hammer carefully across the length of the fret. Clip off each fret with the end nipper (Fig. 12-24). At the fifteenth fret, remove the clamp from the fingerboard-end support block and lock the block (with the neck attached) in the vise. Install the remaining frets.

12–20. Steel-string fingerboard ready for fretting.

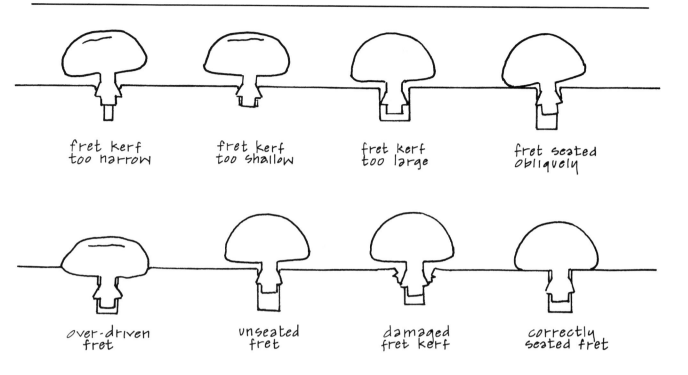

fret kerf
too narrow

fret kerf
too shallow

fret kerf
too large

fret seated
obliquely

over-driven
fret

unseated
fret

damaged
fret kerf

correctly
seated fret

12–21.   Common fretting problems.

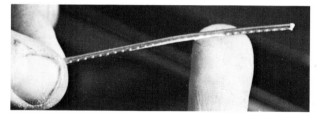

12–22.   Applying a bead of PVA glue to the tang before installing the fret.

12–23.   Driving in the fret from one end to the other. The first blow must keep the fret vertical.

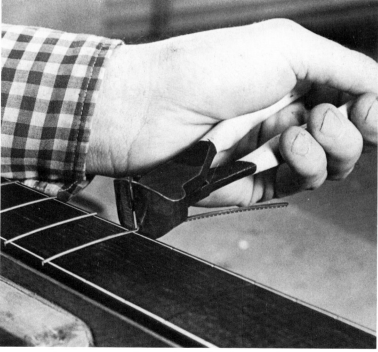

12–24.   Clipping the fret flush with a flush-ground end nipper.

Classical: Take a length of wire and pull it out straight to reduce its curve. Cut off a segment about ¼ inch longer than the first fret slot. Cut about five or six more segments, each successively a little longer than the one before. Line them up in order of length. (After they are installed, you will cut five or six more, and so on.)

The first nine frets on the classical can be hammered in using either a sandbag (Fig. 12-25) or a padded block (Fig. 12-26) for neck support. Remove debris from the tang of the first fret and apply glue, as in Fig. 12-22. Place the fret on its slot and tap in the middle. Make sure that it enters vertically, and then tap toward each end (Fig. 12-27).

After each group of frets is hammered in, clip the ends flush with the end nipper, as in Fig. 12-24.

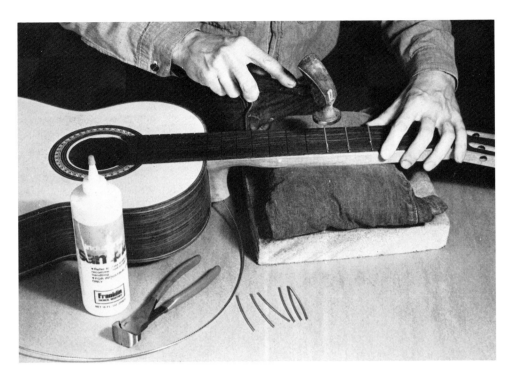

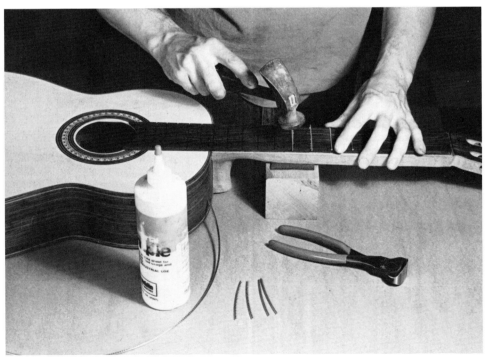

12–25 and 12–26. *Two different neck supports for hammering in frets on the classical neckshaft.*

12–27. *Hammering the fret from the middle outward. Once the fret is seated in the middle, the ends are tapped in.*

Frets ten through fourteen can be tapped in with the guitar on the table, the hammer impact being transferred through the headblock. (See Fig. 12-28.) Frets fifteen, sixteen, seventeen, and eighteen must be struck with the guitar held through the soundhole, off the table, so that the shock of the blow will be transmitted through the box to avoid the possibility of cracking the soundboard. An inertial block (Figs. 12-29 and 12-30) is pressed up against the soundboard under the fingerboard while the fret is held onto the slot with the thumb and hammered in. Do not be perturbed by the loud noise when hammering. For these frets, you may dispense with glue. The nineteenth fret should be

12–28.   The tenth, eleventh, twelfth, thirteenth and fourteenth frets on the classical can be hammered in with the guitar on the table; the headblock and heel provide support.

12–29 and 12–30.   The fifteenth, sixteenth, seventeenth and eighteenth frets must be hammered in with the guitar held off the workbench. An inertial block (any handy-sized chunk of metal will do) is pressed up against the soundboard underneath the fingerboard to prevent dissipation of the hammer impact.

12–31. *Pressing in the split nineteenth fret on the classical with a 2-inch C-clamp. A tiny caul is grooved with a file to fit over the fret, and a small hardwood scrap is placed underneath to protect the rim of the soundhole.*

12–32. *Grinding the fret ends flush to the edge of the fingerboard and beveling back to about 30 degrees off the vertical.*

pressed rather than hammered, to prevent damage to the feathered edge where the soundhole has curved the end of the fingerboard. (See Fig. 12-31.) Shape the fret segments where they will follow the curve of the soundhole before installation. If your fret slot is so large that you can press a nineteenth fret segment in with your fingers, run a dab of epoxy along the tang before inserting.

Step 5—Filing and Beveling the Fret Ends

Mask the soundboard on the classical, and do not strike the guitar body with the file.

File the fret ends flush with the fingerboard edge. Run an 8- to 10-inch mill file along the length of the neck,

mounted on the ledge provided by the overwide neck-shaft.

When the fret ends are flush to the fingerboard edge, tip the file and grind a bevel. (See Fig. 12-32.) Keep the bevel angle consistent at about 30 to 45 degrees off the vertical. Grind until the file contacts the fingerboard, leaving a minute bevel on its edge.

Step 6—Leveling the Frets

We use a 14-inch smooth mill file for leveling frets. A file used for leveling frets should check out dead flat against a straightedge. We do not use this file for any other purpose.

Before leveling, check the frets with a straightedge along the run of the strings to evalu-

ate (Fig. 12-33). If the fingerboard was properly surfaced and the frets properly installed, very little grinding should be necessary. If any fret is noticeably high (causing the straightedge to rock), tap it lightly with the fretting hammer to ensure that it is well seated, and check again before leveling. On the steel-string, you might have to release the truss-rod tension in order to obtain an accurate reading before grinding.

The tops of the frets are ground very gently with the file (Fig. 12-34), using strokes that travel the full length of the fingerboard. The strokes should follow the run of the strings and should not traverse the arch. When the frets are level, file marks should appear on every fret—as long as the file is straight, any missed fret is still low.

If one area is much higher than everywhere else, grind it selectively so as not to reduce the height of the other frets unnecessarily. Use a shorter file (we use a segment cut from a large file that we call a file stub), if necessary, to isolate the grinding on the high area.

Check your progress frequently with the straightedge. When reading the surfaces, make sure that the straightedge follows the run of the strings.

Level frets enable the luthier to maximize playability. If you have problems with this step, however, it is better to stop grinding when the frets are approximately level rather than to remove excessive amounts of material in an attempt to get them perfect on the first try. As all your fingerboard-preparation skills improve, less and less grinding will be necessary.

12–33. Checking frets with a straightedge to make sure they are level. The white backdrop facilitates an accurate reading.

12–34. Leveling frets with a flat mill file.

CHAPTER 13

NECKSHAFT CONTOURS

We have often heard guitarists yearn for some particular instrument that was uniquely comfortable to their hands or especially conducive to their style of playing. Few, however, could pinpoint what made that instrument so special. Perhaps it was just the quality of the guitar's fretwork and adjustment, or perhaps something about its tone; but often the difference may simply have been the contour of its neckshaft.

Luthiers should try to evaluate the comfort of different instruments and learn how the hand can cramp and tire if the shaft is the wrong size or if it is poorly or inappropriately shaped. It is also important for the luthier to become knowledgeable about the elements of individual contours and the range and variety of shapes that have become popular.

The most important variables under the luthier's control are the *fingerboard taper*, the narrowing of the fingerboard width toward the nut;

Final Carving & Finiting

the *shaft taper,* the progressive decrease of the thickness of the shaft from the heel to the headpiece; the *apex,* the area running along the underside of the shaft; and the *shoulders,* the long portions of the shaft that are located between and converge with the apex and the edge of the fingerboard. Sometimes the shoulders start right under the fingerboard and at other times the shoulders extend into and include part of the fingerboard edge.

CLASSICAL NECKSHAFTS

Early multicourse guitars with flush-veneer fretboards characteristically had wide necks to accommodate all the doubled strings. Shafts were typically slender with sloping, flat shoulders and a gently curved apex. The advent of six single strings and the raised fingerboard resulted in a fuller, narrower neck. Typical of this contour is the shape found on most of Torres' guitars. His oval cross-section has become the shape favored on many classical guitars to this day. This shape has a relatively nar-

row, flattened apex and shoulders that recede rapidly from and extend slightly into the fingerboard edge.

One notable variant from this classical practice is the contour favored by several present-day northern and central European makers, such as the successors to Hermann Hauser. This variant, sometimes termed the Mozzani neck, after the guitar teacher and builder Luigi Mozzani, is characterized by its extremely flat and wide apex and its very slender (½-inch) shaft thickness. Its shoulders curve sharply to converge into, without breaching, the fingerboard edge. This contour is preferred by players who feel that the flat bottom lends a sense of security to the left hand and increases the area of the neck against which the thumb actually presses, reducing fatigue.

We favor a classical-guitar neck that is a compromise, in terms of apex width and overall shaft depth, between the Mozzani and the classic Spanish oval.

STEEL-STRING NECKSHAFTS

Modern flat-top steel-string folk guitars evolved from gut-string designs manufactured in this country at the turn of this century. As the steel-string guitar evolved to become a distinct entity and as it gained its own repertoire of styles and techniques, neckshaft contours began diverging from gut-string standards.

The first divergence in contour occurred with the change in the way the neck was actually held. The academic approach to guitar playing requires the neck to be supported by the thumb only and maintains that the thumb should rarely, if ever, venture away from the apex of the neckshaft. The natural tendency of the untutored guitarist is to allow the shaft to rest in the crook of the thumb and forefinger. Classical teachers consider this cradling of the neck slovenly and counterproductive. The practice, they say, discourages the grand barre and leads to the practice of barring the bass strings with the thumb, a technique familiar to ragtime and blues guitarists but shunned by classical devotees. The "slovenly" techniques of the turn of the century became, however, the standard practices of the American folk-guitar tradition.

American guitar manufacturers were at first criticized by teachers for "pandering" to the demands of untutored students by their adoption of the triangular neckshaft at the turn of the twentieth century. Its sharp, prominent apex clearly discouraged the academic playing style, but it appears to have been favored by the masses of players who were turning to the guitar in larger numbers than ever before. The advent of steel strings early in the century only further encouraged the popularity of the triangular neckshaft. It was ideally suited to steel strings, allowing the apex to be much deeper and thus lending greater beam strength to a neck that had already begun to shrink in width. The nearly flat shoulders imparted a feeling of slenderness.

The triangular neck had one serious shortcoming, however, which ultimately rendered it obsolete; its extremely narrow apex locked the player's hand into just one comfortable hand position. As folk music evolved in complexity, musicians demanded contours that were comfortable in many positions requiring extended reaches and frequent barring. As a result, a variety of contours proliferated.

Our preference on the steel-string guitar is a hybrid shape that works well for a variety of hand sizes, playing techniques, and holding positions. It is characterized by a wide, gently curved apex set slightly off center, with flattened, sloping shoulders. In order to allow these elements to converge properly, it is necessary to extend the shoulders rather deeply into the edges of the fingerboard. The very corner edge of the fingerboard must be blunted very slightly to relieve its resultant sharpness.

PROCEDURE: GLUING THE HEEL CAP

The heel cap provides a visual terminus and a measure of protection to the heel end. It is typically a piece of hardwood or other material about the thickness of or a little thicker than the back. The heel cap on the classical guitar usually is flush to the surface of the back; this seldom occurs on the steel-string because of the separate neck/body construction system typically employed.

On the classical guitar in this book, rosewood is used to match the back; on the steel-string, ebony is used to contrast with the mahogany back and sides and to match the ebony binding. Ebony is also sometimes used on classicals; rosewood, maple, ivory, pearl, and plastic are several materials among many commonly used on steel-string guitars.

Both steel-string and classical guitars sometimes feature a veneer sandwich between the heel cap and the heel, producing the illusion that purfling on the sides continues through the heel. Some classical builders make the heel cap by leaving a "tongue" on the back when it is initially cut out of the joined plate. Purfling and binding are let into the tongue, or sometimes even extended around it.

The student building a guitar from this book can make a heel cap out of waste material from a rosewood back or ebony fingerboard. The heel-cap blank should be a rectangular piece a little wider and longer than the required final dimensions. It should be $3/32$ to $1/8$ inch thick, sanded smooth and flat on at least one side.

TOOLS
wide chisel
small sanding board
cam clamps as needed

SUPPLIES
AR glue

Step 1—Preparing the Heel End

Steel-string: The heel end must be tipped back slightly so that the heel cap approximately follows the taper of the back. Clamp the neck in a vise or to the workbench and use short, straight strokes with the small sanding board. *Do not* allow the block to tip sideways, do not tip back too radically, and do not curve the surface.

Classical: The heel end is already tipped to follow the taper of the back, but it usually has a slightly curved surface due to the motion of the sanding board during arching. A wide chisel is the best tool for nipping off the crown of the curved surface, but if you do not have one, the small sanding board will do. Stroke the heel end *across* its grain, taking care to keep your strokes level. Do not exaggerate the backward slant of the heel end. Also, do not sand grooves into the binding with the edge of the block. (This can be avoided by making sure that the sandpaper does not overhang the edge of the small sanding board.)

Step 2—Gluing the Heel Cap

Steel-string: The heel cap must end flush to the end-grain face of the heel. Apply glue to the heel end and place the cap down on it. Align the cap and press until the glue begins to grab, and then clamp with two cam clamps as shown in Fig. 13-1. Make sure that the heel cap does not shift under clamping pressure; if it does, loosen the clamps and realign it.

Classical: The heel cap must butt tightly against the binding. Grind the butting edge on a sanding board until it will sit on the heel end and fit flush against the binding. Apply

glue to the heel end. Slide the cap on, squeezing glue up between it and the binding. Clamp as in Fig. 13-1, but slightly exaggerate the tilt of the clamps to drag the heel cap against the binding.

PROCEDURE: FINISH-CARVING THE NECK

Although many steps are involved in this procedure, to the experienced builder the finish-carved neck emerges from the raw material as the product of a single, integrated act of sculpture, rather than as a result of a series of discrete operations.

The beginner, however, needs a road map of sorts in order to be able to approach the task with a degree of confidence. For instructional purposes, therefore, we are obliged to fragment an otherwise integrated process. Rather than provide a mechanistic series of steps, we will summarize the procedure here in the text while relying upon a "storyboard" photographic sequence as the main instructional device (shown in Figs. 13-2 through 13-24). In the course of actually carving the neck, the student should feel free to vary the sequence in order to be more comfortable with the procedure as a whole.

The heel cap must first be carved flush to the heel end. On the steel-string, the tab

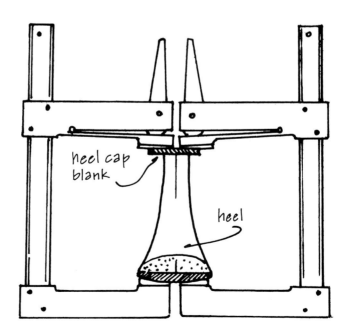

13–1. Clamping arrangement for gluing the heel cap.

may simply be carved to the shape of the bottom of the heel, which remains as carved in Chapter 4. The classical heel cap may be carved similarly *unless,* after assembly, the back centerseam did not come out properly aligned to the point of the heel cap. If so, the centerline of the back must be continued onto the heel cap and a symmetrical heel cap layout drawn in pencil. The heel end must be carved to the new heel cap layout, and the heel recarved to reflect the adjustment.

Before the heel of either guitar is finish-carved, the excess width of the neckshaft must be reduced to the edge of the fingerboard. The sweep of each side of the heel must then be adjusted to end at the fingerboard edge. If reshaping is necessary for heel cap symmetry on the classical, it should be executed during that adjustment. When the sweep of the sides of the heel is brought down to the edges of the fingerboard, the resulting facet must be removed in the same manner as in the initial tial carving procedure in Chapter 4.

The remaining steps involve carving the shaft, finishing the hyoid curves at the throat, carving the back of the throat, and then rounding and smoothing the shaft to link the finished throat to the finished heel.

We leave a visible centerline on the back of the shaft untouched everywhere except at the throat until the very end of the process, at which time lumps or irregularities are removed with a wood file, leaving the silhouette of the shaft dead straight from throat to heel. As a result of that operation, the $1\frac{1}{16}$-inch shaft tapers from the heel to the throat very slightly on the classical and up to (but not over) $\frac{1}{16}$ inch on the steel-string. With thicker stock for the shaft, of course, the taper can be made more pronounced on both instruments.

Our technique emphasizes the primary use of edge tools as opposed to rasps or files. Although the student may feel free to fall back on the rasp or file if a cutting tool proves too challenging to control, we believe that proper woodworking technique ultimately requires mastery over edge tools for carving. In our view, files and rasps should be used only to remove very small amounts of material, and usually only to prepare a surface for finish sanding.

Finally, several caveats are in order. The student must maintain a clear overall perspective as carving progresses, never losing sight of necessary symmetries. Do not linger too long in one area, lest you leave an ineradicable hollow or wind up having to remove excessive material elsewhere to compensate. Be especially sensitive to grain direction in order to avoid tear-out. Above all, the student must be neither too timid nor too aggressive in finish-carving the neck. The former may result in an ungraceful, clublike cross section, while the latter can result in a disastrously excessive removal of material, leaving the neck flimsy and uncomfortable to play. The basic rule of thumb is always to remove material with a specific purpose in mind, continuing only until the neck looks and feels right.

Study Figs. 13-2 through 13-24.

TOOLS
chisel
spokeshave
skew knife
wood file
scraper

SUPPLIES
sandpaper (#100- and #120-grit garnet)

13–2. The heel cap is carved until its edge is flush to the heel end.

13-3. On the classical, the heel cap should be symmetrical to the center-seam of the back. If it is not, the heel may be reshaped slightly to achieve symmetry.

13-4. The excess width of the neckshaft can be pared down with a spokeshave. The tool must be tipped slightly to avoid striking the edge of the fingerboard.

13-5. On the classical, a chisel is used to trim the area adjacent to the body missed by the spokeshave.

13-6. The hyoid curve at the head-piece is faired into the spokeshave facet. The curves on both sides of the head-piece should be symmetrical.

13–7. The sweep of the heel is carried to the fingerboard edge, eliminating the chisel or spokeshave facet. On the classical, the chisel strokes should be kept at least 1/32 inch away from the side.

13–9. A coarse wood file is used to merge the neckshaft edge into the fingerboard edge. The file facet abrades about 1/16 inch of the fingerboard edge most of the way, and then disappears as it approaches the body.

13–8. The contour of the heel is reestablished with a skew knife.

13–10. The square shoulders of the neckshaft are faceted with the spokeshave into rough radius shapes. A centerline down the back of the shaft should remain untouched.

13–11 and 13–12. On the classical, the throat is carved and gently merged into the shaft with the skew knife. Lumps left on the shoulders of the shaft where the spokeshave stopped are removed at the same time.

13–13 and 13–14. On the steel-string, the transition from the headpiece to the shaft must be moved forward to be under the nut. This causes the throat area of the shaft to be reduced in thickness by about $1/16$ inch. The throat is merged into the shaft with the spokeshave and skew.

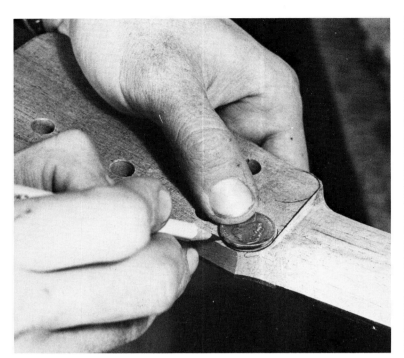

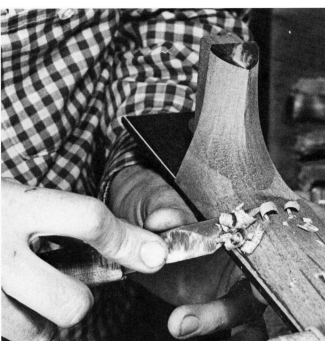

13–15. *We finish the transition by matching the radii of all four corners of the headpiece to produce an interesting segmented appearance.*

13–17. *A lump at the heel is removed with a skew knife and the heel is blended into the shaft.*

13–16. *The shaft must be checked to ensure its straightness and locate remaining lumps. In the photo, the neck is being rotated while silhouetted against a bright background.*

13–18. *The back of the shaft is straightened with a wood file, merging the centerline into the throat area. The flat face of the file also removes tool facets with corkscrew strokes while the half-round can be used to refine the throat and heel.*

13–19. *File marks are removed with a scraper blade. Long, straight strokes will avoid creating hollows.*

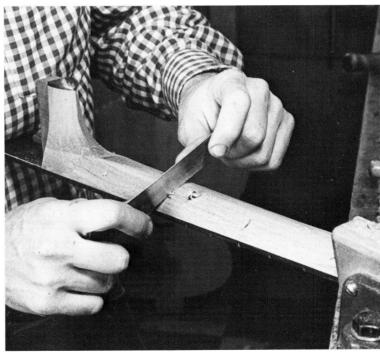

13–20. *The fingerboard end of the steel-string can be pressed into the stomach for support while the shaft is being scraped.*

13–21 and 13–22. The crease of the heel is straightened and finished with a scraper blade and #120-grit garnet sandpaper.

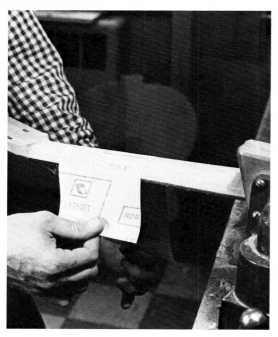

13–23. Irregularities in the shaft can be averaged out by sanding shoe-shine fashion with a wide sheet of #100-grit garnet sandpaper. The widening areas of the heel and throat must be avoided, lest they be scored by the sandpaper edge.

13–24. All surfaces must be trued and smoothed with #120-grit garnet. Running one hand up and down the shaft with your eyes closed is the best way to check for inconsistencies.

PROCEDURE: INLAYING THE EMBLEM AND BINDING THE STEEL-STRING HEADPIECE

In this procedure we provide the option of enhancing the appearance of the steel-string headpiece by binding its edges and inlaying a personal emblem or some other decorative design. Both steps are facilitated by the use of a miniature router, such as the motorized device made by Dremel. We modify its router-base attachment by removing the original plastic base-plate and replacing it with a smaller, more convenient wooden one. We also modify the machine's parallel guide attachment by clamping to it a small wooden "finger" that will serve as an edge guide for routing the ledge for the headpiece binding and purfling strips. (See Fig. 13-28.)

In the absence of a miniature router, the inlay cavity and binding ledges can be excavated with small chisels after the boundaries of the cuts have been accurately delineated with a purfling cutter or a razor knife.

TOOLS
razor knife
small chisel
miniature router or purfling
    cutter
bending pipe
pearl saw
flat file
miniature files

SUPPLIES
PVA (white) glue
five-minute epoxy
#100- and #120-grit garnet
    sandpaper
powdered dye or wood dust
    (see Step 3)

MATERIALS
pearl blank
binding materials (see
    Step 4)

Step 1—Cutting Out the Inlay

Select an appropriate design. Let restraint and simplicity be your guides.

Trace the design, full size, on a piece of stiff paper. Modern luthiers often avail themselves of designs obtained as photocopies from the originals. Cut the design out and glue

it with white glue to a 1/16-inch-thick pearl blank (Fig. 13-25). Allow sufficient drying time to prevent premature delamination. Saw the emblem out from the blank with slow, full-length strokes of the frame saw, following the borderline of the printed design as closely as possible. The edges of the cutout are then trued and irregularities smoothed with miniature files.

Step 2—Routing the Headpiece

Spot-glue the cutout onto the surface where it will ultimately lie. Allow it to dry thoroughly. Pierce its outline deeply and accurately into the surface with the point of a razor knife (Fig. 13-26). The cutout is removed by judicious

13–25. *The emblem is cut out and glued to an abalone wafer, which is sawn to the paper pattern.*

13–26. *The emblem is glued to the headpiece and its outline is deeply scored into the wood with a razor knife. The tuning machine grommets have been mounted as a visual aid for positioning.*

13–27. *An emblem scribed on the steel-string headpiece.*

heating with an iron, and the pierced headpiece surface is deeply scored with additional strokes of the razor knife.

A miniature router with a fine dental burr (Fig. 13-27) is used to excavate the material within the scored lines, leaving a flat-bottomed cavity a bit shallower than $1/16$ inch. After most of the bulk of the cavity is removed, the walls are brought up to the score marks. As the burr travels, it kicks up a fine wooden curl along the rim of its cut. At the instant the burr reaches the scored line, the curl flies off. After routing is completed, the corners of the cavity are cut square with the razor knife. The cutout is fit into the cavity after several trials with the knife and the router. The cutout must finally come to rest on the bottom of the cavity.

Step 3—Inlaying the Cutout

White glue is applied to the bottom of the cutout and the cutout is pressed into place in the cavity; take care not to get any glue in the crevices. After the glue dries thoroughly, the surfaces are leveled with a double-cut flat file; take particular care to concentrate the file's activity solely on the immediate area of the inlay. Sand the file marks off the surface with #100-grit garnet sandpaper wrapped around a flat hardwood block. Blow all the debris out of the crevices. Now pack the crevices with a mixture of epoxy resin glue

and a colorant matching the inlay's background. Five-minute-setting epoxy is used for single inlays and two-hour-setting epoxy is used for multiple-segment inlays. The colorant can consist of powdered japan or aniline colors or matching wood dust. The tinted glue is wiped into the inlay crevices and squished all around and over it. After it sets, the surface is quickly re-leveled by sanding with #120-grit garnet.

Step 4—Preparing Headpiece-binding Materials

Prepare several lengths of binding strips, about $1/8 \times 1/16$ inch in cross section, each long enough to travel around the perimeter of the headpiece. A particularly nice effect is achieved by binding with material that matches the headpiece veneer, separating them with a single white $1/32$-inch purfling line inboard of the binding strip (Fig. 13-28).

We lock a short segment of small-diameter pipe in a metal vise and heat it with a torch to provide a miniature bending iron for the two tight corner bends on the binding strip. Dip the strip in water and apply pressure over the hot pipe gently and carefully. Strive to heat the area of the bend thoroughly before applying any concerted bending force. You may break several strips, but be patient. You have made several extras and will get

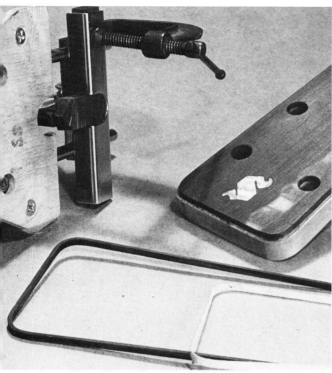

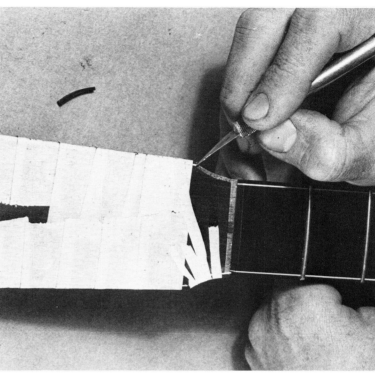

13–28. *Headpiece routed for binding and purfling strips. A wooden finger projecting from the parallel guide of the mini-router serves as an edge guide. The binding and purfling strips have been bent on a small-diameter hot pipe.*

13–29. *Binding and purfling strips glued into the routed ledge. The ends are mitered at the hyoid curve, and the small segments there are bound with thin strips of masking tape.*

closer to your goal each time. If the pieces break consistently, they may be too thick, the material selected may have too many large pores (choose finer-textured pieces) or your corners are too abrupt. Pre-bend your purfling line by first soaking it, then flexing it over the pipe.

A single ledge is routed around the perimeter to accommodate the thickness of the combined binding and purfling strips. For this purpose, the miniature router is fitted with a tiny router bit or end-mill bit. The ledge terminus at the nut may have to be hand trimmed, since the fin-gerboard interferes with the router's progress in that area. A purfling cutter, razor knife, and small chisel will serve to complete the end of the ledge.

The strips are glued into the ledge with white glue and then held in place with masking tape, as shown in Fig. 13-29. At the hyoid, the ends of the bindings must be trimmed and short, prebent binding segments mitered into them. The segments must be long enough to overlap the end of the headpiece veneer and project into the area of the nut. After the curved segments are glued and taped into the small curved ledges, their ends are sawn back and trimmed flush with the end of the headpiece veneer. After forty-five minutes, the tape is rolled off care-fully and the bound headstock surfaces are carefully scraped flush and then leveled with #120-grit and #220-grit gar-net sandpaper (the sandpaper is wrapped around a felt pad during sanding). All the edges are kept sharp until such time as they are finely and uni-formly chamfered with careful strokes of the scraper blade. Further sanding of the pearl inlay with grits down to #500 silicon carbide will refine the pearl surface to its full iridescence.

PROCEDURE: STEEL-STRING ONLY— SETTING THE NECK ANGLE

The angular relationship between the fingerboard surface and the soundboard is crucial to the proper functioning of the guitar. A correctly set neck angle will help ensure that the guitar has available to it an ample range of string-height adjustments to suit the individual player's style and string-tension preferences. In addition, a correctly set neck will provide the guitar with a capacity for adjustment against the progressively distorting effects of string tension.

The lay of the fretboard is compared to the lay of the soundboard by holding a long straightedge down the center of the fretboard and measuring the airspace between the straightedge and the soundboard, precisely at the spot where the saddle would be if the bridge were glued down.

If that airspace measurement is equal to the thickness of the bridge at its middle *plus* (no more than) $\frac{1}{16}$ inch or (no less than) $\frac{1}{64}$ inch, we can expect to end up with an $\frac{1}{8}$-inch-tall saddle and medium string action after the guitar has been strung up and has "settled in"—an optimum situation. On our guitar the bridge will be $\frac{3}{8}$ inch thick; thus the airspace can vary between $\frac{25}{64}$ and $\frac{7}{16}$ inch. We allow a greater airspace if we expect the guitar to flex a greater amount under tension; that is, if our design has a long string length, heavier strings, slender neck, "looser" soundboard, or a combination of these. We allow less airspace on a "stiffer" guitar.

If, after the neck is attached, the airspace is too small, the "back-set" of the neck will be *insufficient* and optimum saddle height will result in excessively *high* string action. Conversely, if the airspace is too large, the back-set of the neck will be *excessive* and optimum saddle height will result in excessively *low* string action.

When the neck tenon is slipped into the headblock mortise, it will stop when the end-grain surface of the heel bears up against the sides of the soundbox. To change the neck angle, we remove material strategically from the end-grain surface, changing the attitude of the entire neck and thus the inclination of the fingerboard relative to the soundboard. Since you can only remove material, think about what you are doing and do not remove any material unless you are certain of what the effects will be.

One of the tools needed for both setting and pinning the neck is a body clamp, which consists of a 4-inch-reach cam clamp with a 30-inch-long bar. These can be mail-ordered from luthier-supply houses or you can make one yourself: Start with a standard 4-inch wooden cam clamp and pop out the "circlip" fasteners that hold the fixed jaw. Use a hammer and narrow punch. Obtain a 30-inch bar with the same cross section as the original from a metal supplier or junkyard. Drill two holes in the end that match the original holes in the fixed jaw. Drive the circlips back into the new bar with a hammer. Put an extra layer of cork on both jaws.

TOOLS
small sanding board
felt block (stiff)
cam clamp
body clamp
small chisel (such as $\frac{3}{8}$-inch)
small sanding block

SUPPLIES
#120- and #220-grit garnet sandpaper

Step 1—Flattening the Bearing Surface of the Sides

To simplify the subsequent neck-set procedure, all the surface irregularities on the soundbox in the immediate area where it contacts the neck must be removed. Lumps, wiggles, or hollows in that region will prevent a fine, tight-looking junction seam when the neck is permanently attached.

Examine the junction area on the soundbox with a straightedge, preferably with a good backlight, to show up hollows and bumps clearly (Fig. 13-30). Take the small sanding board and, securing the soundbox with one hand, stroke the junction area with short, vigorous, unidirectional strokes. Strive to keep the sanding board from tipping or rocking. Now, with #120-grit garnet followed by #220-grit garnet (both wrapped around a stiff felt block), sand the sanding-board scratches away with careful, even strokes, following the grain but taking care that you do not disturb the flatness of the area.

Step 2—Marking the Soundboard

Make a small pencil mark across the soundboard center-line where the saddle would be on the finished guitar. Refer to the layout drawing in Chapter 3 for the distance between the neck/body junction and the theoretical location point of the saddle. A close approximation is all that is necessary.

13–30. *Checking the flatness of the neck junction area of the steel-string soundbox.*

Step 3—Fitting the Neck into the Soundbox

If the neck tenon will not enter the mortise in the sound-box, several things may be hanging it up. The sides may be overlapping the mortise walls; the clearance hole on the soundboard may be too small; the exposed truss-rod adjuster may not clear the hole in the headblock; the tenon may be too deep or too long. You must remove material as necessary with a small rasp or the chisel.

A notch in the bottom of the tenon to clear the binding,

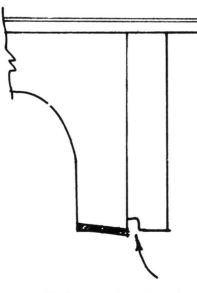

13–31. *Notch cut out from the steel-string tenon to clear binding.*

as shown in Fig. 13-31, may be necessary. Notch it by sawing a cross-grain kerf with a razor saw and snipping material away with a chisel. Be careful not to strike the visible portions of the heel's bearing surface with the saw teeth.

Once the tenon has entered and the neck has "dropped" into the soundbox, you may still notice gaps between the neck and the soundbox. For one thing, the flexible end of the fingerboard is likely to have curved downward slightly by the combined wedging action of the frets. You can gently coax the flexed member downward to conform, using a cam clamp pressed on the fingerboard and the back (mounted across the headblock). The clamp will also hold the neck in place during the subsequent setting steps.

Check the corners of the fingerboard stub. If the neck and soundbox centerlines coincide, the corners will intersect the rosette rings equally. Check also for gaps along the seams of both sides of the heel against the soundbox. You can chisel a small amount of material from the full length of the heel on one side, causing the neck to rotate by the amount necessary to bring the neck and soundbox centerlines into alignment. If you remove material along the heel's edge and no rotation takes place, the tenon is binding in the mortise and you may have to shave material off one side of the tenon to allow the neck to shift in the desired direction. Get it as close as you can.

If the narrow end of the heel does not sit tight against the sides, you must clamp it back with the 30-inch body clamp placed longitudinally across the soundbox.

Step 4—Shaving the Heel-bearing Surfaces to Set the Angle

Clamp up again and hold the long straightedge down the neck centerline (Fig. 13-32). You might have to push the clamp aside a little bit to get a clear shot down the centerline of the instrument. Measure the airspace between the straightedge and the soundbox at the small pencil mark. If it is not the same as the amount specified in the introductory notes to this procedure, you must change the reading by a trial-and-error

13–32. *Checking the lay of the fingerboard to observe the back-set of the neck. Airspace at the saddle location must be 1/64 to 1/16 inch greater than the height of the bridge.*

13–33. *Shaving the bearing surface of the heel to adjust the back-set of the neck.*

13–34. *Cleaning and truing the bearing surface with a sanding block.*

process of removing material from selected points on the heel-bearing surfaces until (a) the airspace measurement is correct, and (b) the seam between the heel and the sound-box is fine and tight.

The main thing to remember is that if a small amount of material (say, ¹⁄₆₄ to ¹⁄₃₂ inch) is removed at the heel, a larger change (¹⁄₃₂ to ¹⁄₁₆ inch) will result at the airspace measuring point. Neck back-set can be increased by removing material from the bottom of the heel in the region of the heel cap. Neck back-set can be decreased (specifically, a reduction in the airspace) by removing material from the top corner of the heel just below the fingerboard. If you go too far in any direction, you can bring the measurement back by carving some bearing surface away from the opposite end.

The best way to chisel is to start at the selected site by removing a wedge-shaped sliver that begins as a full ¹⁄₆₄-inch cut, feathering the cut to zero. (See Fig. 13-33.) You must trim a corresponding amount from the bearing edge of the heel cap when carving at the bottom end of the heel, in order to allow the neck to seat.

If the neck is almost set where you want it, you can improve the quality of the seam by stroking the bearing surface with a square block faced with #100-grit garnet. Hold it tightly against the tenon as it is slid up and down, until the bearing surface is flat once more (Fig. 13-34). Weight the stroke toward the desired final movement of the heel. With chisel strokes, undercut the interior portion of the bearing surface to speed up the sanding of the edge and to allow the heel to "bite" into the sides for a tighter seam.

PROCEDURE: FINITING

After the neck is finish-carved, all surfaces of the neck and body (expect the fingerboard) must be prepared for finishing. We call this process *finiting*. Scraper marks, file marks, and any random nicks or rough spots are removed. Small gaps are filled and sharp edges rounded. On the steel-string, marker dots must be installed on the edge of the fingerboard. On the classical, the nut slot must be cut back and ramps cut at the bottom of the tuning-machine slots. Finally, the surfaces must be sanded with fine sandpaper, leaving no visible sanding scratches.

The finiting procedure involves a variety of simple techniques that are enumerated below. Equally important, however, is the more subtle process of cultivating powers of observation. The experienced woodworker often will see gaps, pits, and masses of sanding scratches where the novice will see no flaws at all, until they are pointed out. By observing a surface under varying angles of illumination after each stage of refinement, over a period of time the student comes to "see" the surface rather than just look at it. Every square inch of the surface should be in a state that reflects intentionality, not accidental configuration. The builder must consciously and critically seek out flaws and correct them, rather than seek merely to verify that the surface is all right.

This process is especially important because flaws that may be hardly noticeable on the bare wood surfaces often become glaringly obvious when the finishing material is applied. Moreover, the builder's ability to apply a thin, even, high-quality finish depends in great measure on the preparation of the surface underneath. The smoother the surface underneath, the easier it is to get a flat, glasslike surface with the finishing material. A poorly refined surface may be difficult, even impossible, to finish properly.

An improperly finished instrument will often obscure the time and care that preceded the refining and finishing steps. Conversely, a clean finish can often effectively camouflage unfortunate earlier mistakes. The student is therefore encouraged to take the time and care necessary to do the following steps thoroughly, and not to let enthusiasm for completing the instrument dilute the quality of energy already invested.

TOOLS
scraper blade
propane torch
palette knife
awl (steel-string only)
drill bit matching diameter of marker-dot material (steel-string only; see Step 4)
hand drill (steel-string only)
fine-cutting flat file (steel-string only)
razor saw (classical only)
narrow chisel (classical only)
round rasp (classical only)
sanding block (cork, rubber, or felt)

SUPPLIES
stick shellac
#120- and #220-grit garnet sandpaper
optional: dyed glue (see Step 3)
marker-dot material (steel-string only; see Step 4)

Step 1—Scraping Plate Surfaces and Binding

The scraper must be well sharpened and burnished for all refining steps.

The binding will have been scraped flush to the plates at the end of the purfling-and-binding procedures, but any remaining irregularities must be eliminated now, while the plates are being scraped. It is important to remember, however, that the binding can easily be scraped too thin when the builder's attention is on the plate surfaces.

Scraping the plates is done to remove both random and regularly occurring flaws. Bits of dried glue must be scraped, rather than sanded. Lingering plane marks or scraper digs from the plate-thinning steps must be eliminated. If the wood has been passed through a thickness sander, it will have combs of sanding scratches that must be scraped to be removed. Just as in neck carving, the edge tool (scraper) should do most of the work. The sandpaper should be used only to smooth the surface just prior to finishing.

The classical can be held by the neck in the vise; the steel-string box must be butted against a stop when being scraped. The scraper can be slightly flexed with both hands as in Fig. 13-35 or in any way that is comfortable. The most important consideration is that it cut a flat swath on flat surfaces, rather than gouge or hollow.

Step 2—Filling in Random Gaps with Stick Shellac

Stick shellac may be clear, or it can be in various shades to match wood pigments. It is most useful for filling in small gaps, such as along the bindings, because it melts easily and then hardens almost instantly upon cooling. We use a palette knife fashioned from a cheap paring knife, ground and bent to a suitable shape for melting and smearing the stick shellac. (See Fig. 13-36.) A burn-in knife can also be purchased from a finishing supplier. The knife is heated with a propane torch and touched to the shellac stick; the melted shellac is then packed into gaps with the knife wherever they are found.

Check along all joints and seams for gaps. Apply stick shellac where necessary, using an appropriate color. Clear shellac will often blend well in a dark background, sometimes

13–35. *Scraping the sides of the steel-string soundbox butted against a stop.*

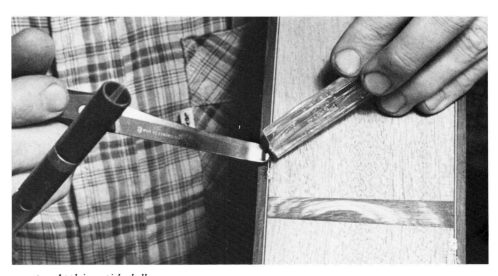

13–36. *Applying stick shellac.*

leaving a less visible filled gap than a matching color. We find it especially useful on the soundhole rosette, where many colors often come together. Darker varieties of stick shellac are sometimes difficult to remove cleanly from spruce; thus, they should be used sparingly along the soundboard bindings. Use clear where possible.

When the stick shellac cools, sand the excess lightly with #100- or #120-grit garnet and then scrape gently until most of the excess is removed. Finally, sand until the gap is smooth and no trace of excess stick shellac remains.

Step 3—Filling End-gaps under Frets

The fret slots are usually somewhat deeper than the tangs of the frets, and the resulting gaps at the ends must be filled before the fingerboard edge can be finished. This step can be done with black stick shellac, as used in Step 2, or with glue dyed black. Liquid aniline dyes or powdered japan color will dye white glue black.

The dyed glue is simply dabbed on each fret-slot end and allowed to dry before being sanded and scraped smooth (see Fig. 13-37). Keep it in an airtight container.

Step 4—Steel-string Only: Installing Marker Dots

Single dots must appear at the third, fifth, seventh, and ninth frets; a pair of dots denotes the octave at the twelfth fret. Marker dots can be added optionally at the fifteenth, seventeenth, and nineteenth frets.

We use thin plastic rods for the dots (diameter approximately .070 inch). These correspond well to a #50 machinist's drill bit. Any similar material can be used, however, as long as a matching drill bit is available.

Find the midpoint between the second and third frets on the fingerboard edge, and mark it with an awl. Drill about ⅛ inch deep at that point with the bit that matches your dot material. If you used dyed glue to fill the gaps under the fret ends in Step 3, use that for gluing in the dot material. If you do not have dyed glue, ordinary white glue will do so long as the dot material fits snugly into the drill holes.

Put a dab of glue into the drill hole and slide in the dot material. Snip it off with a wire nipper, leaving about ⅛ inch excess. Repeat the operation for the other dot locations. Mark and drill for *two* dots between and equidistant from the eleventh and twelfth frets.

When the glue is thoroughly dry, nip back most of the remaining excess on each dot. With a fine cutting file, grind the dot material flush to the edge of the fingerboard. Finally, sand away all traces of glue with a #120-grit garnet paper. (See Fig. 13-38.)

Step 5—Classical Only: Cutting Back the Nut Slot

This operation requires a small block of hardwood about 2 × ⅜ × ⁷⁄₃₂ inches, which is used as a saw guide.

Clamp the neck in a vise (or otherwise secure it) and butt the 2 × ⅜-inch face of the guide block against the end of the fingerboard. Using a razor saw pressed flush against the guide block, carefully saw into the headpiece veneer sandwich (see Fig. 13-39). The saw *must* remain vertical as it enters the veneer. This will be achieved without difficulty as long as the guide block is kept tightly against the fingerboard end and the saw is held firmly against the block.

Progress slowly and carefully, watching *both* ends of the cut. When the saw enters the bottommost veneer, stop the cut and remove the saw and guide block.

Using a narrow chisel, shave away the waste portion of the veneer sandwich and any debris that may have collected in the nut slot (Fig. 13-40). Work from *both* ends of the slot, especially when the depth approaches the mahogany headstock material beneath the veneers. All cuts traversing the ends of the slot should be *entry* cuts. Exit cuts risk severe tear-out of the mahogany edge, a flaw that is very difficult to repair satisfactorily.

If the slot straddles the area where the headstock begins to

13-37.   Filling in gaps at the ends of the fret slots with dyed glue.

13-38.   Marker dots are inserted on the edge of the steel-string fingerboard.

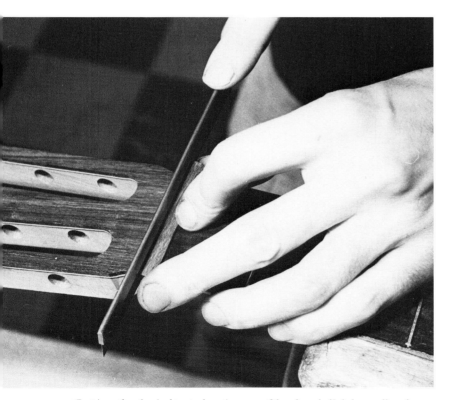

13-39.   Cutting the classical nut slot. A scrap of hardwood slightly smaller than the nut blank is used as a saw guide.

13-40.   Removing waste from the nut slot.

angle back, you must carve a flat floor for the nut without cutting the slot below the level of the seams where the veneer sandwich and fingerboard meet the neckstock. The nut floor will be a facet between the two seams, which is perfectly acceptable. Carefully shave away the peak, again scrupulously avoiding exit cuts.

13–41. Carving the string ramps with a round rasp. The rasp is held above and below the headpiece and is twirled on the cutting stroke for smooth action. The masking tape protects the walls of the slot.

Step 6—Classical Only: Ramping the Tuning-machine Slots

The tuning-machine slots may be ramped as flat channels with a chisel, or as curved troughs with a round rasp. We prefer the latter, but the choice is purely a matter of taste.

Before cutting the ramp with the round rasp, apply a few layers of masking tape to protect the walls of the slot (Fig. 13-41). Pass the rasp through and hold it both above and below the head-piece. Avoid dragging the rasp on the return stroke. You will find that the rasp cuts much more smoothly if it is twirled as the cutting stroke is made.

The curved ramp should travel about halfway down the depth of the slot at about a 45-degree angle. Leave at least ⅜ inch of the veneer surface between the end of the ramp and the nut slot.

When the ramps are mostly cut, remove the masking tape and carefully merge them with the slot walls. The round rasp can still be used, but a fine-cutting round file is better. Do not widen the slots or disfigure their edges. Finish the ramps with sandpaper wrapped around a cylindrical object such as a pencil or razor-knife handle.

Step 7—Sanding the Guitar

Both the neck and body must be thoroughly sanded with #120-grit paper at this point, but what constitutes thorough sanding depends upon what is necessary. The objective of this step is to create a consistent surface on every part of the instrument. Obviously, then, you cannot sand blindly, for some areas will require more attention than others. (*Note:* If your back and sides are made of an open-pored wood, such as mahogany or rosewood, *do not* sand the soundboard at this time. When the pores of the back and sides are filled during the finishing procedure, some of the filler may smudge onto the soundbord; thus, sanding the soundboard is postponed until after that step. This is addressed in Chapter 14.)

If you missed any flaws or deep scratches during the scraping step, scrape them before sanding.

When sanding, never focus on a very small spot—always spread out the sanding area to avoid hollows. Do not sand cross-grain on any surface with #120-grit paper.

When working toward a uniform surface, pay particular attention to areas where the grain changes direction—such as at the throat and heel on the neck.

Always wrap the sandpaper around a sanding block. We use cork, rubber, or felt blocks. Do not use a wooden block.

Step 8—Rounding the Binding and Sharp Edges

Use a scraper to carve a facet into the binding all around. Sand gently with #120-grit garnet, smoothing the facet into a radius. Using long strokes will maintain the evenness of the radius. A very small radius will produce a crisper outline, usually appropriate on the steel-string; a larger radius produces a softer, rounder effect, our preference for the classical.

Other sharp corners such as at the heel cap and on the headpiece should be hit lightly with the sanding block, just enough to knock off the edges. Do not actually radius the corners.

Step 9—Rounding the Soundhole Edge

This is a separate step because of certain caveats that must be heeded to avoid disastrous misshaping. The circular edge of the soundhole intersects both end-grain and side-grain. The side-grain sands away *much* more quickly than the end-grain. Thus, the sides of the soundhole should be just barely touched with the sanding block during the rounding operation. Knock off the edge with long, sweeping motions. Do not try to work a small area—always sweep at least one-third of the circumference with each sanding stroke. (See Fig. 13-42.)

Work both the outer side and underside of the edge until it approximates a radius. If any irregularity begins to develop, do not sand that area any further. Trying to correct an irregularity usually results in a more, rather than less, visible flaw.

Step 10—Final Sanding of the Guitar (#220-grit Garnet)

This step is similar to the #120-grit sanding step in that the objective is to produce a consistent surface. When this step is completed, the instrument is ready for finishing. Wipe or blow off all debris from previous sanding steps before proceeding.

Areas that have not been adequately sanded with #120-grit should be gone over again before #220 sanding. The finer sandpaper should not be used to remove flaws at all, but rather should just eliminate the very fine scratches left by the #120.

13–42. *Rounding the edges of the soundhole. Special care must be taken to ensure that the softer side-grain areas are not cut more heavily than the harder end-grain areas.*

CHAPTER 14

Like most wood finishes, the guitar finish serves to protect and beautify the wood surfaces and to slow down the exchange of moisture between the wood and the surrounding atmosphere. Unlike the almost mystical qualities historically attributed to violin finishes, however, the guitar finish has rarely, if ever, been claimed to have a profound effect on the instrument's sound. A change in sound discernible to a trained ear takes place when the guitar goes from a totally unfinished state to a finished state, but the idea of *controlling* significant aspects of the instrument's voice and tonal response by varying finish coating is rather foreign to most guitar builders.

If more than the minimal amount of finish necessary to protect the instrument is applied, acoustic damping becomes a problem that far outweighs any possible beneficial acoustic effect. The short duration of the plucked-string signal (as compared to the persistent bowed-string signal) exacerbates the impact of damping attributable to a poor

Finishing

finish. Thus, rather than factor the effect of the finish into the instrument's design, as do many violinmakers, the guitar-maker usually designs without regard to the finish, and then simply seeks to apply as little finish as possible.

In order to accommodate problems associated with mass-production finishing, many factories apply thick finishes to their guitars. Some private luthiers do so also, but this is usually out of ignorance about the amount of finish necessary to protect the instrument, or lack of the technical knowledge or skill required to execute a thin finish. We have seen instruments undergo a dramatic increase in volume and clarity simply because a substantial percentage of a thick finish was removed. Learning to apply a thin but durable finish coating can therefore be a crucial element of the luthier's training.

FINISHING MATERIALS

We do not believe that the choice of generic finish coating makes any detectable difference in the luthier's final product. We have seen many great guitars finished beautifully with lacquer, varnish, shellac, or combinations of these materials. Conversely, we have seen all three coatings used disastrously, either because the finishing material was of poor quality or because the builder was incompetent.

The finish coats are typically divided into two layers. The *undercoat* material seals the surface and forms a bond between the wood and the second layer of finish. The *topcoat* material provides actual protection for the instrument and permits polishing to a desired gloss. It is crucial that the undercoat and topcoat be compatible. Lacquer topcoats usually are applied over a sanding sealer undercoat, which is manufactured from the same raw materials as the lacquer but has sealing mediums added to improve adhesion and sand-

ability. Thinned shellac is often applied as an undercoat for a shellac or varnish topcoat; thinned varnish is sometimes used as a sealer coat under a varnish topcoat.

On our guitars we most often use spray lacquer, a nitrocellulose resin in a highly volatile solvent. It dries crystal clear by solvent evaporation. We prefer high-gloss lacquer on our instruments, but flat, semigloss, and "rubbed effect" lacquers are also sometimes used on guitars.

Lacquer is usually sprayed because of its rapid drying time. When sprayed, it will feel dry to the touch in only a few minutes and will be hard enough to handle and recoat within an hour. The addition of a slow-drying solvent (or *retarder*), however, permits application with a brush. "Brushing" lacquer is applied with a soft, flowing stroke, rather than being brushed on like paint. A properly retarded brushing lacquer flows so smoothly that if expertly applied it will be virtually indistinguishable from a spray finish. For builders who seek the fast-drying convenience and working ease of lacquers but have neither the resources nor the technical expertise to employ spray equipment, brushing lacquer is an excellent option. We recommend brushing lacquer in the step-by-step procedure below because we feel that it is the simplest coating finish available to the home craftsperson.

Many great classical guitar-makers choose varnish as a finishing material. Spirit varnishes are gum resins in a volatile solvent; when compounded with an oxidizing oil, they are called oil varnishes. Oil varnishes contain a wide variety of hard and soft resins; spirit varnishes usually contain softer resins with shellac dissolved in alcohol.

Some spirit varnishes dry quickly enough to spray, but we have yet to find one to our satisfaction. The slower-drying characteristic, however, has the major advantage of being very easy to brush on. The varnish will level itself during drying for a while even if applied inexpertly; brushing lacquer is not so forgiving. On the other hand, however, brush varnish must be applied in a dust-free environment, for otherwise it is liable to collect a great deal of dust during its long drying period.

Shellac is an organic material secreted by the lac bug, an insect that lives and breeds on the branches of trees in parts of southern Asia. The secretions encrust the tree branches;

the branches are harvested and then milled and sifted to separate the raw shellac, known as seed-lac. Further refinement of the seed-lac produces shellac flakes and buttons that must be dissolved in alcohol for use. In its natural state, shellac is orange or pale amber. To make a clear coating, the flakes must be bleached before being dissolved. Bleached flakes have a very short shelf life, so we always use a natural amber; we prefer the color anyway.

Shellac can be sprayed, brushed, or padded (French polished), and it dries quickly. It is easily spotted by water and is not heat resistant, however, and it will be immediately damaged by contact with alcohol. It is often used as a sealer coat *under* a varnish topcoat, or used as a topcoat on the soundboard with a varnish or lacquer for the back and sides; it is, however, perfectly suitable for the entire instrument so long as water and alcohol are kept off the finished surfaces when the guitar is in use.

FILLING

Before any finish coating can be applied, the bare wood surface must be as smooth as possible. This is accomplished primarily by the finiting procedure described in the previous chapter, but on certain woods an additional step is required before coating. Hardwoods have vessel elements for

conducting sap, which appear on the lumber surface as pores. (Softwoods are nonporous.) When the pores are easily visible to the naked eye, hardwoods are described as being open-pored; if the pores can only be seen under magnification, the wood is described as being close-pored. Mahogany and rosewood, for example, are open-pored woods; maple is close-pored. Open pores are usually filled with a product composed of a filling medium (usually a crushed stone quartz referred to as silex), a binder (usually a form of varnish), drying additives, and pigments. These are thinned in a reducing medium (we use naphtha exclusively) to the consistency of heavy cream, and brushed on the bare wood surface. When the solvent evaporates, the excess filler is wiped off across the grain with burlap or a shredded fiber sometimes called wood-wool or sisal. The silex filling material is left in the pores when the excess is wiped off, creating a flat surface for the undercoats.

Note: On the classical guitar, the finish coatings are traditionally applied to the bridge as well. Thus, we glue the classical bridge in place after filling but before finishing the classical guitar. The classical builder will be advised at the end of the filling procedure to turn to the next chapter, make the classical bridge, fill it and seal it, and glue it in place before applying the finish coats to the instrument.

PROCEDURE: FILLING OPEN PORES

Silex fillers can be purchased at any finishing-supply store. For filling light-colored woods such as mahogany, precolored fillers will usually do all right, but beware of using them on rosewood or ebony. The darkest shades of precolored filler that are typically available commercially are often not dark enough for very dark exotic hardwoods. The pores must be as dark or darker than the background surface to avoid a speckled appearance. In order to obtain a sufficiently dark filler, it is usually necessary to buy pigments from your finishing supplier and color the natural paste filler yourself.

A wide variety of pigmenting materials is available. The most commonly recommended are dry earth pigments or colors-in-japan. We recommend talking with your finishing materials supplier about available fillers and pigments and then trying them on scrap in your own shop environment before using them on the guitar.

Solvents for fillers include pure gum spirits, turpentine, benzine, varnoline, and even lead-free gasoline, but we always use and exclusively recommend naphtha, which is generally available in paint stores.

When the filler is pigmented, the coloring agent is carried in the solvent as well as the solid material. During filling, the colored solvent inevitably penetrates somewhat into the bare wood surface; this will darken the wood. On woods such as mahogany, this is considered a normal effect; the choice of pigmentation is, in fact, often determined by the desired final shade of the wood. On highly colored rosewood, however, many of the subtle shades of natural coloration can be muddied and lost because of pigmented solvent penetration. To minimize this effect, we use a "wash-coat" on rosewood surfaces prior to filling. A wash-coat is a very thin coat of finishing material that will retard colored solvent penetration. (It also facilitates drying of the filler on resinous hardwoods.) The choice of wash-coat material depends entirely on the coatings to be used in the actual finish. A very diluted coat of any of the final finishing materials will work well.

TOOLS
paintbrush
burlap or sisal
paper towels

MATERIALS
filler and pigment
naphtha

Step 1—Preparing the Filler

The filler will probably have to be diluted for use, although some manufacturers supply it in ready-to-use form. It must be brought to the consistency of heavy cream. A surprisingly small amount of naphtha will be sufficient for reduction. Stir the filler and solvent thoroughly until the solution is smooth and creamy. Ordinarily, about a half cup will do the whole guitar, but mix up a little more to be sure you do not run out.

After the paste has been thinned, add the colors you have chosen (if it is not already pigmented) and stir them in thoroughly. (If you use powdered pigments, dissolve them completely in naphtha before mixing into the filler.)

Step 2—Applying the Filler

Use a clean paintbrush for this step. Put some newspaper on the workbench, lay the guitar on its face, and begin applying the filler with the grain (Fig. 14-1). The wood surface should be completely covered; if it is not, lay on more *across* the grain. Cover the back and sides of the box; on the classical, cover the neck as well. (On the steel-string, do the neck separately.)

Let the filler dry until the wet look is gone and the entire surface is dull. If you are using the right consistency and have applied it properly, the filler will look like a thin coat of dried mud on the guitar.

When dry, begin wiping the filler *across* the grain with the burlap or sisal (Fig. 14-2). Keep changing to fresh wiping material as it gets gunked up

14-1. Applying tinted paste filler. The marquetry centerseam inlay has been masked with a thin strip of masking tape.

14-2. Wiping off the excess filler.

with filler. We usually do a "dirty" wipe to get the bulk of the filler off all parts, and then a "clean" wipe to remove the remnants and thoroughly clean the surfaces.

After the filler has been removed, wait about five minutes for residual drying and then wipe all surfaces *across* the grain with clean paper towels. Finally, wipe *with* the grain, buffing lightly to remove the last bit of excess filler.

Through all of these motions, strive to keep the filler off the soundboard and fingerboard, both when wet and when dry. Do not lay the guitar down on newspaper that is covered with dried filler particles.

It is crucial that the filler be thoroughly dry before any coatings are applied over it. Follow the manufacturer's recommendations for drying time, but in any case wait at least overnight.

When the filler is dry, the soundboard must be #120- and #220-grit sanded as were the other parts of the guitar during the finiting procedure. Make sure that the soundboard surface is clean and free of filler smudges, heavy sanding scratches, scraper marks, gaps, digs, or any other irregularities. If the bindings develop a facet from sanding on the soundboard, round them again with #220-grit garnet.

Important: Classical builders should read the rest of this chapter to familiarize themselves with finishing procedures, but must turn to the next chapter, make the bridge, fill and seal it, and glue it on before applying the finish to the guitar.

PROCEDURE: FINISHING WITH BRUSH LACQUER

Although we have chosen to present a step-by-step procedure for brush lacquer only, the student should feel free to consider varnish, shellac, or spray lacquer if experienced in applying those finishes.

Select a commercially available nitrocellulose (not acrylic) brushing lacquer with compatible sanding sealer, thinner, and retarder. Use a 2- to 2½-inch-wide fitch or ox-hair flowing brush. A new brush should be tapped against the palm of the hand to remove all loose bristles, bristle pieces, and dust. It should then be dipped into a good brush cleaner, dried overnight, and tapped out again.

The wood surfaces must be completely free of dust and grit—"dust-free" drying with lacquer will be useless if the surfaces are not clean to begin with.

We recommend practicing the following steps on scrap until the student is familiar with the flowing characteristics of brush lacquer, before proceeding to apply the actual finish to the instrument. The sealer and lacquer will flow more easily and forgivingly if

thinned out or retarded. In this procedure we recommend thinning up to a point, but if the student has continued difficulty with brush technique, the materials can be further thinned and the number of coats increased. The finish should be applied in an atmosphere that is the same temperature or slightly cooler than the workshop atmosphere to avoid the formation of bubbles caused by air expansion in the vessels of open-pored wood.

TOOLS
2- to 2½-inch brush

MATERIALS
lacquer
sanding sealer
thinner

SUPPLIES
sandpaper (#500-grit Wetordry; #220-, #320-, and #400-grit silicon-carbide paper)
paper towels
rubbing and polishing compounds
cheesecloth or clean rags

Step 1—Preparing the Guitar

Vacuum out any dust or grit that may have accumulated inside the guitar box. Tape several layers of paper towel to the inside surface of the back to catch any lacquer that might drip into the soundhole.

Moisten a double thickness of paper towel *very slightly* with lacquer thinner. It should be just barely damp to the

touch—not quite wet. Wipe down the back, sides, and neck to remove all traces of dust and contaminants; then moisten a fresh piece of paper towel and wipe off the soundboard. Spread some clean newspaper on the work area.

Step 2—Thinning the Sealer

Pour about a cup of sanding sealer into a clean, wide-mouthed glass, metal, or ceramic container. Dip the brush about halfway into the sealer. Do not wipe the brush on the side of the container; instead, just turn it round and round until it stops drooling. Spread some sealer onto a clean, smooth piece of scrap wood.

The material must be *flowed* onto the surface in a continuous, wet coat. The tip of the brush should just barely touch the wood (Fig. 14–3); the liquid should be spread as if you were icing a cake rather than using a paintbrush. The surface should be very wet—almost flooded, but not running. Dip the brush again and spread an adjacent area, merging the fresh material into the material already applied.

As the material flows from the dry area into the wet area, the brush strokes must be *feathered* off the work surface; stopping abruptly will leave little ridges.

Because the sealer has not yet been thinned at all, you will probably notice that the fresh brush strokes do not flow easily into the first area, as it most likely will have begun to skin over. Add some thinner and try again on a fresh piece of scrap. The idea is to stroke with a brushload of material just until the brush begins to run out, and then to redip the brush. Retracing and back-brushing must be avoided or at least kept to a minimum. The work area for each brush-load of lacquer should be kept small enough to avoid stringing out the brush strokes to the point where they must be retraced.

Try to dip the brush the same amount each time, getting a sense of how much material is necessary to cover a given area. This way each section can be started with the same amount and brushed equally.

Keep adding thinner just until the material flows easily from one area into the next. You will note that what may appear to be a very wet, heavy coat will be dramatically reduced by evaporation in a little while.

14–3. *Brushing lacquer. The finishing material must be allowed to flow on rather than being painted on with the brush. This photo shows a steel-string guitar made in the Spanish method by one of our students.*

Step 3—Applying the Sealer Coats

Lay the guitar on its face and apply the first coat of sealer. Getting the sealer undercoats level is not nearly as critical as getting the lacquer topcoats level, so do your best but do not worry if the surface looks uneven. Use the sealer coats as an opportunity to practice for the lacquer.

Always try to work *off* the edges from the middle of the back to avoid buildup on the edges and dripping down the sides. If a drip occurs, wipe it away with a quick brush stroke. When the back is covered, proceed to the sides and neck, including the back of the headpiece.

Wait the amount of time

recommended by the manufacturer for the first coat to dry. Then turn the guitar over and coat the soundboard and the face of the headpiece.

On the classical, be sure to coat the walls of the slots in the headpiece. *Do not* coat the bridge, as it should have enough sealer on it already.

When the first coat is dry on the entire guitar, apply a second coat in the same sequence as the first.

Step 4—Sanding the Sealer

When the sealer is thoroughly dry and hard, it can be leveled with sandpaper. It is best to wait at least overnight after the last coat has been applied.

One caveat is important here. When sanding finishing materials, *never* actually touch the edges anywhere on the guitar (that is, the radius of the binding), for the finish on the edges will be quickly sanded away if you do.

Sand out large irregularities with nonloading #220-grit silicon-carbide paper. (We call it no-fill paper.) You can observe your progress while sanding by noting that the areas hit by sandpaper are dull and unreflective, while the untouched areas are shiny and wet looking. After scuffing the surface with #220, switch to #320-grit and very carefully try to level the surface as much as possible, to eliminate the shiny

areas. Adjust your lighting to be able to see the surface in detail. Although the ideal is a perfectly dull, flat surface all over the guitar, you are likely to sand through the sealer to the bare wood underneath in some spots well before the whole surface is sanded. If this happens, stop sanding in that spot and stay away from the area, even if it obviously is not completely level.

Step 5—Applying and Leveling the Lacquer

Before applying lacquer, the sanded surface of the sealer must be wiped free of dust with paper towels slightly moistened with naphtha.

Go through the same thinning step as you did for sealer. Apply two coats and let them dry thoroughly (for at least twenty-four hours after the second coat). Sand lightly with #400-grit no-fill paper to remove major irregularities, but *do not* try to level the surface.

Wipe off the surface and apply two more coats; let dry for forty-eight hours. Try leveling the lacquer on the back of the guitar with #400-grit no-fill, sanding *across* the grain. If you succeed in leveling the back without going through the finish to the wood, proceed to level the other surfaces on the guitar, also sanding across the grain (except on the neck, of course).

If you find yourself going through the finish on the back

in a lot of places, however, your lacquer surface is too thin. Wipe off the surface and add three coats to the back (which has just been sanded), and two everywhere else on the guitar.

Try leveling the back again. If you sand through again, proceed nonetheless to the other parts of the guitar and try your luck. If you go through all over the place, add a couple of more coats. At this point, we must confess that our ability to help with instructions is limited. The student can absorb the *concept* of applying and leveling the finish from the forgoing instructions but can gain a tactile understanding of the materials only through experience. If you have difficulty, it may be that your coats are too thin or too uneven, or that your sanding technique is insensitive, or a combination of these problems. It may be necessary to build a relatively thick finish in order to be able to level the surface on your first few instruments, but as you gain more experience you will eventually be able to apply a minimal amount of lacquer on the guitar and yet obtain a thoroughly sanded, highly refined surface.

Step 6—Polishing the Lacquer

When you have succeeded in leveling with #400-grit no-fill across the grain, change over to #500-grit Wetordry paper.

Use a sanding block made of a material that will not absorb water (such as rubber). Fill a bowl with water and add a few drops of dish-washing liquid; stir them around until the water appears slightly soapy. Dip the Wetordry paper in the soapy water and begin sanding the lacquered surface *with* the grain. Wipe the surface periodically with a paper towel to observe your progress. Continue until the #400 scratches have mostly disappeared.

The sanded surface must now be polished to a gloss with rubbing and glazing (polishing) compounds. These are very fine abrasives suspended in a liquid or paste medium. Compounds for lacquer are available from some luthier-supply houses, but they may be easier to obtain from your finishing materials supplier. Automotive lacquer suppliers are also a good source for rubbing and polishing compounds.

Compounds are applied to a polishing cloth and rubbed on the lacquered surface. Take a piece of cheesecloth or a rag cut from a clean, well-laundered bed sheet and dip it in water. Wring it out thoroughly so that it is just damp. (Dampening the cloth prevents the compound from drying out too quickly while it is being rubbed.) Fold the cloth neatly, dip it into the rubbing compound, and spread some on the lacquered surface. Rub the surface with the grain, using the heel of the hand on the cloth; use fingertips only to get into tight places. Work one section at a time, alternately rubbing with compound and buffing the surface with a clean cloth. Work the rubbing compound to at least a moderate sheen over the whole guitar, wipe clean with a damp cloth, and then repeat the process with a glazing or polishing compound to bring up the gloss.

Do not let the cloths get gritty with dried particles. Shake them out frequently, replacing them as they become heavily loaded. Do not let a compound cloth become contaminated with dust or grit from the work area.

We sometimes use a polishing cloth wrapped around a felt block or even just use the block itself to work up a high gloss. The block must be dampened and compound applied directly to it. (See Fig. 14-4.) The surface is rubbed until the compound begins to cake on the block; then the block can be used both diagonally and with the grain. The block must be replenished with compound as it dries; if the caked compound starts to slough off, the block must be scraped clean and fresh compound applied. The lacquered surface must be periodically wiped with a clean, dry cloth. Do not buff vigorously with the cloth since small, dried particles of compound can re-scratch the surface. Shake the cloth out often and keep it stored in your shirt pocket when not in use.

We also use an electric polisher to buff the surface to a high gloss (Fig. 14-5).

Examine Figs. 14-6 through 14-8 for visual examples of other methods of finish application.

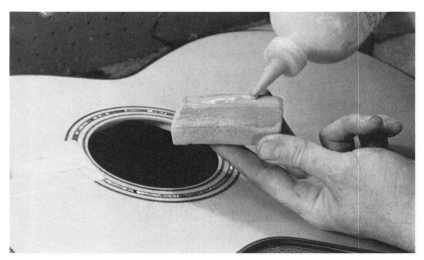

14-4. *Polishing compound applied to a felt block. The polish cakes on the block as it is rubbed, bringing the finish up to a fine sheen.*

14–5. *Electric polishing speeds and improves results. The machine must be handled deftly and carefully, for inattention can cause damage to the finish surface due to excessive heat buildup.*

14–6. *French polishing. A pad, or "rubber" as it is traditionally called, is used to apply a light coat of shellac. As more shellac is applied it is simultaneously flowed out of the pad and leveled by the gentle padding motion. This technique permits an extremely thin finish coat, as no abrasive leveling is necessary.*

14–7 and 14–8. *Spraying is an extremely effective method of applying a thin, even finish coating on the guitar. The soundhole and fingerboard must be masked before spraying, and a handle must be devised to hold the steel-string soundbox.*

CHAPTER 15

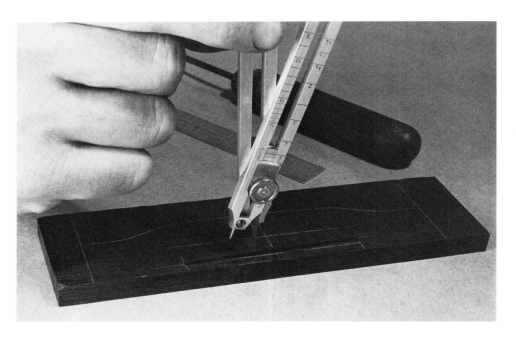

THE BRIDGE: HISTORICAL NOTES

During the first four centuries of the guitar's history, the bridge consisted simply of a rectangular block of hardwood, such as ebony, rosewood, or walnut, drilled through for the strings. In many cases a small flat platform extended behind the block, serving to extend the bridge's gluing surface and influence on the soundboard (Fig. 15-1).

Over the years, the platform extended outward to points beyond both sides of the tie block. Decorative acanthuses or ivy-entwined volutes cut from veneer often grew like branches from the points (Fig. 15-2). Tie block and platform extensions were often bedecked with ivory and shell strips as well as with shell inlays of geometric and floral shapes. Today they help identify the period and country of origin of a surviving instrument.

In the eighteenth century the platform increased in area, in some cases extending the front of the tie block as well, as greater gluing area was re-

The Bridge, & Pinning the Steel-String Neck

quired in response to a progressive increase in string tensions. Then, at the turn of the nineteenth century, there occurred a split in the ranks of the European guitarmakers.

French and Italian builders all but dropped the multi-course guitar in favor of the simpler six-string guitar. At that juncture, they also dropped the tie block design in favor of the pinned bridge. A French guitar built by François Lupot in 1773 shows an early example of a pinned bridge (Fig. 15-3). (It also displays the leafy shrubbery of an earlier time.) Forty years after Lupot, the pinned bridge was

the standard on British as well as central- and northern-European guitars made by such masters as Louis Panormo, René Lacôte, Grobert, and Johann Georg Staufer (Figs. 15-4 to 15-7).

In most cases a raised lip made of the same bridge material served as both a bearing point and string stop on early pinned bridges. By the 1820s, however, many non-Spanish bridges sported a removable ivory or bone saddle in front of the bridge pins.

The Spanish luthiers kept building and developing their six-course (twelve-gut-string) guitar for over thirty years

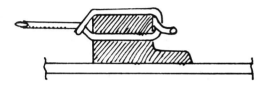

15–1. Early tie block bridge design.

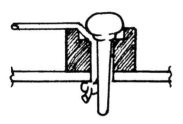

15–3. Cross-section of an early pinned bridge by Lupot.

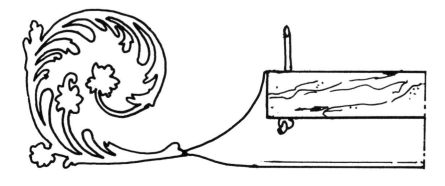

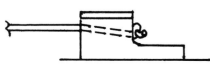

15–2. Bridge with decorative volutes found on eighteenth-century guitar built by Champion (France).

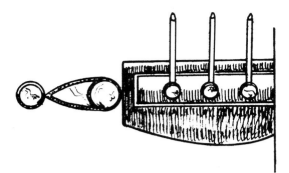

15–4. Pin bridge with raised lip by Panormo.

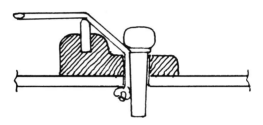

15–5. Pin bridge with removable saddle by René Lacôte.

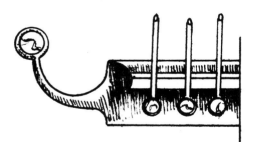

15–6. Early nineteenth-century French pin bridge with removable saddle.

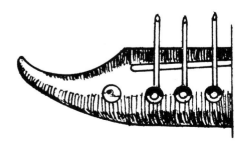

15–7. Viennese pin bridge by Staufer.

longer; they thus retained the archaic tie block bridge design. Even after the six-string guitar finally became popular in Spain, the tie block bridge persisted. By the 1830s, the platform on the Spanish tie block bridge had evolved into the rectangular "wing" extensions familiar to us on modern classical guitars.

By the 1850s the Spanish were experimenting with bridge pins and a removable saddle. About this time, Antonio de Torres was creating his own bridge design. His was a synthesis of several ideas floating around at the time. The design was the Spanish tie block bridge with rectangular wing extensions at either side, but it included a removable bone saddle and moved the tie block to the rear. Torres thus created the modern classical bridge, which has remained virtually unchanged to this day.

C.F. Martin I, who had worked in Austria with Staufer, brought the pinned-bridge design with him to New York in 1833 and proceeded to make guitars in what was then known as the French style. After experimenting with the Spanish style, he too extended the platform into rectangular wings at either side.

Much later, the Martin bridge body was enlarged and deepened by his successors, presumably to better withstand the added stress of steel strings; the modern steel-string bridge was thus born.

THE BRIDGE: TECHNICAL NOTES

The bridge serves as the anchoring point for the strings on the soundboard. It also determines the correct spacing of the strings and provides the means for fine-adjusting their height above the fingerboard. Most important, however, the bridge couples the string's signal to, and distributes the string's tension onto, the soundboard.

The bridge's design and construction determine to a dramatic extent how the guitar sounds and how it plays. Since the total height of the bridge and saddle will determine the height of the strings above the soundboard, it will (like the length of the short arm of a crowbar) also determine the actual amount of string stress "dumped" onto the soundboard. Thus, the bridge's design will affect how long the soundboard will last without distorting.

The luthier selects the finished height of the bridge to be appropriate to the resilience of the braced soundboard and to the soundboard's size. In general terms, the range of appropriate bridge heights is equivalent on both nylon and steel-string guitars. A ¼-inch bridge height is often selected for flamenco guitars and for small, very lightly strung steel-string guitars. A ⅜-inch bridge height is usually selected for use on concert-sized classicals and jumbo (16-inch and greater lower-bout width) steel-string guitars. In the middle of the range, ⁵⁄₁₆-inch bridge heights are found to work well on intermediate-sized instruments.

The inclination of the fretboard surface (which determines the range of available string-height settings on the instrument) is dependent on, and must be set to, the preselected bridge height and not the other way around. The procedures we used in the previous chapters for providing the proper inclination—that is, setting the neck angle on the steel-string or planing a slope into the fingerboard on the classical—were based on this fundamental principle.

A distinguishing characteristic of the steel-string bridge is its slanted saddle slot. This feature provides additional length for the bass strings. This is necessary because as a string increases in mass and in cross-section, it exhibits a proportionally greater propensity toward pitch sharpening when it is pushed out of line down to the fret. Assuming that the bridge is properly located, a saddle-slot slope of ⅛ inch over its 3-inch length will yield excellent pitch intonation for all the strings at normal action height settings.

Another factor in bridge design is the distance between the saddle and the anchoring point of the strings. That distance, along with the height of the saddle above the bridge, will determine the string's

"back angle." Vector analysis can show how, by increasing the steepness of the angle, greater force is brought to bear on the saddle. A steeper angle also increases the tautness of the strings. The result is an increased punch or "pop" to the strings' tone. Many luthiers strive for that effect by reducing the distance between the saddle and the string openings in the bridge; on the classical, the effect can also be produced by slanting the tie block forward toward the saddle, lowering the anchoring point of the strings. The steepest practical back angle is about 45 degrees. A more acute angle risks chronic string breakage and deep dents in the saddle.

The mass and resilience of the bridge itself must be carefully considered, as it will bias the way the entire vibrating system performs. Bridge mass and flexibility are determined by selecting the wood species, the bridge body shape and size, and the thickness of the wings. Indeed, some experienced builders make tonal adjustments by judicious removal of bridge mass after the guitar is strung up.

PROCEDURE: STEEL-STRING ONLY— PINNING THE NECK

The neck-pinning procedure principally involves locating and drilling holes in the neck

tenon which will correspond to the holes in the mortised headblock. Proper location will ensure that, when taper pins are inserted under pressure, the neck will seat tightly against the soundbox.

What follows is a set of steps for pinning the neck to the soundbox, a procedure for removing the pins if neck removal becomes necessary for resetting its angle in the future, and instructions for making or obtaining a number of special utensils that will facilitate both pinning and unpinning the neck.

In order to pin the neck properly, the following utensils and fixtures will be needed:

Pinning pliers: an ice-tong-like tool used to insert and extract the taper pins; it is manipulated through the soundhole against the headblock.

Drilling fixture: a duplicate of the guitar's mortised headblock that is clamped to the heel of the neck, serving to register the neck squarely on the drill-press table when the tenon is drilled to receive the taper pins. It is not needed, however, if the holes are to be drilled with a hand drill.

Pinning awl: a sharp-pointed tool that is inserted in the headblock taper pin holes and pressed into the tenon to mark it for its corresponding pin holes.

Pin popper: a small metal rod that serves to reverse the function of the pinning pliers. The pin popper is inserted into the pinned headblock opposite the taper pin. The pliers are placed on the pin popper and squeezed, driving the taper pin out of its hole.

Inspection light: a wired-up light bulb that illuminates the interior of the soundbox during the pinning procedure so that the pins in the headblock can be more easily seen through the soundhole.

Clamping cauls: a curved fingerboard caul and a fingerboard-end caul that serves to protect the end of the fingerboard from the clamps while it is being glued to the soundbox. These will be described

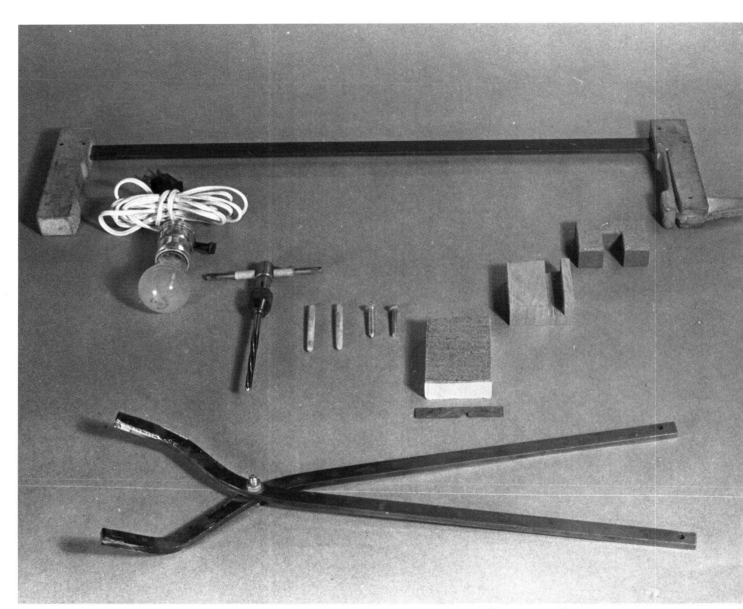

15–8.   Tools and cauls used for pinning the neck. (Note: The drilling fixture is illustrated in Fig. 15-9.)

and made just prior to their use.

Before commencing, retrieve the following items that have already been made and that will be used during the pinning procedure: the upper face brace caul, the angled headblock segment that was cut off the original headblock (pad its angled surface with cork), the long body clamp, and the two taper pins.

TOOLS
pinning pliers
pin awl
4-inch cam clamp
body clamp
small (3-inch) metal C-clamp
two miniature C-clamps, about 1½-inch reach
bar clamp (pad the bar with leather or soft foam)
small sanding block
scalpel or razor knife
single-edged razor blade
ice pick or scratch awl
7/32-inch drill bit (see Step 5)
#4 taper-pin reamer
hand drill or drill press

IMPLEMENTS
drilling fixture block
fingerboard caul
fingerboard-end caul
upper face brace caul
angled headblock caul (headblock segment cut-off)
inspection light

SUPPLIES
masking tape
PVA glue

Step 1—Making the Special Pinning Utensils

The drilling fixture starts with a well-squared block of any wood cut precisely to the dimensions and shape of the mortised headblock. Cut the mortise for a snug fit on the tenon (shim with tape if loose). Notch the back wall of the block, just like the original, to clear the neck's truss-rod adjuster. The cheeks at either side of the mortise will be notched away before the fixture is used to expose to sight (and to the drill) the section of the tenon that has been marked for drilling (Fig. 15-9).

The pinning awl consists simply of a ¼-inch-diameter machine screw, 1 inch long. File the end into a point and dull the threads.

The pin popper consists of a 1-inch length of 3/16-inch-diameter steel rod. File the burrs off the ends.

The light fixture consists of 5 to 10 feet of electric lamp cord, a plug, a bulb socket, and a fifteen-watt light bulb.

The fingerboard caul consists of a ¾-inch piece of scrap wood cut to the same outline as the portion of the fingerboard that sits on the soundboard. It should just span the distance from the fourteenth to the twentieth frets. Hollow one face with a rasp to approximate the curve of the fingerboard, and glue a piece of ⅛-inch cork sheet onto the curved face.

The fingerboard-end caul is simply a thin sliver of hardwood about as long as the end of the fingerboard is wide, and as wide as the distance from the last fret to the end of the fingerboard.

Pinning pliers can be fashioned out of two 18-inch lengths of ¼ × ½-inch steel bar, heated and bent in the following manner:

Trace the full-sized template (Fig. 15-10) and transfer its outline onto a scrap piece of wood or metal. Heat a 1-inch section of one of the bars 1½ inches from one end with a propane torch, until it is cherry red. Insert the bar 1 inch into a vise, flat side up. Slip a length of water pipe over the free end and slide it

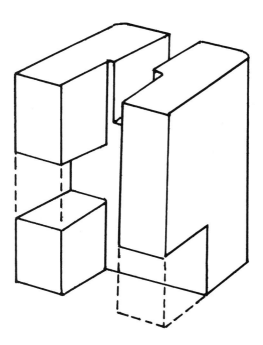

15–9. Support block for drilling steel-string tenon holes.

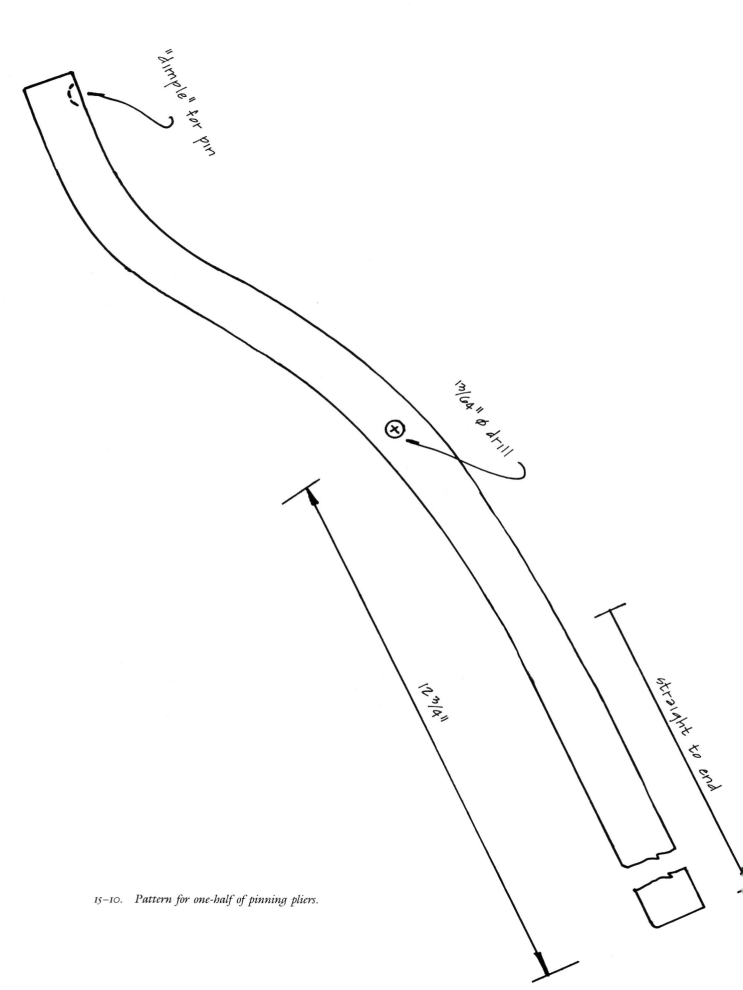

"dimple" for pin

13/64" ∅ drill

12 3/4"

straight to end

15–10.   *Pattern for one-half of pinning pliers.*

near the hot area. Slowly pull the bar toward you and watch it bend. Take the pipe off and place the bar over the template. Reheat the area and readjust the curve as is necessary to match the template. Allow the bar to cool slowly.

Now insert the crooked end into the vise. Heat a 3-inch section starting 2 inches from the first bend. When it is cherry red, push the free end of the bar to make the second bend, which should be gentler than the first. Check your results against your template and reheat and adjust as necessary.

Repeat this procedure on the second bar. Drill the "dimple" in the crooked end as shown in Fig. 15-10. Drill through the bars for the pivot. A ³⁄₁₆-inch-diameter nut and bolt serves adequately as a pivot. You may want to wrap some padding (such as foam, leather, or cork sheet) around the straight portion of the bars to protect the soundhole while the tool is in use.

Step 2—Marking the Tenon and Soundboard

If any significant amount of finish has dripped onto the end-grain bearing surfaces of the heel, it may cause a change in the previously set neck/body angle. Such drips must be removed, but without crumbling or chipping the finish where it will be visible later.

Judicious sanding of the end-grain bearing surface with the square sanding block (used previously during the neck-setting procedures) will remove excess finish without chipping. During sanding, make sure you are registering the block flat against the tenon. Take care that when the block strokes across the heel cap, it does not unduly disturb the bearing edge of the heel cap. Stop stroking as soon as wood

15–11a. *Marking the tenon with the pin awl pressed into the holes in the headblock.*

is exposed, to avoid changing the angle.

Now install the neck into the mortise and secure it temporarily with the body clamp and a 4-inch cam clamp as shown in Fig. 15-11a. If you suspect a change in the neck angle, verify it as described in the neck-setting procedure and correct it, if necessary, with strokes of the sanding block.

Put the pin awl in your hand and, holding the guitar as shown in Fig. 15-11a, put your hand into the soundhole and insert the point of the awl into the *entry* hole of each pin in the headblock. With the awl in the first headblock entry hole, squeeze the point into the tenon, rotating the awl several times between squeezes. Now remove the awl and insert it into the *second* pin entry hole on the opposite side of the headblock. Squeeze it into the tenon on that side. (If you do not own a drill press, mark the tenon on *both* sides for each tenon pin.)

Before removing the clamps and the neck, make a fine line with the point of a scalpel or razor knife right where the stub end of the fingerboard lies on the soundboard. (See Fig. 15-11b.) The tool's point should run along the inside corner formed by the soundboard and fingerboard. Press very lightly while traveling around the fingerboard end. Proceed slowly, taking care not to overshoot and mar the soundboard finish.

15–11b. *Marking the fingerboard outline on the soundboard. The lacquer will be scraped away to provide a gluing surface.*

Step 3—Scraping the Finish

The finish in the area on the soundboard within the fine scratch line must now be scraped down to the bare wood to provide a proper gluing surface for the finger-board stub. You should sur-round the scratch line with masking tape to improve its visibility. Patiently shave the finish away with a single-edged razor blade. It is important that the finish be scraped just shy (within ⅟₃₂ inch) of the scratch line. This will give you some leeway in case the finish chips out. It will also allow the fingerboard edge to bite into the finish when the neck is pinned. Scrape all the finish off within the area and sand the debris away with #220-grit garnet sandpaper. Take care not to dig into the wood too often and thereby hollow the surface.

Step 4—Offsetting the Puncture Marks on the Tenon

The puncture marks previ-ously pressed into the tenon by the pin awl must be offset very slightly relative to the corresponding holes in the headblock. Take an ice pick or a standard scratch awl and press a new puncture mark be-side the originals, as shown in Fig. 15-12. The offset should be minuscule—barely ⅟₃₂ inch. Repeat on the opposite side of

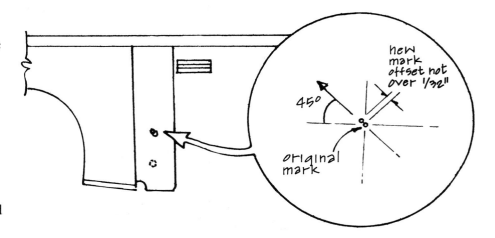

15–12. Offsetting the mark for the drill center on the steel-string neck tenon.

the tenon, precisely in the same way. The new offset puncture marks must be pushed in deeply, causing them to obliterate and com-pletely supersede the originals. The new marks will be drilling centers for the pinning holes. If the holes are offset properly, the squeezed-in taper pins will make the neck tighten in to-ward the sides as well as down onto the soundboard.

Step 5—Drilling the Tenon

Clamp the drilling-fixture block to the tenon, as shown in Fig. 15-13. Clamp or steady the block by hand firmly to the drill-press table, (with the neck attached), exposing the offset puncture mark to the drill bit (Fig. 15-14).

A ⁷⁄₃₂-inch brad-point bit is

installed into the chuck. (You may have difficulty obtaining such a bit. We had ours made specially from a standard ⁷⁄₃₂-inch bit, although they are available ready-made from some machinist-supply houses. An alternative is to use a commercially available ³⁄₁₆-inch brad-point bit and then en-large the hole with a standard ⁷⁄₃₂-inch bit.) The brad point actually seeks out the puncture mark and will not wander around like a standard bit.

If you have no drill press, you must already have marked and offset the puncture marks on both sides of the tenon. Drill in with a hand drill and brad-point bit from both di-rections, meeting in the middle of the tenon.

15–13. *The tenon block clamped to the heel before drilling the taper-pin hole.*

15–14. *Drilling tenon for taper pins.*

Step 6—Reaming the Tenon

The holes drilled through the tenon must now be opened with a taper-pin reamer so they will match the taper of the pins that are to go through them. If they are reamed too deeply, the fine offset might be eaten away. If the holes are not reamed deeply enough, the pins will tighten in the tenon before tightening in the headblock. Use the taper pins themselves as depth gauges. First, insert each pin into its own hole in the headblock and press in firmly with the fingers. Mark precisely on the pins where they intersect the side walls of the mortise. Now take the marked pins and insert them into their corresponding holes in the tenon. *Make sure* that each pin is entering from the correct side. Note whether the tenon falls between the marks on the pins. If it does not, ream the holes some more by twisting the reamer in them once or twice; note that a small amount of reaming causes the pins to drop quite deeply into the holes. Stop reaming when the tenon and pin marks align after pushing the pins in with a little force.

Step 7—Pinning the Neck (Dry Run)

Perform a dry run to check the effectiveness of your previous efforts. Insert the tenon into the mortise. Place a clamp across the fingerboard and headblock. Insert the pins into their proper holes in the headblock and squeeze them in firmly with the fingers. If all has gone well, the pins should enter deeply, but not without some resistance. The heel should "suck in" tight against the soundbox and hold firm even when you tug upward on the end of the neck. If the heel gives slightly when you tug but snaps back tight when you let go, it may only mean that the pins must be pressed in farther. If your fingers are not strong enough to do the job, insert the light and the pinning pliers (do not bump the pliers against the soundhole edge) and vigorously press the pins in (Fig. 15-15a) until you hear a creaking or popping noise. Do not be alarmed: the tightening noise is being amplified by the soundbox. With the pins pressed in, try tugging the neck again. The heel should hold firm. If it gives again but less than before, try reaming the tenon holes by a tiny bit and redo. To remove the pins, insert the pin popper into the headblock hole *opposite* the pin and, placing one arm of the pliers on the protruding pin popper, press the pin out. If all goes well, you are ready for the next step.

What can go wrong? First, one or both pins can simply refuse to enter the tenon, no matter how hard you press with your fingers. (Do not use the pliers—you might break something.) This means the offset is too great. Before redrilling, try as a last resort to ream the tenon deeper by a small amount and try again.

Another thing that can go wrong occurs when you squeeze the pins in and the neck is not drawn into the soundbox. In fact, it may even push *away* from the soundbox. If this is the case, the holes in the tenon have been misdrilled, probably by your letting the drill wander randomly

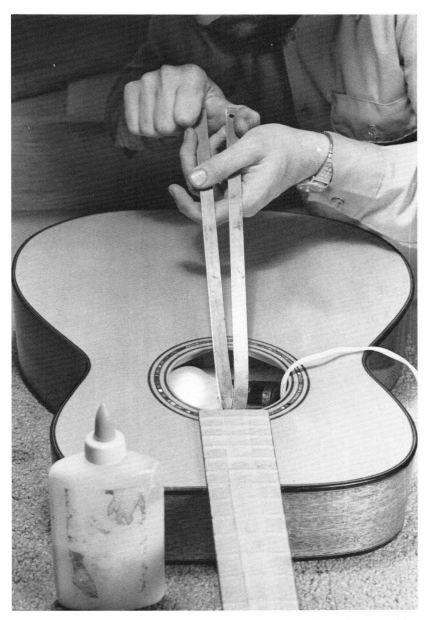

15–15a. Squeezing in the pins with pinning pliers. Care must be taken to avoid hitting the soundhole edge.

away from the offset puncture mark. There is no recourse but to plug the tenon holes and return to Step 3. Most hardware stores supply a small device called a plug-cutter that attaches to a drill. The plug-cutter produces neat, accurate cylinders of wood about ⅜ inch long, and comes in several diameters. If you have obtained a ⅜-inch-diameter plug-cutter, you must drill through the tenon with a ⅜-inch drill bit, obliterating the original hole in the process. Making sure the wood species and grain direction are the same, glue in a plug from each end of the same hole (five-minute epoxy works best for this application). After the glue sets thoroughly, shave the plugs flush with the tenon surfaces if

necessary. Begin the pinning process as if the neck were brand new.

Note: This is also the same procedure to use when resetting the pinned neck joint, which may become necessary much later on, when the guitar has distorted beyond simpler adjustment. The fingerboard end is warmed; the softened glue seam is freed by sliding a spatula or table knife through it, and the neck is removed. The old holes are plugged and material is removed from the heel, as was done during the earlier neck-setting procedure. The neck is reset so that a straightedge on the fingerboard just misses the bridge. The neck is repinned precisely as described in this procedure.

Step 8—Pinning the Neck

Read the following first and run through the sequence once or twice without applying glue (no need to squeeze in the pins until the last time around, when the glue is finally applied).

We will be using a low-temperature-release white glue, such as Elmer's. Apply a moderate quantity of glue to the undersurface of the fingerboard only. With a finger, spread the glue to the edges and corners, but avoid getting any glue on the two square areas on either side of the tenon. These areas will be inaccessible if the glue seam has to be separated in the future. With a clean finger, push the glue away from the edges, thus minimizing squeeze-out and clean-up time. After pushing the glue back, you may also wish to run a fine bead along the edges of the heel where they contact the soundbox. After pinning, the glue serves as a filler to enhance the appearance of the neck-to-soundbox seam.

Now install the neck into the body and apply the long body clamp across the heel and soundbox while holding the guitar upright. Apply the 4-inch cam clamp across the fingerboard and headblock. Working rapidly (the glue on the fingerboard should start setting soon), insert the taper pins into their respective holes and squeeze them in with your fingers as deeply as you can (the pin nearest the finger-

15–15b. Close view of a pin in the dimple ground into the end of the pinning pliers.

board should always be squeezed in first). Remove the clamps. Drop the light into the soundbox and rest the guitar on the padded tabletop. Carefully insert the pliers through the soundhole (Fig. 15-15a). Now squeeze the pins in vigorously. Keep pressing until they stop creaking and popping and the pliers handle starts to flex. Keep the pliers jaws level. Make sure the chamfered ends of the pins seat securely into the dimples in the pliers jaws (Fig. 15-15b). If they do not and you inadvertently jerk or twist the pliers handle, the pin might break or the pliers jaws may slip off, smacking and possibly damaging the back.

Carefully remove the pliers and the light from inside the soundbox. Slip the upper face brace caul into place under the fingerboard, inside the soundbox. Position the curved fingerboard caul on the fingerboard with its end resting on the last fret, leaving the very end of the fingerboard exposed. The caul can be secured with strips of masking tape. (Have it ready.) Also tape the angled headblock caul to the back, right over the headblock.

Apply a bar clamp across the fingerboard and headblock cauls and snug down moderately. Place a 3-inch metal C-clamp through the soundhole, mounted across the fingerboard caul and upper face brace caul, and tighten down firmly. Slip the thin fingerboard-end caul behind the last

fret and manipulate the two miniature clamps over the corners of the fingerboard and through the soundhole onto the upper face brace caul. Snug them down *very gently*.

After ten or fifteen minutes remove the squeeze-out with a pointed spruce stick. The clamps can be removed after an hour. With moistened cheesecloth, rub the seams to remove any remaining smeared glue or squeeze-out.

PROCEDURE: MAKING THE CLASSICAL BRIDGE

The following procedure provides a step-by-step method that requires only hand tools. We note, however, that it is somewhat easier to achieve good results with the use of a hand-held router, and thus we offer an alternative router method on page 348. For those students who have a router and are comfortable with its use, we recommend the alternative method.

The hand method involves cutting out the bridge wings *before* cutting the saddle slot, the valley, and the edges for the tie block decoration. The router method involves making several channels with a 3/32-inch router bit in the billet *before* cutting out the wings.

On our own classical bridges, we make all the straight and angled cuts with a table saw.

TOOLS
scraper
sanding board
dovetail saw
square
razor saw
chisels
file
drill and 1/16-inch bit

MATERIALS
rosewood bridge blank, 3/8 × 1 1/8 × 7 1/2 inches
two 1/16-inch cross-section bone strips
soundboard purfling scraps

SUPPLIES
#120- and #220-grit garnet sandpaper
double-faced tape
masking tape
PVA glue

Step 1—Preparing the Billet

Choose one face of the billet to be the "down" (gluing) face, and clean off saw marks and debris with a scraper. Smooth the down face with circular strokes on the sanding board until it is covered with fresh sanding scratches. Select one long edge and stroke it in one direction on the sanding board until it is straight and square to the down face. This will be the front edge of the bridge.

Step 2—Cutting the Bridge Wings

Tape the down face to the edge of the workboard with double-faced tape. Using a square as a guide, make dove-

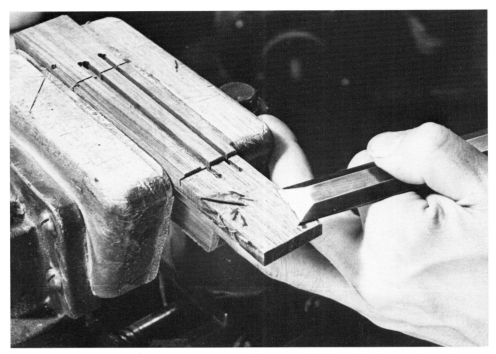

15–16. *Carving out the wings of the classical bridge. The slots in this bridge were cut with a router; if they are cut by hand, the wings must be carved away first.*

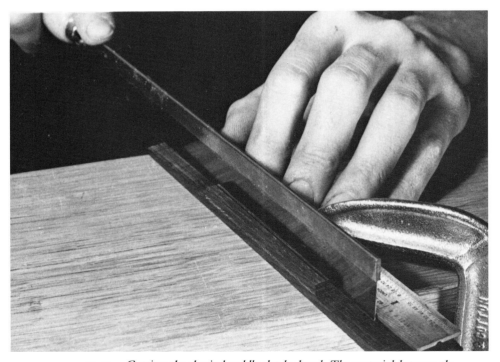

15–17. *Cutting the classical saddle slot by hand. The material between the saw cuts is removed with a 3/32-inch chisel.*

tail saw cuts perpendicular to the front edge, 2⅛ inches from each end of the blank. Stop the cuts about 3/16 inch from the underside of the bridge blank. (On a 7½-inch bridge blank, this will leave 3¼ inches for the body of the bridge; see Fig. 15-18).

Students using hand tools exclusively may proceed to remove sufficient material to leave two flat wings no less than 5/32 inch thick. (Carve cross-grain with a sharp chisel.) Students planning to use the router technique must refer to the sidebar (page 348) and complete all router operations before removing material from the wings. (See Fig. 15-16.) If the router is used, Step 3 below is unnecessary.

Step 3—Making Longitudinal Cuts (Hand-tool Technique Only)

A 6-inch steel ruler and the bridge with wings cut out must be clamped to a work surface, as shown in Fig. 15-17. The ruler (we use the heavy removable ruler from a combination square) must be aligned first to guide a razor-saw cut that is 3/16 inch from the front edge of the bridge.

Make the cut slowly and carefully, keeping the saw level, vertical, and flush to the guide. The cut should be 5/32 inch deep at each end. When it is done, move the guide over to make a parallel cut that will yield a slot 3/32 inch

15–18. Classical bridge layout.

wide when the material between the saw kerfs is removed.

Next, align the guide for a cut that will delineate a ½-inch tie block. Make the cut ³⁄₁₆ inch deep. Finally, make two ¹⁄₁₆-inch-deep cuts that will delineate ³⁄₃₂-inch-wide channels on the front and back of the top of the tie block. (See Fig. 15-18.)

Step 4—Carving Out Saddle Slot, Valley, and Tie Block Decoration Channels

Clamp the bridge in a vise or to the workbench, or tape it down with double-faced tape. If you came to this step from the sidebar on the router technique, you need only carve out the valley, as your saddle slot and tie block decoration channels are finished.

Shave down the material in the saddle slot with the ³⁄₃₂-inch chisel, stopping when you reach the bottom of the saw cuts. To achieve a flat-bottomed slot, use the chisel as a depth-gauged scraper with one fingertip as a guide.

To cut out the valley, shave it with a chisel at an angle until the ramp reaches the bottom of the saw or router cut delineating the front of the tie block (Fig. 15-19). Leave about ¹⁄₁₆ inch between the saddle slot and the line where the ramp begins to angle downward.

Finally, shave the tie block decoration channels at the front and back of the tie block. The channels must be flat bottomed and should go to the depth of the saw cuts.

Step 5—Curving the Bridge Wings and Radiusing the Front Lip

Use a wood file to curve the bridge wings. To avoid frayed edges, the cutting strokes should always be *upward* into the wing, rather than downward and away from it. (See Fig. 15-20.)

A few strokes with a piece of sandpaper wrapped crosswise over the top of the wing will produce a nice, smooth curved surface after the rough work has been done with the file. Finish sanding with the grain to remove the cross-grain sanding scratches. Leave about ¹⁄₃₂ inch on the edges (do not carve a knife edge).

Facet the wing ends by stroking sideways with the file; again, leave a ¹⁄₃₂-inch edge. Remove file marks with sandpaper.

Radius the lip in front of the saddle slot by faceting with the file and rounding with sandpaper.

Step 6—Applying the Tie Block Decoration

The decoration we use on the guitar in this book has two ¹⁄₁₆-inch-square cross-section bone strips bordering two purfling strips taken from left-

15–19. Carving out the valley. The angled ramp is shaved to about ¹⁄₁₆-inch behind the saddle.

over soundboard purfling or rosette lines.

To glue in the decorative strips on the front of the tie block, use small spring clamps as shown in Fig. 15-21. For the strips on the back of the tie block, use masking tape in the same way it was used for binding the guitar. Make sure to get glue in between the purfling strips and the bone, and between the whole sandwich and the channel in the tie block.

When the glue is dry, scrape and sand everything flush, and lightly sand the sharp edges off the bone strips.

For a discussion of tie block decorations, including design variations, see page 343.

Step 7—Drilling the String Holes

This step is a lot easier to do with a drill press, but with a little help from a friend it can be done accurately with a hand drill.

The drill holes enter the back of the bridge ⅛ inch from the bottom face, but they must exit at the base of the tie block, which is about ¹⁄₁₆ inch higher (Fig. 15-18). Thus, the holes must be drilled at a slight slant—easy to do accurately on the drill press but much more challenging to do by hand.

Our bridge design calls for a hole spacing of ¹⁵⁄₃₂ inch, totaling ⁷⁵⁄₃₂ inches (2¹¹⁄₃₂ inches) from the first to the sixth hole. When laying out

15–20. Curving the wings of the classical bridge. The file leaves a ¹⁄₃₂-inch edge all around.

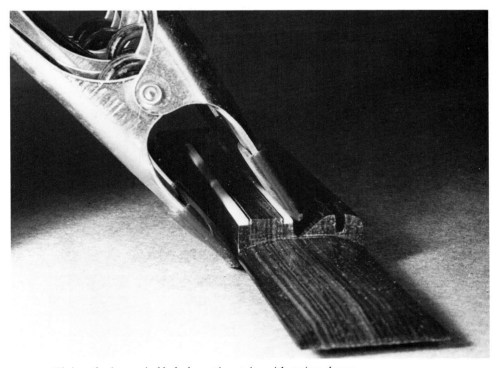

15–21. Gluing the inner tie block decoration strips with spring clamps.

the back of the bridge for drilling, measure the tie block carefully and mark the #1 and #6 holes 2¹¹/₃₂ inches apart and equidistant from the ends of the tie block (Fig. 15-18).

Draw a line on the back of the bridge ⅛ inch from the bottom face and plot out the string-hole locations on the line. Mark the drilling centers with an awl.

Clamp the bridge back-end-up in a vise. Take a ¹/₁₆-inch drill bit and flag a ½-inch depth of cut on it with a piece of masking tape. Check the flagged depth of cut against

your actual tie block—the drill bit must exit from the base of the tie block but should not touch the ramp of the valley.

To achieve the necessary slant with the drill bit on the drill press, we simply prop something under the drill-press vise to angle the bridge correctly (Fig. 15-22). To do it with a hand drill, you need a friend to "spot" for you. Show your friend the angle at which the drill must be held to get it right. Then have him or her stand to the side and coach you as you begin the entry. Once the hole is well started,

the angle will remain constant. Stop at the masking tape flag.

After drilling one hole, take the bridge out of the vise and check the results. If the hole does not go all the way through or if it has nicked the bottom of the ramp, adjust the depth of cut accordingly. If the exit hole is too high or too low, have your friend adjust the spot accordingly. Drill the rest of the holes.

Step 8—Finish Sanding the Bridge

Sand all stray marks off the bridge with #120-grit garnet and then remove the #120 sanding scratches with #220-grit. Wrap a piece of sandpaper around a ruler or a scraper to get into the valley. *Do not* round the corners of the wings.

Note: Our system calls for gluing the bridge on before finishing the classical guitar. The bridge, however, unlike the soundboard, is made of an open-pored wood that must be filled before a finish can be applied. The bridge, therefore, must be filled before it is glued in place. Also, because rosewood will occasionally bleed pigment when coated with a finishing material, the bridge should be sealed before it is glued.

Classical builders should return to the filling and sealing procedures in Chapter 14 and proceed to fill and seal the bridge (including sanding the sealer to level it).

15–22. *Drilling string holes on a drill press. This shows a simple way to slant the bridge while drilling so that the exit holes will be higher than the entry holes. The piece of scrap on which the vise is mounted can be slid in or out to increase or decrease the slant.*

PROCEDURE: MAKING THE STEEL-STRING-BRIDGE

TOOLS
fine-tipped marker or white grease pencil
awl or ice pick
hand drill or drill press
³⁄₃₂-inch twist bit
³⁄₃₂-inch chisel
¹³⁄₆₄-inch twist bit (see Step 3)
optional: #3 taper-pin reamer
coping saw or bandsaw
wood rasps and files
wide (say, ³⁄₄-inch) chisel
scraper blade
optional: buffing wheel

MATERIALS
straight-grain ebony or rosewood bridge blank, about 6¼ × 1¾ × ³⁄₈ inches
set of bridge pins

SUPPLIES
heavy paper (for template)
double-faced tape
#100-, #120-, #220-, #360-, and #500-grit sandpaper

TIE BLOCK DECORATION

Aside from its aesthetic contribution to the instrument, the tie-block decoration performs the important function of preventing string wear on the tie block. For this reason it is traditionally made from very hard materials, usually bone or ivory.

The simplest decoration is a thin sheet of bone or ivory covering the whole tie block. This is also sometimes done with a sheet of mother-of-pearl.

Probably the most common system is the one that we describe, in which two strips of bone or ivory are inlaid into the front and back edges of the tie block. We include purfling lines as an additional aesthetic touch.

Many builders, however, run the strips all around the tie block, mitering at the corners. This can be done as inlay or can be assembled around a separate wafer of wood or marquetry and applied as an overlay. (See below.) We have found it somewhat easier to execute as an overlay; if the tie block is to be slanted (see The Bridge: Technical Notes, page 326), overlay is almost invariably used.

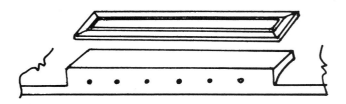

Mitered tie block overlay for classical bridge.

Step 1—Preparation

Begin with a billet of ebony or rosewood, planed to ³⁄₈ inch and large enough to include the outline of the 6 × 1½-inch bridge. Check the ends carefully for splits and cracks. Choose one face and clean off all dirt, cutter marks, and other irregularities by stroking it flat on the sanding board in one direction until the billet's surface is completely covered with fresh sanding marks. This will be the down, or glued, face. Select one long edge and plane or sand it until it is straight and square to the down face. This edge will be the finished front edge of the bridge. Now prepare a heavy-paper outline template by copying the shape suggested in Fig. 15-23, or by devising a template outline of your own of similar size. Trace the outline onto the billet with a fine-tipped marking pen or a sharp white grease pencil. With a square pressed up against the

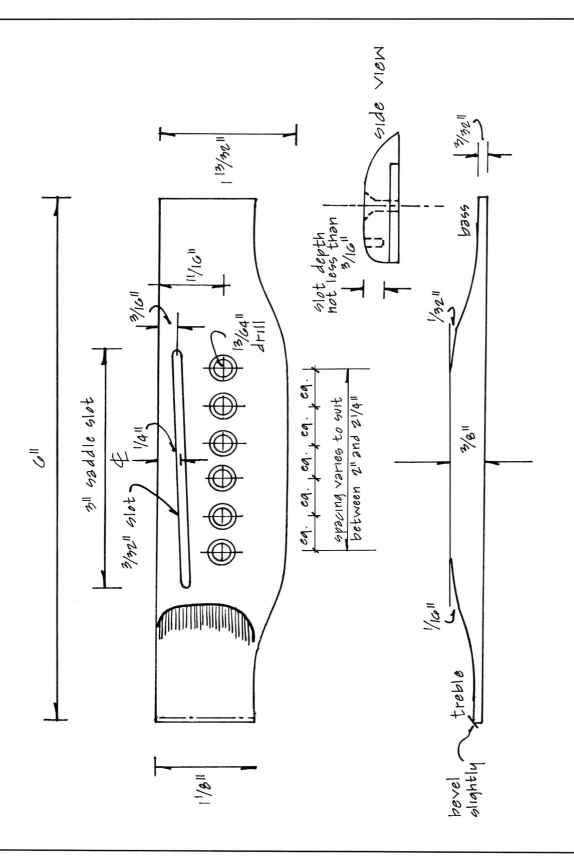

15–23. *Steel-string bridge layout.*

finished front edge, divide the traced outline in half with a line running cross-grain. This line will be the blank center-line, and all drafting of the bridge features will use the centerline as a starting point.

Referring to Fig. 15-23, draft the location of the saddle slot and bridge-pin holes. Press deep point marks precisely at the drill centers of the bridge-pin holes with an awl or ice pick.

Step 2—Excavating the Saddle Slot with Hand Tools

(For power routing of the slot, see sidebar Router Technique, page 348.)

With an awl, press a series of deep point marks along the full 3-inch length of the saddle-slot centerline, spaced about $7/64$ inch apart. Insert a $3/32$-inch drill bit into a hand drill and flag the bit by wrapping a small folded piece of masking tape around it $3/16$ inch from its tip. This will serve as a depth guide. Fix the bridge blank to the table with clamps or with double-faced masking tape. Now drill a series of holes along the length of the saddle slot centerline, using the equally spaced point marks as a pilot for each hole. Hold the drill upright and ask a friend to stand back and help spot your drilling job by advising you if and where you are tipping the drill. You should end up with a series of $3/32 \times 3/16$-inch drilled holes

with an exceedingly fine web of material between each.

Now clamp a straight metal edge (a scraper blade or 6-inch ruler will serve) tangent to the line of small holes. Bearing against the metal edge with a sharp $3/32$-inch chisel, proceed to shave a slot across the tops of all the holes. Do not exert a levering action on the chisel. Instead, shave the material away slowly. Since there is in fact more airspace than wood along its journey, the chisel should produce a slot of fairly good quality rather quickly. If the chisel is not sharp along its entire width, progress will be

erratic and difficult. If you are having trouble, try resharpening your chisel, preferably at a steep (about 35-degree) angle.

To achieve a flat-bottomed slot, use the chisel as a depth-gauged scraper with one fingertip as a guide.

Step 3—Drilling the Bridge-pin Holes

Standard (Martin-style) bridge pins fit too tightly in a $13/64$-inch hole and a bit loosely in a $7/32$-inch hole. This suits us fine, since we can enlarge a $13/64$-inch hole with a #3 taper-pin reamer until we

15–24. *Chamfering bridge pin holes with a countersink.*

15–25. Shaping the belly with a rasp. The bridge is attached with double-faced tape to a piece of scrap.

15–26. Buffing the finished bridge. The wheel is coated with jeweler's rouge, a fine abrasive.

can obtain a fine fit. If you do not wish to invest in this fairly expensive tool, you can elect to drill with the 7⁄32-inch and leave it at that. If you have different bridge pins, your drill size should be selected by measuring across the pin shaft about 1⁄16 inch below its head (if you have a reamer, 1⁄8 inch below the head). Check your pin fit with scrap. If you are not using a reamer, the ideal hole size is the one in which the pin will stop about 1⁄16 inch from its head and can be seated firmly with the thumb the rest of the way.

We use a 13⁄64-inch brad-point bit that we had fashioned from a standard twist drill. If you have a standard brad-point set, we advise you start the hole with the 3⁄16-inch bit and then redrill to the larger size using common twist bits.

Drill the six holes clear through the blank with the bit installed in a twist or electric drill. Have a friend spot the drilling for you. Needless to say, a drill press is the preferred tool for this operation. Now chamfer the holes equally with a countersink bit in the hand drill or drill press, as in Fig. 15-24.

Step 4—Shaping the Bridge

First trim the ends to length with a fine-tooth dovetail saw pressed against a square. Strive to make the cuts perpendicular to the front edge of the blank.

The curved rear outline can be cut with a coping saw (or bandsaw). If you do not feel you can cut down the line accurately, cut about 1⁄16 inch away from it. Rasp down to the line, striving to achieve an edge that is perpendicular to the down face and is as symmetrical to the centerline as possible. You can further improve the outline with greater facility *after* the bridge is closer to its finished state.

Firmly affix the bridge with double-faced tape near or over the edge of a portable flat surface. The bridge and the surface it is stuck to can be easily manipulated and locked into a vise for convenient access during the subsequent shaping steps (see Fig. 15-25).

The wings are shaped next. Note that the curved cutaways for the wings commence as creases at both ends of the saddle slot. Later, after the body is "bellied" or rounded with the rasp and files, the crease migrates about 3⁄16 inch from the saddle-slot ends. The wings can be cut away to their reduced thickness by chiseling and filing. If you have a drum-and-sleeve sanding attachment on a drill press, the wing cutaways can be ground out of the blank accurately by feeding the blank slowly into the spinning abrasive drum while holding it flat against a fence. The bulk of the waste material can be sawn off beforehand and the drum can then be used simply to true up the surfaces.

The bridge body is now shaped with a rasp to a curved cross section (Fig. 15-25). Finally, the front lip is radiused evenly across its length. Reduce all rasp marks with a wood file, defining and refining the two graceful, curved creases that result between the bridge body and wings until they are both similar in appearance. Remove file marks with a scraper blade, keeping the creases sharp. Refine all the forms and edges with #100-grit garnet wrapped around a felt block. Proceed to #120 and #220 garnet, then #360- and #500-grit silicon-carbide paper, blowing or wiping the blank down between grits. With a flat file, cut a minute 45-degree bevel into the top edge of the bridge ends.

If you own a buffing wheel, you can bring the bridge up to a fine polish by pressing the blank up to the the wheel as shown in Fig. 15-26. The rubbing action pulls resins out of the wood and glazes the surface. Hold the bridge firmly, keeping it flat to the wheel. The wheel should always turn *down* onto the bridge; otherwise it will snag and pop out of your hand. Do not let the bridge get too hot; keep it moving against the wheel.

If you do not have a buffing wheel, put a touch of orange (not white or gray) rubbing compound on a rag and rub the surface vigorously. Polish to a luster with a clean, dry rag.

ROUTER TECHNIQUE

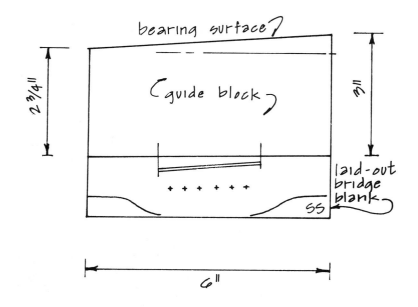

15–27 and 15–28. Layouts for steel-string and classical saddle-slot routing guideblocks.

This is a system for slotting either the steel-string or the classical bridge with a hand-held router. On the steel-string, it is done after the bridge blank is laid out; on the classical, it is done after crosscutting to delineate the bridge wings but before the wing material is removed.

You will need a straight-line horizontal edge guide and a 3/32-inch bit for the router; you will also need to make a guide block the same length and height as the bridge blank, but about 3 inches wide. The long edges of the guide block for the classical bridge must be scrupulously parallel; the edges of the guide block for the steel-string bridge must taper lengthwise (Figs. 15-27 and 15-28).

The guide block must be taped with double-faced tape to the edge of a work surface. The bridge blank is taped to the work surface with its front lip flush against the guide block. Use cam clamps to press the bridge blank down on the tape so that the tape will grip as tightly as possible (to remove it you will need a joint knife or other spatula-type tool).

Steel-string: Because the saddle slot begins and ends within the body of the bridge and does not have open ends, the router bit cannot enter the bridge blank in a waste area. Thus, it must be lowered straight down with no wiggle, must stop precisely at the ends of the saddle layout, and must then be shut off without disfiguring the slot. The best way to accomplish this is to register the edge guide against the guide block with the router tipped *sideways,* lower the bit into the bridge blank with a smooth motion, and then progress into the cut. We recommend practicing on scrap before cutting the actual bridge blank.

Adjust the depth of cut to ³/₁₆ inch and adjust the horizontal edge guide so that the bit follows the saddle-layout lines. The entry should be at the middle of the slot. Progress to one end of the layout lines, and then go back to the middle and progress to the other end of the layout. The router must be registered and held down very firmly throughout this operation. When the slot is done, without moving the router *in any way,* take one hand off it and shut off the motor. Remove the router.

We also use the drill press as a stationary overhead router for this operation. (See Fig. 15-29.)

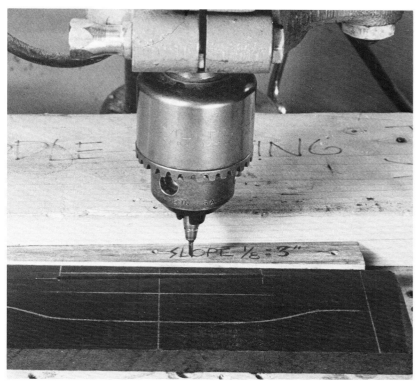

15–29. *Routing the steel-string bridge slot on a drill press used as an overhead router.*

Classical: Adjust the depth of cut to ⁵/₃₂ inch and adjust the horizontal edge guide so that the slot will be ³/₁₆ inch from the front edge of the bridge. Turn on the router and register the edge guide against the guide block. Lower the bit into the bridge blank on the *wing* side of one of the saw cuts. Pressing the edge guide firmly against the guide block and the router firmly downward, make the cut in a smooth, uninterrupted motion, continuing past the other saw cut. Stop, shut off the router, and remove it.

Next, adjust the edge guide to make a cut that will delineate a ½-inch tie block. Adjust the bit to cut ³/₁₆ inch deep, and make the cut in the same manner as the saddle slot.

For the tie-block decoration, adjust the bit to cut ¹/₁₆ inch deep. Make two parallel cuts, leaving ³/₃₂-inch-wide ledges at the front and back edges of the tie block. Remove the bridge from the work surface with a spatula and return to Step 2 of the main procedure to carve away the bridge wings.

PROCEDURE: GLUING THE BRIDGE

The following procedure describes the execution of one of the most critical glue joints on the guitar. The bridge must be accurately placed in order to ensure correct pitch intonation, and its glue seam must be of the highest quality to avoid failure during subsequent years of continuous string tension.

For a good glue seam, the underside of the bridge must be flat, smooth, and free of contaminants; the soundboard surface must be similarly free of debris. Sufficient glue and proper clamping pressure are additional requirements. The bridge must be accurately located in three major spatial relationships: It must be the correct straight-line distance from the nut; its front edge must be parallel to the frets; and the string holes must be centered in relation to the fingerboard.

TOOLS
36-inch ruler
razor knife
inspection mirror
single-edged razor blade
   (steel-string only)
cam clamps, two 6-inch (SS)
   or two 8-inch (CL)
C-clamps, one 5-inch-reach
   (SS) or one 6-inch-reach
   (CL)

IMPLEMENTS
bridge block (see page 219)
various cauls (see Step 6)

SUPPLIES
masking tape
AR glue

Step 1—Locating the Bridge

Lay the guitar on a padded surface; if necessary, place a support under the neckshaft. Wedge a scrap of wood into the nut slot flush to the fingerboard end to act as a zero stop for the ruler. Place the bridge on the soundboard. Using the long ruler, locate the midpoint of the saddle slot at a distance from the nut equal to your string length (25.55 inches SS, or 25.7 inches CL; see Fig. 15-30). The correct string length must fall at a point in space equidistant from the walls of the saddle slot. To make minute adjustments in position, press a finger on the soundboard adjacent to the bridge and "roll" the finger against it.

When the string length measurement is correct, measure from the ends of the body-joint fret (the twelfth or fourteenth) to the front corners of the bridge wings. (See Fig. 15-31.) These two measurements must be exactly equal, to ensure that the front edge of the bridge is parallel to the frets. Nudge the corners by rolling the finger to make corrections. When these distances are equal, go back and check the previous string length measurement. If it has changed at all, go back to square one and measure again for string length; then check again for parallelism.

When both of these measurements are correct, lay the ruler flat on the fingerboard and hold it just above the top of the bridge. Align the end of the ruler to the edge of the fingerboard on the bass side at the nut, and to the middle of the sixth-string hole on the bridge. Note the clearance between the edge of the ruler and the edge of the fingerboard at the body joint. Then move the ruler to the treble edge of the fingerboard at the nut and to the center of the first string hole at the bridge, and again note the clearance at the body joint. For correct centering of the bridge, these clearances must be equal.

Nudge the bridge from side to side to make the clearances equal. When they are, check the two previous measurements again. If they have changed in any way, you must go back to the string length measurement and do the entire locating operation over again. Repeat it as often as necessary until all three spatial relationships are correct.

Note: If you have difficulty gauging the fingerboard edge clearances by eye, measure them with a 6-inch ruler. Also, on the classical, because the string holes are somewhat lower than the top of the tie block, the resulting visual parallax effect may make correct location somewhat difficult. By placing little bits of masking tape on the top of the tie block at the first and sixth string positions and marking the precise locations of the string holes on the masking

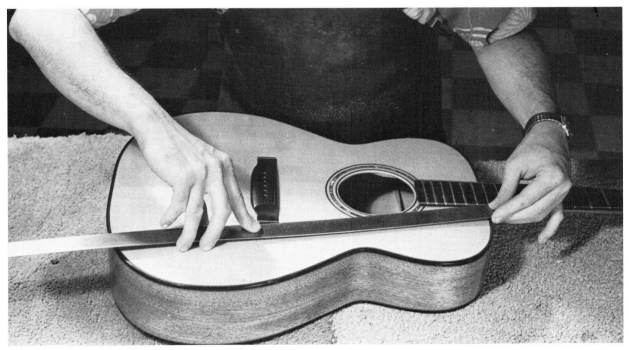

15–30 and 31. Locating the bridge. The first critical measurement is the string length from the nut to the middle of the saddle slot. The next is from the ends of the body-joint fret to the front corners of the bridge. The latter measurement ensures that the axis of the bridge is parallel to the frets. Finally, the bridge must be centered in relation to the edges of the fingerboard (not shown).

tape, the parallax problem can be avoided.

Step 2—Scribing the Bridge Location

The bridge must be immobilized with one hand while a faint scribe mark is made around it with a razor knife. The knife blade must be brand new to ensure that its point is as fine as possible.

To immobilize the bridge, bring one hand over it, about an inch above it. In a gentle, relaxed motion, drop the fingertips on the bridge and press down. If the bridge moves at all, you must return to Step 1 and reposition it.

Hold the razor knife at a slight angle away from the bridge and gently trace a scribe line all around precisely at its bottom edge. (See Fig. 15-32.) The line should be as fine as possible—no more than a scratch—(*especially* on the bare wood surface of the classical) and yet still be visible. Do not dig into the bridge with the knife.

Step 3—Taping the Soundboard

Lay a strip of masking tape along the outside of the scribe mark denoting the front of the bridge. The tape must be precisely adjacent to the line, so lay it gradually, angling your light on the soundboard so that the scribe line remains visible.

Lay a second strip of masking tape and then a third precisely over the first. Apply two strips to the side and back scribe lines in the same manner as you did the front line.

Place the bridge back on the soundboard, imprisoned in the tape boundary. Check all measurements again to ensure that the tape has not somehow been mislocated. If it has, peel it off and adjust it accordingly.

Step 4—Steel-string Only: Scraping Off the Finish

The area bounded by the tape must be scraped with the single-edge razor blade to the bare wood as was done during the pinning procedure in the

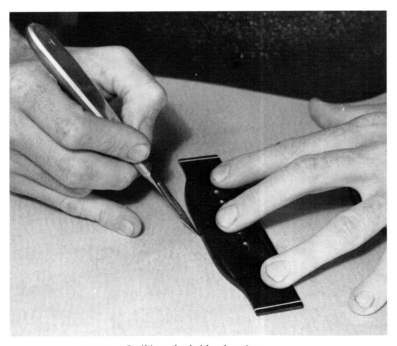

15-32. *Scribing the bridge location.*

15-33. *The scribed lines are bordered with masking tape; on the steel-string, the lacquer must be scraped away within the tape boundary to provide a gluing surface for the bridge.*

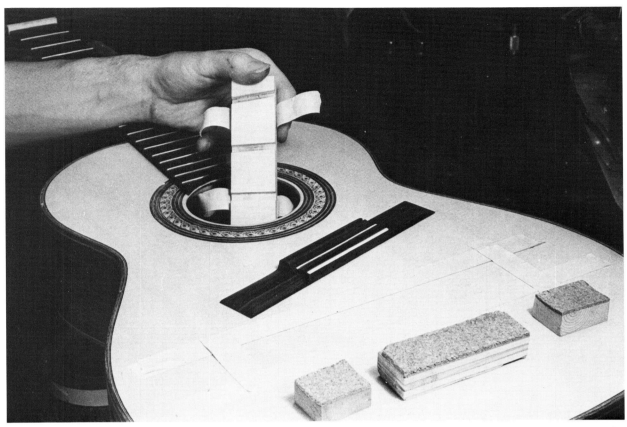

15-34. *Inserting the bridge block with cauls at ready. Note that the two outer cauls are slightly concaved to conform to the curve of the bridge wings.*

area of the soundboard to be under the fingerboard. Scrape just shy (1/32 inch) of the scribe line, removing all the finish within the area (Fig. 15-33). Sand the debris away with #220-grit garnet, leaving the gluing surface smooth.

All scraping and sanding should be done with great care to avoid digging into the wood and hollowing the area.

Step 5—Inserting the Bridge Block

Apply three strips of masking tape to the flat side of the block. Each strip should overhang the block by about 3 inches at either end. Insert the block through the soundhole, taking care not to snag the sticky side of the tape strips on anything. (See Fig. 15-34.) Lay the block on the guitar back, making sure that the strips are spread out and not stuck to anything. Reach under the block and gently bring it up into position. If the block has been made properly, it will fit only in one place. With the fingertips, burnish the tape against the underside of the soundboard.

If the tape does not hold, remove the block, apply fresh tape, and reinsert. When it does hold, check the placement of the block with an inspection mirror held through the soundhole. The bridge block must not be mounted on any of the braces, and it must be reasonably snug against the underside of the soundboard. If it is hanging loosely, there is a danger that it will rack and crush a brace when clamped. A dangling bridge block, therefore, must be removed and retaped.

Step 6—Getting Ready

On both the steel-string and the classical guitars, use a flat 3 × 1-inch caul on the bridge body; on the classical, also use two 1 × 1-inch wing cauls, concaved to fit over the curved wings. All cauls must be padded with cork. (Refer to Fig. 15-34.)

The C-clamp must be opened sufficiently to encompass the bridge block, bridge, and caul. Place the cauls at ready on the soundboard.

On the classical, two 8-inch cam clamps must be inserted through the soundhole before the gluing operation, because the size of the soundhole will not permit their insertion after the C-clamp is applied. If they are difficult to insert, you may need to grind off their bottom corners with a rasp. When they are in, lay them gently against the edge of the soundhole.

Step 7—Gluing the Bridge

Read the following carefully and do this step without glue at least once before actual execution. If you have difficulty with the motions, repeat them until they are comfortable.

Apply a moderate film of glue to the bridge and a light film of glue to the soundboard. Place the bridge down in the masking tape boundary and place the cauls on it. Maneuver the opened C-clamp through the soundhole. Pass one hand through the clamp and support the clamp with the back of the hand while holding the thumb tip and middle fingertip against the

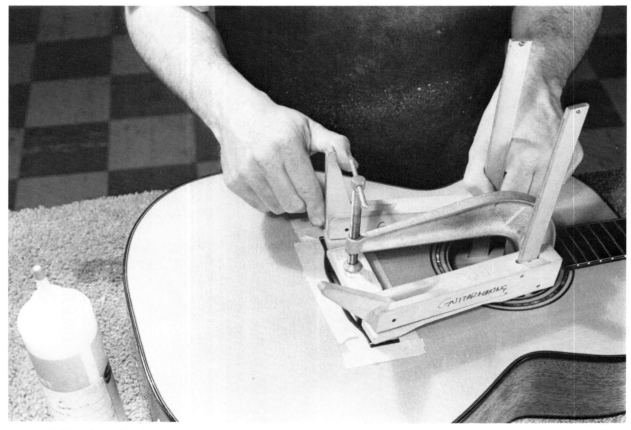

15–35. *Bridge clamped. The clamping arrangement (one deep reach C-clamp and two cam clamps) is the same for both guitars. The classical clamps, however, must have longer reaches than the steel-string clamps.*

front edge of the wings. With the other hand, begin to tighten the clamp, jockeying it with the supporting hand to level it. With the clamp tight enough to easily support itself, remove the supporting hand and check the bridge alignment. If it has begun to mount up on the tape anywhere, support the clamp again with one hand and loosen it. Jockey it again to level it while holding the bridge wings with the fingertips and try again.

On the steel-string, now insert the cam clamps through the soundhole, one on either side of the C-clamp.

On both guitars, as soon as the bridge is stable under the initial pressure of the C-clamp, the cam clamps can be applied. Hold the cam clamp bar with one hand while pressing with the other hand on the back of the upper jaw to close it

tightly before throwing the cam. Apply one clamp gently and then apply the other, watching all the while for movement of the bridge (Fig. 15-35). If the bridge slips in any direction, loosen the cam clamp and jockey it to ensure that it is level. When the bridge is stable and in the correct position, tighten the cam clamps all the way. On the classical, tighten the C-clamp firmly (do not crush it down); on the steel-string, make it very tight.

Step 8—Clean-up

Let the glue squeeze-out dry for about fifteen minutes, or until it is leather hard. Very carefully peel the tape away from the bridge under the clamps. When peeling from bare wood (on the classical), be aware of the direction of grain run-out, exactly as you

were when removing the tape after binding.

Whittle an edge on a long sliver of spruce and use it to slough off any remaining bits of glue squeeze-out. Try not to smear it; if it does smear on the lacquered steel-string soundboard, it can be removed with a bit of moistened paper towel or rag on the end of the spruce sliver. If it smears on the bare wood of the classical soundboard, wipe it away as best you can and then leave it to be sanded when the clamps are removed.

Leave clamped for at least one hour. After removing the clamps, do not forget to remove the bridge block.

The guitar must not be strung up now, nor can any further work be done on the bridge for at least four hours after gluing.

CHAPTER 16

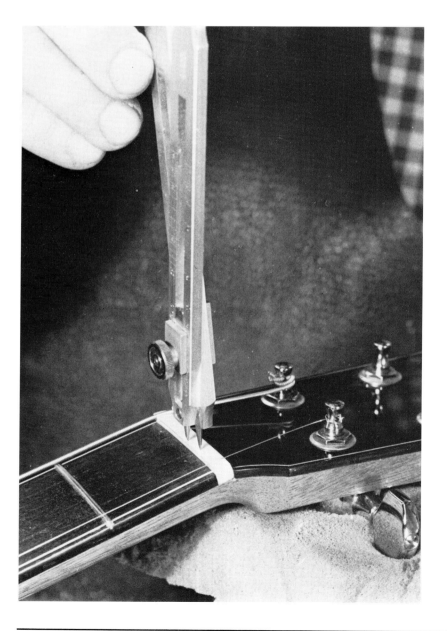

In this chapter the fretboard will receive its final preparation and the guitar's tuning machines, nut, and saddle will be fit up. Finally, the guitar will be strung up and the height of the strings above the fingerboard (the "action") will be determined by a methodical procedure called the set-up.

Up to this point, the maker has been exclusively applying the skills of a precision woodworker and decorative artist. From here on, however, the woodworker becomes instrument maker, employing unique skills that transform the guitar from a small wooden cabinet into a functioning musical instrument.

Regardless of how well designed and well constructed the guitar may be, it cannot perform up to its potential unless it is properly set up and adjusted. Volume, intonation, tonal balance, and playability can be noticeably affected by variations in action settings and by the manner in which these settings are achieved. Moreover, the player will be forced to struggle with his instrument if the set-up is im-

Set-Up

proper. Many an aspiring guitarist has no doubt been discouraged from continuing with the instrument because of playing difficulties that could have been eased dramatically by a few simple adjustments.

In view of this, it seems odd, yet sadly understandable, that this final step is so often given such short shrift. Final set-up on a novice's guitar is often rushed, out of an impatient urge to appraise the outcome of the project. Ironically, carelessness during final set-up will degrade the quality of an instrument's response to a greater extent than any other individual flaw. Even the most inspired design and the most sensitive execution will be effectively nullified by a crude set-up. Conversely, even the most modestly conceived and roughly executed instrument will profit enormously if set up properly. Consequently, builders are urged to rally as much patience as they have left and apply it to these final steps. Our habit is to begin the instrument rapidly and slow down our pace as we approach the crucial final stages, rather than the other way around.

TECHNICAL NOTES ON THE SET-UP

EFFECT OF FRETBOARD INCLINATION

Final action adjustment is made during set-up by cutting the nut and shaping the saddle to produce a desired action height for each string at the first and twelfth frets. The range of available adjustments is entirely dependent, however, on the inclination of the fingerboard that we achieved either by setting the neck angle on the steel-string or planing a slope into the fingerboard on the classical.

If the fretboard is correctly inclined, proper action will be achieved with the saddle at an optimal height: approximately ⅛ inch over the bridge's top surface, as measured down the guitar's centerline. A saddle of greater height is likely to bend forward eventually, causing problems with pitch intonation when the strings are played. In the extreme case, the saddle or even the front lip of the bridge may eventually fracture. Conversely, if the height of the saddle must be reduced radically (to compensate, for example, for incorrect fretboard inclination), tension on the saddle is so reduced as to hush the guitar and, in the extreme, to cause the vibrating string to rub over the saddle with a distinctive and annoying noise.

NUT AND SADDLE MATERIALS

The nut and saddle must be made of a dense material that can bear up to the considerable compressive forces exerted by the strings but can nonetheless be shaped relatively easily and brought up to a fine polish. Traditional materials used for this purpose are walrus or elephant ivory and whale or cow bone. Other materials that have been used are ebony, several types of plastic, brass, and ceramic.

There is little question that the choice of nut and saddle material will significantly affect the quality and character of the instrument's tone. The nut and saddle couple the string's signal to the guitar and will either subtract portions of the signal due to their peculiar damping characteristics or make an acoustic contribution that is distinctive to their density and composition.

The most highly prized material used for nuts and saddles has traditionally been ivory. Cow bone is not as evenly textured or colored, but it polishes nicely and is quite satisfactory acoustically. Due to our concern for endangered species, we have in recent years discontinued the purchase of exotic nut and saddle materials such as ivory and whale bone, and have shifted to the exclusive use of cow bone.

FRETBOARD RELIEF

When a string is plucked, it will vibrate in such a way that all points along its length move within the boundaries of an elongated "envelope" that is very gently curved above and below the position of the string when at rest. The arcs begin at the nut or at one of the frets, widen slowly toward the area of maximum excursion at the string's midpoint, and then gently curve together toward the saddle. Now, if the action is low and the fretboard is absolutely straight, the arcing, vibrating string will contact and rattle on the frets farther down. If the fretboard surface can be curved longitudinally to approximate the string arc, however, lower

action without rattling can be achieved, providing the frets are all level to start with. This curvature is called fretboard relief.

Classical: The nylon strings used on classical guitars have greater elasticity and therefore a greater vibrating arc than do steel strings. They thus require greater clearance all along the fretboard to avoid string rattle. Fortunately, however, nylon strings are soft enough to be comfortable even at action settings significantly higher than those of steel strings. The nature of left-handed attack in classical music is such that, within limits, higher action does not interfere with playing ease. It is also of note that nylon strings will intonate properly at action settings significantly higher than the point at which steel strings would display pitch distortion.

The high string action of the classical thus requires only minimal curvature, or "relief," in the fretboard. Usually the string tension of nylon strings is sufficient to just stress the neck to the fine curvature it needs for sufficient relief.

Steel-String: On the steel-string guitar, one hundred eighty pounds of string tension acting on a long, slender neck can produce excessive relief unless counter-balanced by a reinforcement of the correct stiffness. Our solution is the adjustable truss rod that allows us to determine the degree of resistance in order to obtain the optimum relief.

The existing relief can be measured with a simple test. With the strings up to concert pitch, press one string down to the frets at both the first and the fourteenth fret. A stretched string is dead straight; you can compare it to the fretboard by tapping the string in the middle. No movement whatever betrays one of two conditions: a straight fretboard or a back-bent fretboard, both problematical. Two possible causes are an overtightened truss rod or a neck wedged back by oversize fret tangs. Clearance between the string and the middle fret shows the existence of relief.

On the average, proper steel-string relief varies between $1/64$ and $1/32$ inch. Small relief is appropriate for higher action, gentle attack, or stiffer strings. Greater relief is appropriate for lower action, vigorous attack, or lighter strings. Cross combinations may require some trial and error to optimize the relief for an individual playing situation.

PROCEDURE: DRESSING AND POLISHING THE FRETS AND FINGERBOARD

Fretwork is one of the criteria by which our work is most critically judged, and for good reason: rough, shoddy fretwork not only mars the instrument's visual appeal, but degrades its playability and sound qualities as well.

By this time the fingerboard can look pretty rough: the surfaces may be dented with hammer marks, the fret tops ground flat and faceted unequally, the edges of the fingerboard encrusted with overlaps and runs of dried finish. If the fingerboard has been masked with tape, there is likely to be a dried ridge of finish along the edges of the fingerboard and traces of adhesive on its surface. Our task is to refine the entire playing surface to gleaming perfection by a methodical process that makes considerable demands on our patience and attention to detail.

Tooling the frets, the first step, involves refining the levelness of all their tops, recrowning the ground-down facets, and shaping the ends so they will not abrade the player's fingers. Each of these tooling steps can be adequately performed with several ordinary flat mill files. The process can be optimized using a specialized file that we call a fret file, known to countertop manufacturers as a laminate-edge file (Fig. 16-1). It is made in small quantities and sold to industry for rounding sharp corners on plastic laminate (such as Formica) countertops and the like. It is not, unfortunately, a hardware-store item, but you can buy it from luthier-supply mail-order houses and larger music stores.

On the steel-string, final

shaping of the fret ends can be done with deft strokes of the fret file, but it can be more easily accomplished with a modified miniature file. We use a 4-inch ultra fine flat mill file with the teeth ground off along the narrow edge for about ½ inch from its end.

The fingerboard surface must be scraped free of lacquer, tool marks, and hammer dents. Finally, the scraper marks on the fingerboard and file marks on the frets are removed by thorough sanding.

TOOLS
straightedge
flat fret-grinding file
file stub (see Chapter 12, Fretting Procedures)
modified flat file
soundboard mask
rubber sanding pad
fret file

SUPPLIES
#220-grit garnet sandpaper
#360(400)-, #500-, #600-grit silicon-carbide sandpaper
fingerboard oil

16-1. Recrowning frets with a fret file. The facets left behind by the flat file must be rounded for clarity of tone and correct intonation. Note the sheet-metal mask in place to protect the soundboard.

Step 1—Final Truing of the Frets

With a good backlight, preferably shining off a white surface placed behind the fingerboard, read the accuracy of the frets with a straightedge placed over them. The straightedge must be aligned, in turn, along the "run" of each of the strings. If all your previous assembly, planing, fretting, and leveling steps have proceeded perfectly, you should be able to read the fret tops as perfectly level from the first to the last. Perfection, however, is more commonly a goal than a reality; the beginner may have to be content to concentrate on the first to fourteenth frets and strive to get *them* as level as possible. Touch up the frets with the flat file or the file stub as appropriate.

Note: It may be necessary to accept a compromise in your accuracy rather than grinding away the frets excessively. If you are satisfied that the frets are as level as you can achieve at your skill level, proceed to the next step. Novices may not be able to tell if they are accurate enough until they actually string the guitar up and play it.

Steel-string: Be careful not to lay either the straightedge or the file diagonally across the fretboard arch. All fret-leveling steps must be performed with the truss rod adjusted to provide the straightest reading possible down the centerline. Adjust the truss rod through the soundhole with a ⁵⁄₁₆-inch socket wrench mounted on a ¼-inch driver and extension. After making an adjustment, you may have to "coax" the neck gently against your knee.

Step 2—Recrowning the Frets

Tape and mask the soundboard (Fig. 16-1). (The mask was used previously in Chapter 12 on the classical.)

If you examine the frets closely, you will notice many with flat facets ground into their crowns, widening where the grinding was deepest. Other frets may be just barely scuffed or may even have been ignored entirely by the flat file. We must now recrown only the deeply faceted frets with the fret file. Long, deliberate, unidirectional strokes with the toothed edge of the fret file work best. Do not pump back and forth, since you not only run the risk of inadvertently hopping off the fret and scarring the fingerboard but can also pack metal filings deeply into the file, "blinding" it and slowing down progress. Avoid an extended follow-through that might "clip" the far end

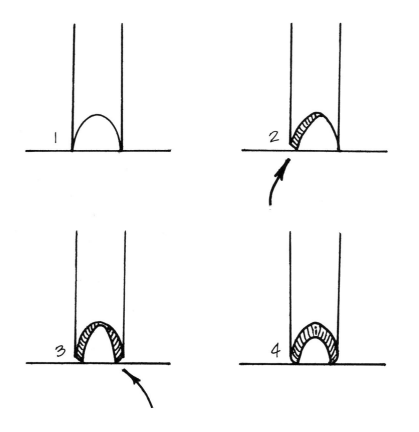

16–2. Sequence for dressing fret ends.

of the fret and remove excessive material there.

As you stroke, you will notice the facet narrowing as the file does its job. The trick is to stop when the facet is *not* entirely ground away but is reduced considerably, ensuring that the original registration against the straightedge remains; the final crowning will be accomplished later with sandpaper.

Step 3—Steel-string Only: Dressing the Fret Ends

Left-hand techniques on steel-string guitars most often require the fingers to be wrapped around the fingerboard edges. If the fret ends are sharp, they can abrade the musician's fingers.

Thus, the steel-string fret ends should be rounded with the small, modified flat file. Place the file upright at the spot indicated by the arrow (Fig. 16-2) with its smoothly ground edge against the fingerboard. Grind off the small sharp corner of the fret right at the bottom of the beveled facet. The smooth edge on the file will prevent marring of the fingerboard. Now, with a pushing stroke, grind the corner of the facet as you turn the file, knocking off the sharp edge toward the top of the fret. Repeat this motion in mirror-image fashion on the adjacent half of the fret end, starting at the fingerboard and ending on top of the fret, as before. A methodical push-and-twist motion with the file on each fret end as you progress down the fingerboard will help you achieve uniformly shaped "domes" over the entire length.

Step 4—Scraping the Fingerboard

Taking care to remove only as much material as necessary and to avoid changing the original contour or flatness of the space between the frets, proceed to scrape the wood very carefully to remove hammer marks and dried finish from the entire fingerboard surface. Push the scraper blade while holding it in a tipped-forward attitude, flexing it little, if at all. Strive to carry your strokes right up to the next fret, rather than stopping short at the same place near it, a practice that may inadvertently create an unsightly ledge that will be difficult to remove. Shear off the hardened bead of dried finish along the top edges of the fingerboard by scraping at an angle from the edge toward the center, rather than the opposite, to avoid chipping the finish off the side of the fingerboard. Remove the fine shavings that may have accumulated next to the frets by lightly drawing the corner of the scraper across the fingerboard adjacent to each fret.

Step 5—Sanding the Frets and the Fingerboard Surface

The technique we favor is to hold a small sheet of sandpaper in such a way that the sandpaper hops over the full width of the fret, supported from behind with the fingers. Try to sand the full radius of the frets rather than just the crowns. The effect is to round the remaining facets on the frets without significantly altering their height, leaving behind, after a dozen or so strokes in each direction, a newly and perfectly beaded surface, free of file marks and other irregularities.

Next, the same grit of sandpaper is wrapped around a sanding pad and the fingerboard surface is sanded *with* the grain in between the frets. Sand first the frets, then the wood, with #220-grit garnet, then with #360, #500 and #600 silicon-carbide waterproof sandpaper (dry), brushing or wiping the surface thoroughly free of debris before going on to each finer grit. A small segment of ¼-inch-thick hard rubber about 2 × 3 inches in size, with one edge beveled, makes an ideal sanding pad that will conform to the fingerboard surface and allow sanding right in close to the frets.

Note: The student will soon discover that final sanding of the fingerboard can be performed with far greater ease and efficacy *before* the frets are installed. This alternative is only practical if the student has become confident and skilled enough not to subsequently mar the polished surface with the fretting hammer and fret files, or to spill filler or finish materials on it. This is, in fact, the sequence we use. It entails final sanding, fretting, masking of the entire fingerboard before finish is applied, and then remasking between the frets just before the fret-dressing step. The tape is removed and the surface is wiped with naphtha to remove traces of adhesive.

Step 6—The Final Touches

Fingerboard oil is now applied to the fretboard surface. This ointment consists of a blend of light oils and lubricants that penetrate and protect the bare fingerboard and leave a fine, nonsticky, and nongumming residue that lubricates the fingers and helps quiet finger "squeek" on the strings. The best fingerboard oil consists of a blend of coconut, lemon, and eucalyptus oils. You can buy commercial liquid preparations made specifically for fingerboards. Avoid creams, aerosols, waxes, or furniture polishes that contain silicones.

Fingerboard oil is applied to the fingerboard with the fingers (taking care not to get any on the *end* of the fingerboard where the nut will be glued). It will be absorbed after about fifteen minutes. Buff away the excess thoroughly with a paper towel.

PROCEDURE: SETTING UP THE ACTION

In this procedure, the nut is rough shaped and fitted into the slot between the fretboard and the headpiece veneer, and the saddle blank is thinned to fit snugly into the bridge slot. What follows is a painstaking and methodical sequence that ensures correct string spacing, correct string clearance over the frets, and proper contouring and polishing of the nut and saddle without sacrificing their tight fit. Final adjustments are made after the strings have been brought up to concert pitch. (Further adjustment will undoubtedly be necessary after several weeks, when the guitar has "settled in" and the clearances have changed.)

The sequence of steps has been carefully considered for maximum efficacy, and we recommend they be strictly followed in the order in which they appear here.

TOOLS
half pencil
sanding board
end nipper
belt sander (optional)
small flat mill file
1/16-inch drill bit
miniature backsaw
needle files (optional)

steel-string only:
    #3 taper-pin reamer (optional)
    hand drill
    13/64- *or* 7/32-inch drill bit (see Step 1 below)
    plumber's reamer
    razor knife
    coping-saw blade

SUPPLIES
masking tape
double-faced tape
white glue
steel-string only:
    quick-setting epoxy
    spray adhesive or contact cement

MATERIALS
bone nut, 2 × 3/16 × 3/8 inches (SS) or 2¼ × ¼ × 3/8 inches (CL)
bone saddle, 3 × 1/8 × 3/8 inches (SS) or 3½ × 1/8 × 3/8 inches (CL)
light- or medium-gauge bronze-wound steel-string set, or good-quality nylon classical string set
set of tuning machines
builder's label (maker's name), paper
steel-string only:
    Martin bridge-pin and end-pin set
    sheet of thin acrylic plastic (black or tortoise-shell pattern), approximately 6 × 9 inches.

Step 1—Steel-string Only: Fitting Up the Bridge

A better fit of the standard-sized bridge pins (such as Martin-style) can be accomplished by drilling 13/64-inch holes through the bridge and fitting each pin with the aid of a #3 taper-pin reamer. An adequate fit can be obtained without this fairly expensive tool by drilling a 7/32-inch hole instead and leaving it at that. You must now use whichever bit you have used for the bridge holes to extend *these* holes fully through the soundboard and bridge patch. Exert very little, if any, downward pressure on the drill as you twist the gear wheel slowly (Fig. 16-3) to lessen chipout as the drill bit emerges through the bridge patch. Be especially careful as you insert the drill bit that you do not strike and mar the bridge or the lacquered surfaces with the tool.

Each bridge pin has a small slot or "flute." These are designed to allow room for both the pin and the string in the hole. The function of the pin is not to wedge the string tightly in the hole, but simply to plug up the hole so the ball end of the string cannot find its way out. Indeed, the string and the pin should in no way compete for the same room inside the hole. When in fact they do, a litany of potential difficulties can arise: jammed pins that must be forcibly pried out just to change

strings, bridge pins that wear out prematurely, bridge pins that get ejected from the guitar when the strings are tightened, bridge pins that stick up at different heights over the surface of the bridge, and so on. The flutes in the bridge pins are, however, too small to allow proper clearance for the doubled-up windings on the ends of the three lowest strings (and, on some string sets, the wound G string as well). Thus we must cut an additional clearance notch in the bridge itself, directly ahead

of the bridge-pin holes. We slot them in our shop using a small portable electric saber saw with a well-padded base and a saw bit that has been ground down narrow enough to slide into the bridge-pin hole. By hand, the notches can be cut with a coping-saw blade manipulated as shown in Fig. 16-4. The notches should be aligned with the holes' centerlines and should be cut neatly; remove only as much material as is necessary to accommodate both the string and the bridge pin comfortably in the hole.

16-3. *Drilling out the bridge-pin holes.*

Step 2—Fitting the Nut and Saddle Blanks into Their Slots

The nut and saddle blanks must fit snugly in order to function properly as acoustic couplers and, in the case of the nut, to facilitate cutting the string notches. The fit should not be so snug, however, that removal becomes inordinately difficult or that the blanks do not fully seat in their pockets. During this step, the blanks will be sized to an overtight fit, which will then be reduced to a fine fit by fine sanding and polishing. To accomplish this, we size each blank first with a file or on a belt sander until it is only slightly oversized, then sand on the sanding board until the blank *just* begins to enter its slot, and finally sand on a sheet of #120-grit garnet taped to a flat surface until the blank seats with overtight fit. The later process of removing the #120-grit scratches with #220-grit and #360-grit papers will yield a good fit.

For grinding with a file, the blank should be taped with double-faced tape to a flat surface.

To size the nut, choose the face that will abut the fingerboard end and level it on the sanding board. Then remove material from the opposite face until the blank seats in its slot. Finally, square or angle the bottom face of the blank to match the angle, if any, of the nut-slot floor.

To size the saddle, smooth one face and remove material from the other until the blank seats. Avoid letting it become tapered in thickness. When it seats (be absolutely certain that it is seating), square the bottom edge to ensure maximum contact with the slot floor.

If the saddle blank jams in so tightly that you cannot remove it with your fingers, pad the jaws of the flush-ground end nipper with masking tape and use it to pry the saddle out.

Steel-string only: The ends of the blank must be rounded to match the ends of the slot. Do not push the blank in crookedly, as it may jam before seating and give the false impression that it is too thick.

Step 3—Preliminary Shaping of the Nut

With the nut blank well seated in its slot, draw a line across its front face, as shown in Fig. 16-5, with the half pencil to denote the height of the first fret. This visual aid will enable you to avoid cutting the string notches too deep or too shallow. If a notch is cut too deep, the "open" or unfretted string will rattle against the first fret when plucked. Cutting too shallow will make fretting difficult and will seriously increase pitch distortion when you fret the string near the nut.

Next, with the half pencil, mark the ends of nut where they emerge from the slot—against the fingerboard edge, against the neck underneath it, and up along the thickness of the headstock veneer behind it. Remove the nut and grind the ends back to these marks, just barely obliterating them. Grind the top of the nut to within

16–4. *Sawing relief notches in the bridge-pin holes with a coping saw blade.*

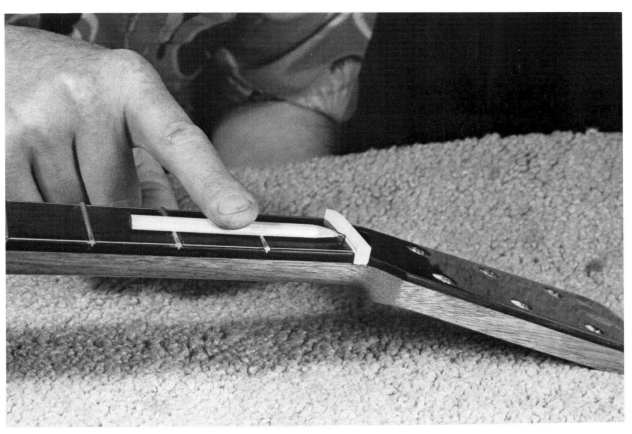

16–5. Marking the height of the first fret on the face of the nut blank with a half pencil.

¹⁄₁₆ inch of the line on its front face; at the same time, tip *back* the top surface of the nut by about 10 degrees so it looks like Fig. 16-6. Now round the two top corners of the nut by a very small amount with a small flat file.

Insert the nut back into its pocket. Make sure that the blank does not overhang the neckshaft at one side or the other.

Step 4—Preliminary Shaping of the Saddle

The top edge of the saddle must be shaped to mimic the contour of the fingerboard and to allow the strings to drop in height evenly and progressively from the bass to treble, the treble string ending up ¹⁄₃₂ inch closer to the fingerboard than the bass string.

Our strategy is to rough-shape the top bearing surface of the saddle to *approximately* the finished contour and inclination, leaving it just a bit taller than necessary. After the instrument is strung up and the strings are spaced and brought to pitch, we will determine the precise contour by a simple calculation.

Steel-string: Draw a line on the front face of the saddle

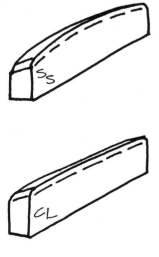

16–6. Contours of steel-string and classical nuts.

right where it emerges from the bridge. Mark a point in the center ⁵⁄₃₂ inch above that line. Remove the saddle. Now file or grind down to that point, gently curving the top edge by a small amount and removing a bit extra from the treble side. Round the edges slightly, but do not crown the bearing surface quite yet. Replace the saddle.

Classical: Draw a line on the front face of the saddle where it emerges above the front lip. Remove the saddle. Draw a parallel line about ⁵⁄₃₂ inch above it, and grind or file the excess down to that line. Round the edges slightly, but do not crown the bearing surface quite yet. Replace the saddle.

Step 5—Installing the Tuning Machines

Steel-string: The headstock holes may need to be reamed to remove dried finish or to expand them slightly to accommodate the tuning machine shafts, or both.

We have found a hardware-store-variety plumber's reamer to be ideal for this purpose. Insert the reamer and twist as shown in Fig. 16-7. Take care not to rack the reamer from side to side. The best technique is to turn the tool with one hand and pull on the tip with the fingers of the other. Twist and check until the shaft enters the hole and the casing stops short of seating fully by ¹⁄₁₆ inch. Put a masking-tape flag on the reamer at this depth. Ream the remaining holes, relying on the flag as a depth gauge. If you have the kind of machine heads with grommets that do not screw down over the shafts, you must also ream the openings on the headstock face until the grommets seat just shy from their top lip. They must then be pressed in the rest of the way with a padded cam clamp.

Insert the tuning machines

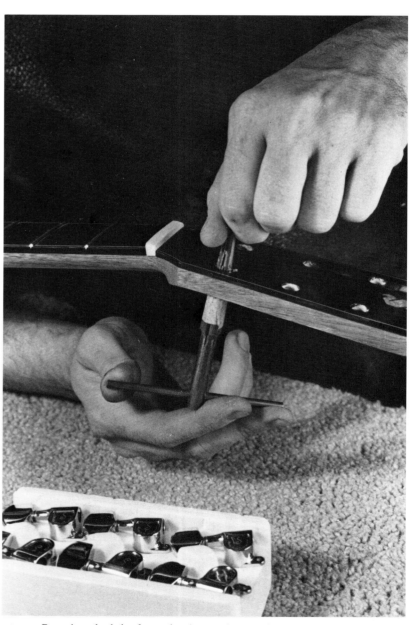

16-7. Reaming the holes for steel-string tuning machines.

into their holes, seating them firmly with thumb pressure. They will hold their positions securely enough to allow proper alignment against a straightedge (Fig. 16-8) or with careful sighting. With an awl, poke through the mounting holes and into the wood underneath to center the subsequent drill holes properly.

A masking-tape flag placed around the shaft of a ⅟₁₆-inch drill bit will prevent drilling entirely through the headstock. The distance between the drill tip and the flag should be equivalent to the length of the screw shaft. Without removing the machines, drill into each screw hole until the flag touches the mounting tabs extending from the casing. Insert the screws and, with the correct-size screwdriver, screw them in carefully and slowly, taking particular care that the screwdriver does not slip in its slot and chew up the screw head. Snug the screws down only; *do not tighten any further*, lest you twist off the heads or strip the screws in their holes.

If the machine-head grommets are the screw-on type, screw them on now, making sure the grommet washer is slipped under the grommet first and is laying on the headstock beveled-side up. (*Note:* Sand the undersurface of the washers to remove burrs that may damage the finish.) Snug down the grommet with the appropriate wrench (Fig. 16-9). As you turn the wrench, note that the machine

casing will start to seat flat against the underside of the headstock. You must stop tightening as soon as the casing has settled against the wood. If you continue tightening past that point, the washer

may crush the finish coating, causing chips or bubbles to appear on the finished surface. Finally, you may have to re-tighten the screws (which may no longer be seated) and snug them down again with the

16–8. *Aligning the steel-string machines prior to drilling for the small screws that fasten the castings to the back of the headpiece.*

16–9. *Snugging down the grommets on the steel-string machines.*

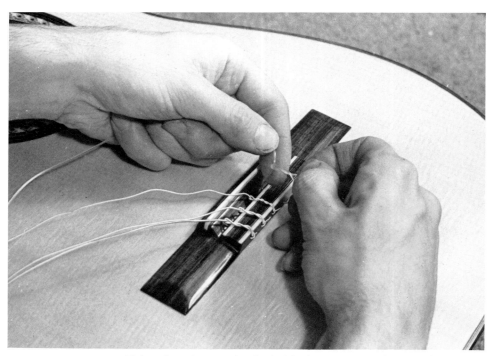

16–10. *Tying the strings on the classical bridge. The sixth, fifth, third, and second strings are twisted two times over the tie block; the fourth and first strings are twisted three times.*

screwdriver until they just stop. Tighten no further.

Classical: Measure the mounting screws. If they are too long, they will poke through the headpiece slots when tightened down; clip and file the screw tips if necessary. If the roller holes have been narrowed by dried finish, twist the original drill bit into the holes to clean them out so the machine rollers can enter them unencumbered and can seat fully. Insert the machines. With an awl, poke through the screw holes in the plates into the wood underneath, taking care that the punctures are well centered to the holes. Remove the machines. Wrap a masking-tape flag around a ⅟₁₆-inch drill bit just under ¼ inch from its tip. Insert the bit into the hand drill and drill into the puncture marks, stopping when the flag touches the surface. Replace the machines. With a screwdriver of the right size, twist the screws in until the plate snugs up against the headstock. Do not tighten them down any further, lest you inadvertently twist the heads off or strip them in their holes.

Step 6—Installing Strings at the Bridge

Remove the strings from their package and uncoil them, taking care not to kink them.

Steel-string: Push the ball end of the string *deeply* into the guitar through its proper hole in the bridge. Plug the hole with the bridge pin, taking care that the flute is facing the saddle. Holding the bridge pin down with your thumb, pull the string up sharply until you hear the ball end come into positive contact with the bridge patch. If the bridge pin pulls up forcibly when you yank the string, the clearance notch cut into the bridge hole in Step 1 must be widened or deepened by a small amount.

Classical: Refer to Fig. 16-10. The wound strings have a floppy end and a stiff end. Plain strings often have one end tinted a bright color. The stiff and tinted ends are tied to the bridge. Insert each string end into its corresponding hole in the tie block from the saddle side and push it through until about 3 inches stick out the other side. Grab that end and bring it back over the tie block. Loop about 1 inch of the string back and around itself and then make one more turn on strings #6, #5, #3, and #2, and two more turns on strings #4 and #1, as shown in the photo. Pull both ends tight. The

16–11. Securing the string for winding on steel-string tuning machine post.

loops will seat flat over the tie block. Take care, however, that the final string crossover occurs *behind* rather than on top of the tie block. If too long a free end still remains after tieing, it may buzz against the soundboard; retie it a bit shorter.

Step 7—Tieing the First and Sixth Strings to the Tuning Machines

Steel-string: Turn the knobs so the holes in the posts are perpendicular to the centerline of the guitar. Pull the free end of the string through its appropriate hole from the middle of the headstock out toward the edges.

Determine the correct winding slack by inserting (three fingers, bass; four fingers, treble) between the string and the fingerboard at the fourteenth fret, and then pull the string taut over the fingers. Loop the string back, around, and over as shown in Fig. 16-11. (Pull the loop tight around the post before folding over.) As you take up the slack by winding the knob counterclockwise, guide the string so it coils neatly *under* the hole without balling up. This will help prevent string breakage. Wind the strings sufficiently to take up the slack.

Classical: Pass each string through the hole in the appropriate roller, pull it nearly taut, bring it back around toward the bridge, and loop it

through on the roller. Hold the loose end and wind the string just enough to take up the slack.

Step 8—Notching the Nut for the First and Sixth Strings

All string notches in the nut must provide adequate, yet not excessive, clearance for the strings so they are secured but not bound up or hindered in any way. Each notch must have an angled floor, ensuring a positive stop for the string at the front face of the nut. The floor of the notch should be shaped to match the cross-section of the string.

Push the first and sixth strings off the ends of the nut. Measure from the edges of the fingerboard to the centerline of the first and sixth string positions (SS: first, 1/8 inch; sixth, 5/32 inch/CL: first, 13/64 inch; sixth, 5/32 inch) and mark them on the nut with a sharp pencil. Saw a scratch line right over each pencil line with the miniature backsaw. The scratch line should be just deep enough to allow the string to stay put. Replace the strings on the nut in their respective scratch lines.

With the half pencil sharpened to a needle point, mark the actual width of the sixth string on the nut by registering the flat side of the pencil against both sides of the string. On the classical, do the same for the first string. Push the strings aside again.

16–12. *Adjusting the string spacing at the nut. The saw cuts with a rotating motion while favoring the direction in which the notch must be moved.*

16–13. *Finishing the notches with a needle file. The file leaves a polished, round-bottom notch.*

Using the saw, create a string notch as follows: Starting the saw at the scratch line, rotate the blade while sawing to create a round bottom notch between the pencil marks. The saw should be tipped at a slightly flatter angle than the angle of the headpiece. Use only the first inch or so of the saw blade to avoid poking the finished surface of the headpiece.

Deepen the notch by sawing while rotating the blade from side to side. Stop when the bottom of the notch almost touches the pencil line drawn across the front face of the nut.

On the steel-string, simply saw the first string notch straight down almost to the pencil line. On the classical nut, repeat the above procedure for the first string notch.

Step 9—Notching the Nut for the Remaining Strings

Tie the remaining strings to the machine heads in the same manner as strings #1 and #6. Take up the slack but leave them loose enough to tuck out of the way to one side of the nut or the other.

The four remaining nut notches must now be properly spaced between the first two so that the string spacing is not mathematically equal but rather visually equal. If we were simply to divide the space up equally, the thicker strings would appear to crowd together. We must begin, however, by marking four equally spaced lines on the nut in between the two outer strings. We have come to be able to eyeball these marks closely, but the beginner might like to measure them. Make a fine scratch line with the saw at each mark. Mount the strings on the scratch lines, and wind the strings up tight enough so that they just become straight, but not so tight that they fly off the scratch marks. One or more scratch marks may have to be deepened slightly to allow this—but avoid deepening the scratch marks unnecessarily. Now put aside the saw and examine the strings and their spacing closely. Ask yourself which strings must be moved in which direction to make the visual field of strings and spaces uniform. Think several strategies through until you arrive at the simplest course of action. Unless you have grossly mismeasured, not more than one or two strings should need to be moved to one side or another. Try out your theory by widening the chosen scratch mark toward the right or left, deepening it very slightly to hold the string in the new position (Fig. 16-12). Replace the string and reassess the situation. Continue until the spacing looks right.

Proceed to mark the string widths and then to notch each one down just barely to the line with the saw. We use a needle file to cut the last bit (Fig. 16-13). *Note:* On the steel-string, the second string, like the first, usually requires only a single saw kerf.

Step 10—Bringing the String up to Pitch and Measuring Clearances

Using a tuning fork, pitch pipe, or electronic tuning standard, bring the strings up to concert pitch. On the steel-string, verify the state of adjustment of the truss rod by checking the relief of the fingerboard. There should be no more than $1/32$-inch clearance and no less than $1/64$ inch between the string and the top of the sixth fret when pressing the string down at both the first and fourteenth frets. Adjust the rod accordingly.

Now we must determine the amount of material that must be removed from the saddle to produce optimal action height. Standard clearance between the underside of the low E string and the crown of the twelfth fret is $1/8$ inch on the steel-string and $5/32$ inch on the classical. (For low action, clearances are $7/64$ and $1/8$ inch respectively; for high action, $5/32$ and $3/16$ inch.) Because the monofilament treble strings do not vibrate in as wide an arc as the wound bass strings, the action on the treble side need not be as high as on the bass side. The clearance under the high E string should thus be $1/32$ inch lower than under the low E string on both guitars, with the string heights graduated in between. The way we determine the proper saddle height is to compare the actual clearances at this stage to the standard and adjust the saddle accordingly.

Measure in sixty-fourths the clearances of all the strings over the twelfth fret. Stand a 6-inch ruler on the fret and measure to the underside of each string. Write the clearances on a scrap of paper. For example, on the steel-string, clearances (in sixty-fourths) may read:

10.5   10   9   9   8.5   8

The fractional numbers represent readings in between two marks on the ruler. Now, immediately below, list the clearances for standard action (in sixty-fourths). On the steel-string, they are:

8   7.5   7   7   6.5   6

Subtract the two lists, yielding the distance each string must drop to reach the standard. In this example, they are:

2.5   2.5   2   2   2   2

The distances the bearing points on the *saddle* must drop are *twice* as much (this is a simple geometric relationship, governed by the fact that the twelfth fret is the midpoint along the scale length). Thus, for the example, the saddle drop will be:

5   5   4   4   4   4

With a pencil, mark the places where the strings touch the saddle. Unstring the guitar and extract the saddle. Measure *down* from the marks and make a pencil point where the drop of each string on the saddle will be, using the last calculations above. The saddle will now have a series of points that, when connected and averaged with a continuous line, will show the final contour of the string-bearing surface.

Note: For purposes of this operation, approximate standard twelfth fret clearances on the classical (in sixty-fourths) are:

10   9.5   9   9   8.5   8

Step 11—Final Shaping of the Saddle

File the saddle down to the line connecting the points, and gently radius the ends. To crown the string-bearing surface, sand the edges with #220-grit garnet, but leave a narrow facet along the top so as not to disturb the measured contour. Finally, switch to sanding the crown "shoeshine" style with a strip of #360 Wetordry, and radius the crown along its length. The faces of the saddle should be smooth and scratch free. If you must resand the faces, fine-sand only the area that lies *above* the bridge to avoid creating a sloppy fit. Buffing the saddle with liquid glazing compound will bring it up to a beautiful luster.

Step 12—Final Shaping of the Nut

It may be necessary to regrind the top of the nut if the notches are much deeper than half of the strings' diameter. This will ensure against binding of the strings in the notches and consequent breakage at the posts. Keep the top of the nut tipped as before. Round the corners generously, taking care not to curve too closely to the outer notches or into the portion that lies inside the slot. Sand and polish the nut as you did the saddle. Avoid getting any polish on the underside of the nut. Put two dots of white glue under the nut and press it firmly into its slot.

Step 13—Finishing Touches

Make up a suitable label and apply white glue or spray adhesive. Insert it through the soundhole; center and smooth it onto the back.

Restring the guitar and bring it back up to concert pitch.

Steel-string only: Make up a pickguard template out of thin wood. Press it firmly on a sheet of thin acrylic, and score a line on the plastic with the point of a razor knife pressed up against the template. The pickguard can be popped out of the sheet by flexing it back and forth across the score lines (Fig. 16-14). Sand the burrs off the edges with fine sand-

paper. Using contact cement or spray adhesive, adhere it to the soundboard as shown in Fig. 16-15.

Select an end pin (this is usually included in the bridge-pin set). Drill through the center of the end graft, after spotting with a deep puncture mark from an awl. The drill diameter should be the same as the diameter of the end pin measured $\frac{1}{16}$ inch from its head. Apply a sparing amount of quick-setting epoxy glue to the end pin. Insert the end pin into its hole and tap it home with a hammer.

After several days or weeks it will be quite probable that string tension has caused the instrument to settle, requiring a final readjustment of the truss rod and a lowering of the saddle to return the action to the desired setting. Saddle adjustment can be accomplished by removing material evenly from the bottom (keeping it straight and square) so as not to disturb the existing contour of the crown.

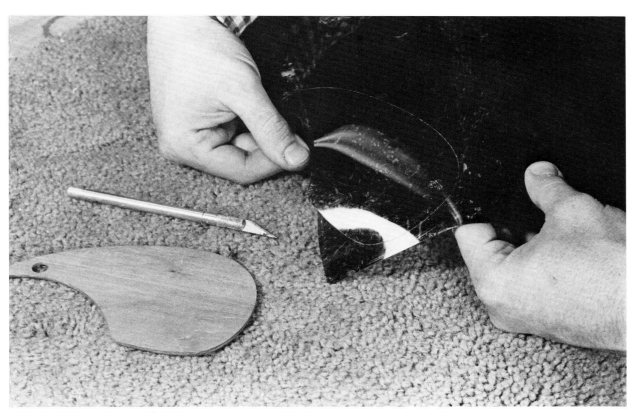

16–14. *Cutting the pickguard out of sheet plastic.*

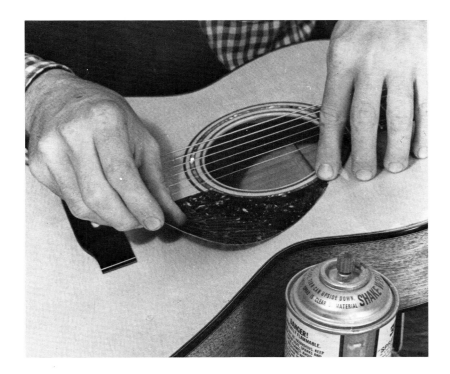

16–15. *Applying the steel-string pickguard with spray adhesive.*

16–16. *The finished classical guitar.*

16–17.   The finished steel-string guitar.

AFTERWORD:

The excitement of first playing a just completed guitar is a truly unique pleasure.

Be aware of the fact that the guitar's intonation and tone will undergo drastic changes in the initial hours of its birth, inevitably for the better. This occurs as tension "soaks in" and the strings straighten slowly between the nut and saddle. Only after several hours of playing will a guitar's character begin to emerge. Thus, do not attempt to judge initial peculiarities in intonation or tone until the guitar is "played-in" for a while.

Some other bugs may appear. String breakage and noises while playing are two of the most commonly encountered problems on the beginner's guitar.

If a string is properly tuned at the correct octave and is not worn out, breakage invariably points to a problem at the nut, bridge, or tuning machines. To pinpoint the problem, ascertain precisely where the string broke. A clean break at the post or roller may result from a balled-up winding of the string. Or, a poorly machined

Troubleshooting & Guitar Care

hole in the post may expose sharp metal burrs and cut the string. If a short length of string remains past the machines, the problem is at the nut. A tapering notch at the nut can scissor or bind the string as it is tightened. If this is the case, broaden the bottom of the notch, taking care not to deepen it. Finally, a long length of string left attached at the post or roller betrays trouble at the bridge (strings almost never break between the nut and saddle). The saddle may be badly crowned or excessively tall; the string angle behind the saddle may be too acute; or the bridge pin holes may be improperly shaped.

On the classical, a monofilament string retied once too often can slip off the tie block. Also, a weak knot can occur if the last crossover of the string lies *on top* of the tie block.

Odd string noises occurring during playing may be trickier to pinpoint and remedy. A continuous noise sounding like an Indian sitar may be caused by an "indefinite" string stop: somewhere the string is being

supported on a level surface rather than at a single point. If the distinctive noise occurs only on the open string (disappearing when the string is fretted), the "flat" is in the nut notch. With a fine file or saw, tip the notch floor down toward the headpiece without

deepening it at its frontal edge. If the noise occurs on some or all of the played notes, the saddle needs to be crowned properly.

The soundbox and neck can convert *any* vibration on the guitar into noise: an overlong string end; a loose brace; a

A–1. *Country-western and folk performer Taylor Pie, the proud owner of the steel-string guitar built for this book.*

floating string ball; a string winding detached from its core; even a player's shirt button in contact with the guitar can produce noise.

Fret buzzes are distinctive noises that occur on a discrete note when a string is plucked and its clearance over one or more frets is insufficient. A slight delay between the plucking and the buzzing may betray insufficient longitudinal curvature of the fretboard ("relief"), especially when the noise occurs on several adjacent frets near the nut. Conversely, buzzing on a succession of several frets nearer the soundhole may indicate excessive relief. An isolated buzz can occur if the fret being played is too low or the next fret is sticking up. Buzzing on the open string may indicate that the nut has been cut too low.

Accurate fretwork is the fruit of much more experience, but there are a few things you can do. If a fret just needs to be seated, tap it down carefully with the fret hammer. If it pops up again, put a drop of cyanoacrylate ("super" or "crazy") glue into the end of the fret kerf and hold the fret down firmly for a minute.

If buzzing continues, before attempting any further fret grinding, try raising the action height by a small amount. Do not expect clean, quiet action at any height setting below the lowest settings recommended earlier in the text. If the frets have been filed unevenly, do not file individual fret tops down: you might end up chasing a buzz all over the fretboard. Use a flat file stub instead, gently stroking the area *ahead* of the buzzing note. Recrown, restring, and try again.

The guitar's worst enemies are a chronically dry environment and direct heat. To minimize the possibility of shrinkage cracks, use a guitar humidifier in the case or, better still, in the soundbox itself whenever the guitar is kept in an artificially heated room. The opposites, extreme cold or high humidity, are not quite as dangerous. The former may cause the finish to "spiderweb" (a pattern of hairline cracks in the finish), and the latter may cause parts of the guitar to swell, changing the action setting. If the guitar soundbox has been assembled in an environment of moderate temperature and humidity, it should weather these extremes very well.

Keep any polishes or ointments containing silicones (such as furniture polish) away from the guitar. Any kind of polish, we believe, is counterproductive, as it simply traps dirt and builds up layers. We use only guitar *cleaners,* which remove, rather than add, dirt. High on our list are the Gurian and Martin brand cleaners, which both clean and renew the luster of the finished surface.

String life will be extended by cleaning the fingerboard occasionally. Scrub with small amounts of a mild solvent such as naphtha, turpentine, or xylol and then apply a specially formulated nonsilicone, nonaerosol ointment such as Gurian Fingerboard Oil.

A–2. *Philo Records recording artist James Thompson in the studio recording with the classical guitar built for this book.*

BIBLIOGRAPHY

GENERAL AND HISTORICAL REFERENCES

Achard, Ken. *The History and Development of the American Guitar*. London: Musical News Services Ltd., 1979.

A history of the steel-string guitar, with special emphasis on the major guitarmaking companies.

Baines, Anthony, ed. *Musical Instruments Through the Ages*. London: Penguin Books, 1961.

A concise work by a distinguished instrument historian.

Bellow, Alexander. *The Illustrated History of the Guitar*. Bellwin/Mills, 1970.

A description of the guitar from its most primitive beginnings.

Buchner, Alexander. *Folk Instruments of the World*. New York: Crown Publishers, 1972.

Covers all major ethnic groups and reveals the cross-cultural nature of instrument design. Fascinating photographs in large format.

Denyer, Ralph. *The Guitar Handbook*. New York: Alfred A. Knopf, 1982.

Information on many aspects of the history, construction, and music of the guitar. Primarily for musicians but of interest to the luthier.

Evans, Tom and Mary Ann. *Guitars: Music, History, Construction and Players from the Renaissance to Rock*. New York: Paddington Press, 1978.

A monumental work that addresses every aspect of the guitar and its world.

Ford, Charles, ed. *Making Musical Instruments*. New York: Pantheon Books, 1979.

Concise summaries of the construction process of various bowed and plucked instruments; written by distinguished instrument makers in each field.

Grunfeld, Frederic. *The Art and Times of the Guitar*. London: Macmillan & Co., 1969.

An overview of the guitar's history, its music, and its performers.

Longworth, Mike. *Martin Guitars—A History*. New Jersey: Colonial Press, 1975.

A major source of information not available elsewhere in one volume.

Wheeler, Tom. *The Guitar Book: A Handbook for Electric and Acoustic Guitarists*. rev. ed. New York: Harper & Row, 1978.

Focuses on the steel-string and electric guitar; well written and researched; lively text and superb illustrations.

Winternitz, Emanuel. *Musical Instruments of the World*. New York: McGraw Hill, n.d.

An extraordinary look at some of the greatest feats of workmanship in the history of instrument making. Awe-inspiring photographs.

The Lute Society (see Societies, below) publishes various booklets on relevant historical subjects:

Harwood, Ian. *A Brief History of the Lute*. Lute Society Booklet 1, 1976.

Short but satisfying description of the design evolution of the lute.

Gill, Donald. *Gut-String Instruments Contemporary with the Lute*. Lute Society Booklet #2, 1976.

Essential description of the historical evolution of the four and five course guitar.

Gill, Donald. *Wire-String Instruments Contemporary with the Lute*. Lute Society Booklet #3, 1977.

Precious tidbits on such ancestors of the steel-string guitar as the orpharion, the bandora, the polyphant, the chitarra, and the stump.

TECHNICAL

Feirer, John L. *Cabinetmaking and Millwork*. Peoria, IL: Chas. A. Bennett Co., 1967.

An excellent reference for the serious woodworker.

Hoadley, Bruce R. *Understanding Wood*. Newtown, CT: Taunton Press, 1980.

Wood technology for the craftsperson. Essential reading.

Dresdner, Michael M. *The Woodfinishing Book*. Newtown, CT: Taunton Press, 1992.

A clear treatise on every aspect of the subject.

Patterson, J.E. *Working with Mother-of-Pearl*. Santa Cruz, CA: self-published, 1978.

Everything you need to know about cutting and inlaying shell materials.

United States Department of Agriculture, United States Forest Service, *Air Drying of Lumber*, Report 1657. (Madison, WI: Forest Products Laboratory.)

United States Department of Agriculture, United States Forest Service. *Properties of Imported Tropical Woods*, Research Paper FDL 125. (Madison, WI: Forest Products Laboratory).

United States Department of Agriculture, United States Forest Service. *Shrinking and Swelling of Wood in Use*, Report 736. (Madison, WI: Forest Products Laboratory).

United States Department of Agriculture, United States Forest Service. *Table of Relative Humidity and Equilibrium Moisture Content for Dry-and-Wet Bulb Hygrometers*, Technical Note 156. (Madison, WI: Forest Products Laboratory).

United States Department of Agriculture, United States Forest Service. *Wood Handbook: Wood As An Engineering Material*, Handbook 72. (Madison, WI: Forest Products Laboratory).

For technical information on specific woodworking processes, we write to the customer service departments of major manufacturers for free pamphlets on many subjects, such as: finishing materials; spray equipment and spray finishing; glues and basic adhesive technology; and coated abrasives (sandpaper, etc.).

REPAIR AND MAINTENANCE

Kamimoto, Hideo. *Complete Guitar Repair*. New York: Oak Publications, 1975.

Excellent; required reading for all aspiring luthiers.

Teeter, Don E. *The Acoustic Guitar*. Vol. I and II. Norman, OK: University of Oklahoma Press, 1975, 1980.

Another fine collection of intelligent problem-solving techniques.

Erlewine, R. Daniel. *Guitar Player Repair Guide*. San Francisco: Miller-Freeman Publications, 1990.

Expert guitar repair advice.

ACOUSTICS

Benade, Arthur H. *Fundamentals of Musical Acoustics*. New York: Oxford University Press, 1976.
Rossing, Tom. *The Science of Sound*. New York: Addison-Wesley, 1982.
White, Tim, ed. *The Chicago Papers*. Journal of Guitar Acoustics, Issue #6 (see Journals and Periodicals, below).

JOURNALS AND PERIODICALS

Early Music Quarterly
Oxford University Press
Ely House
37 Dover Street
London W1X 4AH
England

Fine Woodworking Magazine
Taunton Press
Newtown, CT 06470

GPI Publications
Guitar Player Magazine
20085 Stevens Creek
Cupertino, CA 95014

Acoustic Guitar Magazine
412 Red Hill Avenue #15
San Anselmo, CA 94960

Journal of Guitar Acoustics
(Published irregularly since 1980)
Back issues available from:
Tim White
146 Lull Road
New Boston, NH 03070

SOCIETIES

Association of Stringed Instrument Artisans (ASIA)
"Guitarmaker" (pub.)
14 South Broad Street
Nazareth, PA 18064

Catgut Acoustical Society
Bi-annual Newsletter
Sec. Carleen Hutchins
112 Essex Avenue
Montclair, NJ 07042

Fellowship of Makers & Restorers of Historical In-
  struments (FOMRHI)
Quarterly Bulletins
Hon. Sec. J. Montague
c/o Faculty of Music
St. Aldate's
Oxford OX1 1DB
England

Guild of American Luthiers (GAL)
Data Sheets and Quarterlies
8222 South Park Avenue
Tacoma, WA 98408

Guitar Foundation of America
"The Soundboard" (pub.)
P.O. Box 1090A
Garden Grove, CA 92642

Lute Society
Francesca McManus, Administrator
Priory Road
Kew Gardens
Richmond
Surrey TW9 3DH
England

BILL OF MATERIALS

Below is an alphabetical list of all the major parts of the guitars built in this book. Excluded are some very small parts that will be made from scrap during the procedures. Refer to the designated chapter for materials selection criteria, possible alternate materials, and quantities required. The column headed "Where to Obtain" indicates three choices: "G" means that you must buy the item from a guitarmakers (or luthiers) catalogue supplier; "C" means that the item is made from material commonly found, as the case may be, at lumberyards, art/hobbyist supply stores, hardware stores, or industrial suppliers; "S" means that the item will be most easily obtained by retrieving scrap or cut-off material from other parts of the instrument.

ITEM	MATERIAL	DIMENSIONS	CHAPTER REFERENCE	WHERE TO OBTAIN
Back	Mahogany; Maple; Rosewood; Walnut; book-matched pair appr. 3/16″ thick	8″ x 20″ min. (SS) 7½″ x 19¼″ min. (CL)	5	G
Back Braces	Spruce; Mahogany; Spanish Cedar (CL only)	See text	10	G, C
Back Graft	Cross-grained Mahogany or Spruce; 1/8″ thick	5/8″ x total of 18″ (SS) 1/2″ x total of 18″ (CL)	10	G, C, S
Back Stripe	Marquetry strip (SS only) or veneer lines	21″ (SS) 19″ (CL)	5, 10	G
Bindings	Maple (SS only); Rosewood; 3/32″ thick	3/16″ x 32″ (SS) 3/16″ x 30″ (CL)	11	G, S
Bridge	Rosewood or Ebony; 3/8″ thick	1½″ x 6″ (SS) 1⅛″ x 7½″ (CL)	15	G
Bridge Patch (SS only)	Rosewood or Maple	3/32″ x 2″ x 6½″	7	G, C, S
Bridge Pins (SS only)	Plastic or Ebony (Martin std.)	N/A	16	G
End Graft	Hardwood; match bindings; 1/16″ thick	See text	11	C, S
End Pin	To match bridge pins	N/A	16	G
Fingerboard	Rosewood or Ebony; 5/16″ thick	2½″ x 18½″ (SS) 2¾″ x 18½″ (CL)	12	G
Frets	Medium fretwire; tang to match saw kerf	50″	12	G
Headpiece Face Veneer	Hardwood sheet 1/16″— 3/32″ thick	3″ x 7″ (SS) 3″ x 8″ (CL)	4	G
Headpiece Laminations (CL only)	Hardwood veneer(s); 1/40″ thick	3″ x 8″	4	G,C
Heelcap	Hardwood scrap; 1/8″ thick	2″ square	13	S
Linings (SS; kerfing)	Honduras Mahogany; 1/4″ stock	3/4″ x total of 128″	9	G, C
Linings (CL; top kerfing)	Basswood; 3/16″ stock	5/8″ x total of 56″	9	G, C
Linings (CL; back)	Basswood; 5/32″ stock	5/8″ x 28″ (2 pcs.)	10	G, C

ITEM	MATERIAL	DIMENSIONS	CHAPTER REFERENCE	WHERE TO OBTAIN
Neck Shaft & Headpiece	Honduras Mahogany; (11/16"—3/4" stock)	3" x 24" dressed	4	G, C
Nut	Bone blank	3/16" x 3/8" x 2" (SS) 1/4" x 3/8" x 2¼" (CL)	16	G
Pickguard (SS only)	Black or tortoise-shell acrylic plastic	6" x 9"	16	C
Purflings	Veneer lines; marquetry strips (SS only)	32" min (SS) 30" min (CL)	11	G
Rosette lines	Natural or dyed 1/40" veneer strips	3/32" x 16"—24"	6	G
Rosette marquetry (SS only)	Herringbone or other marquetry strip 1.5 mm. thick	3.5 mm. x 20"	6	G
Rosette mosaic pieces (CL only)	Natural or dyed veneer	See text	6	G
Saddle	Bone blank	1/8" x 3/8" x 3" (SS) 1/8" x 3/8" x 3½" (CL)	16	G
Sides	Mahogany; Maple; Rosewood; Walnut; bookmatched pair appr. 1/8" thick	4" x 30" (CL) 5" x 32" (SS)	5, 8	G
Side Dots (SS only)	White plastic rod; 1/16" diameter	See text	16	C
Shell Inlay (SS only)	Pearl or Abalone wafers or strips	See text	6	G
Soundboard	Spruce; Red Cedar; Redwood; bookmatched pair appr. 3/16" thick	8" x 20" min. (SS) 7½" x 19¼" min. (CL)	5	G
Soundboard braces	Sitka or Alpine Spruce; cut from billets (preferably split)	2" x 3" x 22"	7	G, C
Tailblock	Honduras Mahogany; Basswood (CL only)	3/4" x 3" x 4" (SS) 1/2" x 2½" x 3¾" (CL)	9	G, C
Truss Rod (SS only)	Mild steel rod; 3/16" dia. stock (see text for other parts of Truss Rod)	36" length	4	C
Truss Rod Spline	Hardwood	See text	4	C, S
Tuning Machines	Chrome or gold plate; Schaller; Grover; Gotoh; Van Ghent; etc.	N/A	4, 16	G

SOURCES OF GUITARMAKING SUPPLIES

GUITARMAKER'S CONNECTION—all woods, tools, materials, books and supplies. Division of C.F. Martin.
Box 329
Nazareth, PA 18064
(800) 247-6931

THE LUTHIER'S MERCANTILE—all tools, materials, books and supplies. Highly informative catalog.
P.O. Box 774
412 Moore Lane
Healdsburg, CA 95448
(707) 433-1823

ELDERLY INSTRUMENTS—tools, books, supplies.
1100 N. Washington
P.O. Box 14210
Lansing, MI 48901
(517) 372-7890

EUPHONON CO.—all tools, materials, supplies. Owned and operated by luthier Walter Lipton.
Orford, NH 03777
(603) 353-4882

METROPOLITAN MUSIC CO.—all tools, materials, books and supplies.
Mountain Road R.R. #1
Box 1670
Stowe, VT 05672-9598

STEWART-MACDONALD—all tools, materials, books and supplies.
21 N. Shafer St.
Box 900
Athens, OH 45701
(800) 848-2273

EXOTIC WOODS COMPANY—all woods; specializing in Rosewood and Ebony.
P.O. Box 532
Sicklerville, NJ 08081
(800) GIDWANI

BRIDGE CITY TOOLWORKS—tools, books, supplies.
1104 N.E. 28th Avenue
Portland, OR 97232
(800) 253-3332

LEE VALLEY TOOLS, LTD—tools, books, supplies.
1080 Morrison Drive
Ottawa, Ontario
Canada K2H 8K7
(613) 596-0350

INTERNATIONAL VIOLIN COMPANY, LTD.—most tools, materials, books and supplies.
4026 West Belvedere Avenue
Baltimore, MD 21215-5597
(301) 542-3535

CONSTANTINE'S—all woods, materials, books and supplies.
2050 Eastchester Road
Bronx, NY 10461
(800) 223-8087

GARRETT WADE COMPANY, INC.—fine tools, books and supplies.
161 Avenue of the Americas
New York, NY 10013
(800) 221-2942

WOODCRAFT SUPPLY CORP.—fine tools, books and supplies.
41 Atlantic Ave.
Box 4000
Woburn, MA 01888
(800) 225-1153

THE WOODWORKER'S STORE—tools, wood, books, supplies.
21801 Industrial Boulevard
Rogers, MN 55374
(800) 279-4441

LEICHTUNG, INC.—tools, books, supplies.
4944 Commerce Parkway
Cleveland, OH 44128
(800) 321-6840

WOODWORKER'S SUPPLY OF NEW MEXICO—tools, books, supplies.
5604 Alameda, NE
Albuquerque, NM 87113
(800) 645-9292

INDEX